The Life of **Jane Austen**

147 Mrs Bates

(Frontispiece)
Portrait of Jane Austen from the 1870 *Memoir* by James Edward Austen-Leigh; engraving, probably from Cassandra Austen's pen and pencil sketch portrait of her sister (c. 1810)

The Life of Jane Austen

John Halperin

*Centennial Professor of English,
Vanderbilt University*

THE HARVESTER PRESS • SUSSEX

First published in Great Britain in 1984 by
THE HARVESTER PRESS LIMITED
Publisher: John Spiers
16 Ship Street, Brighton, Sussex

Reprinted 1986

British Library Cataloguing in Publication Data
Halperin, John
    The life of Jane Austen.
    1. Austen, Jane—Biography   2. Novelists,
    English—19th century—Biography
    I. Title
    823'.7   PR4036

    ISBN 0-7108-0526-8

Typset in 10 point Garamond by
Photobooks (Bristol) Ltd.
Printed in Great Britain by
Whitstable Litho Ltd, Whitstable, Kent

To
Max F. Schulz and Robert J. Dilligan
and
Gillian Tindall and Peter M. Stevens

I think I may boast myself to be, with all possible vanity, the most unlearned and uninformed female who ever dared to be an authoress.
— Jane Austen in 1815

Practically anything may be the business of the unattached woman . . . An unmarried woman just over thirty, who . . . has no apparent ties, must expect to find herself involved or interested in other people's business, and if she is also a clergyman's daughter then one might really say that there is no hope for her . . . Being a clergyman's daughter is a good training . . . It is a known fact that people like clergymen's daughters, excellent women in their way, sometimes rush in where the less worthy might fear to tread.
— Barbara Pym, *Excellent Women*

Jane Austen might have said, with Henry James, 'I have the imagination of disaster—and see life as ferocious and sinister.'
— A. Walton Litz, *Jane Austen*

'It is very unfair to judge of any body's conduct, without an intimate knowledge of their situation. Nobody, who has not been in the interior of a family, can say what the difficulties of any individual of that family may be.'

— *Emma*

She sat musing on the difference of woman's destiny.

— *Emma*

'I will not allow books to prove any thing.'
— Anne Elliot in *Persuasion*

It is a riddle wrapped in a mystery inside an enigma; but perhaps there is a key.

— Winston Churchill on Russia (1939)

The enthusiasm of a woman's love is even beyond the biographer's.
— *Mansfield Park*

Contents

List of Illustrations

Foreword

'The biographer becomes attached to his subject in a way that cannot be duplicated in other relationships,' Ted Morgan has written in his life of Somerset Maugham. 'In many cases he knows a great deal about someone he has never met. Upon his work depends the way that person will be remembered.'

I do not for a moment believe that Jane Austen's memory will be much affected by what I—or any individual, for that matter—may say about her. Possibly the greatest of the English novelists, Jane Austen's reputation enjoys a position too solid to be raised or lowered with the publication of a single book. Still, since what some people think of her may in some measure be affected by what I write, I have tried in this new life of the novelist to be careful without being overly cautious, to be conservative in my assessment of facts without being uninteresting or unoriginal, to express views strongly held without being inflammatory. Whether or not I have succeeded in these aims I must leave to the reader to decide.

Many people already have a fixed image of Jane Austen. I have heard acquaintances say that Elizabeth Bennet is their idea of what the novelist must have been like. If one accepts this proposition, he is unlikely to think that Fanny Price, to take just one example, is a 'typical' Jane Austen heroine. It is my feeling that none of the heroines is any more or less 'typical' than any of the others—and that each of the novels is equally 'typical' of Jane Austen. She was a woman of many moods, like the rest of us; and the mood in which *Pride and Prejudice* was composed was quite different from that in which, fifteen years or so later, *Mansfield Park* was written. Neither of these novels can be more or less 'typical' of Jane Austen than the other, as I shall take some pains to show; indeed, each of the books is equally a Jane Austen performance.

Not everyone, of course, is so certain that he knows what Jane

Austen must have been like. I myself have been unsure for years
about a number of aspects of the novelist—not so much about the
quality of her work, which strikes me as indisputably first-rate ('of all
English and American novelists Jane Austen is perhaps the most
secure in her reputation,' A. Walton Litz has aptly written), but
rather the more personal questions. What kind of woman was she?
What sort of personality did she have? What was her life like when
she was not writing novels (i.e., most of the time)? We know
remarkably little about this great woman—certainly the first great
woman writer in English. There are a good many books about Jane
Austen, but few detailed critical biographies. The last, indeed, was
published by Elizabeth Jenkins in 1938. In the intervening years there
have been a number of coffee-table picture-books, but few genuine
attempts at a full-dress life. Of those studies of the novelist which
have at least made the biographical attempt, the most underrated in
my opinion is that by Joan Rees, the most overrated that by David
Cecil. In fact we have nothing in print remotely close to the
achievement of Miss Jenkins.

Some people, inevitably, will not like this book because it assumes
unhesitatingly that Jane Austen was a real person with problems and
idiosyncrasies and failings real people often have. For once I agree
with A.L. Rowse, who declares in his life of Marlowe: 'Far too much
is made of the merest textual *minutiae* . . . the law of diminishing returns has long ago set in. Meanwhile, the real and actual
contribution which historical knowledge has to make—of time and
circumstance, dating and conditions, personal and biographical—is
absolutely neglected.' I wish to make Jane Austen come alive for the
reader, if I can—to make her real, actual. With those who think the
great should never be criticized, I simply cannot agree. On the
contrary, I think Somerset Maugham is quite right when he says
that the more we know about the great the better off we are.
Maugham—who, to be sure, gave his own would-be biographers no
help—wrote in *The Summing Up*: 'I do not believe they are right who
say that the defects of famous men should be ignored. I think it is
better that we should know them. Then, though we are conscious of
having faults as glaring as theirs, we can believe that that is no
hindrance to our achieving something of their virtues.' And he said in
Ten Novels and Their Authors: 'The sort of books an author writes
depends on the sort of man he is and so it is well to know what is
relevant in his personal history.' I believe this absolutely.

*   *   *

I wish to thank Alistair Duckworth, Donald Greene, Elaine Halperin, Sidney Ives, John Spiers and Joseph Wiesenfarth for reading this entire book in manuscript and making, each of them, many invaluable suggestions of which I have taken advantage in the present volume. Professor Greene has been especially helpful in elucidating for me—insofar as these matters are at all capable of elucidation—the complicated ancestry and wide family connections of the Austens and the Leighs. I am also indebted to Elizabeth Jenkins and Sir David Smithers, both of whom discussed Jane Austen with me at some length, led me to new insights into the novelist and her work, and inspired some of the surmises I make in following pages. I have had the benefit of Sir David's medical expertise, as well as that of Dr Donald Atlas, Dr Abraham Braude, and Dr Michael Safdi, in connection with the conclusions I draw in Chapter 8 on the subject of Jane Austen's last illness, and for this too I am grateful. Needless to say, any errors in fact or judgment are my own responsibility.

I have chosen not to interrupt the narrative flow of this book with footnotes. John Barrymore supposedly remarked that having to stop for a footnote in the middle of an otherwise interesting passage one was reading was like having to answer the doorbell while making love. In the interests of telling a story, I have relegated to the end of this volume all notes; in them the reader will find a detailed accounting of the works that have influenced my view of Jane Austen, of those without which a book such as this could not have been written. Certainly no one who works on Jane Austen can help but be indebted, for example, to the scholarship of R.W. Chapman and Brian Southam. Among the critics, I have been inspired chiefly by the work of Walton Litz and Marvin Mudrick. But I hope the reader will find that my discussion of Jane Austen's life and work together results in a book that is as a whole different from those of the many talented scholars and critics who have preceded me into this fascinating field.

My interest here, as elsewhere, is in the relation between the life of the artist and the work produced rather than in either by itself. My discussions of the fiction centre on this question instead of attempting full-scale critical evaluation, which seemed to me inappropriate given the rich critical literature we already possess on the novelist's work and the biographical focus of the present study. I perhaps read the work more 'biographically' than my predecessors; this has been intentional. Commenting on James Joyce's 'incessant joining of event and composition,' Richard Ellmann writes in his splendid biography of that novelist:

> The life of an artist . . . differs from the lives of other persons in that its events are becoming artistic sources even as they command his present attention. Instead of allowing each day, pushed back by the next, to lapse into imprecise memory, he shapes again the experiences which have shaped him. He is at once the captive and the liberator. In turn the process of reshaping experience becomes a part of his life, another of its recurrent events like rising or sleeping. The biographer must measure this participation of the artist in two simultaneous processes.

Searching out the links between the life and the work as I have done—measuring 'this participation of the artist in two simultaneous processes'—seems to me to require no apology.

In quoting from the letters of Jane Austen, her relations and contemporaries, I have retained original spellings (and mis-spellings), punctuation, and vagaries of capitalization rather than taken it upon myself to make corrections so as to bring those who lived nearly two centuries ago 'up to date.' As L.P. Hartley reminds us, the past is a foreign country; they do things differently there. Why pretend otherwise?

The discussion in Chapter 7, Section II, of popular attitudes toward the novel in the early years of the nineteenth century is indebted in part to a previously published essay of my own—the 'Introduction' to *Jane Austen: Bicentenary Essays*, ed. John Halperin (Cambridge, London, and New York, 1975); I am grateful to the syndics of the Cambridge University Press for their permission to reprint some of that material here. A small part of the discussion of *Mansfield Park* in Chapter 7, Section V, is indebted to another previously published article of mine—'The Trouble with *Mansfield Park*,' in *Studies in the Novel*, 7, No. 1 (Spring 1975); a larger part of the same section appeared, in altered form, as 'The Novelist as Heroine in *Mansfield Park*: A Study in Autobiography,' in *Modern Language Quarterly*, 43, No. 2 (Summer 1983); much of the first section of Chapter 3 appeared previously as 'Unengaged Laughter:

Jane Austen's Juvenilia,' in the *South Atlantic Quarterly*, 81, No. 3 (Summer 1982); and Chapter 8, Section III, appeared in altered form as 'Jane Austen's Anti-Romantic Fragment: Some Notes on *Sanditon*,' in *Tulsa Studies in Women's Literature*, 2, No. 2 (Fall 1983). I am grateful to the editors of these journals for permission to reproduce this material here.

The passage in Chapter 4 from W.H. Auden's 'Letter to Lord Byron' is quoted, with permission from Faber & Faber in England and Random House/Alfred A. Knopf in America, from Auden's *Collected Poems*, ed. Edward Mendelson (copyright Edward Mendelson, William Meredith, and Monroe K. Spiers).

Lastly, I am indebted to Yvette Soto and Alberta Martin for their dedicated and skilful typing, and to Laura Mooneyham for helping me to correct proofs.

J.H.
London, May 1984

A PARTIAL PEDIGREE OF JANE AUSTEN, DEVISED BY DONALD GREENE

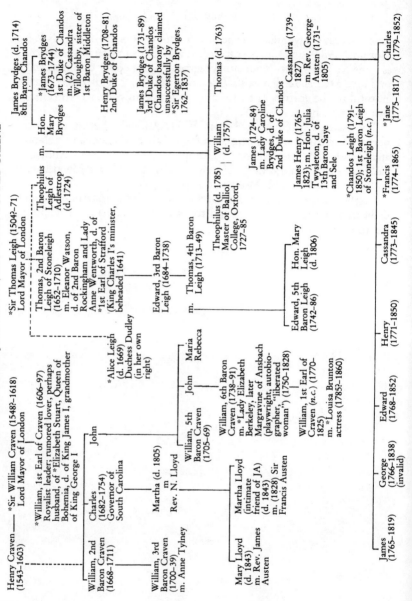

JANE AUSTEN'S BROTHERS AND SOME OF THEIR DESCENDANTS

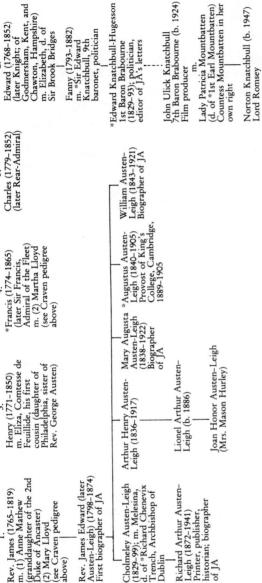

1.
Rev. James (1765–1819)
m. (1) Anne Mathew
(granddaughter of the 2nd
Duke of Ancaster)
(2) Mary Lloyd
(see Craven pedigree
above)

Rev. James Edward (later
Austen-Leigh) (1798–1874)
First biographer of JA

Cholmeley Austen-Leigh
(1829–99); m. Melesina,
d. of *Richard Chenevix
Trench, Archbishop of
Dublin

Richard Arthur Austen-
Leigh (1872–1941)
Printer, publisher,
historian; biographer
of JA

Arthur Henry Austen-
Leigh (1836–1917)

Lionel Arthur Austen-
Leigh (b. 1886)

Joan Honor Austen-Leigh
(Mrs. Mason Hurley)

Mary Augusta
Austen-Leigh
(1838–1922)
Biographer
of JA

*Augustus
Austen-Leigh
(1840–1905)
Provost of King's
College, Cambridge,
1889–1905

William Austen-
Leigh (1843–1921)
Biographer of JA

3.
Henry (1771–1850)
m. Eliza, Comtesse de
Feuillide, his first
cousin (daughter of
Philadelphia, sister of
Rev. George Austen)

4.
*Francis (1774–1865)
(later Sir Francis,
Admiral of the Fleet)
m. (2) Martha Lloyd
(see Craven pedigree
above)

5.
Charles (1779–1852)
(later Rear-Admiral)

2.
Edward (1768–1852)
(later Knight; of
Godmersham, Kent, and
Chawton, Hampshire)
m. Elizabeth, d. of
Sir Brook Bridges

Fanny (1793–1882)
m. *Sir Edward
Knatchbull, 9th
baronet, politician

*Edward Knatchbull-Hugesson
1st Baron Brabourne
(1829–93); politician,
editor of JA's letters

John Ulick Knatchbull
7th Baron Brabourne (b. 1924)
Film producer
m.
Lady Patricia Mountbatten
(d. of *1st Earl Mountbatten)
Countess Mountbatten in her
own right

Norton Knatchbull (b. 1947)
Lord Romsey

NOTES

'It is pleasant to be among people who know one's connections and care about them,' Jane Austen wrote in 1808 to her sister Cassandra (named, like their mother, after their collateral ancestress, Cassandra, Duchess of Chandos). The main point of this selective excerpt from her family tree is to combat the myth that Jane Austen was a cloistered spinster familiar with little beyond the bounds of a country parsonage. Her family's connections with nobility and even royalty, with the worlds of politics, learning, and high society from the seventeenth century to the twentieth, are remarkable, and Jane Austen was well aware of them, as a glance at her letters and the names she gives the major characters in her novels will show. When the snobbish Sir Walter Elliot says of the hero of *Persuasion*, 'Mr. Wentworth was nobody . . . quite unconnected, nothing to do with the Strafford family. One wonders how the names of many of our nobility become so common,' it adds to the piquancy of the satire that Jane Austen's family was in fact 'connected' with the Strafford Wentworths, who, incidentally, were ancestors of the Earls Fitzwilliam, of Wentworth Woodhouse, Yorkshire—the hero of *Pride and Prejudice* is the nephew of an earl named Fitzwilliam. As for his obnoxious aunt Lady Catherine de Bourgh (*née* Fitzwilliam), it is interesting to learn from Jane Austen's equally snobbish would-be cousin Sir Egerton Brydges that his family name and that of Jane Austen's great-grandmother, of the ducal house of Chandos, was earlier written 'De Burgh.'

Asterisks designate individuals who are the subjects of articles in the *Dictionary of National Biography*. Broken lines indicate omissions in the direct line of descent. 'N.c.' means a new creation of a peerage. I am indebted to Joan Corder, *Jane Austen's Kindred* (typescript in the College of Arms, London) for information in the more recent part of the listing.

—D.G.

There is always a living face beneath the mask.

—Yeats

'Writers in time transfer the mendacity of their craft to the other areas of their lives . . . In my sad trade, we can never be really devout or pious. We lie for a living.'

—Anthony Burgess, *Earthly Powers*

Like many other great moralists and preachers, she had been eloquent on a point in which her own conduct would ill bear examination.

—*Persuasion*

'Even the smooth surface of family-union seems worth preserving, though there may be nothing durable beneath.'

—*Persuasion*

'She has no more heart than a stone to people in general; and the devil of a temper.'

—*Emma*

'Those who tell their own Story . . . must be listened to with Caution.'

—*Sanditon*

CHAPTER 1

The End, July 1817

Early on the morning of Friday, 18 July 1817, in a house in College Street in the city of Winchester, a woman lay dying. She was forty-one, and she was dying painfully. She had lived in Steventon, in Hampshire; in Bath and Southampton; in Chawton, also in Hampshire; and she had visited a good deal in London and in Kent: never had she been out of England. She had six brothers and a sister and a host of nieces and nephews, some cousins and a mother living—but no children of her own. She had never married.

Her sister Cassandra asked her if she wanted anything. 'Nothing but death,' was the clear reply: 'God grant me patience, Pray for me oh pray for me.' Her physician gave her something to relieve the pain: half an hour later she was unconscious. 'During that half-hour was her struggle, poor soul!' Cassandra wrote two days later. 'She said she could not tell us what she suffered, though she complained of little fixed pain.' The sufferer reached a state of quiet insensibility, scarcely moving a limb. Except for a slight movement each time she drew breath, she lay still. Her head, nearly off the bed on which she reposed, rested on a pillow on her sister's lap. 'There was nothing convulsed or which gave the idea of pain in her look; on the contrary . . . she gave me the idea of a beautiful statue,' Cassandra said later. At 4:30 that morning, in Cassandra's arms, her sister's struggles came to an end. Cassandra closed her eyes.

'In her coffin,' Cassandra wrote, 'there is such a sweet serene air over her countenance as is quite pleasant to contemplate.'

On the 24th of July—early in the morning, so as not to interrupt the regular 10 a.m. service—the body was buried in Winchester Cathedral, near the centre of the north aisle and the chantry tomb of William of Wykeham—founder of Winchester College and of New College, Oxford—and close too to the final resting-place of Izaak

Walton. 'It is a satisfaction to me to think that [she is] to lie in a Building she admired so much,' Cassandra said. The burial was private; three brothers and a nephew attended. A black marble slab marked the place.

Cassandra remained at home. The little procession from College Street to the nearby Cathedral started from the house so quietly that she would not have known it was on its way had she not been 'upon the listen.' But she was determined to see the last of her sister. 'I watched the little mournful procession the length of the street; and when it turned from my sight . . . I had lost her for ever.'

The dead woman's family missed her. 'Never was human being more sincerely mourned by those who attended her remains than was this dear creature,' Cassandra declared. 'She was the sun of my life, the gilder of every pleasure, the soother of every sorrow . . . it is as if I had lost a part of myself. I loved her only too well, not better than she deserved.' Each of her brothers, her nephew was to write, 'loved afterwards to fancy a resemblance in some niece or daughter of his own to the dear sister . . . whose perfect equal they yet never expected to see.' He added: 'She was a humble, believing Christian. Her life had been passed in the performance of home duties, and the cultivation of domestic affections, without any self-seeking or craving after applause. She had always sought . . . to promote the happiness of all who came within her influence . . . Her sweetness of temper never failed. She was ever considerate.' And he also said this: 'Of events her life was singularly barren: few changes and no great crisis ever broke the smooth current of its course . . . There was in her nothing eccentric or angular; no ruggedness of temper; no singularity of manner . . . I have no reason to think that she ever felt any attachment by which the happiness of her life was at all affected.' One of her nieces, who was all of ten when her novelist-aunt died, solemnly declared in later years: 'I do not suppose she ever in her life said a sharp thing.' Her brother Henry felt that he should 'never look upon her like again' and that the Cathedral at Winchester could not 'contain the ashes of a brighter genius or a sincerer Christian.' In words which were to provoke much hostility among future generations of readers, Henry went on. She was witty and candid, he said in the 'Biographical Notice' he published, but never unkind or affected.

Faultless herself, as nearly as human nature can be, she always sought, in the faults of others, something to excuse, to forgive or forget. Where extenuation was possible, she had a sure refuge in silence. She never uttered either a hasty, a silly, or a severe expression. In short, her temper was as polished as her wit . . . She was tranquil without reserve or stiffness; and communicative without intrusion or self-sufficiency.

His sister, he added, was modest and unpretending, religious and devout: 'fearful of giving offence to God, and incapable of feeling it towards any fellow creature.' Her religious opinions, he declared, 'accorded strictly with those of our Established Church.' He concluded: 'Every thing came finished from her pen. For on all subjects she had ideas as clear as her expressions were well chosen . . . she never dispatched a note or letter unworthy of publication.'

Of course this sort of thing would be more likely to infuriate than to impress, to provoke guffaws rather than veneration. The ritual closing-of-ranks among the family in so unsubtle a fashion helps explain why so many have laboured so long to discover what was hidden. Surely something was being hidden. Why else call her flawless? Could this life, could any life, have been lived devoid of 'events,' of 'crisis,' of 'attachment'? Could this woman who never said an unkind or even a sharp thing and to whom nothing ever happened be the same woman whose ironic moral vision the world has celebrated for a century and a half? Could the family's touched-up portrait be a faithful likeness of her who laughed so unrestrainedly at the absurdities of her neighbours? How is it that the brothers who loved to fancy in some daughter or niece a resemblance to the dear sister departed named only one of them after her? And what about all that burning and pruning of her letters carried out so assiduously by Cassandra a few years before her own death—and witnessed by a niece? The effect of the destruction and the bowdlerisation was to suppress anything of a peculiar intimacy. As one critic has surmised, 'the gaps in the letters can be expected to correspond with crises in their author's life.' But she is not supposed to have had any crises. Another critic has said: 'If, as some have thought, [she] was a woman of sterling character and strong family attachments, but of a repellent personality—worldly, censorious, and hard—it is possible that her genius might have promoted the growth of a family legend about her, which would have softened her asperities and made the most of her sterner virtues and her intellectual gifts.' Surely this may account for the 'mass of cozy family adulation,' as another writer has characterised it.

Perhaps, then, hers was a personality entirely different from that promulgated by family legend. Consider these two comments—made, respectively, by Elizabeth Hardwick and Ian Watt:

> there is simply too much knowledge of wickedness, too much skill in the portrayal of contemptible characters, for us to feel unengaged . . . The ability to nail down unpleasant bits of character . . . must inevitably be the fruit of intense intro-spection. . . . I believe the records that say [she] was taciturn and stiff. I don't think her superb intelligence brought her happiness.

*   *   *

> pessimistic, she saw the individual life less as a series of pinnacles to be scaled than as . . . a set position to be maintained against the forces of selfishness, unreason, and emotional excess; nor . . . were silence and cunning too high a price to pay for maintaining it at home.

Hardwick suggests that the lady's knowledge of unpleasantness was the fruit of self-scrutiny, Watt that 'silence and cunning' were weapons used by her to mask her true feelings. Was she herself without 'feeling'? 'In [her] unpleasant people it [always] boils down finally to a lack of capacity for feeling,' Donald Greene has written. D.H. Lawrence commented on her 'sharp knowing in apartness,' and added: 'this old maid is . . . thoroughly unpleasant . . . bad, mean, snobbish.' Another critic has called her 'England's finest hater.'

Undoubtedly this goes too far; critics have done so from time to time. Surely it is unfair to say, as Frederic Harrison did, that the lady in question was a 'heartless little cynic . . . penning satirettes about her neighbours while the Dynasts were tearing the world to pieces and consigning millions to their graves.' One wonders about Frank O'Connor's assertion that she 'was a woman afraid of the violence of her own emotions, who rode the nightmare and sometimes rode it on too tight a rein.' But it is true, as others have said, that she was fond of exposing 'the economic basis of social behaviour with an ironic smile'; that she saw 'not a good society but a bad one, a predominantly vulgar society'; that she had a 'constant awareness of the many grotesque forms which the perversion of native human potential can take, and the dangers inherent in that perversion.' R.F. Brissenden has written that 'it is her ability to include the potential cruelty and nastiness of ordinary people together with their more admirable and pleasant qualities in one balanced image of humanity that in part makes [her] a great novelist.' Brissenden links our lady with her contemporary Sade as a deflator of the sentimental 'image of man as a social, sympathetic, generous, benevolent, and good-natured being' and says that she pictures him instead as 'an isolated, anarchic, selfish, cruel, violent, and aggressive being.' Her work, Brissenden declares, demonstrates her insight into the depths of human perversity. The novelist George Moore wrote:

> We do not go into society for the pleasure of conversation, but for the pleasure of sex, direct or indirect. Everything is arranged for this end: the dresses, the dances, the food, the wine, the music! Of this truth we are all conscious now, but should we have discovered it without [her] help? It was certainly she who perceived it, and her books are permeated with it.

Perhaps the lady was one person with intimates and another person at other times. Thus Virginia Woolf described her as probably 'Charming but perpendicular, loved at home but feared by strangers, biting of tongue but tender of heart.'

Whatever the truth, none of these things, needless to say, could or would be said by the lady's family, then or later. Instead, putting 'up the densest screen around her,' as one critic has remarked, 'they created a monstrous figure of sweetness,' wishing us to take her corrosive wit for genteel (and gentle) humour. The inscription on the tomb in Winchester Cathedral reflects the family's undeflectible solidarity:

In Memory of
JANE AUSTEN
youngest daughter of the late
Rev GEORGE AUSTEN
formerly Rector of Steventon in this county
she departed this life on the 18th of July, 1817,
aged 41, after a long illness supported with
the patience and the hopes of a Christian.

The benevolence of her heart,
the sweetness of her temper, and
the extraordinary endowments of her mind
obtained the regard of all who knew her, and
the warmest love of her intimate connections.

Their grief is in proportion to their affection
They know their loss to be irreparable
but in their deepest affliction they are consoled
by a firm though humble hope that her charity,
devotion, faith and purity have rendered
her soul acceptable in the sight of her
REDEEMER

What is perhaps most striking about these tributes—particularly the inscription on the tomb—is that each ignores the most interesting fact of all in the life of the recently departed: the lady wrote novels. Since her name never appeared on the title-page of any of her books during her lifetime, the secret of her authorship was not widely known outside the family circle.

It was not until 1872 that, on the north wall of the Cathedral's nave, an additional brass tablet was erected. It reads:

JANE AUSTEN

known to many by her writings,
endeared to her family
by the varied charms of her Character
and ennobled by Christian faith and piety,
was born at Steventon in the County of Hants.
Dec. xvi mdcclxxv,
and buried in this Cathedral
July xxiv mdcccxvii

"She opened her mouth with wisdom
and in her tongue is the law of
kindness."

Prov. xxxi. v. xxvi

You cannot write about Euripides and ignore Athens.
                                    —Ford Madox Ford, *Henry James*

'I dearly love a laugh . . . but . . . I hope I never ridicule what is wise or good. Follies and nonsense, whims and inconsistencies *do* divert me, I own, and I laugh at them whenever I can.'
                                    —Elizabeth Bennet in *Pride and Prejudice*

And Jane Austen. The daughter of a rather dull and perfectly respectable father, a clergyman, and a rather silly mother. How did she come to write *Pride and Prejudice*? The whole thing is a mystery.
                                    —Somerset Maugham

'Yes, indeed,' cried Mrs. Bennet, offended by his manner of mentioning a country neighbourhood. 'I assure you there is as much of *that* going on in the country as in town.'
                                    —*Pride and Prejudice*

'I could not preach, but to the educated.'
                                    —Edmund Bertram in *Mansfield Park*

CHAPTER 2

Steventon, 1775-1787

The best of times and the worst of times, certainly. An age of elegance and taste—and of squalor and callousness beyond imagination. An age of vanished loveliness—in which roughly a thousand people annually starved to death in London. An age of rigid class distinctions, in which the prosperous and the destitute inhabited two different worlds, both physically and morally. The age of Rowlandson and the age of Gainsborough.

The eighteenth century in England was the first great age of newspapers and advertising—and the bow window, built to allow more goods to be displayed. Early in the century the circulating library came into being, and stimulated interest in science, philosophy, history, divinity, and travel. Magazines of all sorts flourished; for the first time anywhere writers could actually make a living by their pens alone. The numbers of readers increased; much of the new readership was female. As the century wore on, the novel and the drama came to be more and more in demand. It was an age which considered fiction a frivolous amusement, but witnessed such steady growth in the novel's popularity as to make it, along with the drama, among the most ubiquitous of *genres*. Indeed, the Georgians became passion-ately addicted to plays—so much so that they grew fond of reading and acting them at home as well as watching them in theatres. As never before, perhaps, the imagination was excited, the appetite whetted, some part of the populace enticed to participate in the expanding world of culture. Prints of contemporary events and personalities filled the shops and were bought up at a tremendous rate. The new vogue for travel enriched both innkeepers and highwaymen; visits to such mountainous parts of Britain as Wales, Scotland, and the Lake District became fashionable. 'By 1800,' J.H. Plumb has written, 'all towns south of the Trent and east of the Severn were within a comfortable day's journey from London, whereas in 1700 it had taken three days to reach the city from Southampton.' It was the age of the horse and the road, of the coach and the carriage; all were constantly being refined in an attempt to attain higher speeds. Savage traffic accidents, then as now, were commonplace. The newly paved roads were an inducement to travel; they also helped to initiate a more regular, and expensive, postal service.

In the country much of England's rural beauty was unspoiled, and here many of the horrors of the time were easier to forget—though there were plenty of poor villagers in evidence. Indeed, in the last half of the eighteenth century more people still lived in towns and villages than in London and the smaller cities, though the proportions were beginning to change.

In genteel households small matters of etiquette were of greater importance than they are today, largely because the eighteenth-century gentry belonged to a society more formal than anything we know. There was more outward courtesy and ceremony of manner. It was an age of deportment: the way one moved was a badge of one's social class; to walk clumsily or make an awkward bow could be embarrassing. Manners were seen as a reflection of morals: one's outward decorum was likely to be carefully scrutinised. So the manners of the time were elaborate, and had to be learned. How to enter a room, how to go in to dinner, how to sit a horse, how to dance, how to draw or paint—these were things 'accomplished' Georgians were supposed to do effortlessly. The age's social concerns rendered it highly moral, interested in good works and prone to a rational, untheoretical piety. The evangelicals made swearing and drinking less fashionable than they had been early in the century; and they attacked slavery, frivolity, and religious inertia. Social hierarchy was an unquestioned fact of life, democracy of any sort virtually unknown. As David Cecil has written, by 1775 England had become 'a hierarchic society run by a hereditary oligarchy of nobles and squires, in which everyone, high or low, accepted distinctions of rank as part of the natural order as ordained by God.' It was an age of militant patriotism—'Rule Britannia' is an eighteenth-century song —and, among the upper classes, of laxity and licence (following the example of the Prince of Wales).

The Georgians loved to dance. In the provinces balls were often organised, in assembly rooms or in rooms at an inn specially designed for the purpose, by subscription—usually on the night of a full moon to make travelling easier. If it was a dancing age, the later eighteenth century was also a fighting age—an age of war, of war after war; an age of upheaval, and great inflation; of pluralism and hunting parsons; of Mary Wollstonecraft's *Vindication of the Rights of Women* (1792).

It was an age of practical realism, of 'good sense.' People believed in the family, in moderation and balance, in the good things money and social position brought with them. Landscape gardening became a passion among those who could afford it. Formal gardens disappeared and were replaced by planned 'natural' landscapes which 'copied' nature. Famous gardeners like Humphry Repton and Capability Brown rearranged landscape to create spectacular effects; the result often was a prospect that looked natural but was in fact man-made. The Georgians loved the out-of-doors, and spent as much time as was compatible with fashion in the countryside. Hunting and shooting were the most popular rural sports.

And what of indoor sports? Educated women without money of their own had to marry if they wanted to avoid being teachers or governesses; the professions and the universities were not open to them. For an education they substituted 'accomplishments'—drawing, music, languages. Nor was marriage easy for them, especially if they were not rich: they were not supposed to do anything or go anywhere without a chaperon or companion. A suitable match for a woman meant what was called in those days 'equality of fortune.' Still, taste and style and learning and intelligence and a sense of humour were valued.

Men stopped powdering their hair and curled it instead; they stopped wearing knee-breeches and embroidered waistcoats and full-skirted coats and started to wear trousers. Women threw off their stiff hoops and full-skirted gowns and began to wear high-waisted flowing skirts. They dressed their hair in a fine cloud of little curls over neck and shoulders, as Margaret Kennedy has described it, as if rejoicing in release from powder and pomatum. In the 'morning,' which lasted until 4 p.m., it was generally swathed in a loose muslin cap so as to save the wearer having to curl it at the back until evening. At formal events elaborate, enormous hats often were worn; on such occasions some women might resemble ambulatory birdcages or greenhouses. The dinner hour tended to vary with the degree of fashion of the diners—the more 'fashionable,' the later the hour—but most people ate their dinners before nightfall. Few dining-room tables had candlesticks on them; lights were brought in as needed.

Vegetables and potatoes were less popular than they are today; meat of all kinds, beer and home-made wines, especially mead, were more in vogue. Food was plentiful and relatively inexpensive for the well off; overeating and obesity were common. Yet at least half the population still lived meanly, possessed little, and often went hungry.

Changes in style and taste, of course, exhibited themselves in the towns before they reached the villages. Town life was fashionable, country life shrinking. *Persuasion* tells us that men in a country family could interest themselves only in game, horses, dogs, and newspapers, while the ladies must make do with housekeeping, neighbours, dress, dancing, and music.

Many parts of the countryside would still, in 1775, have been recognisable to Chaucer.

It was in the country that Jane Austen was born, and in the country that she lived most of her life. In fact the first twenty-five years of her life were spent largely in the place where she was born: Steventon, in Hampshire.

North Hampshire in those days, as in these, abounded in lanes, farms, and cottages which kept an air of privacy and peace. Steventon lay south of the main road from London to Basingstoke, Andover, and Salisbury. Basingstoke was seven miles to the east; Overton, the post-town, was only about a mile and a half away. Coaches could be caught twice each evening at Deane Gate on the main road, or at the Wheatsheaf Inn in Popham Lane, about the same distance away but south of Steventon, on the road from London to Winchester and Southampton.

Steventon was located in what has been described as 'fresh upland country, which holds copses tucked into folds of the ground and lanes sunk in the chalk' and overhung by yew, elm, chestnut, fir, and juniper. Set amidst thick hedgerows in the chalk hills, it was small and probably not very exciting, though the work of the parish, the farms, and the village itself would have made it a bustling little place, a self-contained world, in Jane Austen's day. The village consisted of a row of cottages between the Rectory at the eastern end and a road running north-south at the western end—and little else. The cottages had gardens and were scattered haphazardly along the village's main (and only) street. The more prosperous families of the district lived a few miles away, on their estates.

Steventon Rectory was pulled down in 1826 and a new one built in its place, but the older house has been described in detail by several of the generation which knew it best. It was an unpretentious, two-storeyed square Georgian building with a flat facade, two square sashed windows flanking the front door and five above on the upper floor, a trellised porch, and a sloping, narrow roof with attic dormer windows and two chimneys. It contained seven bedrooms. In front was a wide, curving, gravelled drive and an informal garden. A bow window looked out onto the old-fashioned back garden which was framed by a thatched wall and sported a shadowed walkway under elms. Along the upper or southern side of the garden ran a terrace of fine turf bordered by strawberry beds. The garden was studded with rustic seats and a sundial and was planted with hedgerows, which formed within them some pleasant walks. There was farmland attached to the house (used partly for the pleasure of the family and partly to increase its income) and a spacious barn. The Rectory stood in a shadowed valley surrounded by sloping meadows sprinkled with elms. There were servants and a carriage, though the two horses probably were used for farming when they were not pulling the carriage. The family kept five Alderney cows. Later on the Austen boys had riding horses of their own.

The church and manor were at the southern end of the village, down an unpaved road whose surface was repaired with shovelfuls of stones whenever a company larger than usual was expected. The Church of St Nicholas was plain, simple, and small, but set charmingly apart on a hill near some sycamore trees. A thirteenth-century building, it had whitewashed walls and dark beams: since Jane Austen's day a steeple and a memorial window to the novelist are virtually the only additions.

Nothing now remains of the old Rectory except its pump. The sitting-room, also used as a dining-room, was on the ground floor, as was the kitchen and a small parlour where the Rector's wife did her sewing. Also on the ground floor was the Rector's study, which looked out into the back garden. On the floor above were the bedrooms and a dressing-room, which contained a modest library and a piano. In mid-Victorian times J.E. Austen-Leigh, Jane Austen's nephew, looked back upon the house and found it wanting: 'the rooms were finished with less elegance than would now be found in the most ordinary dwellings. No cornice marked the junction of wall and ceiling; while the beams which supported the upper floors projected into the rooms below in all their naked simplicity, covered only by a coat of paint or whitewash.' The drawing-room was sparsely furnished with straight-backed, hard chairs, a table, an uncushioned sofa, and a glass-fronted cupboard containing a gilt china tea-service. On the wall was a tall pier-glass. There was little carpeting. Still, most of Austen-Leigh's contemporaries who knew the place in their younger days found it pleasant enough.

Here, at Steventon Rectory, on 16 December 1775, Jane Austen was born.

Her father's family had been clothiers in Kent from the Middle Ages. They were substantial landowners in the Sevenoaks area, mostly at Horsmonden and Chevening, in the sixteenth and seventeenth centuries, and they are landowners there still. The Austens were what was known as gentry—vigorous landowning families which in the eighteenth century carefully educated its scions and sent them into the Church, the law, and the military. The upper reaches of this class joined the aristocracy, while its lower ranks embraced the attorneys, apothecaries, and the surgeons of the country towns. All that separated the gentry and aristocracy were income and politics (the nobles were generally Whig, and country gentry usually Tory). The gentry, like most middle classes, was prone to snobbery, since it had the best opportunity for social advancement; it was also prone to culture, refinement, and pragmatism in commonplace matters. It was this class—the hereditary ruling class of England, in fact—into which Jane Austen was born, in the midst of which she would be brought up, and about which she would write.

The Austens had their financial and social ups and downs. Having become prosperous in the cloth trade, the family acquired two small manors—Broadford and Grovehurst, in Kent; there followed a period during which a struggle to maintain appearances and educate children back to a larger fortune and greater prosperity became the hallmark of this family of good property but only moderate wealth.

As Sir David Smithers has found, the family fortunes were spectacularly revived by Jane Austen's father's uncle, Francis Austen. He became a solicitor, agent to the Duke of Dorset at Knole in Kent, and Clerk of the Peace for the County. Ultimately he married two heiresses—and persuaded the godmother of his eldest son, Viscountess Falkland, to will him a legacy of £100,000. This was around the time of Jane Austen's birth.

The novelist's father—George Austen (1731-1805), the Rector of Steventon—was a strikingly handsome man with hazel eyes and curly hair (prematurely grey), a sweet temper, and genteel, cordial manners. He came from a poor branch of the family. His father was a surgeon—then near the bottom of the middle-class scale. His grandmother had remained in the Sevenoaks area so that her sons might have a good classical education at the grammar school there. George's father married a widow with a son; of his many children only two survived—George, and his half-sister Philadelphia Walter, later Mrs Hancock. It was she who was to bring Warren Hastings and, through her only daughter Eliza (Hastings' god-daughter), the French Revolution into Jane Austen's life. The Walters were a vigorous and long-lived family. Philadelphia's brother James met his end in the hunting-field at the age of eighty-four by falling into a snow-drift.

By the age of nine George Austen was orphaned. He was adopted by his wealthy solicitor uncle in Sevenoaks, who had been buying up all the land he could find with the proceeds of his inheritances. George was sent to the Tonbridge School, from which he obtained an Open Scholarship to St John's College, Oxford. At Oxford he became an accomplished classical scholar and English grammarian. Indeed, he went on from Oxford to teach at his old school at Tonbridge, where he was appointed Second Master in 1758 (he taught all his own children in their early years and took pupils into his house—educated in the company of his sons—to augment his income; one of these was the young Lord Lymington, son of the great local magnate the Earl of Portsmouth: in later years, after he had succeeded his father, the young man would invite the Austen girls to attend the annual ball at Hurstbourne Park, always a great event during Jane Austen's girlhood). George Austen became a Fellow of St John's in 1759; he was known there as 'the handsome Proctor.' In 1760 he took orders, and in 1761 he was given the Steventon living by his kinsman Thomas Knight of Godmersham Park, a mansion near Canterbury, and Chawton, in Hampshire. Probably he did not take up any parish duties before 1764. As it turned out, Knight's son, also a Thomas, was childless, and made George Austen's third son, Edward, his heir. Edward Austen inherited the properties in Godmersham and Chawton in 1794, and took the name of Knight in 1812. In 1773 George's uncle Francis purchased for him the nearby living of Deane, about a mile and a half away from Steventon; the population of the two livings together amounted to no more than three hundred.

At Steventon George Austen largely lived the life of a country gentleman and a scholar, devoting much time to books, some to supervising the farm attached to the Rectory, and some to his clerical duties. Mr Knight had leased the manor house at Steventon and much of the land around it to a family named Digweed, and the Rector was a sort of acting squire, the closest thing to a lord of the manor in the tiny village. He was also to become an affectionate family man.

On 26 April 1764 in Bath—where his bride's father had recently died, and where, forty-one years later, his own body would be laid to rest—George Austen married Cassandra Leigh (1739-1827) in Walcot Church. The pair probably had met through some Oxford connections. If his origins lay near the bottom reaches of the gentry, hers were decidedly near the top. Though her family was only a little older than his—some Leighs had settled in High Leigh in Cheshire at the time of the Norman Conquest—it was distinctly more illustrious. One of the Leigh ancestors, Sir Thomas White, had founded St John's College, Oxford, and another, Sir Thomas Leigh, was Lord Mayor of London at the time of Elizabeth I's accession. The Queen, as a matter of fact, rode behind him to be proclaimed at Paul's Cross. When Coventry shut its gates against Charles I, that ill-fated monarch found shelter with Sir Thomas's son—like all succeeding Leighs (including Jane Austen) a staunch supporter of the Stuarts—at his place in Warwickshire, Stoneleigh Abbey. Sir Thomas's granddaughter Alice had the distinction of being married and deserted by Robert Dudley, son of the Queen's great favourite (Charles I made her a duchess).

Stoneleigh Abbey was the family seat of the ennobled branch of the family, the Leighs of Warwickshire. Cassandra's grandfather, a Brydges, was the brother-in-law of that famous Duke of Chandos who was the patron of Handel. Her father—Thomas Leigh, of Adlestrop, Gloucester—was early in life elected a Fellow of All Souls College, Oxford. Later he became Rector of Harpsden, near Henley-on-Thames, in Oxfordshire. This is where Cassandra Leigh grew up. She had a sister, a Mrs Cooper, who had also married a clergyman and lived with her husband and their two children near Bath—but the Coopers died young, and Jane Austen hardly knew this aunt and uncle; and a brother, James, who in 1751 inherited some property from a great-uncle on his mother's side named Perrot and called himself Leigh Perrot thereafter. The Perrots had settled in Pembrokeshire as early as the thirteenth century. The last of them died in 1778: James Leigh Perrot pulled down the family mansion and sold the estate to the Duke of Marlborough. Mr Leigh Perrot also had a life-interest in the Stoneleigh property in Warwickshire. He married a niece of Sir Montague Cholmeley of Lincolnshire. The Leigh Perrots were wealthy, childless, and long-lived, and Jane Austen was to know them well. They spent part of the year in Bath and the other part at Scarlets, their house in Berkshire.

The daughter of a clergyman, Cassandra Leigh fell in love with another one, and married him. She was considered sensible, distinguished, and good-looking—but not beautiful. She had an aquiline nose, which she apparently enjoyed looking down, and a sharp, epigrammatic turn of speech—inherited, perhaps, from her father's elder brother, Dr Theophilus Leigh, Master of Balliol College, Oxford, for more than fifty years, whose quick wit was praised by Mrs Thrale in a letter to Dr Johnson. The Master of Balliol's daughter married Samuel Cooke, vicar of Great Bookham, Surrey; he was to be Jane Austen's godfather (she had two godmothers: Mrs Musgrave, a connection of her mother's, and the second Mrs Francis Austen, the wife of her father's generous uncle), and his children were among her earliest friends. Cassandra was said by all who knew her to be a serious, pious, and unpretentious woman, practical and hard-working. She was small and slight and in her early years had enormous energy; she was an untiring sempstress and gardener. In later years she became something of a hypochondriac.

The happy couple—'well-connected, well-mannered, and tradition- ally Tory'—went on a brief honeymoon which consisted of a journey from Bath to Steventon with a one-day stopover in Andover. They lived first at Deane, moving to Steventon a few years later. Oddly enough, they commenced their married life with a small child who was not their own but in their care—the son of the celebrated Governor-General of British India, Warren Hastings. The little boy had been left at the age of three in the guardianship of George Austen in 1761, three years before his marriage to Cassandra Leigh, through the influence of his half-sister Philadelphia Hancock, whose husband was an English surgeon working in India and a friend of Hastings. Hancock died a month before Jane Austen was born, and his widow spent most of the next few years with her brother's family at Steventon. Little George Hastings, who may have been the illegitimate offspring of Warren Hastings and Philadelphia Hancock —when Hancock died, Hastings made over to the widow a trust fund worth £10,000—died of diphtheria at the age of six in 1764, during the first year of the Austens' marriage. Warren Hastings was nonetheless always grateful to the Austens for their care of the lad; indeed, they themselves were deeply attached to the child and missed him terribly. Hastings was also an early admirer of *Pride and Prejudice*. The Austens in their turn were fanatical defenders of Hastings some years later during his spectacular trial by the House of Lords of his impeachment by the House of Commons for misconduct (the trial lasted from 1788 to 1795). Philadelphia Hancock was in London during much of this time and sent dispatches back to Steventon. In one of the more interesting of these she writes:

> I had the satisfaction of hearing all the celebrated orators— Sheridan, Burke, and Fox. The first was so low we could not hear him, the second so hot and hasty we could not understand, the third was highly superior to either, as we could distinguish every word, but not to our satisfaction, as he is so much against Mr Hastings whom we all wish so well.

It should be understood that Jane Austen was related, if distantly, to the nobility. She was the great-great-granddaughter of the eighth Lord Chandos, and the great-grandniece of the first Duke of Chandos. Her mother, her elder sister, and one of her cousins (Mrs Cooke) were all named Cassandra after her mother's great-aunt Cassandra, Duchess of Chandos. Cassandra Leigh's family had several aristocratic forebears; two of her sons would marry cousins of the Earl of Craven, one of them a duke's daughter. Jane Austen's kinsman Sir Samuel Egerton Brydges for many years fought an epic but unsuccessful campaign to persuade the House of Lords to resurrect the extinct Chandos peerage. He also boasted that his name derived from the Norman 'Bourgh'; this amused Jane Austen, who adapted the surname for one of her more snobbish upper-class characters, Lady Catherine de Bourgh in *Pride and Prejudice*. Brydges's sister, Mrs Isaac Lefroy, was one of the novelist's neighbours at Steventon and among her most intimate friends.

Jane Austen could not have remained unaware either of her ancestry or her contemporary connections. There were still an abbey and a barony in the family. The class to which she belonged, the gentry, was at the height of its power, prestige and influence as she was growing up. If her plots are conservative ones—'fearing subversion, advocating the values which in times past justified the rule of the gentry,' as Marilyn Butler characterises them—we must not be surprised; nor should we be surprised if her books sometimes rebuke individualistic female initiatives and imply, as they all do, that the consummation of a woman's life lies in marriage to a commanding man. Hers was a conservative class, and hers a conservative nature.

Each of the Austen's eight children was born at the Steventon Rectory, though the family lived at Deane, in less comfortable circumstances, until 1771.

The Rectory had seven bedrooms, but Jane Austen never possessed a room of her own. All of the children shared—Jane with her sister Cassandra until her death. She was the seventh of eight children, six boys and two girls, and the youngest to die—although the second son, George (1766-1827), was mentally handicapped and lived quietly away from home in the neighbourhood of Steventon. The only mention of him in surviving correspondence among the Austens occurs in a letter written by his mother in December 1770, when he would have been four: 'My poor little George is come to see me to-day, he seems pretty well, tho' he had a fit lately; it was near a twelve-month since he had one before, so was in hopes they had left him, but must not flatter myself so now.' We can surmise from Jane Austen's knowledge of the dumb alphabet—in 1808 she said she could talk to the deaf with her fingers—that he remained deaf through all or much of his life.

The eldest child, James (1765-1819)—named for his mother's brother—was educated as a boy by his father and later at St John's College, Oxford, where he got a scholarship as Founder's Kin. He became a Fellow of St John's and while there helped establish and contributed to *The Loiterer*, a periodical modelled on *The Spectator*. He took orders, and had livings at Overton and at Deane, ultimately (in 1805) succeeding his father as Rector of Steventon and residing for the rest of his life in the house in which all the Austen children were born. His first wife was the daughter of a general and related through her mother to the second Duke of Ancaster. James Austen's first wife died within three years of the marriage, leaving one daughter, Anna. His second wife was Mary Lloyd, a clergyman's daughter. She and her sister Martha would become important figures in Jane Austen's life. James and his second wife had two children. All three of his offspring—Anna Austen Lefroy, Caroline Austen, and James Edward Austen-Leigh—were to become fruitful sources of information about their novelist-aunt. James Austen seems to have been a reflective, cultured, scholarly man; he may, as his son declares, have helped direct Jane's early reading. It is known that he wrote parts of some of the plays the family put on for its own amusement (in the barn in summer and the dining-room in winter). He was apparently semi-invalid, of an uncertain temper, and rather impractical.

The third son, Edward (1768-1852), the future heir of Godmersham and Chawton, was no scholar but a clever man of business. He was from all accounts generous, indulgent, and easy-going. The Knights, George Austen's connections, took a fancy to the boy which his mother encouraged; after becoming their heir, he took their name, as we have seen. Edward married the daughter of Sir Brook Bridges of Goodneston, near Canterbury (the Bridges and the Brydges were different families altogether). After her husband's death, Mrs Knight (Catherine Knatchbull) chose to surrender Godmersham and most of her income to Edward and his wife and move to Canterbury. Edward's sisters came often to visit this pleasant brother and his growing family (ultimately eleven children). Edward's wife died after the birth of their last child in 1808, from which time the visits of his sisters (especially Cassandra) to the motherless family became more frequent—thus, happily for us, providing the occasion for much letter-writing back and forth. One of the Knight daughters, Fanny, the future Lady Knatchbull, would become Jane Austen's favourite niece, and the recipient of some of her most interesting letters. Edward lived mainly at Godmersham and did not marry again.

The fourth son, Henry (1771-1850)—supposedly the handsomest of the handsome Austens—was Jane Austen's favourite brother (Edward was Cassandra's) and acted as the novelist's adviser in literary and practical matters. Henry's life was less placid than those of James and Edward. Like James, he was educated by his father and as Founder's Kin at St John's, where he too contributed to *The Loiterer*. Although very clever, some said brilliant, he did not win a fellowship, and indeed took many years to settle himself professionally. His earliest ambitions were military, and he became an officer in the Oxford Militia. After an engagement to another lady, in 1797 he married his cousin Eliza, the Comtesse de Feuillide, whose first husband had been guillotined in 1794. Eliza, ten years older than Henry and the daughter of the Rector's half-sister Philadelphia—and possibly of Warren Hastings—had a little boy of her own called Hastings de Feuillide. During the short Peace of Amiens in 1802,

Henry and Eliza went to France in the hope of recovering some of her late husband's property. They had a narrow escape. Napoleon had issued orders to detain all English travellers, and they would have been 'detained' had not Eliza ordered horses in perfect French, her husband keeping his mouth shut. Upon their return to England they settled in London, and Henry became a banker. At first he prospered, being appointed Receiver-General of Oxfordshire in 1813. When, in this year, Eliza died, he engaged himself to another lady, but did not marry her. In 1815-16 his bank failed. Casting around for something to do, Henry decided to follow in the relatively safe footsteps of his father and eldest brother, and took orders. He settled down to curacies at Farnham and Bentley near Alton in Hampshire. He was a lively, witty, cheerful but unstable and hapless man who grew pompous in late middle age and never fulfilled his youthful promise. He spent the last thirty-four years of his life as a conscientious but obscure parish clergyman. The family always admired his sermons.

After Henry came Cassandra (1773-1845), two and a half years older than Jane and the recipient of most of her letters. In her early twenties Cassandra became engaged to one of her father's former pupils, Thomas Craven Fowle, a clergyman who died of a fever while serving as an army chaplain in the West Indies. Cassandra never married. She lived with her mother and sister until the latter's death, and then with her mother until Mrs Austen's death in 1827. In her last years Cassandra lived alone at Chawton and interested herself in the poor of the parish—though she frequently went off on visits to other members of the large Austen family. She died in her brother Frank's house near Portsmouth and was buried beside her mother at Chawton. Cassandra, clearly, was an intelligent and clever woman but apparently undemonstrative and sometimes moody. Contemporaries are agreed that her habits were regular and her opinions on most matters conventional. There can be no question, however, that, alone with her sister, the cool front she presented to the world came down. Cassandra was the single most important person in Jane's life. Their innermost thoughts were shared, and shared with no one else, nor did they confide their deepest feelings to any other persons— though the letters Jane wrote to Henry which were destroyed by Cassandra might have made interesting reading. Mrs Austen once remarked that if Cassandra were to have her head cut off, Jane would insist on having hers cut off too.

The fifth son, Francis (1774-1865)—neat, practical, and intrepid as a child—had a spectacularly successful career in the Navy. He died Sir Francis, G.C.B., Admiral of the Fleet. He sailed in the East Indies and the Mediterranean as well as in home waters. He served under Nelson; during the Peninsular War he took charge of the disembarkation of General Moore's troops. Like Edward, he had eleven children. Francis's first wife died in 1823. Five years later he married Martha Lloyd, the sister of his eldest brother's second wife. Francis (called Frank by the family) had a reputation for piety and sternness, but was considered just by the men who served under him.

The youngest son, Charles (1779-1852), followed in the footsteps of his naval brother. Both boys entered the Royal Naval Academy in Portsmouth around the age of twelve. Charles served in the Mediterranean and the West Indies, becoming a rear admiral, a C.B., and later Commander-in-Chief of the East India Station. Unlike Frank, he was never knighted—and he was regarded by his men with unbounded affection. He married twice, fathered seven children, and died in China. He was the only one of Jane Austen's brothers younger than she—her 'own particular little brother,' as she sometimes called him. He was apparently more easy-going and demonstrative than his brother Frank, and his letters home were more lively.

Five years younger than Wordsworth and three years younger than Scott, Jane Austen, called 'Jenny' as a child, derived her given name from her great-grandmother on her mother's side; her godmother Mrs Francis Austen, the wife of her father's uncle; and her mother's sister, Mrs Cooper. By all accounts, Jane was a general favourite in the family circle—engaging, vivacious, and of course witty. By our standards her life might seem limited and narrow. She never travelled abroad—never saw much of England, for that matter, beyond Hampshire and Kent. She had few acquaintances outside the family. But she drew great pleasure from living in the midst of the affectionate, cultured, lively household at Steventon—though, as we shall see, there is ample evidence to suggest that Jane Austen's childhood was not all sunshine and smiles.

George Austen's income, in the year of his younger daughter's birth, was probably a little under £600 after he had paid his two curates. He kept a carriage, and he and his wife were very much part of the society of the county. They were not rich, says Jane Austen's nephew, 'but, aided by Mr Austen's power of teaching, they had enough to afford a good education to their sons and daughters, to mix in the best society of the neighbourhood, and to exercise a liberal hospitality to their relations and friends.' Still, one hears of Mrs Austen being without a new gown for two years at a stretch, and of her cutting up some of her worn clothes to make a suit for one of her boys. George Austen decided not to send his young sons away. As we have seen, he educated them at home, along with several carefully selected pupils he took in as boarders to increase his income. After 1778 he no longer had to give a home to Eliza Hancock, his half-sister's child and his future daughter-in-law; the girl's mother took her to Paris to finish her education. There she met the glamorous, wealthy Jean Gabriel Capotte, Comte de Feuillide, an officer in the Queen's Regiment of Dragoons and owner of an estate called Le Marais, near Gaboret, in Guyenne (bought by his father, a speculator in grain).

The boys stayed at home for their schooling and enjoyed the hunting and riding around Steventon, which was in the centre of the Vine Hunt district. The two girls, Jane and Cassandra, could not hunt or shoot. Their mother being too busy with the cares of a growing household to instruct them herself, the sisters were sent away to school at an early age. In addition to her eight children, Mrs Austen had the brewing and baking and laundering to look after, and her girls were too young to help her with the chores. The Rectory was full to overflowing. So off they went to Oxford in 1783—Jane was seven—with their cousin Jane Cooper to a Mrs Cawley, Dr Cooper's sister and widow of a master of Brasenose College. Mrs Cawley was stiff and formal and unpopular with her charges. When she moved her household to Southampton the three girls went with her. There they caught what was called a putrid fever (probably diphtheria, possibly typhoid) from which Jane nearly died and which was to kill her aunt Mrs Cooper, who took her daughter home with her to nurse. In 1784 Cassandra and Jane were also fetched home. In the following year Cassandra, Jane and their now motherless cousin were sent to the well-known Abbey School in the Forbury at Reading. It was run by a Mrs Latournelle, an amiable, elderly Englishwoman married to a Frenchman. Her chief claims to culture were a vast knowledge of the contemporary theatre and an artifical leg made of cork. The girls liked her, but learned little at her school. There were just a few hours of casual lessons each day; Mrs Latournelle's most engaging interests were cooking, sewing, and gossip.

A contemporary tells us that the Abbey school-house at Reading was an ancient building consisting of 'a gateway with rooms above, and on each side of it a vast staircase. . . . The best part of the house was encompassed by a beautiful, old-fashioned garden, where the young ladies were allowed to wander under tall trees in hot summer evenings.' 'One may imagine Jane' at this time, Elizabeth Jenkins writes, 'a small, slender child with a round face and big black eyes, following Cassandra like a shadow, shy, but ready at once to be friendly and merry with anyone who was kind.' One may also imagine the girls lounging in the romantic, spacious, tree-lined garden of the old Abbey School, gossiping and laughing. It was an easy-going regime. George Austen was paying just under £40 a year for the schooling of his two daughters. After nearly two years—summer 1785 to spring 1787—he grew dissatisfied with the place. When she was eleven, in 1787, Jane Austen's schooldays came abruptly to an end. It is perhaps significant that Anne Elliot is the only one of her heroines who goes to school. Most of the others have the sort of education Jane Austen herself had—largely the result, as one critic puts it, of 'plenty of books, plenty of time, and plenty of good talk.'

Cassandra, now nearly fourteen, was old enough to help her mother with the household, and soon Jane would be able to do the same. So they remained at home, where Jane's education was completed. It was probably directed by her father, an excellent classical scholar with a good library, assisted by James and Henry. We know that in addition to Shakespeare and Milton, she read Pope, Thomson, Gray, Hume, Sherlock, Sheridan, Baretti, Price, Blair, Gilpin, Payne Knight, and the *Spectator*. Her favourite contemporary writers were Johnson, Cowper, Crabbe, and Goldsmith. She also read an enormous amount of eighteenth-century fiction—Fielding, Richardson, Sterne, Charlotte Smith, Charlotte Lennox; later, Ann Radcliffe, Fanny Burney, Maria Edgeworth, Scott and others. She learned French and some Italian, a good deal of history, played the pianoforte with some skill, and was taught to draw, sew, and embroider. There can be little doubt that the years of her real education were those which she spent under her father's tutelage— the years, that is, following those of her so-called formal education. Henry Austen's 'Biographical Notice' of his sister tends to confirm this. So does the scene in *Pride and Prejudice* in which Lady Catherine de Bourgh cross-examines Elizabeth Bennet on the subject of her education.

'Then, who taught you? who attended to you? Without a governess you must have been neglected.'

'Compared with some families, I believe we were; but such of us as wished to learn, never wanted the means. We were always encouraged to read, and had all the masters that were necessary. Those who chose to be idle, certainly might.'

When Jane and Cassandra returned home in 1787, the population of the Rectory was thinning out. James was at Oxford, Henry about to go. Edward was on the Grand Tour arranged for him by the Knights. Frank was at the Naval Academy in Portsmouth; in the following year, 1788, he went as a volunteer on the *HMS Perseverence* to the East Indies. Of the six brothers only Henry and little Charles were still at home, though James and Frank spent their holidays there. Certainly there was no time to be bored. Under their mother's supervision, the girls would have done all of the hemming and stitching now done by machine; they would have looked after the men's linen and their own bonnets; they would have been involved in preparing some of the family recipes; they would have visited the local poor and gone regularly to church; they would have taken walks in the countryside—but not too far from home, for these were rough times. Cassandra and Jane occupied together two rooms on the upper storey—a bedroom and a combination sitting- and dressing-room. It was furnished, a visitor recalls, with a chocolate-coloured carpet, bookshelves—among the books were Dodsley's *Collection of Poems* and Richardson's *Clarissa* in five volumes—a desk, Jane's piano, Cassandra's sketching materials, and an oval mirror between the windows.

Jane Austen was a Georgian, and brought up in the frank atmosphere of the age—an atmosphere which eschewed restrictions on reading or the subject-matter of conversation. While her education was somewhat haphazard, it was a liberal one. It is not surprising, then, to find that much of her earliest writings are burlesques and parodies of fashionable literature. She was taught to question rather than to accept blindly; and the satirical vein very early became a favourite with her, not least because she could be certain of addressing an audience—the family—familiar with the objects of her mirth and sympathetic to her irreverent treatment of them. But the parodic vein suggests other things as well about these childhood years, as we shall see.

II

The Austen family enjoyed what society the neighbourhood of Steventon offered. Such local magnates as Lord Bolton, Lord Dorchester, and Lord Portsmouth were to be seen for the most part only at the occasional balls they gave at Hackwood, Kempshott Park, and Hurstbourne, and at county balls held each month during the winter at Basingstoke. Nobility and gentry did not see too much of one another. The Austens were country Tories of the deepest dye. Most of the families Jane Austen knew as a girl in Steventon were gentry.

Mrs Nowes Lloyd, the widow of a clergyman and the daughter of Governor Craven of South Carolina, resided with her three daughters at nearby Deane, where her husband had the living, and later at Ibthorp, near Andover, about twenty miles from Steventon. Mrs Lloyd's mother was the melodramatic Mrs Craven, who was known to have treated her daughters brutally—beating, starving, and incarcerating them until, in desperation, they left home and made safe marriages. Jane Austen heard the well-known story from the Lloyds; undoubtedly there is a hint of it in the youthful 'Lesley Castle,' and more than a hint of Lady Craven in Lady Susan. In any case, between the Austens and the Lloyds there was much visiting back and forth. The middle Lloyd daughter, Eliza, married a Fowle, a brother of Cassandra Austen's future fiancé (the Fowles and the Lloyds were cousins). The eldest Lloyd girl was Martha, who, as we have seen, lived with the Austen ladies in later years and ultimately became Frank Austen's second wife. Mary, the youngest Lloyd girl, would be James Austen's second wife.

An interesting cousin by marriage of the Lloyd girls was Elizabeth, Lady Craven, wife of the sixth baron (patron of Cassandra Austen's fiancé Thomas Fowle)—a notorious libertine whose second husband was related to Queen Caroline, George II's consort. Some of her plays—written, after her second marriage, under the name of Margravine of Ansbach—were produced at Drury Lane and Covent Garden; in later life she specialised in 'private theatricals' at her home in Hammersmith. Jane Austen must have known of her.

Another nearby family was the Bigg Withers of Manydown. Again, three daughters (called simply Bigg) were intimate friends of the Austen girls: Elizabeth, the future mother of Sir William

Heathcote, prominent in the Oxford Movement and the sole patron of John Keble; Catherine, who married the father-in-law of Southey's daughter; and Alethea, who remained a spinster. The Digweeds, who had rented the manor-house at Steventon from the Knights, later moved to Alton when the Austens were at Chawton, becoming neighbours once again.

Most important during these years were the Lefroys. Isaac Lefroy—the grandfather of Mary Russell Mitford—was the Rector of Ashe; his wife Anna was a sister of Sir Egerton Brydges. Though she was twenty-five years older than Jane Austen, the two were intimate friends until Mrs Lefroy died, thrown from her horse, on Jane Austen's twenty-ninth birthday; a two-column obituary notice was published in the *Gentleman's Magazine*, suggesting that Mrs Lefroy's prominence was more than local. A woman of unusual culture, elegance, and grace, Anna Lefroy was apparently the first to encourage her young neighbour Jane Austen in her work. She was also a pioneer in health matters and an early advocate of vaccination. In his autobiography, Sir Egerton Brydges remarks that Jane Austen 'was very intimate with Mrs Lefroy, and much encouraged by her.' In a memorial poem she wrote four years after Mrs Lefroy's death, Jane refers to 'Her partial favour from my earliest years.' Mrs Lefroy's nephew Tom—later the Right Hon. Thomas Lefroy, Lord Chief-Justice of Ireland (1852-66)—figures in Jane Austen's story; and Mrs Lefroy's son Benjamin married Jane's niece Anna. At Ben Lefroy's ordination, it is said, the Bishop asked him just two questions: Was he the son of Mrs Lefroy of Ashe? And had he married a Miss Austen? The connections between the two families were many and close.

One thing the Austens had in common with their neighbours was a love of amateur theatricals. Between 1784 and 1790 a good many plays were put on in the Austens' barn or in their dining-room, depending on the season; Christmas and midsummer were favourite times of the year—most of the younger generation were at home then. This was in some measure the work of the Comtesse de Feuillide, who had a passion for the stage. Among the plays known to have been performed at the Rectory during these years were *The Rivals*, Thomas Francklin's *Matilda*, Mrs Cowley's *Which Is the Man?*, Bickerstaffe's *The Sultan: or A Peep into the Seraglio*, Garrick's *Bon Ton, or High Life above Stairs*, Townley's farcical *High Life below Stairs*, Mrs Centlivre's *The Wonder: A Woman Keeps A Secret*, and Garrick's adaptation of Fletcher's *The Chances*. Plays were a family custom for some years: James Austen often wrote the prologues, and Henry Austen and the Countess Eliza frequently played the leading roles. Inevitably the young Jane would have been fascinated by the preparations, rehearsals, performances, and offstage complications. Inevitably she would have learned the language of the theatre. Nor is there any doubt (as we shall see) that she continued to enjoy the theatre into middle age. Sir William Heathcote remembered being with her at a Twelfth Night party when he was a child, on which occasion she acted the part of Mrs Candour 'with appreciation and spirit.' The Austens were always fond of drama, charades, riddles, conundrums, and impromptu games of various kinds. They were an articulate family: probably they learned much from hearing George Austen read aloud to them night after night. He was said to read with great feeling and skill.

III

When she was twelve, Jane, along with Cassandra, went with their parents to visit her great-uncle Francis Austen at Sevenoaks. She had been to Oxford, Southampton, and Reading: this was her first visit to Kent—and, undoubtedly more interesting even than this, her first to London as well. We know the foursome stopped in town because one of Eliza de Feuillide's letters to Philadelphia Walter mentions that they dined with Eliza and her mother on the way home to Hampshire. At Sevenoaks Jane and Cassandra met their aunt Philadelphia, who has left this account of the future novelist: 'The youngest (Jane) is very like her brother Henry, not at all pretty & very prim, unlike a girl of twelve. . . . Jane is whimsical & affected.' The bad impression Jane made undoubtedly was due in some measure to shyness. Several years later Jane and Cassandra were described by the Comtesse de Feuillide as being 'greatly improved . . . in manners as in person' and as 'two of the prettiest girls in England'; they 'are perfect beauties and of course gain "hearts by dozen."' Anna Lefroy's brother Sir Egerton Brydges characterised Jane as a teenager as 'fair and handsome, slight and elegant, but with cheeks a little too full.'

In the *Memoir* he wrote of his aunt, J.E. Austen-Leigh described her in her thirties thus:

In person she was very attractive; her figure was rather tall and slender, her step light and firm, and her whole appearance expressive of health and animation. In complexion she was a clear brunette with a rich colour; she had full round cheeks, with mouth and nose well formed, light hazel eyes, and brown hair forming natural curls close round her face. If not so regularly handsome as her sister, yet her countenance had a peculiar charm of its own to the eyes of most beholders.

One of Austen-Leigh's nieces, who was still a child when her aunt died, recalled the novelist as having had 'large dark eyes and a brilliant complexion, and long, long black hair down to her knees.'

Henry Austen's portrait in the 'Biographical Notice' is not, of course, disinterested:

> Of personal attractions she possessed a considerable share. Her stature was that of true elegance. It could not have been increased without exceeding the middle height. Her carriage and deportment were quiet, yet graceful. Her features were separately good. Their assemblage produced an unrivalled expression of that cheerfulness, sensibility, and benevolence, which were her real characteristics. Her complexion was of the finest texture. It might with truth be said, that her eloquent blood spoke through her modest cheek. Her voice was extremely sweet. She delivered herself with fluency and precision. Indeed she was formed for elegant and rational society, excelling in conversation as much as in composition.

Again one wonders about this picture of perfection. The reference to 'her real characteristics' is especially interesting: was his sister falsely believed, by anyone, to be the opposite of cheerful, sensible, and benevolent? The business about 'eloquent blood' and 'modest cheek' is a misquotation of Donne's 'Second Anniversary.' Like most pronouncements upon Jane Austen by the Austen family, we need not take this too seriously. Still, a portrait of a sort begins to emerge—that of a shy, sometimes awkward, but unusually articulate girl who grows into a graceful, elegant, more self-assured adolescent —into, perhaps, a girl like Catherine Morland in *Northanger Abbey*. Her form fills out, her dark eyes take on the light hazel cast of her father and her favourite brother—and she begins to write.

'I would wish not to be hasty in censuring any one; but I always speak what I think.'

—Jane Bennet in *Pride and Prejudice*

'It is my wish to be candid in my judgement of every body.'
—Elinor in *Sense and Sensibility*

So often what one observed was neither amusing nor interesting, but just upsetting.

—Barbara Pym, *No Fond Return of Love*

'There is a safety in reserve.'

—Frank Churchill in *Emma*

'God forbid that I should undervalue the warm and faithful feelings of any of my fellow-creatures.'
—Anne Elliot in *Persuasion*

Who can understand a young Lady?

—Jane Austen in 1817

We are each of us filled with a perfect blackness.
—John Updike, *Rabbit Is Rich*

CHAPTER 3

The Juvenilia and Beyond, 1787-1795

Jane Austen's 'Juvenilia,' of which about 90,000 words—written in three slim quarto notebooks between 1787 and 1793—survive, are mostly farcical and satirical in nature. Some of the twenty-nine extant pieces, which come down to us in a selection made by the mature author for her family from among her early productions, were written by her for the amusement of her younger brother Charles, and several for her elder brother Frank, who was away in the Navy. Some of the items in the Juvenilia are relatively serious; it is interesting to note that as late as 1809 Jane Austen was still tinkering with a few of the things in the three little volumes. The first of these early works was not published until 1871, though they were in circulation among the Austen family for many years.

The Juvenilia—short tales, sketches, fictional letters, scraps of epistolary novels, bits of plays, some highly imaginative English history—show among other things that as a girl Jane Austen was already well-read. By the time she was in her 'teens her literary taste was set. Above all, she was addicted to novels—novels of all kinds. Richardson was her favourite novelist and she knew his works intimately, but she read all the fiction she could get her hands on. She was less tolerant of contemporary novels. As an adolescent she already viewed popular and sentimental fiction with the critical eye of the satirist; her early works ridicule the sentimental excesses and sensational unrealities of current popular fiction—mostly the novel of 'sensibility' and the Gothic novel of 'terror.' If it is unusual to find an eleven- or twelve-year-old girl spending much of her time writing so determinedly, it is even more unusual to find her, at so tender an age, already a confirmed parodist and cynic. She read nothing without passing judgement upon it. The ironic, satirical vein was one Jane Austen was of course to mine so skilfully in later years and works. The well-known 'Love and Freindship' (spelled that way),

'The History of England,' and the later Juvenilia, especially 'Catharine,' show unmistakable signs of comic talent; by the time of the last-named work the writer was seventeen years old. Much of the contents of the three volumes probably was composed by Jane Austen between the ages of fourteen and eighteen. Since we have no letters written by her before 1796, the Juvenilia are the surest guide to the things she thought about and interested herself in during her adolescence. Above all, they are the surest guide to *her*—to Jane Austen herself.

The earliest of the Juvenilia (1787–1790 or thereabouts; few of the pieces are actually dated) is largely literary satire, the later Juvenilia (roughly 1791-1793) largely social comedy. Between the two lies a fine line. What distinguishes both, perhaps, is an element of ridicule, of mockery, of contempt even, which emphasises the faults and vices of others. There is a lot of hostility in satire. To write in the satirical vein demands a certain detachment, a moral distancing from the object of criticism. It demands a cold-blooded assessment of aesthetic and moral values. To this challenge Jane Austen, even as an adolescent, was equal. She seems by this time already to have acquired that detachment, that moral distance—that coldness. As we have seen, she was prone to judge everything she read. At the very least, by the time she was a teenager she knew a great deal about what, as a writer, she ought to avoid. As one critic has said, she 'began by defining herself through what she rejected.' What she valued above all, in literature as in life, was common sense. Or so it would seem.

What sort of teenager was this? It seems appropriate to inquire, at this point, what this early penchant for mockery and ridicule may tell us about Jane Austen's adolescent personality. What does it mean to say, as an early reviewer of Jane Austen's work did, that she 'began by being an ironical critic . . . This critical spirit lies at the foundation of her artistic faculty'—? Parody, says one critic, 'begins in antagonism'; parody, says another, 'tends . . . to become an affirmation of superiority,' and parody, for Jane Austen, was always 'the simplest reaction to feeling.' Donald Greene has written: 'One needs to remember that [Jane Austen] grew up in the great age of caricature, when Hogarth's engravings were on every wall, and Gillray, Rowlandson, and the Cruikshanks were producing their twisted, grotesque distortions of the human frame.' It is indicative that her only known attempt at sustained playwriting (*Sir Charles Grandison*) should be a burlesque. But Marvin Mudrick has argued persuasively in his famous study of Jane Austen that the parodic, the ironic mode was especially favoured by her for reasons more purely personal— largely because such forms enabled her as a writer to remain 'detached, from oneself as from others' and from 'personal commit- ment.' Irony is Jane Austen's defence 'not only against the world, but against herself, against the heart of passion.' It is a kind of repression, practised by her and in her from her earliest years—a preservation and a protection of her essential reserve, her essential distance. From the beginning, Mudrick declares, Jane Austen was a spectator; she is always subject in her work to her own 'hard compelled detachment,' a 'conscious shying from emotion' which took the form of ironic writing—parody and burlesque of others as a smokescreen to hide her own feelings. 'Her temperament chose irony at once . . . She maintained her distance by diverting herself and her audience with unengaged laughter.' Irony, an instrument of laughter without personal involvement, was Jane Austen's conscious preference, the mode she always liked to use in portraying life. She saw life only 'as material for comedy . . . with a detached discrimination.' As another critic has noted, comedy was for Jane Austen a way of both expressing and controlling her critical spirit.

Mudrick tests his hypotheses against the Juvenilia, which he labels 'close observation without sympathy, common sense without tenderness, densely imagined representation without passion.' Certainly these earliest works are startling in their hostility and cold detachment, and no one who studies Jane Austen can altogether escape Mudrick's conclusions. He was writing at a time (1952) when the things he wished to say about Jane Austen had to be overstated: because they had never been said in so many words before (though Reginald Farrer and D.W. Harding had started the demythologising process), because there was so much to unsay, so much accumulated undiscerning admiration of the novelist to flatten, he had to speak loudly. Whether or not he overstates his case as a result is a question which cannot be answered with certainty. What is clear is that what he said needed saying and that any reader of Jane Austen who dismisses his conclusions out of hand is a foolish one. The Juvenilia betray many of the personality traits Mudrick insists are present in all of the works; in many ways they are precursors of almost everything that was to come. Often enough, after all, bright children cover up their sense of being different with feverish affectations of ease, and their insecurity with denigrating others—until the sneer is permanent.

The Juvenilia are precocious and sometimes amusing but they are by no means brilliant, as those who view them with passionate hindsight like to make out—nor are they more than intermittently entertaining. They are chiefly interesting in illuminating for us Jane Austen's first struggles to find a literary voice of her own. When she found it, it did indeed turn out to be the voice of irony—which she never abandoned. Irony, we have seen, suggests detachment. It makes, as Mark Schorer has written, 'no absolute commitments and can thus enjoy the advantage of many ambiguities of meaning and endless ambiguities of situation.' It is, he concludes, 'at the same time an evaluative mood, and, in a master, a sharp one.' Schorer was speaking of Ford Madox Ford here, but what he says about irony is apt enough for our purposes. For Jane Austen was already on her way to being a mistress of the ironic mode. 'Her capacity for ironic detachment was inborn,' as Brian Southam says. 'The conditions of her childhood favoured the cultivation of an aesthetic objectivity, without which her later development in the creation of comic art . . . would not have been possible.'

What conditions? Chiefly the vogue for literature of a peculiarly burlesqueable type; and the Austen family's passionate interest in literature of all kinds, and in responses to it. They encouraged the budding parodist to perform; she found plenty of material to hand. In the 1780s romances and sentimental novels, written largely by would-be but inept imitators of Richardson, would have provided the most spacious targets for literary satire. *The Loiterer*, in whose publication James and Henry Austen played such conspicuous roles, frequently warns against the excesses of sensibility in sentimental literature. It is in the vein of *The Loiterer* that the initial quarto notebook of the Juvenilia, *Volume the First*, commences.

'The earliest Juvenilia are the work of a high-spirited child set on amusement, delighting in knockabout farce, fanciful extravagance, solemn nonsense, and word-play,' Southam has written in his definitive study of the early manuscripts. But the underlying seriousness of the comedy is also noted: 'For all its exuberance the wit is shrewdly applied in exposing the false values and absurd conventions of sentimental fiction, and in general the flaws of bad writing.' Probably Brecht was right to say that tragedy deals with the suffering of mankind in a less serious way than comedy does.

And let us remember, along with Christopher Fry, that comedy is an escape not from truth but from despair. Like comedy, satire is often deadly serious; equally often it is written out of despair (one thinks of Dickens). The satirist must be both serious and angry if he is to succeed in his chosen role of literary demolition-expert. Such is the role chosen by the young Jane Austen.

One of the first tales, 'Frederic & Elfrida,' though largely burlesque, contains some revealing passages. Frederic and Elfrida, says the author, 'loved with mutual sincerity but were . . . determined not to transgress the rules of Propriety by owning their attachment.' Very early—this piece probably was written either in 1787 or 1788—Jane Austen seems to have been aware of the advantages of holding back from the world's view one's feelings—of revealing as little as possible about oneself to others. She accepted the idea current in the eighteenth century that excessive indulgence of emotion was bad—in literature, as in life. Of her heroine, the youthful Jane writes: 'Elfrida . . . had found her former acquaintance were growing too old & too ugly to be any longer agreeable.' Such heartlessness on Elfrida's part is of course condemned and laughed at; but the young author's perception and understanding of heartlessness are impressive.

One of the most striking characters in *Volume the First* is the strong-minded part-time surgeon Lady Williams in 'Jack & Alice,' who 'was too sensible, to fall in love with one . . . much her Junior'—which she does—and who in a memorable moment describes herself as 'a sad example of the Miseries, in general attendant on first Love.' 'I am determined for the future,' Lady Williams declares, 'to avoid the like Misfortune . . . Preserve yourself from first Love,' she tells the heroine, whose addiction to claret prevents her from paying much attention, '& you need not fear a second.' Also noteworthy here is Charles Adams, whom Jane Austen describes as 'polite to all but partial to none . . . lovely . . . lively but insensible.' Pursued by an unwanted suitor, he lays a steel bear-trap for the lady, into which she obligingly steps. Later, considering a proposal of marriage from an elderly duke, this same lady, her leg healed, is tempted to accept it, on the ground 'That one should receive obligations only from those we despise.' Instead, she is poisoned; the duke 'mourned her loss with unshaken constancy for the next fortnight.' The 'high-spirited child' whom Southam describes as the author of the Juvenilia is also capable, it seems, of biting sarcasm. So much for 'Jack & Alice,' little more than a series of disconnected fictional autobiographies spoken by the characters largely in a parody of the manner of Defoe.

In the next piece, 'Edgar & Emma,' the hero never appears, while the heroine does little but cry—indeed, at the end she retires to her room in a fit of weeping and, we are told, 'continued in tears the remainder of her Life.' 'Henry & Eliza' traces the fortunes of its amoral, Moll Flanders-like heroine, who, during an escape from prison, throws her two young sons out of the window before her in order to allow herself to descend unencumbered. Several unfinished tales follow. There is also 'The Visit,' a short play, remarkable chiefly for its accomplished dialogue, though once again burlesque is the dominant motif.

In 'The Three Sisters,' probably written in 1792 (when Jane Austen was sixteen; one must remember that she was born in December), Mary Stanhope asks her future husband to build a theatre in their home and put on Mrs Cowley's *Which Is the Man?*, which had been presented at Steventon at Christmas in 1787. Mary is uncertain whether to go ahead with her marriage to Mr Watts because, though 'He is extremely disagreeable & I hate him more than any body else in the world,' and though 'If I accept him I know I shall be miserable all the rest of my Life,' there is the equally important fact that 'He has a large fortune & will make great Settlements on me.' Nor can she bear that he may offer himself to one of her sisters should she refuse him, thus robbing her of her 'triumph' over them; she prefers 'everlasting Misery' to such a humiliation. While Mr Watts cannot make Mary happy, reasons one of her sisters, 'his Fortune, his Name, his House, his Carriage will.' Ultimately Mary decides that 'if he will promise to have the Carriage ordered as I like, I will have him.' One of the sisters concludes: she 'is resolved to do *that* to prevent our supposed happiness which she would not have done to ensure it in reality.' For his part Mr Watts—like Mr Collins later on—doesn't especially care which girl he marries, so long as he marries one of them; they are all young and pretty. Mary finally accepts him with a reminder of 'the pinmoney' he has promised her, mumbling under her breath: 'What's the use of a great Jointure if Men live forever?' She goes on to urge such egregious material demands upon Mr Watts as to make him demur. When he tries one of the other sisters and is told she expects him to be good-tempered, cheerful, considerate, and loving, he is equally shocked. After much protracted negotiation Mary and Mr Watts agree on settlements, and he leaves. 'How I do hate him!' says Mary, adding that she wishes never to see him again. There are a number of ironic touches here characteristic of Jane Austen's later work—perhaps chief among them Mary's remark, upon being asked by a neighbour if she likes Mr Watts, that 'when there is so much Love on one side there is no occasion for it on the other.' 'The Three Sisters' is clever—and very cynical. The youthful author was aware early of the mercenary nature of many marriages—she heartily makes fun of them—and of the roles vanity, desire for position, fear of being an old maid, and the wish to shine at others' expense may all play when decisions of this sort are taken. The tale also shows her very much aware of sibling rivalry. It is after all virtually impossible for siblings not to compete in some way; this must have played a part in the formation of Jane Austen's personality. In *Pride and Prejudice*, *Northanger Abbey*, and *Mansfield Park*, as we shall see, there are overt references to sibling rivalry in romantic matters. In *Sense and Sensibility* sibling rivalry is not specifically alluded to—but there is plenty of it, especially between the Steele sisters. In *Persuasion* two of Sir Walter Elliot's three daughters are irrationally competitive.

Volume the Second, the second quarto notebook of Juvenilia, opens with 'Love and Freindship' (dated June 1790), an epistolary 'novel' of just under 10,000 words. This is one of the most important items among Jane Austen's earliest writings. Primarily it is a spoof of the novel of sensibility and its characteristically improbable romantic elements. The word 'sensibility' is repeated again and again throughout the tale. Most of the characters are obsessed by their own sensibilities; being so self-absorbed, they do little but exhibit their sensibilities to others. 'Love and Freindship' is about emotional self-indulgence. At its centre are two heroines who behave in such a way as to leave us in little doubt about the focus of Jane Austen's satire: 'She was all Sensibility and Feeling. We flew into each others arms and after having exchanged vows of mutual Freindship for the rest of our Lives, instantly unfolded to each other the most inward secrets of our Hearts—.' At a crisis the two ladies faint alternately upon a sofa—and they continue to faint whenever an 'expected . . . Blow to our Gentle Sensibility' is sustained. One of the heroines faints once too often, however, and dies as a result of a chill caught while lying on damp ground. She admonishes the other with her last breath(s) to 'Beware of fainting-fits . . . though at the time they may be refreshing and agreeable yet beleive me they will in the end, if too often repeated

and at improper seasons, prove destructive to your Constitution . . .
One fatal swoon has cost me my Life. Beware of swoons Dear Laura.'
Perhaps the single funniest moment occurs when the hero, covered
with blood and dirt and speaking from the remains of a carriage that
has been wrecked in the course of an arduous journey, remarks
languidly to the hysterical heroine: 'I fear I have been overturned.'
Everything in the tale happens because someone possesses either too
much or too little 'Sensibility.' Jane Austen is laughing here at
sentimental behaviour that, taken to an excess of self-indulgence, has
become a form of affectation. She is also, incidentally, showing what
happens when the epistolary novel falls into the wrong hands—those
of the sentimental romancers, who have learned nothing from her
favourite Richardson. 'Love and Freindship' is an amusing, though
not very subtle, burlesque of the sentimental novel—written,
astonishingly, when Jane Austen was just fourteen.

'Lesley Castle,' the next item in *Volume the Second*—at 12,000
words slightly longer than 'Love and Freindship'—was written when
the author was sixteen. Like 'Love and Freindship,' it is an epistolary
'novel.' 'Lesley Castle' is interesting chiefly in demonstrating the
advancing sophistication of Jane Austen's prose style—and her
steady progress toward the form of the novel. It is in the old vein of
burlesque: the target is again excessive sensibility. But one sees here
the beginnings of the future novelist's dissatisfaction with mere
parody as a personal style. More is needed—and found.

In a striking passage in 'Lesley Castle' the weepy Charlotte writes
of her disinclination to marry: 'I never wish to act a more principal
part at a Wedding than the superintending and directing the Dinner,
and therefore while I can get any of my acquaintance to marry for me,
I shall never think of doing it myself.' This may remind us of Emma
Woodhouse, so fond of finding sexual proxies for herself in the dance
of desire by which she is both fascinated and repelled. But for the
most part 'Lesley Castle' is another burlesque of the sentimental
novel. 'You must expect from me nothing but the melancholy
effusions of a broken Heart,' declares Charlotte to her correspondent,
'which is ever reverting to the Happiness it once enjoyed.'

'The History of England from the reign of Henry the 4th to the
death of Charles the 1st,' written in 1791 (between 'Love and
Freindship' and 'Lesley Castle') 'by a partial, prejudiced, and
ignorant Historian,' so the author confesses, is genuinely witty. It
attacks partisan, romanticised, trivialised, popularised history-

writing, seeing it as false to reality as the sentimental novel. A comic adaptation of Goldsmith's *History of England* (1764) and subsequent *Abridgement* (1774), it eschews dates and leaves out almost all the facts (as Goldsmith did); gives an enlightened (i.e., Yorkist) account of the fifteenth century; quite rightly identifies Henry VII as a 'Monster of Iniquity and Avarice' and 'as great a villain as ever lived'; attacks Elizabeth I with venom; and lavishly praises the Stuarts, especially Mary Queen of Scots (Goldsmith was anti-Stuart). The account of the civil wars is a Royalist one; 'Never certainly,' says the author of this 'History,' 'were there before so many detestable characters at one time in England as in this period . . . never were amiable men so scarce.' The Leighs, of course, gave Charles I shelter at Stoneleigh Abbey; loyalty to the Stuarts ran in the family. Among other things the 'History' shows us that at fifteen many of Jane Austen's historical and political loyalties, like her attitudes toward fiction, were firmly set.

There follows, in *Volume the Second*, 'A Collection of Letters' (1791). The second of these is remarkable chiefly for anticipating some of the names used later in *Sense and Sensibility*: a family named Dashwood, a hero named Edward, a jilt named Willoughby—and a Colonel. In the third letter appears Lady Greville, a brutal snob, who, in a memorable scene, rudely abuses a younger woman of humbler status while leaning out of a carriage—readers of *Pride and Prejudice* may be reminded of Lady Catherine de Bourgh. The fifth letter may suggest *Persuasion* in having at its centre a family named Musgrove, but it is memorable primarily for its loutish hero and heroine, both of whom constantly pray for the deaths of her relations so they may have an income to marry on.

In the group of fragments called 'Scraps,' written mostly in 1793, there appear two sisters two years apart in age. The younger of the two is described, in a piece called 'The Female Philosopher,' in a way that may encourage us to see her as a laughingly complacent self-portrait.

> Charlotte who is just sixteen is shorter than her Sister, and though her figure cannot boast the easy dignity of Julia's, yet it has a pleasing plumpness which is in a different way as estimable. She is fair and her face is expressive sometimes of softness the most bewitching, and at others of Vivacity the most striking. She appears to have infinite Wit and a good

humour unalterable; her conversation . . . was replete with humourous sallies, Bonmots and repartees.

Three or four additional scraps bring 'Scraps' to a conclusion—among them a playlet called 'The First Act of a Comedy,' which contains these deathless lines:

> I am going to have my dinner
> After which I shan't be thinner.

Volume the Third, subtitled 'Effusions of Fancy by a very Young Lady, consisting of Tales in a Style entirely new,' and dated August 1792, is the last book of the Juvenilia. It contains only two tales—'Evelyn' and 'Catharine,' both written when Jane Austen was sixteen. Of 'Evelyn' comparatively little need be said. It continues the attack on sentimental fiction; almost all of the characters are motivated exclusively by an oversupply or an undersupply, as the case may be, of sensibility. Example: the owner of a gloomy Gothic fortress who refused to give his consent to the marriage of his recently deceased son is harangued by the tale's hysterical hero, who wishes to know if the father isn't sorry now that he withheld that consent. The father isn't; the situation is made ludicrous by the confrontation between excessive and non-existent 'sensibility.' A chief thrust of 'Evelyn' is its attack on misplaced or distorted benevolence, a sort of sub-*genre* under the heading of excessive sensibility. 'The bulk of the irony' here, as Walton Litz says, 'is reserved for emotional and irrational generosity, Benevolence uncontrolled by Judgment.' It is indicative that already, at sixteen, Jane Austen preferred hardness to softness, sense to sensibility.

The story is also significant in that it contains her earliest and most exact landscape-description—though some of this undoubtedly is a burlesque of methods of describing landscape in fiction then current—and in suggesting the young writer's amusement with some Gothic fashions. By the early 1790s Gothic fiction had reached its full flower; in the next few years, in works by Horace Walpole, Clara Reeve, Sophia Lee, Ann Radcliffe and others, its bloom was to remain undiminished.

'Catharine,' written both under and against the influence of such novels by Fanny Burney as *Evelina* (1778) and *Cecilia* (1782), is the first of Jane Austen's longer tales to eschew the epistolary form. A little more than 15,000 words of third-person narrative uninterrupted by chapter divisions, 'Catharine,' though at times awkwardly written, shows the youthful novelist coming closest, among all the pieces of the Juvenilia, to the form she ultimately found in her major works. It is, at last, less literary criticism than genuine fiction. 'Catharine' bids a temporary farewell to epistolary fiction—Jane Austen was to use the form again a few years later in 'Lady Susan'; indeed, Mrs Percival, Catharine's aunt and guardian, responds to Mrs Stanley's pronouncement that 'nothing forms the taste more than sensible & Elegant Letters' by replying that 'a correspondence between Girls [is] productive of no good, and [is] the frequent origin of imprudence & Error by the effect of pernicious advice and bad Example. She . . . had lived fifty Years in the world without having ever had a correspondent, and did not find herself at all the less respectable for it—.' That Jane Austen takes Mrs Percival's side in this argument is made clear when the brainless Camilla Stanley remarks that correspondence 'is the greatest delight of my life, and you cannot think how much . . . Letters have formed my taste,' which is non-existent.

'But 'Catharine' is interesting chiefly for the autobiographical echoes one hears in it, and for the ways in which it anticipates some future works. Catharine's bosom companions, the Wynne sisters, bear some resemblance to the Lloyd and Lefroy girls. The eldest of them goes off to Bengal to marry under circumstances which obviously point to the story of Jane Austen's aunt Philadelphia Hancock. And Catharine shares some characteristics of the young authoress herself. She is described as 'a great reader'; 'she had always [a book] about her.' And: 'The expectation of a Ball was indeed very agreable intelligence to [her], who [was] fond of Dancing and seldom able to enjoy it . . . The very few Times that [she] had ever enjoyed the Amusement of Dancing was an excuse for *her* impatience, and an apology for the Idleness it occasioned to a Mind naturally very Active.' Thus the sixteen-year-old country girl defends her passion for one of the pleasures of life to which she always looked forward.

Other things in Catharine's make-up may suggest Jane Austen at sixteen. Catharine is said to have 'too much good Sense to be proud of her family, and too much good Nature to live at variance with anyone'; and to know that 'Youth and Beauty . . . is but a poor substitute for real worth & Merit . . . there is certainly nothing like Virtue for making us what we ought to be, and as to a young Man's, being young & handsome . . . is nothing at all . . . for he had much better be respectable.' Catharine is nonetheless 'in love with every handsome Man I see.' By the end of the story she has learned '*not* to think Every Body is in love with me' and to absorb such home truths as this one: 'a young Man would [not] be seriously attached in the course of four & twenty hours, to a Girl who has nothing to recommend her but a good pair of eyes!' Jane Austen, remember, was sixteen. Of course some self-scrutiny is going on here. Among other things the young writer is looking at her own sentimental excesses and laughing at them. She may also be recalling, more ruefully, her dowerlessness.

There is a bitter statement in 'Catharine' about the education many women of the time were likely to have. Camilla Stanley's life 'had been dedicated to the acquirement of Accomplishments which were now to be displayed and in a few Years entirely neglected . . . those Years which ought to have been spent in the attainment of useful knowledge and Mental Improvement, had been all bestowed in learning Drawing, Italian and Music . . . and she now united to these Accomplishments, an Understanding unimproved by reading and a Mind totally devoid of Taste or Judgment.' Jane Austen's novels often attack this method of 'educating' women and heap scorn upon the 'Accomplishments' women were forced to substitute for genuine learning—as Mary Wollstonecraft does in her Introduction to the *Vindication of the Rights of Women*, published in 1792.

Some other themes of the later works are anticipated here, albeit vaguely. Like Elizabeth Bennet, Catharine tends to store up prejudices about people based on their personal appearance. Edward Stanley's arrogance and vanity—he is described as having 'a vivacity of temper seldom subdued, & a contempt of censure not to be overcome, [and] possessed an opinion of his own Consequence, & a perseverance in his own schemes which were not to be damped by the conduct of others'—reminds one of Darcy's. Catharine, '[addressing] him with so much familiarity on so short an acquaintance, could not forbear indulging the natural Unreserve & Vivacity of her own Disposition, in speaking to him, as he spoke to her.' This sounds like a warm-up for some of the exchanges between the hero and heroine of *Pride and Prejudice*. There are echoes, too, of *Sense and Sensibility* in the predicament of the Wynnes, who through a series of calamitous deaths 'had been reduced to a state of absolute dependance on some relations, who though very opulent and very nearly connected with them, had with difficulty been prevailed on to contribute anything towards their support'; and of Frank Churchill (in *Emma*) and Sir Edward Denham (in *Sanditon*) in Edward Stanley's peculiar combination of gallantry towards women and egregious self-absorption.

Catharine herself, as Southam has observed, is a significant departure from the usual type of heroine found in the Juvenilia—a woman of spirit and intelligence, with a touch of irreverence, very much in Jane Austen's distinctive tradition, to be continued in the heroines of *Pride and Prejudice* and *Sense and Sensibility*. Miss Lascelles has suggested that the heroine of 'Catharine' more nearly resembles her namesake in *Northanger Abbey*. In any case, it is clear that in 'Catharine' Jane Austen was edging towards the major works she would begin to write during the latter half of the 1790s.

While the date of the composition of 'Lady Susan' is disputed, it most likely belongs to the years 1793-94 and should thus be considered as belonging to the period of the late Juvenilia, though not nominally a part of them. 'Lady Susan' is an epistolary 'novel' of a little under 25,000 words. Jane Austen was about eighteen when she wrote it.

The heroine of 'Lady Susan' is one of Jane Austen's most disagreeable, unpleasant creations. Vain, greedy, heartless, cynical, and dishonest, she dominates this dark story. Perhaps the most striking thing about the tale is the young Jane Austen's insight into the lower depths of the human character. Where, one cannot help wondering, did such a perspective come from? Here is a mother who hates her own daughter; who declares that stubborn people must be 'tricked' into doing what they don't want to do; whose considered opinion it is that 'where there is a disposition to dislike a motive will never be wanting'; who feels drawn only to those 'easily imposed on'; who looks 'with a degree of contempt on the inquisitive & doubting Fancies of the Heart which seems always debating on the reasonableness of it's Emotions'; who believes that 'Jealousy' is the best 'support of Love' and indeed that 'There is something agreable in feelings so easily worked on'; whose chief efforts throughout the story are devoted to 'making a whole family miserable'; and yet who complacently remarks that she 'never was more at ease, or better satisfied with myself & everything about me, than at the present hour.' Somehow, for all her bad-tempered guile, Lady Susan remains a convincing character—a tremendous accomplishment for the young author. Where did Jane Austen acquire the sort of insight and understanding needed to draw such a character and make us believe in her? We shall see that she and her mother were not always congenial together—that the mother may have preferred Cassandra to Jane and that the younger daughter was often critical of the mother—but this alone would not explain the character of Lady Susan, whose vulgarity and cruelty Mrs Austen, from all contemporary accounts, certainly could not match. It has also been suggested that there is something of Jane's cousin Eliza de Feuillide in Lady Susan (as in Mary Crawford in *Mansfield Park*), but the novelist knows so much about the sort of personality described here that one must conclude some of that knowledge was instinctive rather than merely contextual—intrinsic rather than purely extrinsic. One notes that almost all of the characters are catty. Every letter in the series brims with nasty cracks about others—cracks of the sort to be found in some of Jane Austen's extant letters, as we shall see. Almost everyone seems to be wishing inconvenience, pain, torment, and death upon everyone else; and within the confiding limits of letters, at least, there is little dissembling about true feelings. 'Facts are such horrid things!' Lady Susan's only friend admits to her, '& there is no defying Destiny.'

The other characters in 'Lady Susan,' though some of them are likeable, concern themselves generally, like most of the cast of *Sense and Sensibility*—the first draft of which was written in 1795, soon after 'Lady Susan'—with questions of money, settlements, inheritances, entails, and speculations on the length of life of fathers, uncles, and guardians, as if the world revolved around the issues of possession and ownership of land and houses. This world does so revolve; clearly it is a reflection of how the adolescent novelist, in certain moods, saw her own world. As Lady Susan herself so candidly puts it, 'where possessions are . . . extensive . . . the wish of increasing them . . . is too common to excite surprise or resentment.' Thus speaks Jane Austen's Madame Merle.

'Lady Susan' also provides some lessons in behaviour. 'Where Pride & Stupidity unite, there can be no dissimulation worthy notice,' declares the story's hero. 'Consideration & Esteem as surely follow command of Language, as Admiration waits on beauty,' declares the anti-heroine—quite clearly, for once, in the novelist's (hopeful) voice. And: 'Artlessness will never do in Love matters.' At the end of the tale Jane Austen steps in, in her own voice, as she would so often do in her novels, to resolve all things unresolved, tie up loose threads, and provide a catalogue of last things. 'This Correspondence,' she remarks, obviously having grown tired of the novel in letters, 'could not, to the great detriment of the Post Office Revenue, be continued longer,' and so it abruptly terminates with a third-person account of the ultimate fate of everyone. There is some humour in the last few pages—and a good deal of cold-hearted summary, in the mode of the endings of most of the novels. Lady Susan, we are told, finally forgets altogether the existence of her own daughter; in her next marriage 'She had nothing against her, but her Husband, & her Conscience.' And so on. It is an astonishing, frightening performance by an eighteen-year-old girl—who somehow, within the confines of the Rectory at Steventon, acquired vision into the heart of darkness within man (or, more properly, woman) and learned to articulate her vision of that darkness with unerring conviction. 'The aesthetic distance between the author and her subject is strictly preserved,' as Southam remarks. But she must have found her subject somewhere—inevitably from her vision of the universe she inhabited. Clearly the Rectory at Steventon was no Garden of Eden: indeed, the monsters may have seemed, to the young writer, always on the verge of taking it over. Reginald Farrer regards 'Lady Susan' as of a piece with the major writings—in fact as simply the first of them: 'the cold unpleasantness of *Lady Susan* is but the youthful exaggeration of that irreconcilable judgment which, harshly evident in the first book, is the essential strength of all the later ones.'

'Lady Susan' represents an advance in some ways. We see the protagonist not through her own letters only but also through the eyes (and letters) of others, which gives us what amounts to the fullest human portrait Jane Austen had yet attempted. In Lady Susan there is no progress toward self-knowledge, as there would be in some of the later heroines. Brilliance without sense, breeding without principle, were for Jane Austen not enough: in this there is a foreshadowing of the mature author's perspective. Indeed, the psychological richness of 'Lady Susan' anticipates much of what was to follow.

In all likelihood Jane Austen began to write her play *Sir Charles Grandison* in 1791 or 1792, but she worked on it desultorily for a number of years and did not complete it until 1800—we shall glance at it in its place. Despite failures of other sorts, one can say of the Juvenilia as a whole that they are lucidly written. They are of course by no means

uniform in quality or success. Most of them are of a mixed nature—
light-hearted and sombre, full of laughter and serious satire both. Inevitably this was a reflection of the writer. 'Laughter,' the late Joe
Orton remarked, 'is a serious business, comedy a weapon more dangerous than tragedy . . . One does not kill by anger, but by laughter.' The
detachment of the young Jane Austen seems evident in some of these
early works; most are burlesques, many are precociously witty. But
laughter kills. She must have been a disconcerting teenager. Joan
Rees has written that Jane Austen's earliest work 'demonstrates her
acute sensitivity to the fine differences of human relationships, her
wit and humour, and her exceptional intelligence, all qualities which
must have been observable in her life.' She had already learned to
laugh at her fellow men and women—a sign of detachment as well as
humour. Indeed, the darker hues of this early work, its inherent
cynicism, are often glossed over; the vision is sharp, sometimes
unforgiving, often mocking. Clearly it is a mistake to regard the
Juvenilia as being separated, by chronology and subject-matter, from
the maturer productions. We know that the first versions of what
were to become *Pride and Prejudice*, *Sense and Sensibility*, and
Northanger Abbey were written, all of them, in the middle and later
1790s. The Juvenilia and the later work may equally be seen as sharing
a community of theme and vision. Indeed, the Juvenilia help prepare
us for what is to come.

Catharine muses: 'Sorrows are lightened by Communication.'
Jane Austen's youthful communications make it plain that she had
other things on her mind besides comedy. As Virginia Woolf has
observed, the second-rate writings of first-rate writers are often most
revealing. At fifteen, Mrs Woolf surmises, Jane Austen 'had few
illusions about other people and none about herself.' One does not
become less cynical with the passage of time.

II

Catharine, remember, is said to be 'in love with every handsome Man
I see.' Her aunt lectures her on virtue: 'The welfare of every Nation
depends upon the virtue of it's individuals, and any one who offends
. . . against decorum & propriety is certainly hastening it's ruin.' At
fifteen or sixteen or seventeen a young lady's fancy turns to love, and
the Juvenilia demonstrate among other things that Jane Austen was
no exception. Certainly there was plenty of it around: it was in the air.

During the last years of Jane Austen's 'teens there was a good deal of love-making and marriage in the Austen family. Her eldest brother James, in 1792, married Ann Mathew, daughter of the owners of the neighbouring manor house of Laverstoke, and took curacies first at Overton and later at Deane. Mrs James Austen kept a carriage; the hunting parson kept a pack of harriers. Edward Austen had married Elizabeth Bridges in 1791. Indeed, romance had come into Jane Austen's very bedroom, for Cassandra had fallen in love with Thomas Craven Fowle, a cousin of Lord Craven and a kinsman of the Lloyds. Eliza Lloyd had married the Reverend F.C. Fowle, later vicar of Kintbury in Berkshire. Thomas Fowle was his brother, and a former pupil of George Austen. At the time of his engagement to Cassandra, Fowle was Rector of Allington, in Wiltshire. Ultimately he accepted the chaplaincy of Lord Craven's regiment in the West Indies. There could be no marriage until he had a safe income; Lord Craven had promised him the rich living of Ryton in Shropshire whenever it should fall vacant. And the Austens' cousin Jane Cooper, who had been to school with Cassandra and Jane, was actually married from Steventon in 1792 (both of her parents were dead by the time of her marriage) to Lieutenant Thomas Williams.

Now that Jane's only sister was engaged, she could 'come out' whenever she liked—even though Cassandra was not actually married. Thus far the only romantic interest in her life, and a shadowy one at that, seems to have been Isaac Lefroy's nephew Tom. But Jane only saw him when he visited the Lefroys at Ashe or the Biggs at Manydown, and the 'romance,' such as it was, was given little fertile soil in which to bloom.

Surely she had romance on her mind. One day she playfully forged in her father's parish register, in the Entry of Publication of Banns, the announcement of a proposed marriage between 'Henry Frederick Howard Fitzwilliam of London and Jane Austen of Steventon.' As Miss Jenkins has pointed out, the hypothetical gentleman whose banns were to be published bore the names afterwards given to Henry Crawford, Frederick Wentworth, the Mr Howard who was to marry Emma Watson, and Fitzwilliam Darcy. In the Entry of Marriage register itself there is an account in Jane Austen's hand of a marriage between Jane Austen of Steventon and one Arthur William Mortimer of Liverpool.

We know that Jane Austen started to visit relatives and friends and go to dinner parties during the first half of the 1790s. She paid short visits to the Biggs and the Lloyds in the neighbourhood. Farther afield were the Leigh Perrots, and, while they lived, the Coopers, both in Bath. She also visited some connections—probably the Fowles—in Gloucestershire. She stayed with Edward Austen and his wife in his new home at Rowling in Kent in 1794—stopping off with Cassandra in London on the way. We may surmise that she had been at least twice to the metropolis by the time she was eighteen. There were dances at Basingstoke and in private houses in the immediate neighbourhood. In September 1792 Jane and Cassandra together paid a long visit to the Lloyds at Ibthorp. Several months later, when their brother Frank came home on shore leave, he took his two sisters to a dance at Southampton. These various expeditions widened the circle of Jane Austen's acquaintance and showed her a good deal more of life than she had seen at Steventon. Still, her life at home would have been busy, despite the depleted household (Henry had by this time given up his plan to become a clergyman and gone off to the Oxfordshire Militia). Jane kept up her piano-playing, receiving lessons on the pianoforte from Mr Charde, the assistant organist at Winchester Cathedral. She went for long walks in the Hampshire countryside. She helped her mother with the daily chores. She sewed. She read. And she wrote.

This was not, however, a time of unalloyed happiness or tranquillity for the young Jane Austen. The death of her cousin Eliza de Feuillide's husband on the guillotine in 1794 brought home to the family at Steventon tragedy of a real sort. The Count was condemned to death by the citizen government in Paris for attempting to assist his friend the Marquise de Marboeuf by suborning and seducing witnesses when she was tried by the state on the trumped-up charge of failing to cooperate in food production. In 1793 the Marquise was accused of conspiring against the Republic by planting at her estate at Champs, near Meaux, lucerne, sainfoin, and clover, with the object of producing a famine. The Comte de Feuillide attempted to bribe one of the secretaries of the Committee of Safety to suppress the so-called incriminating documents and to testify in the Marquise's favour. The secretary betrayed the Count. He and the Marquise of Marboeuf, along with her agent, were condemned to death. The Count was executed on 22 February 1794. Eliza was left with an invalid child and little income; she took refuge at Steventon, where the barbarity of the Revolution across the Channel must have made its impact. It is interesting to note that Jane Austen hated France all of her life—the francophobia of *Emma* is just one manifestation of this.

The death of James Austen's wife the following year, in May 1795, was a disaster even closer to home. His two-year-old daughter Anna—another refugee from premature and tragic death—was transferred to Steventon, where she was brought up largely by her two youthful aunts. A measure of relief must have come to the family around this time from the acquittal of Warren Hastings, Philadelphia Hancock's friend and benefactor, after a trial of seven years' duration.

Some months later Jane and her brother Frank visited Edward and his family at Rowling. At nearby Goodnestone there was a ball, and it was Jane Austen's honour to open it. She was in her twentieth year, and an unkind observer might have thought her practically on the shelf. Girls married early in those days. Her sister was already engaged. But where was the man for her? For a young lady in her position, marriage had to be the ultimate object of social life; there is no evidence that Jane Austen ever questioned this. The dilemma of Charlotte Lucas in *Pride and Prejudice*, faced with the attentions of Mr Collins, is indicative: 'Without thinking highly either of men or of matrimony, marriage had always been her object; it was the only honourable provision for well-educated young women of small fortune, and however uncertain of giving happiness, must be their pleasantest preservative from want.' She accepts Mr Collins 'solely from the pure and *disinterested* desire of an establishment' (my italics). 'I ask only a comfortable home,' Charlotte tells Elizabeth Bennet, and she is not likely to have another chance to get one. Charlotte, and Mrs Smith in *Persuasion*, are instructive examples, Alistair M. Duckworth has argued, 'of a fate that haunts all [of Jane Austen's] novels . . . the entirely unsupported woman, reduced to bare existence without husband, society, or friends.' Of Mrs Smith, Duckworth adds: 'Though she appears at the end of Jane Austen's writing life, Mrs Smith has always existed as a latent possibility in the novelist's thought . . . this is the danger facing many of Jane Austen's heroines, that present security may become total isolation.' He sees in Jane Austen's concern over income, status, and the rise and fall of families an autobiographical relevance. This is just. In the 1790s, terror of spinsterhood would have been very much on the mind of an unmarried twenty-year-old girl without prospects—a 'well-educated young [woman] of small fortune,' like Jane Austen. To remain a spinster was to admit failure—to be patronised by other women and ridiculed by men. One married for love if one could; if one could not, one married, like Charlotte Lucas, as painlessly as possible (awful as Mr Collins is, he will not beat his wife)—for a home and independence and companionship and children, and to avoid diminishing consequence, and financial and social dependence on others. It is impossible to believe that Jane Austen could ever have expected to remain a spinster or chosen such a fate willingly. All of her novels are concerned with love that leads to marriage. Still, she must have observed the dance of desire with some detachment—the detachment, perhaps, of the artist who is storing up material for use. And she must have seen early on that finding a match for herself, a man suitable in intellect and humour as in other things, would be no easy task. 'Jane Austen's sense of a hidden difference between herself and the people she met in company cannot but have increased her innate reserve and confirmed her in any shyness she may have retained since childhood,' as one critic surmises. Surely she had begun to understand by the time she was twenty that loneliness is the human condition. It may well have been in this frame of mind that she began, in 1795, another epistolary novel called 'Elinor and Marianne.'

While outsiders were later to be surprised by the well-kept secret of Jane Austen's authorship, the members of her family, among whom she was more prone to open up, were not surprised at all. They had experienced at firsthand her wit, her irony, her cold-blooded judgment, her irreverence, her occasional malice. This may go far toward answering the question with which this study began—the question of what it was the family wished to conceal about Jane Austen. Her detachment and her coolness and perhaps a certain old-maidish waspishness need not, after all, accompany the reputation for brilliance and humour she would take down to posterity.

The money-making opportunities available to needy women of the middle classes were few indeed. Foremost among them was marriage, but for a secure and attractive match, a girl without a portion was at a disadvantage. For a woman prepared to capitalize on her charms, there were the higher reaches and more sophisticated branches of prostitution. For the talented, there were the theatre and music. For the reasonably educated, there were the usually dreaded roles of governess and companion, or, depending on available capital, the possibility of starting a school.

And there was the profession which had once been a male prerogative, but to which women were steadily infiltrating, that of writing.

—Joan Rees

If you describe things as better than they are, you are considered to be romantic; if you describe things as worse than they are, you will be called a realist; and if you describe things exactly as they are, you will be thought of as a satirist.   —Quentin Crisp

Because they were fond of reading, she fancied them satirical: perhaps without exactly knowing what it was to be satirical; but *that* did not signify. It was censure in common use, and easily given.

—*Sense and Sensibility*

Why he should say one thing so positively, and mean another all the while, was most unaccountable! How were people, at that rate, to be understood?   —*Northanger Abbey*

Once, slumped over a biro-scarred school copy of *Pride and Prejudice*, he had perceived suddenly the nature of wit.

—Penelope Lively, *Treasures of Time*

'Oh! the blessing of a female correspondent, when one is really interested in the absent!'   —*Emma*

'Women are the only Correspondents to be depended on.'

—*Sanditon*

Nothing is ever quite what it seems to be, that is what being grown-up adds up to, that is the one thing you do find out.

—Penelope Lively, *Treasures of Time*

CHAPTER 4

The Years of the First 'Trilogy,' 1796–1799: *Pride and Prejudice, Sense and Sensibility, Northanger Abbey*

The years 1796–99 were crucial ones in Jane Austen's life. In October 1796 she began a novel called 'First Impressions,' which was finished in August 1797 and eventually renamed *Pride and Prejudice*. 'Elinor and Marianne,' begun in 1795 as a novel in letters, was largely recast in November 1797 and later given the title *Sense and Sensibility*. The tale which would be published as *Northanger Abbey*—originally called 'Catherine'; *not* the 'Catharine' of the Juvenilia—was written in the years 1798 and 1799. Between 1796 and 1799, then, three of the six novels were composed. Each was revised during the long period between their original drafting and their eventual publication—*Northanger Abbey* less than the other two. But still, in these three short years, between the ages of twenty and twenty-three, Jane Austen wrote most of the three great books that have come down to us. It is interesting to note that her other three completed novels—*Mansfield Park, Emma*, and *Persuasion*—were also composed in just a few short years of creative activity, between February 1811 and August 1816. She did not of course plan it this way, but a result of these two bursts of sustained composition was two 'trilogies'—not groups of three novels narrating a series of consecutive events happening to the same cast of characters, but rather two groups of three novels each, the three books in both instances written virtually one on top of the other. In any case, by 1796 Jane Austen's apprenticeship to fiction was over. She had learned her trade.

From 1796 onwards we also have her letters—those not destroyed by Cassandra. Their somewhat chequered publishing history is conveniently summarised by Austen bibliographer David Gilson:

> Extracts from Jane Austen's letters were first quoted by her brother Henry in the 'Postscript' dated 20 December 1817

which he added to the 'Bibliographical notice' of his sister written to preface the first publication of *Northanger Abbey and Persuasion* (1818). Some entire letters and many extracts were printed in James Edward Austen-Leigh's *A memoir of Jane Austen* (1870) . . . but the first collected edition appeared in 1884, edited by Edward Knatchbull-Hugessen (1829-93), first baron Brabourne, comprising 96 letters which came into his possession at the death of his mother, Lady Knatchbull (Jane Austen's favourite niece, Fanny Knight, 1793-1882) in her ninetieth year. These letters are additional to those appearing in the *Memoir*. Some of the novelist's letters to her brother Francis Austen were first printed in *Jane Austen's sailor brothers* (1906), by J.H. and E.C. Hubback, while *Jane Austen: her life and letters* (1913), by W. and R.A. Austen-Leigh . . . quoted from almost all the extant letters; but all previous publications were superseded by R.W. Chapman's *Jane Austen's letters to her sister Cassandra and others* (2 vols., 1932; second edition, 1 vol., 1952), the fullest edition of the letters to date.

Most of the letters were written to Cassandra; and the reticent, undemonstrative Cassandra was not a woman to whom one unbosomed oneself in correspondence. Writing to her, one would be unlikely to indulge in personal disclosure or irrelevant digression; 'It would not have suited Jane Austen's sense of propriety to charge her sister sixpence (or thereabouts) for opinions on religion or politics, on life or letters, which were known already, or would keep,' Chapman reminds us. In those days the addressee, not the sender, paid the postage. 'But news would not wait, and news must always give satisfaction.' Thus most of Jane Austen's letters are chatty rather than deep, and focus on local rather than metaphysical matters. Cassandra knew her sister's mind; they had no secrets to betray in correspondence. What was not written could be spoken of at the next opportunity; a great deal undoubtedly was not written precisely because it had already been the subject of conversation between the sisters. Owing to the gossipy nature of many of the letters, the novelist has been called trivial, and uninterested in the issues of her time or in contemporary events. That she should have been called these things by, of all people, E.M. Forster—reviewing Chapman's edition of the *Letters*—is a spectacular piece of irony. It is also nonsense, like so much of Forster's criticism. Her letters to correspondents other than Cassandra range more widely; neither her letters nor her fiction suggests that she was indifferent to current events. Indeed, Jane Austen was not at all the inhabitant of a small, cosy world, her mind firmly withdrawn from the horror outside. 'I think of her as a war novelist,' V.S. Pritchett has said, 'formed very much by the Napoleonic wars, knowing directly of prize money, the shortage of men, the economic crisis and change in the value of capital.' 'It is characteristic of Jane Austen,' another critic has written, 'that, though she seems always to have been *au courant* with the affairs of the nation, she tends only to mention them when they affect the family. In those days when postage was paid by the recipient, one would not fill one's page with information that could be culled from any newspaper.' There is also the fact that, in those days, women were not supposed to have opinions on politics—much less express them; Fanny Burney, who lived in a circle of politicians, hardly mentions politics anywhere in her Diary.

As we shall see, Jane Austen knew what was going on around her. W.H. Auden certainly found her very much a woman of the world:

> You could not shock her more than she shocks me;
>   Beside her Joyce seems innocent as grass.
> It makes me most uncomfortable to see
>   An English spinster of the middle class
>   Describe the amorous effects of 'brass',
> Reveal so frankly and with such sobriety
> The economic basis of society.

The letters after all are *family* documents—written by one member of a family to another, and in some cases meant to be read aloud in a family circle as the most efficient means of conveying family news. Of course they are not full of Napoleon and Nelson, Wellington and Metternich. And we must not forget that Cassandra apparently destroyed more letters than she preserved; and that *all* of the letters to Henry were destroyed. Those letters which remain are not uninteresting—not by any means. Surely H.W. Garrod's characterisation of them as 'a desert of trivialities punctuated by occasional oases of clever malice' is unfair—though no one who reads them carefully can deny that many of them are malicious enough, and cynical. Harold Nicolson labelled them 'old-maidish and disagreeable,' the product of a mind 'like a very small, sharp pair of scissors.'

Forster claimed he heard 'the whinnying of Harpies' in them. But they reveal more than a cold, hard heart and a petty, censorious spirit. And they brim with portraits of persons as vivid as many of those in the novels—and with much the same sort of wit, malicious and otherwise. Surely A.C. Bradley is right when he says that Jane Austen's letters are interesting chiefly because 'the Jane Austen who wrote the novels is in them.'

The letters, after all, were not meant to be heard or seen beyond the Austen family circle. Anne Elliot in *Persuasion*, being given a letter to read not intended for her eyes, is 'obliged to recollect that her seeing the letter was a violation of the laws of honour, that no one ought to be judged or to be known by such testimonies, that no private correspondence could bear the eye of others.'

Jane Austen's earliest surviving letters were written from Steventon in January 1796 to Cassandra, who was staying with the Fowles, the family of her fiancé. The first paragraph of the first letter mentions the birthday of Tom Lefroy, a month younger than she, who was visiting his aunt and uncle at Ashe Rectory. He had just come down from Trinity College, Dublin. There are subsequent references to him in this letter: 'he has but one fault, which time will, I trust, entirely remove—it is that his morning coat is . . . too light'—she surmises he dresses in imitation of his namesake Tom Jones. She dares not, she says, tell Cassandra how badly she and Tom have been behaving: 'Imagine to yourself everything most profligate and shocking in the way of dancing and sitting down together.' She adds: 'He is a very gentlemanlike, goodlooking, pleasant young man, I assure you.' They seem only to meet, however, at dances; he hates to call. She refers to him as 'my friend' and assumes Cassandra must be 'impatient to hear something about him.' The letter goes on to describe the ball of the previous evening, at which the writer, arrayed in a rose-coloured silk dress, obviously enjoyed herself. There was one disagreeable man there, a friend of her brother Edward's, whom she managed to escape altogether: 'I was forced to fight hard for it, however.' She declares that all of her money has been 'spent in buying white gloves and pink persian' (figured silk). Even in this first letter there is a touch of the cold-hearted humour that was to shock and exasperate some of her future readers: 'I am sorry for the Beaches' loss of their little girl, especially as it is the one so much like me.'

A few days later we find her writing to Cassandra again. She expects, she says, in the course of a party the next night, 'to receive an offer from my friend. . . . I shall refuse him, however, unless he promises to give away his white coat.' She adds that she plans 'to confine myself in future to Mr Tom Lefroy, for whom I do not care sixpence,' and to give up her other admirers. The next morning she writes: 'The day is come on which I am to flirt my last with Tom Lefroy, and when you receive this it will be over. My tears flow as I write at the melancholy idea.' It is unclear whether for Jane Austen this was a pleasant flirtation or a serious affair of the heart: we must not take her flippancy at face value. Certainly the Lefroy 'affair' took on more meaning for her in later years, after the friendship between them had been abruptly terminated; we shall see this in *Northanger Abbey* and *Persuasion*, among other places. At any rate, Jane concludes the letter to Cassandra thus: 'I am very much flattered by your commendation of my last letter, for I write only for fame, and without any view to pecuniary emolument.'

Among all of the novelist's surviving letters there is only one other reference to Tom Lefroy—in November 1798. Mrs Lefroy, she tells Cassandra, has been to call. 'She did not once mention the name' of her nephew Tom 'to *me*, and I was too proud to make any enquiries; but on my father's afterwards asking where he was, I learnt that he was gone back to London in his way to Ireland, where he is called to the Bar and means to practise.' So much for the future Chief Justice of Ireland. He brought the first bit of romance into Jane Austen's life, and certainly the outcome could not be described as happy. Whether or not she was in love with him, the passages quoted above suggest that he was not as ardent a suitor as she might have liked: this rankled with her for years afterwards. Apparently Mrs Lefroy sent her Irish nephew packing 'at the end of a *very* few weeks, that no more mischief might be done' between two young people who had, together, nothing to live on—and that was that. One of Jane Austen's nieces recalled later that there was ill usage on neither side 'and no very serious sorrow endured,' though she had some idea that if there was any 'heartlessness' in the matter it was the gentleman's, not the lady's. The ambitious young man got over his infatuation quickly enough. He was called to the Irish bar the following year, in 1797. In 1798 he became engaged to a wealthy Irish girl, and married her in 1799. He settled down in Ireland, and he and the novelist never set eyes on one another again after that hectic month of January 1796. He was nonetheless undoubtedly her first romantic interest. Years later the old Chief Justice told his nephew that he had once been in love with the famous Jane Austen, but 'he qualified his concession by saying that it was a boyish love.' The available evidence suggests that he recovered more quickly than she from whatever disappointment there may have been. A major theme of *Persuasion* is that woman's love is more enduring than man's; it is likely that Jane Austen never entirely forgot Tom Lefroy.

In September 1796 Jane visited Edward and his family in Kent. The letters written during these months contain mostly family news and local gossip—and a few characteristic touches. 'Pray remember me to Everybody who does not enquire after me,' Jane tells Cassandra. Of a Miss Fletcher, encountered at a recent gathering: 'Miss Fletcher and I were very thick, but I am the thinnest of the two—She wore her purple Muslin, which . . . does not become her complexion. There are two Traits in her character which are pleasing; namely, she admires Camilla, & drinks no cream in her Tea.' Fanny Burney brought out *Camilla*, her third novel, in 1796. The public had been invited to subscribe, and several pages of the first volume were taken up with a long list of those who did. Among the subscribers is Miss J. Austen, Steventon: the subscription was a present from her father. Edmund Burke, incidentally, put his name down for five sets of the five-volume work. Of a local family, the novelist writes: 'Mr. Children's two Sons are both going to be married, John & George—. They are to have one wife between them; a Miss Holwell, who belongs to the Black Hole at Calcutta.' There is also a tantalising if droll reference to what may have been a past flirtation with Edward Taylor of Bifrons in Kent, one of the five sons of the Reverend Mr Taylor: 'We went by Bifrons, & I contemplated with a melancholy pleasure, the abode of Him, on whom I once fondly doated.'

Cassandra destroyed any of Jane's letters written in 1797, the year in which, in February, Thomas Fowle died of yellow fever in San Domingo in the West Indies. The sad event took place just a few weeks before he was scheduled to return to England and his fiancée. Undoubtedly much of whatever correspondence may have passed between the two sisters in this year betrayed, to Cassandra's thinking, too much of her own state of mind during this most tragic period of her life. It is also likely that Jane left Cassandra as little as possible during the year, and thus wrote few (if any) letters. Now twenty-four, Cassandra seems to have given up any idea of marriage from this time forward, though there is evidence that she bore the blow bravely. 'Jane says that her sister behaves with a degree of resolution and propriety which no common mind could evince in so trying a situation,' Eliza de Feuillide told a correspondent. We remember Cassandra's reputation for undemonstrativeness and inscrutability, and are not surprised. Fowle left her a legacy of £1,000. Lord Craven declared that he would not have let Fowle go off to such a dangerous climate had someone told him of the engagement to Miss Austen.

So between September 1796 and April 1798 we have no letters at all. That is unfortunate: a good deal happened during this time. There is some evidence to suggest a rather one-sided (on the gentleman's side) love affair between Jane and a Mr Blackall, a friend of the Lefroys, around Christmas 1797—of this there will be something more to say shortly. During these eighteen months Jane wrote 'Elinor and Marianne' and 'First Impressions.' And in November 1796 James Austen remarried—his second wife was the novelist's friend and neighbour Mary Lloyd. Eliza de Feuillide told her mother (Jane's aunt Philadelphia): 'Jane seems much pleased with the match, and it is natural she should be having long known & liked the lady.' The lady, added the Comtesse, was 'not either rich or handsome, but very sensible and good-humoured.' As it turned out, Mary Lloyd Austen was never a favourite relative of Jane's; the novelist would have a good many sharp things to say about her old friend and sister-in-law. Extant is an interesting note to Mary from her new mother-in-law, Cassandra Leigh Austen: 'I look forward to you as a real Comfort to me in my old age, when Cassandra is gone into Shropshire [that is, to Fowle's promised living at Ryton], and Jane—the Lord knows where.'

One always looks for signs, for clues, for explanations of Jane Austen's early and lifelong ironic detachment. Certainly one reason for an unhappy nature could have been the sense that her sister—or her brothers—was preferred by one or both of her parents to herself. There is no evidence of this—quite the reverse, given his interest in her work—in George Austen. One is less sure about the mother. The letter quoted above sounds good-humoured enough, but it might well point toward an important source of unease during Jane Austen's early years. Could Mrs Austen have preferred Cassandra to Jane? If only one of her parents seemed to favour her sister over herself, this would account for much of Jane's adolescent bitterness, obvious everywhere in the Juvenilia: think, for example, of 'Lady

Susan,' in which there is a mother who hates her daughter and ultimately forgets her existence altogether. In *Sense and Sensibility*, the first draft of which was begun during the period of the last Juvenilia, there is a mother—Mrs Ferrars—who devotes much of her energy alternately to disinheriting and forgiving her unoffending children. The number of unpleasant mothers in the fiction is striking—but then there are plenty of unendearing fathers too. A sense of inadequacy within the family or of being unloved by one of her parents, whether imagined or somehow valid, might also account for the theme of sibling rivalry which recurs in Jane Austen's books; for the succession of silly ladies she puts into the novels—Mrs Bennet and Miss Bates are especially astonishing creations; and for the obvious impatience with which, later on, the novelist treated her mother's growing hypochondria. Perhaps her early years at home were more stressful than has been imagined.

Another marriage which took place during this period of Jane's life was that of her brother, now Captain Henry Austen, to the widowed Comtesse de Feuillide, at the Church of St Marylebone, on 31 December 1797. No family were present. The lady was ten years the senior of the two; according to her, Henry had been proposing at frequent intervals for the past two years. The marriage came immediately in the wake of Henry's affair with, and brief engagement to, a Miss Pearson, and despite the opposition of Mrs Austen, who disliked the match (nevertheless it turned out a successful one).

In 1797 too, in November, Mrs Austen took her two daughters to Bath for some weeks, where they probably stayed with her brother James Leigh Perrot and his wife. It was here that Jane began to recast 'Elinor and Marianne' into what was to become *Sense and Sensibility*. Also in 1797 the widow of Thomas Knight—he had died three years earlier—offered her estates at Godmersham and Chawton, along with their substantial income, to her late husband's heir Edward Austen. Edward had four children, and the early inheritance was welcome. From this time on, Edward's sisters lived in the luxury of the classical mansion at Godmersham Park whenever they visited their prosperous brother in Kent. Cassandra, whose favourite brother was Edward and who seemed to like children more, went oftener than Jane. To two unmarried women who had allowances of only twenty pounds a year (from the family; assuming that Cassandra drew the income from Fowle's legacy, she had more), visits of this sort now and then were a welcome diversion—though there is some evidence to suggest that as Edward's family continued to expand, Jane's impatience with the lack of peace and quiet in the Godmersham household grew.

II

In August 1797 'First Impressions' was completed, having been begun the previous October; and while it underwent some revision— in the years 1809–13, but primarily in 1810—before its publication as *Pride and Prejudice* in 1813, there can be little doubt that Jane Austen had it down in fairly finished form by the time her father offered it to a London publisher—Cadell—on 1 November 1797. He had in his possession, said George Austen, 'a manuscript novel, comprising 3 vols., about the length of Miss Burney's *Evelina*.' He wished to know 'what will be the expense of publishing it at the author's risk, and what you will venture to advance for the property of it, if on perusal it is approved of.' The book was declined by return of post. Cadell preferred to publish Mrs Radcliffe.

Critics have surmised that the original title was discarded following the publication of *First Impressions* by Mrs Holford in 1801, and that the final title might well have been suggested by the last pages of Fanny Burney's *Cecilia* (1782), in which the phrase 'pride and prejudice' is printed in capital letters three times in a single perorational paragraph. The original title may well have been taken from the opening chapter of Mrs Radcliffe's *The Mysteries of Udolpho* (1794), in which we see St Aubert instructing his daughter Emily 'to resist first impressions, and to acquire that steady dignity of mind, that can alone counterbalance the passions'—a lesson of Jane Austen's novel as well. The initial version of 'Elinor and Marianne' was drafted before 'First Impressions'; but 'Elinor and Marianne' was completely recast in 1797-98, when the novelist, having discarded the epistolary form in the course of writing 'First Impressions,' decided to scrap the earlier tale in letters ('Elinor and Marianne') and rewrite it along the lines of the story she had just completed ('First Impressions'). So, while 'Elinor and Marianne,' the skeletal beginning of *Sense and Sensibility*, predates 'First Impressions,' the latter was in fact the first of the novels to be written in something resembling its final form.

Those who dispute this chronology sometimes do so on the ground that *Pride and Prejudice* is too great a novel to be a first novel, or that it is a better novel than the next two or three Jane Austen wrote. But all of her novels are—in various ways, it may be—great, and one of them had to be first. What of *Wuthering Heights*—not only a first, but an only novel? And who would like to argue that novelists invariably get better with each book they produce? Jane Austen did revise *Pride and Prejudice* in the years between its original composition and its publication. She may have employed almanacs for the years 1811 and 1812 in polishing the book's chronology, and she could have used a possible visit to Chatsworth in 1806 to fill out her description of Pemberley, and there is a reference in the novel to the restoration of peace which might indicate the Peace of Amiens in 1802, and it is unlikely that a twenty-one-year-old girl would refer to twenty-seven-year-old Charlotte Lucas as 'a young woman,' whereas a lady in her thirties could easily do so—but none of these things is incompatible with the theory of composition and revision outlined here. Indeed, those who believe that the book was written wholly between 1809 and 1812 cannot be right. Jane Austen conceived the action of the tale as belonging to the last decade of the eighteenth century. There can be no doubt that the dates Cassandra gives for the writing of the book (October 1796-August 1797) George Austen offered to Cadell in November 1797 are those for 'First Impressions'; Cassandra's dating of the composition of the novels can hardly be disputed. As Chapman has pointed out, the militia camps at Brighton were notorious in the years 1793-95, but not afterwards. Probably *Pride and Prejudice* began as a burlesque, principally of *Cecilia*. Elizabeth, as several critics have noted, is patently anti-Cecilia—though Jane Austen's heroine does resemble Camilla and Evelina in some ways; and Darcy is not unlike some of Fanny Burney's patrician heroes. If, as Mrs Leavis says, *Pride and Prejudice* is Jane Austen's effort to 'rewrite the story of *Cecilia* in realistic terms,' this would also tie it to the 1790s—a period during which, as we have seen, the novelist came to literary flower principally as a parodist. Southam sees *Pride and Prejudice* as a response as well to such other novels as *Sir Charles Grandison*—a dramatic version of which Jane Austen was working on in the nineties—and *The Mysteries of Udolpho*. He identifies elements of burlesque in *Pride and Prejudice* and argues that in its earliest stages it might have been written in letters. In all of these lights *Pride and Prejudice* may be seen as the natural spiritual heir of the Juvenilia and a work of the nineties.

Recently some additional information has come to light (see Notes) which further confirms *Pride and Prejudice* as a novel of the 1790s. It must be fairly certain that Chevening Park, in Chevening, Kent, along with its parsonage house, provided the basis for Rosings and Hunsford parsonage, the homes of Lady Catherine de Bourgh and Mr Collins in *Pride and Prejudice*. Jane Austen did some visiting in Kent in 1796 while she was writing 'First Impressions.' The most direct route from Steventon to Goodnestone, Godmersham, and so on to London would have taken her through Guildford, Reigate, and Westerham, over the Sundridge Cross by Chevening and onwards via Borough Green and Maidstone. A section of the road at one time actually ran through Chevening Park—built originally around 1630 for the thirteenth Lord Dacre, later (1717) bought by the first Earl of Stanhope, whose family, the Lennards, employed George Austen's uncle Francis as their solicitor during the latter third of the eighteenth century. Old Francis Austen owned property in and around Chevening, and may well have taken his grand-nieces over some of the ground. Certainly Jane Austen had the opportunity to know the Chevening area well. Due to the absence of letters before 1796 we cannot be sure exactly where she went in her late 'teens, but we do know that she visited her uncle Francis Austen, and that between 1792 and 1796 she stayed with relations in Kent on several occasions.

Rosings is described in *Pride and Prejudice* as being 'well situated on rising ground' and 'a handsome modern building,' which fits the account of Chevening Park given in *Paterson's Roads* (1826); in Jane Austen's day it would have been about 165 years old, but it had just undergone extensive renovation. From 1813 the parsonage house near the Great House at Chevening Park was occupied by the Rev John Austen, Jane Austen's cousin. But the novelist, as we have seen, had ample opportunity to know the area well long before 1813, the year in which *Pride and Prejudice* was published.

Rosings and Hunsford are almost perfect fits for Chevening Park and its parsonage house. Sir David Smithers reminds us that, according to *Pride and Prejudice*,

> Rosings . . . lay in the village of Hunsford near Westerham, a
> convenient distance from London and nearly fifty miles from

the Bennet home at Longbourn . . . Records of journeys between the two, with pauses made in London at the home of Mr and Mrs Gardiner in Gracechurch Street, reveal that the drive from Hunsford to the Gardiners was completed within four hours, changing horses at The Bell . . . in Bromley. From Gracechurch Street to the unnamed town . . . near Longbourn where the travellers were met by Mr Bennet's carriage was a distance of twenty-four miles. It is to be concluded, therefore, that Rosings also lay some twenty-four miles from London to the south near Westerham on a route through Bromley which would be roughly half way.

But there is more than this. Rosings Park and Hunsford parsonage are described in some detail in *Pride and Prejudice* when Sir William Lucas, his daughter Maria, and Elizabeth Bennet visit Charlotte Lucas Collins and her husband at the parsonage house. Once in Hunsford Lane, Rosings Park is said to form the boundary on one side, and the parsonage house to stand opposite the gate to the Great House, and to be separated from it by a lane. This perfectly recapitulates the geographical relationship of Chevening Park (still extant) to its parsonage house (since pulled down). The parsonage is described as having a short gravel walk and standing in a large garden—with walks and cross-walks—which sloped down to the road fronted by green pales and a laurel hedge. Two glebe meadows are said to be adjacent to it. Its back room, from which Mr Collins watches the road for the approach of Lady Catherine's carriage, fronts the road itself. Elizabeth's walks in garden and meadow while at Hunsford parsonage are described in language which easily fits the topography of the parsonage house at Chevening Park. Indeed, the architect's plans confirm that *Pride and Prejudice* gives an accurate picture of the parsonage at Chevening as it existed in the 1790s.

Lady Catherine de Bourgh, both physically and temperamentally, bears many resemblances to the Dowager Lady Stanhope (wife of the second Earl and mother of the third), who would have been in her seventies in the 1790s. Contemporaries describe Lady Stanhope as a very 'determined' woman who dominated her husband while he was alive and his descendants when he was dead. One source refers to her as 'a rather fierce old lady.' In the 1790s the dowager was living at the Dower House across the park from the Great House at Chevening, but was frequently at Chevening Park. It is interesting to note that the first Earl of Stanhope's mother—the dowager's mother-in-law—was named Catherine Burghill. The first Lady Stanhope's portrait hung in the Great House. Jane Austen probably appropriated both her name and her daughter-in-law's character with a minimum of alteration.

The extent to which Jane Austen, by writing for publication at all, was flouting a convention of the period probably has not been adequately realised. At the time she began to write in earnest, professional women writers were still regarded with suspicion. Of course there were exceptions. Fanny Burney had the help of royal patronage, her father's wide circle of cultivated friends, and Dr Johnson; Maria Edgeworth also enjoyed the encouragement and even the collaboration of her father, and had written works on education as well as novels. But the extent of Jane Austen's distance from the official world of letters of the time is reflected in the fact that all of her books published during her lifetime appeared anonymously. It was still forward for a woman, except an already famous one, to put her name on a title page. Nevertheless, Jane Austen wrote for publication—there is no doubt about that—making, as Joan Rees has put it, her own quiet revolution in the novel, and becoming in the process the first great woman writer in English.

It can hardly be disputed that *Pride and Prejudice* is one of the greatest novels in any language. It is about the difference between true and false moral values. It is about the difference between the appearance of things, the ways in which they may be perceived, and their true reality, the ways in which they exist. Like all great literature, it seeks to identify what is true and expose what is false—and to separate the two from one another. It accomplishes these things brilliantly.

Critics have tended to agree with much of this, though in recent years *Pride and Prejudice* has been relegated by some of them to an inferior position among the six novels. This may be a mistake; it is probably the best of Jane Austen's books, for all the changes in modern taste. It has many virtues beyond those already mentioned. It is not only a very funny novel, it is also highly suspenseful—elements not always noticed by its readers. The events of the last half of the book race toward resolution at a breathless pace: it must be one of the most perfectly plotted novels in English. And its dialogue—much of it worthy of a Congreve, a Wilde, an Orton—is often brilliantly witty. If the book reminds some readers of Mozart's music, one may recall that the composer died just five years before Jane Austen began to write 'First Impressions.'

Our concern here must be chiefly with what *Pride and Prejudice* may tell us about its author. It is unnecessary to rehearse again the process by which Darcy's pride is humbled and Elizabeth's prejudices exposed—'*your* defect is a propensity to hate every body,' she tells him early in the novel; 'And yours . . . is wilfully to misunderstand them,' he replies; or how conceit, self-importance, avarice, arrogance, materialism, hypocrisy, and snobbishness are all attacked; or how 'first impressions' are shown to be, so often, merely a self-indulgent exercise in egotism, dependent upon the perceiver and his own complicated psyche rather than the thing or person perceived. 'My first impressions of people are inevitably right,' the erring Gwendolen remarks complacently to Cecily in Wilde's *The Importance of Being Earnest* (1895); this is what Jane Austen's heroine believes, but never quite manages to say. 'If gratitude and esteem are good foundations of affection, Elizabeth's change of sentiment' as far as Darcy is concerned 'will be neither improbable nor faulty,' the novelist declares. 'But if otherwise, if the regard springing from such sources is unreasonable or unnatural, in comparison of what is so often described as arising on a first interview with its object, and even before two words have been exchanged, nothing can be said in her defence, except that she had given somewhat of a trial to the latter method, in her partiality for Wickham, and that its ill-success might perhaps authorise her to seek the other less interesting mode of attachment.' Nor need one list contrasts between right and wrong moral conduct in the novel, which sets out very precisely to define these things, and does so. Such matters have been amply discussed by others. As in all of Jane Austen's novels, in *Pride and Prejudice* the true, the rational way of looking at things emerges out of the false, the unreliable point of view, so that we, like the characters, receive an education in perception as the story unfolds.

But how does the novel reveal the novelist herself? At the centre of the story are two sisters, close in age and inseparable in most things. There is something of Jane Austen in both Jane and Elizabeth— though she is present chiefly in the latter. When the family is assembled in the evening, the conversation among the Bennets loses 'much of its animation, and almost all of its sense,' if the sisters are absent—which must have been true of the Rectory household when the three elder brothers had gone off to Oxford. Both sisters love to dance. Jane Bennet—though wishing, as she says, 'not to be hasty in censuring any one'—always says what she thinks. Elizabeth, who 'dearly love[s] a laugh,' 'had a lively playful disposition, which delighted in any thing ridiculous': she 'shares her author's characteristic response of comic irony,' it has been noted. Yet there is also a side of her that is reserved, 'unsocial, taciturn,' as she tells Darcy— 'unwilling to speak' without being able 'to say something that will amaze the whole room and be handed down to posterity.'

Darcy says he is the same sort of person—and defines, perhaps, Jane Austen's special brand of shyness: 'I . . . have not the talent which some people possess . . . of conversing easily with those I have never seen before. I cannot catch their tone of conversation or appear interested in their concerns, as I often see done.' 'We neither of us perform to strangers,' Elizabeth says. Shyness and arrogance are often confused; and perhaps some of those who found Jane Austen cold simply encountered her reserve. There is a reserve in Elizabeth, gay as she can be. Like Jane Austen at the Rectory, Elizabeth at Longbourn is fond of going to a little copse in a back garden to think over important matters. She is not easily attached to others. She tells her aunt Mrs Gardiner that she has never been in love—but wishes she could find an intelligent, interesting man to fall in love with. After her first failures with Darcy, she declares petulantly: 'Stupid men are the only ones worth knowing, after all.' Mrs Gardiner replies that 'that . . . savours strongly of disappointment.' One is reminded of Tom Lefroy, and possibly Taylor and Blackall too—of each of whom, perhaps, the novelist had some hopes which, for different reasons, came to nothing.

The 'disappointment' Mrs Gardiner refers to is responsible for Lydia's torment of Jane: 'Jane will be quite an old maid soon . . . she is almost three and twenty! Lord, how ashamed I should be of not being married before three and twenty!' Here is sibling rivalry articulated with a vengeance. Jane Austen was twenty or twenty-one when she wrote that—Elizabeth's age. Unlike her sister, she had never been engaged. Clearly enough, Darcy is the sort of man she was looking for.

> She began . . . to comprehand that he was exactly the man, who, in disposition and talents, would most suit her. His understanding and temper, though unlike her own, would have

answered all her wishes. It was an union that must have been to
the advantage of both; by her ease and liveliness, his mind might
have been softened, his manners improved, and from his
judgment, information, and knowledge of the world, she must
have received benefit of greater importance.

Jane Austen undoubtedly saw 'ease and liveliness' as being among the
contributions she could bring to marriage with a knowledgeable,
discriminating (and wealthy) man. 'He wants nothing but a little
more liveliness,' Mrs Gardiner says of Darcy, 'and *that*, if he marry
prudently, his wife may teach him.' Mr Bennet tells Elizabeth: 'I
know that you could be neither happy nor respectable unless you
truly esteemed your husband; unless you looked up to him as a
superior. Your lively talents would place you in the greatest danger in
an unequal marriage. You could scarce escape discredit and misery.'
These passages may help explain why Jane Austen never married.
Where was the man for her? She found them only in her novels—in
extraordinary men like Darcy, Henry Tilney, and Mr Knightley. The
men she met in real life suffered by comparison.

An important theme of *Pride and Prejudice* is the danger of
detachment. It seems as if Jane Austen—aware, perhaps, of her own
temptation to withdraw, to stand back—exhibits for herself, by
putting them into a novel, some of the possible penalties of such
conduct.

Elizabeth's tendency to observe others from afar is clearly
delineated.

> 'I did not know before,' continued Bingley . . . 'that you were
> a studier of character. It must be an amusing study.'
> 'Yes; but intricate characters are the *most* amusing. They
> have at least that advantage.'
> 'The country,' said Darcy, 'can in general supply but few
> subjects for such a study. In a country neighbourhood you
> move in a very confined and unvarying society.'
> 'But people themselves alter so much, that there is something
> new to be observed in them for ever.'

Mrs Bennet's assurance that there is quite as much of '*that*' going on
in the country as in town follows, but Elizabeth's character as an
amused observer, a student of human nature 'for ever,' is established.

Admitting to Darcy moments later that she loves a good laugh, she adds: 'I hope I never ridicule what is wise or good. Follies and nonsense, whims and inconsistencies, *do* divert me, I own, and I laugh at them whenever I can.' At the end of the novel she has to hold in check her desire to laugh at her husband-to-be: 'he had yet to learn to be laught at, and it was rather too early to begin.' The habit of laughing at others may bespeak a lively sense of humour or the characteristic of easy amusement; but it may also signal a tendency to distance oneself from such objects of amusement as other people. Satire embodies both hostility and detachment; and in this sort of laughter—what we might call moral laughter—there is usually an element of satire.

That Jane Austen is fully aware of these possibilities and these dangers is apparent in the character of Mr Bennet, a frightening exemplar of the perils of detachment. He is a terrible father precisely because of his bottomless capacity to be amused by others. He could be a warning: don't become like this, Jane Austen may be telling herself. After all, Mr Bennet's brand of mockery is not unlike her own. He says some witty things, but there can be no doubt that he is dealt with unsympathetically by the novelist. His most spectacular abandonment of duty comes in connection with his daughter Lydia's proposal to go to Brighton. 'Lydia will never be easy till she has exposed herself in some public place,' says Mr Bennet, 'and we can never expect her to do it with so little expense or inconvenience to her family as under the present circumstances.' Fatherly sentiments indeed! The expense and inconvenience turn out to be enormous. As Mr Bennet rightly says later, after the Brighton debacle: 'Who should suffer but myself? It has been my own doing, and I ought to feel it.' Elizabeth's judgment of her father is harsh, but just. She sees that his only response to his wife's ignorance and folly is to be amused; he won't take the trouble either to correct or quiet her. Elizabeth, says Jane Austen, had never been 'blind to the impropriety of her father's behaviour'—a strong word indeed ('impropriety') to use in connection with a gentleman. Elizabeth reflects on 'that continual breach of conjugal obligation and decorum which, in exposing his wife to the contempt of her own children, was so highly reprehensible.' And she feels markedly 'the disadvantages which must attend the children of so unsuitable a marriage,' and the potential 'evils arising from so ill-judged a direction of talents; talents which rightly used might at least have preserved the respectability of his daughters.' Again, strong words: this man has failed to preserve 'the respectability of his daughters.' So that when, at the end of the novel, Mr Bennet makes his famous pronouncement—'For what do we live, but to make sport for our neighbours, and laugh at them in our turn'—it is the uninformed reader who takes this as a declaration of the novelist's faith. On the contrary, everything in the book up to this point asks us to read Mr Bennet's statement ironically—as the speech of a man who, by practising the kind of detachment he defines here, has ruined the life of one of his daughters and made possible one of the most ill-assorted and unpleasant marriages in English literature. The only real question is whether or not Mr Bennet is *speaking* ironically here—whether he is *aware* of the monstrous nature of the philosophy he articulates in the 'making sport for our neighbours' speech. If we can see him as speaking ironically, we may get closer to Jane Austen's point of view. Mr Bennet has now experienced at firsthand the perils of detachment; surely he has no further desire to make sport for his neighbours. It is an important moment in *Pride and Prejudice*. His sort of 'detachment' is shown to be highly irresponsible. Mr Bennet is morally defective in becoming 'an ironic spectator almost totally self-enclosed, his irony rigidly defensive'; in him 'the irony of the detached observer has become sterile.' Critics have noted this. Mrs Bennet, being stupid, can almost be forgiven her silliness, but 'there is something more ominous in Mr Bennet.' 'Ominous,' one feels, is just the right word; and it is especially 'ominous' that many readers of *Pride and Prejudice* are so ready to see Mr Bennet as the author's spokesman. This far she doesn't go: there is such a thing as excessive detachment, and Mr Bennet personifies it. As Donald Greene says, Mr Bennet winds up being an object of contempt, not pity. Susan Morgan has written that Mr Bennet's chief weakness, 'the weakness which must finally make him more culpable than his intolerable wife, is his refusal to be responsible for his life . . . Retiring to his library, he has retired from his life.' If any part of Jane Austen wished to do this, Mr Bennet is a frightening warning to herself not to 'retire.'

There can be no doubt, however, that in the novel appear unmistakable strains of cynicism and nastiness—strains which seem to have made up a part of Jane Austen's personality. Some of them we find in the novel's celebrated irony, some in an attitude of mind which must be characterised by stronger words. The irony begins, as everyone knows, in the very first sentence, perhaps the most famous opening of any novel in English: 'It is a truth universally acknowledged, that a single man in possession of a good fortune, must be in want of a wife.' The novel's nastiness is everywhere—spectacularly in Lady Catherine de Bourgh, but elsewhere as well. Mrs Bennet to one of her daughters: 'Don't keep coughing so, Kitty, for heaven's sake! Have a little compassion on my nerves. You tear them to pieces.' Mr Collins to Elizabeth: 'Your portion is unhappily so small that it will in all likelihood undo the efforts of your loveliness and amiable qualifications.' The novelist on Sir William Lucas's younger daughter: 'Maria, a good humoured girl, but as empty-headed as himself, had nothing to say that could be worth hearing, and [was] listened to with about as much delight as the rattle of the chaise.' The gossips of Meryton on hearing that Wickham has finally consented to marry Lydia: 'the good-natured wishes for her well-doing, which had proceeded before, from all the spiteful old ladies of Meryton, lost but little of their spirit in this change of circumstances, because with such an husband, her misery was considered certain.' Charlotte Lucas on marriage: 'If a woman conceals her affection . . . from the object of it, she may lose the opportunity of fixing him. . . . In nine cases out of ten, a woman had better shew *more* affection than she feels . . . There is so much of gratitude or vanity in almost every attachment, that it is not safe to leave any to itself . . . considering Mr Collins's character, connections, and situation in life, I am convinced that my chance of happiness with him is as fair as most people can boast on entering the marriage state.' The significance of Charlotte's marriage has been discussed. As Mrs Gardiner reminds Elizabeth, in matrimonial affairs there is very often no difference 'between the mercenary and the prudent motive.' The cynicism of all this is striking—especially the suggestions that human attachments spring largely from selfish motives, and that women who do not feign affection for men are likely to be left on the shelf.

There is a measure of cynicism too in Darcy's declaration that no more than half a dozen women among his large acquaintance are genuinely 'accomplished'; no woman who refuses to cultivate her mind by 'extensive reading' can be truly accomplished, he says. The speech he makes to Elizabeth about his own prickly nature savours strongly of self-scrutiny on the part of the novelist: 'I cannot forget the follies and vices of others so soon as I ought, nor their offences against myself. My feelings are not puffed about with every attempt to move them. My temper would perhaps be called resentful.—My good opinion once lost is lost for ever.' He adds a sentiment which, if it is the novelist's, may help explain much of the pessimistic assessment of human nature to be found in all of Jane Austen's books: 'There is, I believe, in every disposition a tendency to some particular evil, a natural defect, which not even the best education can overcome'—thus the detached irony and cynicism with which human nature is often depicted in the novels. Elizabeth's speech to her sister on the unsatisfactory nature of the human race—and the reasons she gives for not being specially fond of people—seems to be spoken directly from the novelist's heart and mind, and in her own sad voice:

> There are few people whom I really love, and still fewer of whom I think well. The more I see of the world, the more am I dissatisfied with it; and every day confirms my belief of the inconsistency of all human characters, and of the little dependence that can be placed on the appearance of either merit or sense.

None of this detracts from the novel's comedy, black though some of it may be. Indeed, the razor-sharp wit which flashes through *Pride and Prejudice* is one of its most striking features—and proof, among other things, that Jane Austen's sense of humour was fully developed at an early age. Among many possible examples, one might cite these. Elizabeth on Bingley: 'Is not general incivility the very essence of love?' On Sir William Lucas: 'his civilities were worn out like his information.' On Darcy and Wickham: 'There certainly was some great mismanagement in the education of those two young men. One has got all the goodness, and the other all the appearance of it.' On Darcy, at the end: 'Perhaps I did not always love him so well as I do now. But in such cases as these, a good memory is unpardonable.' On Lady Catherine's meddling: 'Lady Catherine has been of infinite use, which ought to make her happy, for she loves to be of use.' Mr Bennet, after hearing of the engagements of Jane and Elizabeth: 'If any young men come for Mary or Kitty, send them in, for I am quite at leisure . . . I admire all my three sons-in-law highly. . . . Wickham, perhaps, is my favourite.' This is indeed the wit of a Congreve, a Wilde, an Orton: Jane Austen has the same sort of comic genius. It is not always so pronounced in her books—perhaps never, after *Pride and Prejudice*, allowed such free rein.

The novel may also tell us something about her views on a few issues, for there is a good deal of old-fashioned, unashamed preaching in it. Some examples:

'Happiness in marriage is entirely a matter of chance.'

'Do any thing rather than marry without affection.'

'How little of permanent happiness could belong to a couple who were only brought together because their passions were stronger than their virtue.'

'Nothing is more deceitful . . . than the appearance of humility. It is often only carelessness of opinion, and sometimes an indirect boast.'

'It is very often nothing but our own vanity that deceives us.'

'Think only of the past as its remembrance gives you pleasure.'

And there is the irrepressible Mary Bennet's lecture on female virtue: 'loss of virtue in a female is irretrievable . . . one false step involves her in endless ruin . . . her reputation is no less brittle than it is beautiful . . . she cannot be too much guarded in her behaviour towards the undeserving of the other sex.'

These pronouncements are quite sensible. Elizabeth, however, remarks at the end of the novel: 'We all love to instruct, though we can teach only what is not worth knowing.' Some things cannot be taught; some things cannot be learned. It would make an appropriate epigraph for a novel which laughs at human nature without any real hope of changing it—an appropriate mixture of the comedy and pessimism that run in parallel streams throughout the book. Like Byron, Jane Austen laughs so as not to weep. The melancholy of Thackeray, another comic genius, is made of similar stuff. You laugh because people are ridiculous; you cry because they will never change; and again you laugh because you know it is useless and unproductive to try to change what is both unchangeable and amusing.

A word on the dramatic method of *Pride and Prejudice*. It is of course a novel about psychological growth and moral education, and as such its focus is largely on the developing minds of the major characters. The central moment of the book is that during which Elizabeth realises that many of her judgments of others have been mere errant prejudices. The chapter in which this happens—Volume 2, Chapter XIII—gives us in miniature the method and the substance of much of the rest of the novel. It is therefore a great disappointment—in

Volume 3, Chapter XVI—to be told in cool third-person commentary, without dialogue or any direct access to the minds and thoughts of either character, of the final reconciliation of Elizabeth and Darcy and their agreement to marry. It is an anticlimax of awful proportions, and it is a mistake Jane Austen makes in all of her books. If she has one overriding fault as a writer, it is her obvious and over-hasty desire, near the ends of her novels, to wrap up loose ends and get the thing over with, once the *dénouement* has been reached, as quickly as possible. It is as if she has had enough of her people by the end of the book and cannot wait to get rid of them once they have reached their happy ending. Their distress interests her more than their happiness. She is too impatient. The result, inevitably, is something unsubtle, undramatic, and ineffective. She does this again and again. Still, one may admire her eagerness and her energy. She began to rewrite 'Elinor and Marianne' in November 1797, within three months of finishing 'First Impressions.'

III

In October 1798 Jane wrote from Dartford, to Cassandra at Godmersham, of the coach trip taken with her parents home from Kent, where all had been paying a visit that autumn to Edward and his family—Cassandra had been left behind to help with the rapidly growing household. They began the day in Sittingbourne, the novelist says, travelled through Ospringe to Rochester, then through Surrey to Staines, Basingstoke, and Hartley via Croydon and Kingston. Back at Steventon, she writes to Cassandra again. This letter (27 October 1798) contains the first hint of displeasure with James Austen's second wife: her eldest brother, she says, has come to Steventon 'in spite of Mary's reproaches.' She herself, Jane tells Cassandra, has bought some material to make a hat—'on which you know my principal hopes of happiness depend.'

The same letter contains one of Jane Austen's most celebrated comments, and if she could have known of the storm of controversy it would cause over the years undoubtedly she would have left it unsaid. Giving Cassandra the news of the neighbourhood, she remarks: 'Mrs Hall, of Sherborne, was brought to bed yesterday of a dead child, some weeks before she expected, owing to a fright. I suppose she happened unawares to look at her husband.' This is identified by some as an example of the novelist's heartlessness. It is

malicious, nasty, and tasteless, certainly; Jane Austen was frequently
malicious and nasty, though not often tasteless. And undoubtedly
there was a streak of heartlessness in her, a pitilessness—a coldness, as
has been suggested; but she was by no means the bitch-monster of
E.M. Forster, H.W. Garrod, D.W. Harding, Harold Nicolson, and
others. To retain a sense of humour amidst the tragedies and ironies
of life counts for much. If it is a defence against them, a way of
detaching oneself from them, then so much the better for the mental
health of the possessor. Even at her most malicious and nasty, Jane
Austen is *sane*. Probably her sense of humour, which hardly ever
failed her—even when it should have, if some of her critics are to be
believed—is largely responsible for such admirable sanity.

She goes on to tell Cassandra of a new maidservant at Steventon:
'She does not look as if anything she touched would ever be clean, but
who knows?' Of a woman she has heard of who married a peer who
keeps a household devoid of servants in order to maintain privacy:
'What a prodigious innate love of virtue she must have, to marry
under such circumstances!' And she describes an invitation from her
aunt (Mrs Leigh Perrot) in Bath as 'a kindness that deserves a better
return than to profit by it.' One does have the feeling, reading Jane
Austen's letters, that the milk of human kindness was often kept in
the larder, and the tea served with lemon.

Cassandra remained at Godmersham with Edward's family throughout the last two months of 1798, and her sister wrote to her at length.
In one letter there is an interesting reference (though not by name) to
a 'friend'—the Reverend Samual Blackall, a Cambridge don who
seems to have fallen briefly in love with Jane. They probably met at
Steventon during Christmas 1797, and the likelihood is that Blackall
came there in the course of a visit he was paying to the Lefroys. Much
of this is conjecture, but it is conjecture solidly based on what little is
known of the affair. Four years older than the novelist, Blackall,
great-grandson of the Bishop of Exeter in the time of Queen Anne,
became a Fellow of Emmanuel College, and was ordained, in 1794. In
later years (from 1812 onwards) he was Rector of North—not
'Great,' as Jane Austen has it in a letter—Cadbury in Somersetshire.
In the autumn of 1798 he wrote to Mrs Lefroy that he wished to
improve his acquaintance with the Austens, and especially with Jane,
'with a hope of creating to myself a nearer interest. But at present I
cannot indulge any expectation of it.' Mrs Lefroy showed Blackall's
letter to the novelist, who wrote of it to Cassandra: 'This is rational

enough; there is less love and more sense in it than sometimes appeared before, and I am very well satisfied. It will all go on exceedingly well, and decline away in a very reasonable manner.' She tells Cassandra that Blackall will not come into Hampshire this Christmas (1798), 'and it is therefore most probable that our indifference will soon be mutual, unless his regard, which appeared to spring from knowing nothing of me at first, is best supported by never seeing me.' Clearly it was a one-sided, as well as a brief, romance; Jane Austen seems not to have cared for Blackall, whose name she never mentions to Cassandra. As she predicted, he soon left her alone; and in 1813 he consoled himself at the altar with another woman. Hearing of his acquisition of the Somersetshire living and of his marriage, Jane wrote years later with some complacency of Blackall's 'succeeding . . . to the very Living which we remembered his talking of and wishing for'; and she went on: 'He was a piece of Perfection, noisy Perfection himself whom I always recollect with regard.' 'Pictures of perfection,' the novelist told one of her nieces a few months before her death, 'make me sick & wicked'; so her characterisation of Blackall here need not be seen as especially complimentary. She could never summon up more than 'regard' for him; indeed, she seems to have found him pompous and didactic. We know so little of Blackall that it would be presumptuous to accuse her of coldness. We do know that she did not care for the gentleman. When she goes on to tell us what she hopes for in his wife, we may see something of what he might have been like: 'I would wish Miss Lewis to be of a silent turn & rather ignorant, but naturally intelligent & wishing to learn;—fond of cold veal pies, green tea in the afternoon, & a green window blind at night.'

This letter also contains several passages in a characteristic vein. 'Mrs Portman is not much admired in Dorchester; the good-natured world, as usual, extolled her beauty so highly, that all the neighbourhood have had the pleasure of being disappointed.' In Cassandra's absence a good deal of the housekeeping duties have fallen to her: 'I am a very good housekeeper . . . I really think it my peculiar excellence, and for this reason—I always take care to provide such things as please my own appetite, which I consider as the chief merit in housekeeping.' Of the imminent birth of her nephew (and future biographer) James Edward, son of James and Mary Austen, Jane writes that the mother will be 'glad to get rid of her child, of whom she is heartily tired.'

It is this same letter in which the novelist—by this time (November 1798) having finished the revised version of *Sense and Sensibility* and begun to write what would eventually be *Northanger Abbey*—remarks to her sister, apropos of some designs she has sent her young nephew George Austen, Edward's son, that she wishes they had been less elaborately finished: 'but an artist cannot do anything slovenly.' It is a remark justly celebrated. Among other things it pinpoints Jane Austen's perfectionism and helps to explain the minute care with which, as long as she was physically able to do so, she revised and polished everything she wrote for publication. A true artist, she could do nothing slovenly.

Henry is now a colonel in the Oxfordshire Militia, Jane tells Cassandra. Their kinsman Egerton Brydges has written a new book, *Fitz-Albini*: 'I expected nothing better. Never did any book carry more internal evidence of its author. Every sentiment is completely Egerton's. There is very little story, and what there is told in a strange, unconnected way. There are many characters introduced, apparently merely to be delineated.' They have bought Boswell's *Tour to the Hebrides* and ordered his *Life of Johnson* and a set of Cowper's works. 'Altogether I am tolerably tired of letter-writing,' the novelist concludes, 'and unless I have anything new to tell you . . . I shall not write again for many days; perhaps a little repose may restore my regard for a pen.' She was deep into *Northanger Abbey* and jealous of her writing time.

But she could not resist for long the urge to share news with Cassandra. She reports she has heard from their brother Frank, who has just arrived with his ship at Cadiz. He says there may be long gaps between his letters in the future due to poor communications and that the family should not alarm itself at his silences. 'I address this advice to you two,' Jane tells Cassandra and their brother Edward, 'as being the most tender-hearted in the family.' She, apparently, is made of sterner stuff. As for James's wife—she is recovering from child-birth, but Mary's state is not one, says the novelist, to induce her to become a mother herself. 'She is not tidy . . . in her appearance; she has no dressing-gown to sit up in; her curtains are all too thin, and things are not in that comfort and style about her which are necessary to make such a situation an enviable one.' One of the maids, Jane tells Cassandra, has departed, to apprentice herself to a dressmaker: 'we may hope to see her able to spoil gowns in a few years.' Humour? Crabbiness? Probably more of the former than the latter, but it is this sort of thing that over the years has sustained those who wish to read the letters as cross and spiteful.

The novelist declares she is delighted to hear that her young nephew George was allowed to drink a toast in honour of her birthday (on 16 December; she was twenty-three): 'I am sincerely rejoiced . . . that I ever was born, since it has been the means of procuring him a dish of Tea.' The Austens have become subscribers of a local library, Jane tells Cassandra. The librarian has announced that every branch of literature will be stocked—not just novels: 'She might have spared this pretension to *our* family, who are great Novel-readers & not ashamed of being so.' She hears that her old beau Edward Taylor has come into a substantial inheritance. A neighbour's wife has been 'discovered to be everything that the Neighbourhood could wish her, silly & cross as well as extravagant.' They eat their dinner now at 3:30 in the afternoon and have their tea at 6:30. During the past few evenings their father has been reading Cowper to the family: 'I listen when I can,' but she spends much of her time these days in the dressing-room upstairs rather than in the parlour—to write, presumably. She has designed a new cap for herself, along lines suggested by Cassandra, which makes her resemble a fashionable lady—'which is all that one lives for now.' The cap was designed primarily to hide—and thus to minimise the amount of washing and brushing necessary—her curly brown hair. If both sisters, as some have surmised, were a bit dowdy in later years, Jane seems to have got a head start. Had she given up already? A ball, she announces, is soon to take place in the neighbourhood, but it will probably be 'very stupid, there will be nobody worth dancing with, and nobody worth talking to.' Shades of Darcy. That is a note of sexual desperation, surely. She had reached the age at which Lydia Bennet proclaimed her sister Jane an old maid; the novelist obviously was feeling low. 'People get so horridly poor & economical in this part of the World, that I have no patience with them,' she writes snappishly to Cassandra. 'Kent is the only place for happiness. Everyone is rich there.' George Austen was now sixty-seven. He had relinquished the curacy of Deane, worth £50 annually, to his son James, and stopped taking pupils. His health was growing precarious. He had saved no money. Economies must be made; the Austens gave up their carriage. This would have been a blow to the daughters of the family, who had no dowries, and found it difficult enough as it was to get themselves to all the local balls. Perhaps the string of unsatisfactory suitors—Lefroy, Taylor, Blackall—was taking its toll on Jane Austen's good humour; she sounds exasperated and lonely at the end of 1798. She attacks materialism and snobbishness in her books, but she was always very much aware of the advantages of wealth, comfort, good society, and peace—and undoubtedly a well-heeled suitor would have been a welcome change.

The family's exertions in official circles on behalf of Frank are likely to pay off in a promotion before long, the novelist tells her sister. She hopes that young Charles may be as lucky—'But I will not torment myself with conjectures and suppositions; facts shall satisfy me.' She has made no new friends lately: 'I do not want people to be very agreeable, as it saves me the trouble of liking them a great deal.' Darcy and Elizabeth do not make friends easily; neither did their author. Lady Dorchester's ball at Kempshott was not as dull as Jane had feared. 'There were twenty dances, and I danced them all, and without any fatigue . . . I fancy I could just as well dance for a week together as for half an hour.' Elizabeth, of course, loves to dance—as do Marianne and Willoughby in *Sense and Sensibility*, who have an endurance on the dance floor similar to that of the novelist. Jane writes she is impressed to hear that Cassandra has 'supped' with Prince William of Gloucester—son-in-law and nephew of George III—at Ashford. George Austen's reputation and his wife's aristocratic connections guaranteed that their children would be asked to meet fashionable people as well as the leading families among the landed gentry. As for herself—she has nothing to wear, says Jane: she is 'tired and ashamed' of her clothes. She apologises for the shortness of this particular note: 'You deserve a longer letter than this; but it is my unhappy fate seldom to treat people so well as they deserve.' Said playfully—but perhaps with a flash of insight as well.

A few days later came the happy news that Captain Frank Austen had been made a Commander and given a sloop, the *Petterel*; and that Charles Austen, at his brother's request, had been appointed to a second lieutenancy. 'Interest'—of the sort William Price would benefit from in *Mansfield Park*—apparently had been brought to bear in the right quarters.

IV

'Elinor and Marianne,' as we have seen, was originally a novel in letters written sometime before 1796—probably in 1795, when it was read to the family. It was completely rewritten in 1797-8 and given

something very like the final form of *Sense and Sensibility*. The title
was changed as well at this time. As in the case of *Pride and Prejudice*,
internal evidence suggests minor revisions made later, during the
long period between composition and publication—mention of the
two-penny post, which did not come into being until 1801, and of
Scott as a popular poet, not possible before 1805, and use of several
names the novelist may have got from a marriage register for 1810.
There was a final revision at Chawton in 1809-10, and some further
corrections made in proof before the appearance of this first of Jane
Austen's novels to be published—in November 1811. The apprentice
quality of the first (epistolary) version of 'Elinor and Marianne' has
been surmised from the fact that no attempt was made to place it,
whereas Jane Austen's father offered 'First Impressions' to a London
publisher only three months after its completion. It is appropriate,
then, to consider *Sense and Sensibility* Jane Austen's second finished
novel, though it was published first, and an early version of it
preceded 'First Impressions.' In any case its background and
atmosphere relate it to the earliest period of Jane Austen's novel-
writing—of that there can be no doubt.

If *Pride and Prejudice* is light and bright and sparkling, *Sense and
Sensibility* is bleak and black and nasty. What Lionel Trilling said of
Mansfield Park might better be said of *Sense and Sensibility*: its
greatness is commensurate with its power to offend. Sartre's 'Hell is
other people!' might well be its epigraph, as another critic suggests.

Mr Palmer in this novel unfortunately possesses 'an aptitude to
fancy himself . . . much superior to people in general,' and *Sense and
Sensibility* among other things demonstrates clearly that the young
Jane Austen was subject to something like the same fancy. She is
undeviatingly judgmental—and most of the characters in the book
deserve to be judged harshly indeed. One might sum up the message
of *Sense and Sensibility* in this crabby leavetaking, near the end, of the
odious Lucy Steele, the unprincipled mercenary warrior in the
matrimonial jungle: 'The whole of Lucy's behaviour . . . and the
prosperity which crowned it . . . may be held forth as a most
encouraging instance of what an earnest, an unceasing attention to
self-interest . . . will do in securing every advantage of fortune, with
no other sacrifice than that of time and conscience.' There is no
wholesale meting out of poetic justice at the end of *Sense and
Sensibility*, though the two heroines get their men. The evil continue
to prosper as unfailingly as the virtuous. The world of this tale is a

dark, dark place, populated by the most astonishing cast of villainous characters assembled by the novelist in any of her books. Lucy Steele's elder sister, as W.A. Craik remarks, 'is the most vulgar and the most stupid person Jane Austen ever uses' in a story. Compared with that of *Sense and Sensibility*, the world of *Mansfield Park* is a paradise.

There is far too much of the Steele sisters, who are great bores. Lucy is described variously as 'capable of the utmost meanness of wanton ill-nature'; 'ignorant and illiterate,' with a 'deficiency of all mental improvement' and 'want of information in the most common particulars'; and again 'illiterate, artful, and selfish.' As Henry James said so persuasively, the intelligent reader cannot interest himself for long in a character incapable of intellectual and moral growth. Why, one wonders, should such a character as Lucy Steele occupy so many pages of a novel? Jane Austen clearly wrote the book in a foul mood; the nastiness is everywhere. It is indicative that Lucy is described as 'superior in person and understanding to half her sex.' Sir John and Lady Middleton, meanwhile, 'strongly resembled each other in that total want of talent and taste which confined their employments.' Lady Middleton 'had nothing to say one day that she had not said the day before. Her insipidity was invariable.' She rates 'good-breeding as more indispensable to comfort than good-nature.' She is of course a natural ally of Fanny Dashwood: 'There was a kind of cold hearted selfishness on both sides, which mutually attracted them; and they sympathised with each other in an insipid propriety of demeanour, and a general want of understanding.' The portrait of Mrs Ferrars is another piece of nastiness: 'A lucky contraction of brow had rescued her countenance from the disgrace of insipidity, by giving it the strong characters of pride and ill nature.' She not only disinherits her elder son, but threatens to block his advance in any profession should he marry against her wishes. Indeed, she is constantly casting her children off and grudgingly letting them back into her good graces, for ridiculous reasons—an odd sort of mother indeed. There is an impatient swipe taken here at ladies' 'accomplishments': Charlotte Palmer's landscape in coloured silks is 'proof of her having spent seven years at a great school in town.' Even parties are described with scathing sarcasm. Guests who come to one are 'permitted to . . . take their share of the heat and inconvenience, to which their arrival must necessarily add.' And: 'The party, like other musical parties, comprehended a great many people who had real taste for the performance, and a great many more who had none at all; and the performers themselves were, as usual, in their own estimation, and that of their immediate friends, the first private performers in England.' At a party given by John and Fanny Dashwood 'no poverty of any kind, except of conversation, appeared.' The host 'had not much to say for himself that was worth hearing, and his wife had still less. But there was no peculiar disgrace in this, for it was very much the case with . . . their visitors, who almost all laboured under one or other of these disqualifications for being agreeable—Want of sense . . . want of elegance—want of spirits—or want of temper.' That covers just about everything. Surely the clergyman's daughter from the country village missed the society of intellectual equals outside her family; surely she was exasperated with what little society she could find in Hampshire.

One of the most unappealing things about the characters in *Sense and Sensibility* is their preoccupation with money: it is virtually the only thing that gets talked about in the novel, and it is the only yardstick many of them use to measure the 'respectability' of others. Is he rich? Then he can be visited. Is he poor? Then avoid him at all costs. The extent of a girl's prettiness, it is suggested, will determine how rich a husband she may catch. 'What have wealth and grandeur to do with happiness?' asks the romantic Marianne early in the book. The 'sensible' Elinor replies: 'Grandeur has but little . . . but wealth has much to do with it.' Statements like this abound: 'She seems a most valuable woman indeed.—Her house, her style of living, all bespeak an exceeding good income'; and: 'I assure you they are very genteel people. He makes a monstrous deal of money, and they keep their own coach.' To be sure, it is the silly people who say these things, but since most of the people are silly much of the novel's content is correspondingly disagreeable. The avarice, stinginess, and dishonesty of this cast of characters are astonishing in the mass. The word 'insipid' keeps reappearing; *Sense and Sensibility* boasts more insipid characters than any novel one can think of (Lady Middleton, Mrs Palmer, John Dashwood, Robert Ferrars, Nancy Steele—even the good-hearted Mrs Jennings). Fanny Dashwood and Mrs Ferrars are just bitchy. Many of these people are awful snobs in the tradition of Lady Catherine de Bourgh, a type which reappears in the novels. There are others. The mindless mother doting on her spoiled children—Lady Middleton's type—is familiar to readers of Jane Austen. So is Mrs Jennings's type—the garrulous but well-meaning old lady, helpful and boring. Mr Palmer, like Mr Bennet, is an intelligent man whose marriage to a stupid woman has made him neurotically detached. Other types repeated from *Pride and Prejudice* include the handsome and dashing but wicked seducer-villain who takes advantage of a young lady who happens to be related to the hero; the upright but diffident man (Brandon sometimes sounds like Darcy: 'I never wish to offend, but I am so foolishly shy, that I often seem negligent'); and of course, at the centre of the book, the two sisters.

This leads us back to the question of autobiography—the question of what the novel may tell us about Jane Austen beyond the fact of her obvious moodiness, her occasional bad temper, her inclination toward sarcasm, cynicism, and harsh judgment of others.

Certainly it tells us a good deal about her attitude, at twenty-two, towards men and marriage. Again the emphasis seems to be on the difficulty an intelligent, quick-witted, sensible woman may have in finding the right man. That Jane knew, as she was writing *Sense and Sensibility*, the time left to her for finding a husband was not limitless, is reflected in Marianne's comment that a woman in her twenties living in cramped quarters on a small income might never 'inspire affection.' The years between nineteen and twenty-three, Elinor reflects, 'if rationally spent, give . . . improvement to the under-standing' and open one's eyes to a great many things. On the other hand, as Mrs Dashwood says, 'It is not time or opportunity that is to determine intimacy;—it is disposition alone.' Did Jane Austen worry that her 'disposition'—arch, satirical, prickly—was likely to put men off? Surely the subject was on her mind in 1797-8.

The novel also shows her, however, being wary of men: the number of unsuitable or disastrous marriages in *Sense and Sensibility* amply demonstrates this. Observing the Palmers, for example, Elinor wonders 'at the strange unsuitableness which often existed between husband and wife,' and resolves not to let such a fate overtake her. She ponders that 'worst and most irremediable of all evils, a connection for life' with the wrong man. And she tells Marianne that, despite 'all that is bewitching in the idea of a single and constant attachment, and all that can be said of one's happiness depending entirely on any particular person, it is not meant—it is not fit—it is not possible that it should be so.' This is revealing. It shows the novelist coming to grips with the possibility of life without marriage—with the necessity of cultivating inner resources, the capacity for self-dependence. Elinor says of herself: 'She was stronger alone, and her own good sense . . . supported her.' When, near the end of the novel, she leaves London with her sister, she reflects that 'she left no creature behind, from whom it would give her a moment's regret to be divided for ever.' We know that in Jane Austen's time an unmarried woman in her twenties was considered an old maid. *Sense and Sensibility*, it may be, shows the novelist viewing the possibility of spinsterhood with a peculiar combination of reluctance and resignation. This may help account for the book's mixed, uneven tone.

Elinor may be viewed as at least a semi-autobiographical figure. It is said of her (by her mother) that she loves to doubt where she can; she replies: 'it is my wish to be candid in my judgment of every body.' Again the emphasis on judging others—on the importance of accurate perception of one's fellow creatures. Not that Elinor is an infallible judge of others—she is taken in by Willoughby's muddled protestations of good will at the end; on the contrary, like Elizabeth Bennet she finds that the first impressions one forms of other people are often way off the mark.

> I have frequently detected myself in such kind of mistakes . . . in a total misapprehension of character in some point or other: fancying people so much more gay or grave, or ingenious or stupid than they really are, and I can hardly tell why, or in what the deception originated. Sometimes one is guided by what they say of themselves, and very frequently by what other people say of them, without giving oneself time to deliberate and judge.

Her romance with Edward Ferrars is a prudent one—neither of them, as Jane Austen says, is 'quite enough in love to think that three hundred and fifty pounds a-year would supply them with the comforts of life.' Elinor is consequently delighted when Mrs Ferrars relents and gives Edward some money—'for at my time of life you know,' the heroine remarks, 'everybody cares about *that*.' The novelist's romance with Tom Lefroy had been thwarted, and Cassandra's marriage to Thomas Fowle had been fatally postponed, in each case because there was not enough money: we understand this remark. (Yet £350 would have been an ample income on which to marry; one wonders how smitten Edward and Elinor really are.) And

Elinor dislikes noisy children—a trait which became more pronounced in Jane as she grew older. We may be warned by the fact that it is Lucy Steele who expresses a preference for children who are 'full of life and spirits; I cannot bear them if they are tame and quiet.' Elinor dislikes unruly children, observing that 'a fond mother . . . in pursuit of praise for her children' is 'the most rapacious of human beings,' and 'the most credulous . . . she will swallow any thing.'

But we must not see Elinor as the sole or consistent representative of Jane Austen in *Sense and Sensibility*. Probably Elinor's restraint and self-discipline are the novelist's, and many of the things she says and does Jane approves of; but undoubtedly, in the undemonstrative elder sister, there is something of Cassandra too. Surely Elinor's self-control under provocation is partly a portrait of Cassandra's deportment after Fowle's death—and an argument that self-discipline need not denote insensibility or lack of feeling. In the less restrained, more emotional, more romantic younger sister, there may also be a dash of the novelist herself. Elinor is sometimes prudish and priggish, and she has little humour: she is an ancestress of Fanny Price. Marianne is described as 'brown,' with an 'uncommonly brilliant' complexion, good features, a 'sweet and attractive' smile— 'and in her eyes . . . there was a life, a spirit, an eagerness which could hardly be seen without delight.' She loves to dance; and she 'had the knack of finding her way in every house to the library.' These things are suggestive. When Marianne says that she 'could not be happy with a man whose taste did not in every point coincide with my own. He must enter into all my feelings; the same books, the same music must charm us both,' we may conclude that this is the novelist speaking. That Marianne eventually settles for less than she wished for is simply the way of the world. It is natural to hope. Idealists, however, are often chastened by events. So when Marianne says that 'the more I know of the world, the more I am convinced that I shall never see a man whom I can really love,' she is also speaking with the author's voice. Indeed, the chastening of idealism, the destruction of romance, is one of the novel's chief themes—as so often in Jane Austen's work. Marianne may well be a sort of warning to the writer not to let her romantic idealism go too far—as Mr Bennet was a warning against excessive detachment.

As on other occasions, the author is fond of using names already known to her rather than unfamiliar ones. Cassandra, Duchess of Chandos, after whom Jane's mother and sister were named, was the sister of the first Baron Middleton (father of the second Duke of Chandos); Duchess Cassandra's family name was Willoughby.

Sense and Sensibility among other things is a novel about how much emotion and feeling it is right to have, and how much it is right to show. It attacks the deliberate stimulation of feeling, the cultivation of emotion for its own sake. At the beginning of the story, when Mr Dashwood dies, Marianne and her mother, though they feel real grief, are said to 'voluntarily renew' and 'create' additional grief for themselves by 'seeking increase of wretchedness in every reflection that could afford it.' The attack on artificial stimulation of emotion is Jane Austen's retort to the novel of sensibility then in vogue. When Willoughby goes away, Marianne is described as indulging every feeling—as in fact 'nourishing' her grief in new ways every day. 'Misery such as mine has no pride,' she declares. Throughout the novel she savours 'moments of precious, of invaluable misery,' even though the cause and object of it—Willoughby —is utterly undeserving of a moment's thought. Elinor observes to Brandon that Marianne's 'systems have all the unfortunate tendency of setting propriety at nought; and a better acquaintance with the world is what I look forward to as her greatest possible advantage.' Experience destroys romance. A cynical view, perhaps: at any rate, this is the educational process Marianne undergoes. In the novel's first two volumes she is often led to 'injustice . . . in her opinion of others, by the irritable refinement of her own mind, and the too great importance placed by her on the delicacies of a strong sensibility.' She 'was neither reasonable nor candid.' It is only at the end of the novel—when, having what is called 'a better knowledge of mankind,' she accepts Brandon—that Marianne also perceives the wisdom of governing her feelings, improving her temper, and lowering her expectations. She sees, as she says herself, that 'my own feelings had prepared my sufferings.' Jane Austen sums up: 'Marianne Dashwood was born to an extraordinary fate. She was born to discover the falsehood of her own opinions, and to counteract, by her conduct, her most favourite maxims.' It is important, the novelist shows us in *Sense and Sensibility*, to see what is there, and not just what one wishes to see. Though it may be a disillusioning process, it is a necessary one. Moral vision must come—even at the expense of romance. The novel argues, as Marilyn Butler says, that strong feelings and those who have them should not be regarded as innately good.

Surely Edward speaks with the novelist's approval when he describes his taste in landscape to an astonished Marianne:

> I like a fine prospect, but not on picturesque principles. I do not like crooked, twisted, blasted trees. I admire them much more if they are tall, straight and flourishing. I do not like ruined, tattered cottages. I am not fond of nettles, or thistles, or heath blossoms. I have more pleasure in a snug farm-house than a watch-tower—and a troop of tidy, happy villagers please me better than the finest banditti in the world.

It is a plea for realism—in life as in art. And it is probably an oblique attack on the cult and jargon of the 'picturesque' found in Gilpin, Price, and others, including some of the Gothic novelists (especially Mrs Radcliffe). Nor should one forget that in 1798 appeared the first edition of *Lyrical Ballads*. Jane Austen's work shows that she preferred a countryside that gave social value by being both handsome *and* useful; to be one without being the other would have seemed to her anomalous.

Ultimately—between the sisters, as in landscape—the novelist takes a middle course. Marianne, the partisan of the picturesque, is too emotional and unrestrained; Elinor, always so useful to everyone, is too repressed. Marianne learns to govern her emotions, Elinor to express hers. Somewhere between sense and sensibility lies what is just plain *sensible*, and it is here that Jane Austen wishes us to stand. If it is a conservative message, it is also a rational one.

In connection with questions of landscape and autobiography, it may be relevant to point out that the countryside around Barton, though supposed to be located in Devonshire, bears a striking resemblance to the Hampshire environs of Steventon as they have been described to us. 'The whole country about them abounded in beautiful walks. The high downs . . . invited them from almost every window,' it is said of Barton. 'I call it a very fine country,' Edward declares. 'The hills are steep, the woods seem full of timber, and the valleys look comfortable and snug—with rich meadows and several neat farm houses scattered here and there . . . it united beauty with utility,' as the novelist liked land to do. At the end of the book we find that 'between Barton and Delaford, there was that constant communication which strong family affection would naturally dictate'—as there were strong family ties between Steventon and

Godmersham, and Steventon and Deane. Jane Austen was neither the first nor the last writer to describe her home country while calling it, for novelistic purposes, something else. One thinks, for example, of Virginia Woolf, who describes so vividly the summer home in St Ives she lived in as a child, yet calls it, in *To the Lighthouse*, the Hebrides rather than Cornwall.

Sense and Sensibility, as we know, was originally an epistolary novel. Remnants of the original form remain—chiefly in the huge speeches the characters make to each other in lieu of dialogue, a residue of the third-person reportage of letters. The lithe and sparkling ambience of *Pride and Prejudice* is flattened here into something like heaviness. *Sense and Sensibility* is less dramatic, less 'scenic,' than its predecessor. It too focuses on the psychological processes of its protagonists, emphasising the ordeal of moral education going on in some of them—an education in values and feelings. As such it succeeds admirably. But the ending is badly botched, much more so than that of *Pride and Prejudice*, and it is partly this which prevents *Sense and Sensibility* from being as great a novel as its predecessor.

As in *Pride and Prejudice*, Jane Austen makes the mistake of summarising in third-person commentary important late scenes rather than giving them to us directly, dramatically. While this is a minor fault in *Pride and Prejudice*—there is relatively little to be resolved in the final chapters there—it is a major matter in *Sense and Sensibility*, in which a great many threads are left hanging until the end. Will Elinor and Edward marry at last? Will Marianne accept Brandon? How can Willoughby's extraordinary behaviour be explained? What will Mrs Ferrars do? And so on. The opportunity exists for some marvellous 'scenes.' But instead Jane Austen lets the dramatic structure of the novel collapse. In four cold sentences she gives us, in third-person narrative, Elinor's description to Marianne of Willoughby's nocturnal visit to Cleveland. Edward's proposal to Elinor is summarised, again in third-person voice, in just two sentences—though the whole book has been, in a sense, a prelude to this dramatic moment. Here is all that we get: 'This only need be said;—that when they all sat down to table . . . he had secured his lady, engaged her mother's consent, and was . . . one of the happiest of men.' So much for Edward and Elinor. In the same disastrous way Marianne's acceptance of Brandon is described in a few lines of third-person narration. 'What else could she do?' Jane Austen lamely asks of Marianne. Certainly she herself could have found something else to do. These are terrible lapses after so many interesting pages of high drama. Once again the novelist seems too anxious to wind up her story and dispose of her characters; once again she is noticeably dismissive of those who have been brought to final happiness.

The worst element of the awful ending is of course the scene between Elinor and Willoughby in the final pages, his 'explanation' of his past actions. When he tells Elinor that he felt his intentions were honourable and his feelings blameless, and that he should be pitied for being 'forced to play the happy lover' to a woman he doesn't love, and that he simply forgot he never told poor Eliza Williams where he lived, and when he calls himself a 'hard-hearted rascal' and declares what comfort it gives him to look back on his own misery, any sensible reader must find him ludicrous. Willoughby is still lying. Yet this hardly serious defence of the indefensible moves the sensible Elinor. For once Jane Austen's heroine and the reader must part company; it simply doesn't work. Most readers have quite rightly rated this sequence embarrassingly inept, a failure in writing. Elinor finds him 'less faulty' than she had believed, which is nonsense, and reflects sadly 'on the irreparable injury which too early an independence and its consequent habits of idleness, dissipation, and luxury, had made in the mind, character, and happiness of a man who . . . united a disposition naturally open and honest and a feeling, affectionate temper.' This is an odd description of a cold-hearted, vain, grasping scoundrel—who is about as open and feeling as a clam. One may be tempted to read the scene ironically and see Elinor as taken in by Willoughby, her own sense turned to sensibility as Marianne moves from sensibility to sense in the novel's closing pages. But this won't wash: if we cannot believe in Willoughby's sincerity, then we can hardly believe that Elinor should be moved by him; or we must believe that she is a fool—which, the book has made amply clear, she is not. The novelist's grip on her heroine loosens again in the last pages when Elinor gives Edward the astonishing advice to humble himself to his awful mother—to apologise for having 'offended' her, presumably to ensure the future financial support of the impecunious couple grudgingly promised by Mrs Ferrars. Money, it seems, is very important after all, despite the ironic treatment throughout the novel of the people who value it too much. The excuse, apparently, is that marriage, especially marriage on a competence, justifies almost anything. One wonders how desperate Jane Austen really was.

It is no coincidence, as Edmund Wilson pointed out, that all of her books are about 'young provincial girls looking for husbands.' Another critic—finding, like many readers, the novel's ending oddly unsatisfactory—has remarked of it: 'not treated at all adequately in the final chapters are the implications and consequences of the moral themes central to the plot and given such prominence' throughout most of the book. This is a sweeping condemnation of the last sections of *Sense and Sensibility*—and a just one.

It is a strange performance. *Sense and Sensibility* holds the attention, it contains some marvellous writing, it is cleverly conceived—but it just misses being a masterpiece. It is intermittently great, prevented from being truly great by the author's ill-temper and impatience with her own characters. Its greatness comes in patches. With Marianne principally in mind, George Moore commented that *Sense and Sensibility* 'gives us all the agony of passion the human heart can feel . . . it is here that we find the burning human heart in English prose narrative for the first, and, alas, for the last time.' But for most readers this would be an exaggeration; many dislike the novel altogether. Jane Austen does make some terrible blunders here. It is a mistake to devote so many pages to Lucy and Willoughby and so few to the dramatic reconciliations of the four central characters at the end. When Kingsley Amis accuses Jane Austen of taking 'a long time over what is of minor importance and a short time over what is major,' he might have had *Sense and Sensibility* in mind.

The book remains, nevertheless, powerful and engaging. Perhaps its chief interest is the glimpse it gives us into the dark side of the novelist's personality. 'Her object is not missionary,' D.W. Harding has written; 'it is the more desperate one of merely finding some mode of existence for her critical attitudes.' In *Sense and Sensibility* she found it. Sometimes 'it seems as if her creatures were born merely to give Jane Austen the supreme delight of slicing their heads off,' Virginia Woolf declared.

The Austen family hadn't the same affection for *Sense and Sensibility*, rarely mentioned in surviving letters, that it had for *Pride and Prejudice*. It is indicative too that in the book written just after *Sense and Sensibility*, Jane Austen returned to the lighter vein. Part of the unpleasantness of *Sense and Sensibility* springs from the subtle, undeclared rivalry of the Dashwood sisters in romantic endeavours and the more savage, brutal competitiveness of the Steele sisters for the attentions of men (the betrayal of Lucy Steele by her elder sister is of course no accident). We note again that sibling rivalry is often an underlying theme in these novels; in *Sense and Sensibility* there are *two* sets of competing sisters, and this contributes to the novel's dark landscape.

If nice things are nicer than nasty things, then surely *Pride and Prejudice* is a more engaging novel than *Sense and Sensibility*.

V

In January 1799 Jane Austen attended a ball; it wasn't a personal success. Writing from Steventon to Godmersham, where Cassandra was still staying with Edward and his family, the novelist described her outfit for her sister. She wore green shoes, she says, and carried a white fan. Also in attendance were the Miss Blackstones, whom she dislikes: 'Indeed, I was always determined not to like them, so there is the less merit in it.' She goes on: 'I do not think I was very much in request [to dance]. People were rather apt not to ask me till they could help it; one's consequence, you know, varies so much at times without any particular reason.' Her own stock apparently was low at the moment; she was twenty-three, and not a popular partner. However, not all of her inaction was involuntary. 'One of my gayest actions was sitting down two dances in preference to having Lord Bolton's eldest son for my partner, who danced too ill to be endured.' A particular young lady indeed. There follows a catalogue of the latest marriages, as well as a list of couples in the process of breaking up. Of one local lad, Jane writes: 'It is to be hoped' that he will soon jilt his lady 'for the sake of a few heroines whose money he may have.' She reports that she has a new 'mamalone' cap which is all the fashion now; undoubtedly she meant 'mamalouc' or 'mamaluke,' a sort of fez—the Battle of the Nile the previous year had created a craze for everything Egyptian. But she says she will write no more about it: 'I hate describing such things."

She goes on to remark, obviously in response to something Cassandra had told her, that she is 'glad to hear that Edward's income is so good a one—as glad as I can be at anybody's being rich except you and me.' There follows either an ill-natured or an ironic remark about Mrs Knight. Her 'giving up the Godmersham estate to Edward was no such prodigious act of generosity after all . . . for she has reserved herself an income out of it still; this ought to be known, that her conduct may not be overrated.' Mrs Knight took an annuity for herself of £2,000. The novelist speaks of some (obviously inimical) acquaintances who have threatened to come and see them: 'perhaps they may be overturned in their way down, and all laid up for the summer.' She complains of a weakness in one eye which makes writing difficult for her; she has used the time to improve her music. A visit she recently paid to friends has not been sufficiently inquired after by Cassandra: 'You express so little anxiety about my being murdered [on the way] . . . that I have a great mind not to tell you whether I was or not.' She refers to her first novel: 'I do not wonder at your wanting to read "First Impressions" again, so seldom as you have gone through it, and that so long ago.' The moodiness—the writer is alternately sunny and snarling—is not unlike that of *Sense and Sensibility*.

Jane reports that her eye is better, and that she has been to a rather dusty ball—'chiefly made up of Jervoises and Terrys, the former of whom are apt to be vulgar, the latter to be noisy.' Second Lieutenant Charles Austen, now twenty, had been visiting Steventon; he has just left for Sheerness, says the novelist, to join his ship. This was the *Endymion*, under command of Sir Thomas Williams, Jane Cooper's widower. He had been knighted for the capture, after a two-hundred-mile chase, of a French frigate while commanding the *Unicorn*, in which Charles was serving in 1796. She wishes, says Jane, that she could have travelled with Charles to Deal, 'that I may explain the country to him properly between Canterbury and Rowling.' She tells Cassandra that Mrs Lefroy thinks Charles handsomer than Henry—high praise indeed. (Henry was with his regiment in Ireland at this time.) Their cousin Edward Cooper has got the living of Hamstall-Ridware in Staffordshire: 'Staffordshire is a good way off; so we shall see nothing more of them till, some fifteen years hence, the Miss Coopers are presented to us, fine, jolly, handsome, ignorant girls . . . Our first cousins seem all dropping off very fast. One is incorporated into the family [Eliza de Feuillide], another dies [Lady Williams, in August 1798], and a third goes off into Staffordshire.' The death of Lady Williams—formerly Jane Cooper, the little cousin who had gone to school with Jane and Cassandra when all three were girls, been orphaned at an early age, and married from Steventon—must have been distressing to the Austen sisters, though little feeling is expressed in this letter. While driving herself in a light carriage, Lady Williams had been in collision with a runaway dray horse and killed instantly.

In this same letter there is a first fleeting reference to Harris Bigg Wither of Manydown—who, as we shall see, proposed marriage to Jane Austen in 1802. Six years younger than the novelist and in uncertain health, Bigg Wither later married another lady. The Austen family kept the story under wraps for many years because, it has been suggested, Bigg Wither's children lived in the same neighbourhood as the Austens and might have been embarrassed by any discussion of his unsuccessful suit. We shall come to this later. Jane goes on in the letter to tell Cassandra, somewhat impatiently, that their mother, now sixty and growing more hypochondriacal with the passing years, complains a good deal about colds but in fact is quite well: 'I have not much compassion for colds . . . without fever or sore throat.' The novelist says she is going to visit the Lloyds at Ibthorp soon; she looks forward to Cassandra's return to Steventon in March.

Jane went to Ibthorp, and Cassandra came home. During May and June 1799 the novelist visited Bath in company with her mother (and possibly her father: it is not clear whether he went or not), her brother Edward and his wife Elizabeth, and their two eldest children—Fanny, aged six, and Edward junior, aged five. The other three children of Edward and Elizabeth were left with attendants at Godmersham. Edward senior was feeling poorly and wanted to take the waters at Bath. They set up house in rooms on Queen's Square, from which they could see part of Brock Street and a slice of Queen's Parade.

Bath, which was destined to play an appreciable role in Jane Austen's life and work, had been a fashionable place for 'taking the waters' ever since the Romans discovered its hot springs. It was only in the later seventeenth century, however, that the city began to acquire a significance social as well as medicinal. Bath became boisterous when gamblers, prostitutes, and widows and widowers looking out for a good match followed the sufferers to the waters' edge. In Queen Anne's day the place was cleaned up a bit by 'Beau' Nash, who outlawed riding-boots, swords, aprons, and indecorous behaviour, and introduced music, balls, and the theatre. He permitted gambling and intrigue—so long as it was discreet. Soon Bath became 'the summer colony of the beau monde, the home of heads of fashion, who drew crowds in their wake,' as J.H. Plumb has written. The young came as well as the old. The ancient city was torn down, and the 'new' Bath—the city which exists today, 'its squares and crescents and terraces all in the great tradition of classical architecture'—replaced it. Jane Austen was to spend a significant amount of time in Bath, and to use it as a setting in *Northanger Abbey* and *Persuasion*.

Writing to Cassandra, who had by now returned to Steventon, the novelist describes the journey to Bath. From Steventon they travelled via Andover and Devizes. Along the way they met a man 'in such very deep mourning,' says Jane, 'that either his mother, his wife, or himself must be dead.' She observes that 'Bath has been as gloomy as it was last November a twelvemonth'—that is, in November 1797, when she had visited the city with her mother and begun to turn 'Elinor and Marianne' into *Sense and Sensibility*. Two weeks later she writes again. Cassandra had conveyed several requests for purchases from various members of the family unable to do their shopping in so large a city as Bath, and Jane says she will attend to some of these—but not all: 'I am not fond of ordering shoes.' The waters of Bath, she reports, have not improved Edward's gouty complaints. She has received word that Charles's ship has sailed. They have seen the Leigh Perrots; her uncle sometimes travels in a chair now. There is much discussion of materials Cassandra needs to make an artificial sprig to wear in her hair: 'Flowers are very much worn, & Fruit is still more the thing.' They all recently took a long walk in the country with some acquaintances; of one of them: 'considering how fair she is, [she] is not unpleasant.' A Mr Gould walked home with her: 'he is a very young Man, just entered of Oxford, wears Spectacles, & has heard that Evelina was written by Dr Johnson.' She looks forward to 'a grand gala' in Sydney Gardens on the King's birthday—a concert, with illuminations and fireworks: 'even the Concert will have more than it's usual charm with me, as the gardens are large enough for me to get pretty well beyond the reach of its sound.' This is the first of a number of indications we have that Jane Austen's musical taste was by no means highbrow.

The novelist betrays her homesickness for Steventon; despite all the things Bath had to offer, she never really enjoyed herself there. She asks Cassandra if the people they have planned to visit during the coming summer couldn't be made to visit Steventon instead. Edward seems to be much improved in health. She declares that she 'had some thoughts of writing the whole of my letter in [the style of Mrs Piozzi—that is, Hester Thrale, who in 1788 had published her correspondence with Johnson], but I believe I shall not.' On the subject of Cassandra's sprig: 'I cannot help thinking that it is more natural to have flowers grow out of the head than fruit.' She tells Cassandra not on any account to let Martha Lloyd, who has asked to do so, read 'First Impressions' again: 'She is very cunning, but I [see] through her design; she means to publish it from memory, and one more perusal must enable her to do it.' Here is further evidence of the popularity of Jane Austen's first novel within her circle. She asks Cassandra if Martha has admitted yet that, as she herself believes, 'fair men are preferable to black.' She goes on: 'I do not know what is the matter with me to-day, but I cannot write quietly; I am always wandering away into some exclamation or other. Fortunately I have nothing very particular to say.' She was restless, probably lonely. Her letters, like her novels, dwell on marriage. There has recently been a wedding in Bath: 'Dr Gardiner was married yesterday to Mrs Percy and her three daughters.' Edward is feeling badly again, and complains of gout. He has bought some coach-horses at the instigation of his friend Mr Evelyn: 'if the judgement of Yahoos can ever be depended on, I suppose it may now, for I believe Mr Evelyn has all his life thought more of Horses than of anything else.' The doctors of Bath, in her opinion, are too apt to write prescriptions. She sees her friends 'the Miss Mapletons very often, but just as often as I like; we are always very glad to meet, & I do not wish to wear out our satisfaction.'

One bizarre event belongs to the years 1799–1800, and it occurred in Bath. The Leigh Perrots had a comfortable home in Twyford, Berkshire, called Scarlets; among their neighbours and friends there was Richard Lovell Edgeworth, the father of Maria Edgeworth. As the Leigh Perrots were childless, it was assumed among the Austens that their heir would be their eldest nephew, James Austen. James Leigh Perrot was Mrs Austen's brother; the relationship was close even if affectionate feelings were not always in evidence. He suffered badly from gout, and he and his wife spent a good deal of time at Bath so he could take the cure there. In August 1799, just two months after the Austen party had left Bath, the Leigh Perrots became involved in an unlikely and costly (the legal costs were between one and two thousand pounds) scandal. The rich, respectable Mrs Leigh Perrot was accused, in a lace shop of somewhat dubious reputation— Miss Gregory's, near Walcot Church; not Smith's, as some have surmised—of shoplifting, and arrested on a charge of theft. At the subsequent trial, presided over by Sir Soulden Lawrence, son of

Johnson's friend Dr Thomas Lawrence, it was suggested that the accusation was a trumped-up one with extortion and blackmail as its object, the idea being that Mr Leigh Perrot, wishing to hush up the matter, would bribe the shopman to withdraw his charge. But Mr Leigh Perrot, backed by his wife, refused to be drawn. So the shopman swore he saw Mrs Leigh Perrot steal some white lace, and she was taken into custody pending trial. Mr Leigh Perrot stayed with his wife of thirty-five years during the eight months she spent among the Hogarthian delights of the local gaol, and later at the gaol-keeper's house, at Ilchester. He was sixty-three at the time; she was fifty-four. It could not have been pleasant. Jane and Cassandra offered to come to the couple, but were told to stay home. They also offered to give their aunt moral support at her trial at the Taunton assizes on 29 March 1800; it was here, in the Old Castle Hall, that Judge Jeffreys sat on his 'Bloody Assizes.' But Mrs Leigh Perrot remarked that 'to have two young creatures gazed at in a public court would cut me to the heart!' The case had aroused a good deal of interest in the press; as it turned out, over two thousand spectators watched Mrs Leigh Perrot's trial. Again the two sisters were told, very kindly, to stay home.

The penalty, had she been convicted, would probably have been transportation to Australia for Mrs Leigh Perrot, and she and her husband were prepared for that eventuality should the case go against them: in those days stealing anything worth more than a shilling could be punishable by death or transportation. She had already been incarcerated in miserable conditions for more than eight months: before the reforms of Sir Samuel Romilly, magistrates could not allow bail for a person accused of felony theft if the stolen article were actually found in his possession; the shopman apparently planted some lace not bought by Mrs Leigh Perrot in the package he wrapped up for her while she was not watching. After her ordeal, Mrs Leigh Perrot was acquitted by a jury in fifteen minutes. She resolved in future to do without lace.

There has been some questioning in recent years of Mrs Leigh Perrot's innocence—based in some part on an anonymous report that at a later date she was also charged at Ilchester with stealing plants. But it is a matter of record that the shopman at Miss Gregory's who wrapped up Mrs Leigh Perrot's purchase had been involved in several of these attempts at extortion; and Miss Gregory's female clerks were probably coached by him and his co-

conspirators as to what to say at the trial about Mrs Leigh Perrot's behaviour in the shop. The most important proof of the attempted extortion plot was the receipt by the Leigh Perrots of several letters threatening blackmail if money were not paid. One of the letters stated plainly the disappointment of the extortionists that no attempt by Mr Leigh Perrot had been made to buy off the potential witnesses against his wife; it suggested to him that he should 'gladly pay rather than have a Wife, you are so fond of, exposed.' One assumes that if there had been anything in the charge, Mr Leigh Perrot would have paid a few hundred pounds to protect his wife from public scandal; instead they both paid a great deal more to protect and maintain her good name.

Among those most outraged by the ordeal of the Leigh Perrots was Richard Lovell Edgeworth, whom James Leigh Perrot had assisted some years earlier in his experiment of telegraphing from Hare Hatch to Nettlebed by means of semaphores. Mr Edgeworth wrote to his friend 'with tears of indignation in my eyes—aye Sir!—with actual, not sentimental, tears in my eyes.'

As the year 1799 drew to a close, the 'innocent country girl' who had already written *Pride and Prejudice* and *Sense and Sensibility* stayed home in Hampshire, finishing yet another novel. Begun in 1798 and called at first 'Susan,' it would appear many years later, after the author was dead, as *Northanger Abbey*.

VI

If the letters of 1799 show Jane Austen in a bittersweet mood— alternately light-hearted and restless, perky and distressed—the new book, *Northanger Abbey*, is of a correspondingly mixed *genre*. It is satirical yet light, judgmental yet amusing. Its elements of burlesque may remind us of some of the earlier writings.

When Jane Austen began it in 1798 there was no doubt as to the form it would take: she chose that of 'First Impressions' over that of 'Elinor and Marianne.' Insofar as we know anything about the original manuscripts at all, the likelihood is, as Southam cogently argues, that *Northanger Abbey* was never a novel in letters. It has an odd, sad history. It was finished in 1799, put away for several years, and taken out and revised in 1803. In the spring of that year, entitled 'Susan,' it was sold (for £10) to the publisher Crosby. He advertised 'Susan; a Novel in 2 Volumes'—but never published it. In the

'Advertisement By The Authoress' appended to the posthumous first (1818) edition of *Northanger Abbey and Persuasion*, Jane Austen wrote that she had never been able to learn why Crosby behaved in this mysterious fashion. 'That any bookseller should think it worth while to purchase what he did not think it worth while to publish seems extraordinary,' she said. Perhaps Crosby decided after his purchase that its burlesque of Gothicism tied the book too specifically to a particular period, and that it could not have a continuing sale. To the extent that it is dated at all, 'Northanger Abbey is dated mainly because it is a literary burlesque,' as one critic puts it. In any case, Crosby offered in 1809 to return it to the author's agent if he could get his £10 back; this being a period of relative poverty in the novelist's life, the offer was declined. Crosby sat on the book until 1816, when Jane Austen, flush from the success of *Emma*, bought it back from him. Even then he could have had no idea that the anonymous writer was also the author of *Sense and Sensibility*, *Pride and Prejudice*, *Mansfield Park*, and *Emma*; as we know, the novelist's name never appeared on the title-page of any of her books during her lifetime, and the secret of her authorship was fairly well-kept outside of the family. When she got the manuscript back in 1816, Jane Austen revised it again—very lightly, in all probability, though the reference to a mob seizing the Tower could have been suggested by the Spa Field riot of 2 December of that year—and in 1816-17 she prepared it for the press. At the time of her death she could not have been certain whether it would ever be published, though she had written the brief 'Advertisement' for it in the event that it did appear. It was published a year after her death, along with *Persuasion*.

The few scholars who have concerned themselves with the subject largely agree that the revisions of 1803 and 1816-17 must have been very slight indeed: there is almost nothing in the book to suggest that it belongs to any period other than that of the late 1790s. The title was altered in 1816—first to 'Catherine,' later to *Northanger Abbey*. At some point the heroine's name was changed from Susan to Catherine; a novel called *Susan* was published anonymously in 1809. The only specific post-1790s reference in *Northanger Abbey* is that to Maria Edgeworth's *Belinda* (1801). One of the chief elements of the original story which would have been relevant in 1798-9 but not in 1816-17 is the good-natured attack on Gothic fiction, and this survived the few revisions that were made. Much of the rest of the story concerns a young girl's entrance into society, a subject in which Jane Austen was always interested. In the brief period during which she was able to work early in 1817, she was occupied chiefly with the unfinished *Sanditon*. Her 'Advertisement' declares that she left *Northanger Abbey* virtually untouched after 1803. There is even internal evidence to suggest that the novelist could not have looked closely at the manuscript after 1805. It has also been demonstrated that the schedule of evenings in the public rooms at Bath as it is given in *Northanger Abbey* is as it was in (and preceding) the year 1802. There is no reason to doubt that the book belongs to the years 1798-9, as Cassandra's note on the composition of the novels indicates, or that *Northanger Abbey* was published in 1818 in something very like the form in which it was completed in 1799.

Northanger Abbey differs from Jane Austen's other novels in at least three important ways. It is set in a city (Bath) and an isolated country house rather than in a village; it is almost wholly satirical from beginning to end; and the heroine is one with whom, for once, the novelist is not in sympathy. These last two elements of *Northanger Abbey* make of it the most 'detached' of all of Jane Austen's novels, the book in which she maintains the most distance between herself and her subject-matter. No longer can we assume an identification between the writer and a leading lady. What ties her to the novel, what prevents her from being so distant from it as to be virtually out of sight, is the book's hero: for once, there is more of Jane in her hero than her heroine. As one critic has noted, 'Henry Tilney is the only one of Jane Austen's heroes who shares her ironic viewpoint, the only one who ever threatens the primacy of her heroine.' Never far from the author, Henry, it has been pointed out, comes to be accepted as her spokesman in *Northanger Abbey*. It may well be these things which make him her greatest leading man: among them all, surely, he is the most witty, the most incisive, the most charming, the most *interesting*. Among them all he is the most like the novelist herself. Darcy lacks his vivaciousness; Mr Knightley, for all his virtues, can be arid, stiff, even pompous (he can also be irrationally jealous). But Henry is nearly perfect. He is a male Elizabeth Bennet— like all of Jane Austen's most engaging characters ironic, irreverent— and detached. He is indeed 'fully the equal of a charming heroine.' Like the usual Austen heroine, he is our chief observer and interpreter in the novel. Marvin Mudrick adds:

> Henry Tilney is the willfully ironic and detached spectator as
> no one except the author herself is in any other of Jane Austen's
> novels . . . he is allowed to know about as much as the author
> does, to pass similar judgments, to respond with a similarly
> persistent and inviolable irony toward all characters and events
> that come within his range.

Henry Tilney stands in for Jane Austen in *Northanger Abbey*; this
would seem to be indisputable.

Who is this paragon? Henry Tilney is a respectable bachelor-
clergyman from Gloucestershire. Loving Catherine for her virtue,
honesty, guilelessness, and lack of sophistication, he stands miles
away from the other men in the book, many of whom—slaves of
convention—see in her little more than an inexperienced, naive girl.
He loves her for what she is not, and this also contributes to his
appeal for us. 'Your mind is marked by an innate principle of general
integrity, and therefore not accessible to the cool reasoning of family
partiality, or a desire of revenge,' he tells Catherine late in the novel.
The possessor of a brilliant sense of humour, he is one of the most
accomplished ironists Jane Austen ever drew. 'He talked with
fluency and spirit—and there was an archness and pleasantry in his
manner which interested,' according to the narrator of *Northanger
Abbey*. His 'archness,' his tendency—as his sister Eleanor puts it—to
'find fault,' often reminds one of the novelist herself, especially the
novelist of the letters. When, for example, Catherine tells him that at
home in Fullerton she has few opportunities for social intercourse
except calling on her friend and neighbour Mrs Allen, Tilney replies:
'Only go and call on Mrs Allen! . . . What a picture of intellectual
poverty!' Catherine says of Isabella Thorpe: 'I was never so deceived
in any one's character in my life before.' 'Among all the great variety
that you have known and studied,' Tilney responds. On the intellect
of women: 'No one can think more highly of the understanding of
women than I do. In my opinion, nature has given them so much, that
they never find it necessary to use more than half.' Some of his verbal
exchanges with the unsophisticated Catherine give Jane Austen the
chance to write her wittiest dialogue since *Pride and Prejudice*:

'I do not understand you.'
'Then we are on very unequal terms, for I understand you
perfectly well.'

'Me?—yes, I cannot speak well enough to be unintelligible.'
'Bravo!—an excellent satire on modern language.'

A gathering of characters in this novel that does not include Henry tends to be a dull affair.

In one of his best moments, Henry uses many of the clichés of Gothic fiction to prepare Catherine for her stay at Northanger Abbey. He reminds her of possibly wild storms, dimly lit halls, gloomy tapestries, immovable chests, haunted corridors, secret passages, hidden chapels, mysteriously locked doors. 'Oh! Mr Tilney, how frightful!—This is just like a book!' replies the delighted heroine. Tilney's ironic perspective on Gothic romance is the author's. Tilney and Jane Austen know that Catherine's reading has overexcited her mind; her illusions of romance will be punctured by Northanger Abbey—a remodelled, highly undramatic building. He and the Abbey together are responsible for much of the destruction of romance in Catherine which the novel traces—thus its title. In this role Henry is particularly an instrument, a creature, an extension of the novelist: the two are closely identified throughout.

While the destruction of romance was an issue in the preceding works, especially *Sense and Sensibility*, here it is the single most important one. Catherine has to unlearn a vision of existence picked up from her reading of Mrs Radcliffe and other Gothic novelists, and learn instead to see things as they are. *Northanger Abbey*, it has been said, is about the 'ability to distinguish between the valuable and the worthless, in literature and in life'; the novel both demonstrates and recommends 'invulnerability to illusions.' In this process of moral education, Henry Tilney is of course of prime importance.

Jane Austen's satire is not specially subtle here, but it is highly effective. The mysterious chest in Catherine's room is found to contain nothing more exciting than a white cotton counterpane. When she finally manages to open a drawer of the enigmatic ebony and gold cabinet, she finds it empty. In another drawer is discovered an inventory of linen and a washing bill. 'If Wednesday should ever come! . . . It did come, and exactly when it might be reasonably looked for.' Here, as elsewhere, the writer attacks the distortions of an overactive imagination, the absurdities of excessive fancy. Catherine has been reading Gothic novels, most recently *The Mysteries of Udolpho* (1794). *Northanger Abbey* is a response to books like *Udolpho*, Charlotte Smith's *Emmeline* (1788), Matthew Lewis's

The Monk (1796), and Mrs Radcliffe's *The Italian* (1797). The heroine of *Northanger Abbey*—whose behaviour at the Abbey may recall that of Adeline in Mrs Radcliffe's *Romance of the Forest* (1792)—moves through the story towards rejection of the Gothic in favour of the ordinary, just as Jane Austen, in all of her works, demonstrates the moral advantages of realism, in life as in literature. Ultimately Catherine learns to 'scorn the causeless fears of an idle fancy . . . Nothing could . . . be clearer than the absurdities of her recent fancies.' She comes to see 'how grossly mistaken in every thing' her romantic imagination has rendered her.

Henry Tilney is the chief instrument of her conversion to realism. The novelist's alter-ego in *Northanger Abbey*, he bids Catherine in judging the world around her to 'Consult your own understanding, your own sense of the probable, your own understanding of what is passing around you,' rather than the pages of Gothic novels. From her earliest writing days, as we know, Jane Austen had parodied and satirised the improbable in fiction; now, in 1798-9, she wrote a novel on the subject. Much of the book is literary burlesque. By the end of it Catherine's 'visions of romance were over. [She] was completely awakened.' She understands 'the extravagance of her late fancies . . . the anxieties of common life began soon to succeed the alarms of romance' in her mind. She sees that her reading has principally given her a 'craving to be frightened': as in *Sense and Sensibility*, the artificial stimulation of excessive emotion is lampooned. In a climactic moment in *Northanger Abbey*, Catherine comes to a conclusion her author had already reached and which in some measure prompted her to write this third of her novels: 'Charming as were all Mrs Radcliffe's works, and charming even as were the works of her imitators, it was not in them perhaps that human nature, at least in the midland counties of England, was to be looked for.' The writer argues instead for her own kind of fiction: 'Human nature,' she declares, may 'be more easily discovered in novels of domestic realism than those of Gothic romance.' It is better to see things as they are than to see them as they might be. In all of Jane Austen's novels correct vision is important: to that end 'domestic realism' is the means. Typical, in this connection, is a passage and a scene at the end of *Northanger Abbey*, when Catherine returns home to Fullerton. The novelist tells how she might have written such a scene, and where in fact the true boundaries of realism lie. It is a mode Thackeray was to find congenial.

A heroine returning, at the close of her career, to her native village, in all the triumph of recovered reputation, and all the dignity of a countess, with a long train of noble relations in their several phaetons, and three waiting-maids in a travelling chaise-and-four, behind her, is an event on which the pen of the contriver may well delight to dwell; it gives credit to every conclusion, and the author must share in the glory she so liberally bestows.—But my affair is widely different; I bring back my heroine to her home in solitude and disgrace; and no sweet elation of spirits can lead me into minuteness. A heroine in a hack post-chaise, is such a blow upon sentiment, as no attempt to grandeur or pathos can withstand.

Here is deliberate anti-climax with a vengeance—another version of the empty drawers and the laundry lists of Northanger Abbey.

The destruction of romance and its replacement by 'domestic realism' is one of several familiar themes in *Northanger Abbey*. In the Allens we have yet another mismatched married couple—an intelligent man married to a stupid woman. As in *Sense and Sensibility*, the poverty of real conversation in polite society is displayed. Again the jargon of the 'picturesque' school of Gilpin and Price is attacked: after Catherine's lesson in how to admire landscape, 'she voluntarily rejected the whole city of Bath.' Again, 'first impressions'—such as Catherine's of Isabella—are found to be incorrect much of the time. As in *Pride and Prejudice*, the meddling of a proud and snobbish parent helps bring the hero and heroine together at the end. Once again the hero is dark, intelligent, well-heeled, and has a sister.

And again the ending is bungled. The dialogue, or 'scenic' portion, of *Northanger Abbey* comes to an end eleven pages before the finish; the last pages are composed entirely of third-person omniscient commentary which ties up all loose threads, including Henry's proposal of marriage to Catherine and her acceptance of him. Yet again we are not allowed to 'see' with our own eyes that one event towards which the novel has moved from its earliest pages. Here is Jane Austen's cold report: 'She was assured of his affection; and that heart in return was solicited, which, perhaps, they pretty equally knew was already entirely his own.' The explanation of General Tilney's conduct, like that of Willoughby at the end of *Sense and Sensibility*, is utterly unconvincing. There is an equally unconvincing and indeed embarrassingly clumsy account of Eleanor Tilney's marriage. The novelist comments wryly on 'the tell-tale compression of the pages' of the final chapters and confesses herself anxious to bring her hero and heroine 'to perfect felicity' as quickly as possible. It is a rehearsal of the ending of *Mansfield Park*, her next full-length novel—though the later book ends in a paroxysm of rage rather than mere impatience.

That these abrupt endings keep punctuating Jane Austen's books suggests that they are not accidents. 'The conclusions to all the novels bear a certain resemblance to one another,' it has been noted. 'They all end . . . with a conventional summary of the events which take place after the climactic point in the narrative has been reached.' Exactly. Why did Jane Austen, we may well ask, consistently shy away from detailed treatment of the fulfilment of romantic expectations at the ends of her novels? Is it because 'life isn't like that'—her ongoing emphasis on the importance of correct vision, the destruction of romance? That she provided happy endings at all suggests that she was aware of her readers' (and publishers') expectations. Probably Jane herself did not see life as being happy, or ending happily, most of the time—and in all likelihood not ending happily for her. Could she have been jealous and resentful of the happiness she was forced to provide her own characters—resentful that such endings were possible in her books but not in her life? If her heart doesn't seem to be in the nominally happy endings, these might be some of the reasons why. *Northanger Abbey*, more clearly than its two predecessors, shows her disillusionment and disappointment with life: the 'distance' between her and her happily fulfilled characters has never been wider.

The consistently satirical slant of *Northanger Abbey* carries down to its very last sentence, which puts a question largely irrelevant to everything that precedes it: 'I leave it to be settled by whomsoever it may concern, whether the tendency of this work be altogether to recommend parental tyranny, or reward disobedience.' On this note of Chaucerian irony, *Northanger Abbey* comes abruptly to an end. It is, as Mudrick says, an 'absurd finishing-off.'

There are other familiar elements here, among them some autobiographical ones. Though none of the heroines, it might seem, could be less like Jane Austen, she and Catherine resemble one another in several ways. Catherine goes to Bath to visit wealthy, childless connections; the novelist stayed in Bath with the Leigh Perrots in November 1797. While there she enjoyed dancing in the public rooms, as Catherine does. Catherine, it is said, was an unpromising child, but as she grew into adolescence her appearance was 'mending; she began to curl her hair and long for balls; her complexion improved, her features were softened by plumpness and colour, her eyes gained more animation, and her figure more consequence.' She loves to read—especially novels: 'provided they were all story and no reflection, she had never any objection to books at all.' Eleanor Tilney feels the same way—preferring, she says, historical reconstructions to history itself, and being, as a reader, 'very well contented to take the false with the true.' Catherine's writing-desk is momentarily lost during a journey; Jane Austen's mahogany lap desk suffered a similar mishap in October 1798 (she was undoubtedly working on *Northanger Abbey* at the time) while the novelist was *en route* from Godmersham to Steventon. Like her author, Catherine loves to walk, especially in the country. When James Morland becomes engaged to Isabella Thorpe, Catherine's reaction is to note 'what *could* be done'—and 'she had got so far as to indulge in a secret "perhaps."' Probably Jane felt something like this when Cassandra became engaged to Thomas Fowle. In the novel it is brother and sister, in real life sister and sister, in both cases a touch of that phenomenon mentioned earlier: sibling rivalry. Mr Morland's offer to give over one of his livings to his son James may recall George Austen's similar kindness to *his* son James upon the latter's marriage.

Except insofar as it reflects the novelist's state of mind in 1798-9, there is probably less direct autobiography in *Northanger Abbey* than in preceding books. Certainly there is more satire—more distance, more irony, more hostility. No one is spared the rapier—least of all the hapless heroine (for once without a sister). Catherine's own mother calls her 'a sad little shatter-brained creature'; she is declared by the novelist herself to be 'a great simpleton.' Ignorant, foolish, and vague, she can't remember whether or not John Thorpe proposed to her, but on the whole thinks not. She has little self-consciousness, or knowledge of contemporary manners: in part, as we have seen, this is what endears her to the ironical Henry Tilney. She is always the last to understand anything; her opinion on most matters is formed as a result of what has been said to her most recently on the subject. Her passion for everything ancient is theoretical rather than real, the result of reading rather than observation. This is a source of great amusement for Jane Austen: 'she cared for no furniture of a more modern date than the fifteenth century . . . Her passion for ancient edifices was next in degree to her passion for Henry Tilney.' The suspicions about General Tilney Catherine entertains while staying at Northanger Abbey are those of an imbecile reader of Gothic trash; the novelist tells us directly that 'Catherine had read too much.' And—a serious fault in an Austen character—Catherine is immune to irony: 'why he should say one thing so positively, and mean another all the while, was most unaccountable! How were people, at that rate, to be understood?'

For irony, bitter irony, is the mode of *Northanger Abbey*. It is not as black a book as *Sense and Sensibility*; much of the satire of the later novel, especially the literary satire, is done with a relatively light touch and a hearty laugh. But nonetheless is *Northanger Abbey* the work of a caustic, disappointed woman. In Catherine's early failures with men, we may perceive the novelist's. 'She had reached the age of seventeen, without having seen one amiable youth who could call forth her sensibility; without having inspired one real passion, and without having excited even any admiration but what was very moderate and very transient.' What heartbreaking disappointment lies behind those words! Catherine aches to be popular. Instead, when she enters a public room in Bath no one notices her, no one asks who she is, no one sings her praises. Jane Austen's own despondency is clear in this. No one had inspired passion in her, nor had she inspired passion in anyone—and mere esteem was not enough. When Isabella says, 'I have no notion of loving people by halves. . . . My attachments are always excessively strong,' we may catch the novelist's tone in her voice. 'I believe my feelings are stronger than any body's; I am sure they are too strong for my own peace,' Isabella adds. That last phrase is a telling one. Jane Austen's 'peace' was surely on the brink of destruction, in her early twenties, as a result of loneliness, of sexual longing. *Northanger Abbey* shows her asking the old question: Where is the man for me? She was twenty-three and had no prospects, no prospects at all. What man would make it a point to look for such an exceptional woman—what man would be able to find her—in a village rectory?

A fully conscious artist, Jane Austen includes in *Northanger Abbey* several passages which describe, bitterly and sarcastically, some of the difficulties young ladies may encounter once they embark on the husband-hunting route. 'Dress is at all times a frivolous distinction,' snarls the novelist, and adds that 'It would be mortifying to the feelings of many ladies, could they be made to understand how little' attention men generally give to clothes. This sounds like disappointed experience speaking. You don't get a man with a gown, says Jane Austen. Nor do you get one, apparently, with a good mind. The novelist goes out of her way to make, scathingly and sarcastically, this point:

> Where people wish to attach, they should always be ignorant. To come with a well-informed mind, is to come with an inability of administering to the vanity of others, which a sensible person would always wish to avoid. A woman especially, if she have the misfortune of knowing any thing, should conceal it as well as she can . . . though to the larger and more trifling part of the [male] sex, imbecility in females is a great enhancement of their personal charms, there is a portion of them too reasonable and too well informed themselves to desire any thing more in woman than ignorance. But Catherine did not know her own advantages—did not know that a good-looking girl, with an affectionate heart and a very ignorant mind, cannot fail of attracting a clever young man, unless circumstances are particularly untoward.

Clever woman are at a disadvantage: it is more difficult for them than for stupid women to massage, with a straight face, the male ego. Jane Austen had the 'misfortune' of knowing a great deal and not being able to 'conceal' it very well. Her chances in the marriage market were perhaps diminished because she was *not* 'a good-looking girl, with an affectionate heart and a very ignorant mind.' She was attractive, it seems—pleasing. She was perhaps less 'affectionate' than open-minded; having high standards, her affections were not easily bestowed. Disposition determines intimacy, as Mrs Dashwood says; if Charlotte Lucas is right, a woman has to show more affection than she feels to get a man, and Jane Austen's disposition did not encompass dissembling of this sort. And of course she was by no means 'ignorant.' Most revealing of all is the bitterness in the declaration that 'a woman . . . if she have the misfortune of knowing any thing, should conceal it as well as she can.' The novelist understood that men do not easily attach themselves to women they suspect of being cleverer than themselves—thus 'Stupid men are the only ones worth knowing, after all,' as Elizabeth Bennet says. Did Jane despair of finding a man clever enough both to perceive and to value her own cleverness? Probably. All of this helps to explain why, in *Northanger Abbey*, the novelist makes her heroine both stupid and successful. In 1796-7, when she was writing 'First Impressions,' Jane Austen still believed that a witty woman might get the man she wanted, as Elizabeth does. Two years later that optimism had evaporated; cynically, the heroine is turned into a fool in order to let her get her man. What happened between 1796 and 1798? Well, there was Tom Lefroy, for one; and the shadowy Taylor; and Blackall, though she seems not to have cared much for him. Perhaps her disappointment over the Lefroy affair went deeper than we know, deeper than anyone has surmised; perhaps there were other disappointments we shall never know anything about. At any rate, there were to be no more heroines like Elizabeth, ever again.

In *Northanger Abbey*, then, the perspective we are given on the dance of desire, the marriage game, is a cynical one. Lucy Steele is repeated in Isabella Thorpe, who wishes to marry only to see 'herself at the end of a few weeks, the gaze and admiration of every new acquaintance . . . the envy of every valued old friend . . . with a carriage at her command, a new name on her tickets, and a brilliant exhibition of hoop rings on her fingers.' Isabella wishes to marry solely for the comfort and convenience of herself. Even Catherine is alive—as Jane Austen so obviously was—to the advantages of snaring a rich husband. The novel reminds us that for a woman without a dowry, one fortune—the man's—is all that is required. As Catherine puts it: 'If there is a good fortune on one side, there can be no occasion for any on the other. No matter which has it, so that there is enough. I hate the idea of one great fortune looking out for another.' And well she might, since she has little fortune of her own. Surely this is the novelist thinking aloud once again. A single fortune would do. But there must be one—as Jane learned well enough when Mrs Lefroy sent her nephew packing. 'After all that romancers may say, there is no doing without money,' Isabella says. Where was the man and the fortune for Jane Austen? In *Northanger Abbey* we come upon her musing in her own voice more often than in any of the other novels.

Between 1796 and 1798 she had learned that it is dangerous and disappointing to become infatuated with a man who hasn't the means to marry. 'Dearest Catherine, beware how you give your heart,' her brother implores her. Catherine's mother bestows upon her advice that the novelist must have heard, and loathed hearing: 'Wherever you are you should always be contented, but especially at home, because there you must spend the most of your time.' What awful, what frightening words those must have been to write—to din into the ears of a heroine. Is it any wonder, after all, that *Northanger Abbey* is such a sarcastic, cynical, caustic, and ironic performance? Is it any wonder that Jane Austen remains detached from her heroine? As the storyteller her presence in *Northanger Abbey* is more intrusive than in any of her other novels because here, more than anywhere else, she must continue to assert her own separation from the events and the people she has created, as Mudrick says. The ending of the novel may be seen, he argues, as a logical and 'final flourish of unconcern,' proof positive that in *Northanger Abbey* irony has overridden the artist and become 'rejection unlimited'—of everyone and everything.

Nor is it any wonder that in his speech to Catherine on the uses of common sense and the absurdities of an overactive imagination, Henry Tilney, the only character in the book treated without irony, notes that such things as Catherine imagines General Tilney to have done are simply not possible to do without detection in a society such as theirs, in which everything is open and 'voluntary spies' watch over everyone and prevent the untoward, the unusual, from going unnoticed or unrecorded. There is more than a little paranoia here; no wonder Jane Austen's books teem with gossipy women living on scandal. The novelist, herself an unusual woman, must have felt trapped and helpless in the country rectory, shut away from eminent contemporaries and discerning men of the marrying kind, and prevented by the 'voluntary spies' around her from doing anything out of the ordinary, from breaking away—had she wanted to do so. Perhaps she did. Her wariness of others may be glimpsed in the tradition, repeated by all the family, that Jane Austen at Chawton allowed the door of her sitting-room, in which she wrote, to squeak when opened, thus giving her a warning—an opportunity to put her work away before being found out. There were 'voluntary spies' everywhere.

'The person, be it gentleman or lady, who has not pleasure in a good novel, must be intolerably stupid,' declares Henry Tilney. *Northanger Abbey* may attack Gothic fiction, but it also goes out of its way to defend the *genre* of the novel. Indeed, it contains the single most passionate defence of the profession she adopted ever written by Jane Austen. In an unusually long aside, the writer speaks directly to the reader about the notion current at the end of the eighteenth century in England, due largely to the untiring efforts of evangelical tract-writers, that fiction was at best only a frivolous amusement, at worst a pernicious interference in and interruption of the serious concerns of people's lives. Novelists, Jane announces in the fifth chapter of *Northanger Abbey*, should stick together and defend their craft against the attacks of prudes and bores.

> Let us not desert one another; we are an injured body. Although our productions have afforded more extensive and unaffected pleasure than those of any other literary corporation in the world, no species of composition has been so much decried. From pride, ignorance, or fashion, our foes are almost as many as our readers . . . there seems almost a general wish of decrying the capacity and undervaluing the labour of the novelist, and of slighting the performances which have only genius, wit, and taste to recommend them. 'I am no novel reader—I seldom look into novels—Do not imagine that *I* often read novels—It is really very well for a novel.'—Such is the common cant.—'And what are you reading, Miss—?' 'Oh! it is only a novel!' replies the young lady; while she lays down her book with affected indifference, or momentary shame.—'It is only Cecilia, or Camilla, or Belinda;' or, in short, only some work in which the greatest powers of the mind are displayed, in which the most thorough knowledge of human nature, the happiest delineation of its varieties, the liveliest effusions of wit and humour are conveyed to the world in the best chosen language.

In this famous passage, written when she was twenty-two, Jane Austen announces her commitment to her art. She had the disadvantages of being a woman, knowing no single person who had any professional connection with literature, having her early work praised by no person outside her family circle. 'Only a novel' it might be to some; to her it was the one form in which, as she says here, the greatest intellectual powers could be displayed and the most thorough knowledge of human nature and its varieties expressed—and in which alone her lively wit, her wonderful humour, and her perfect sense of style could have free play. As yet she had no audience—and she would have none for another dozen years. Many a would-be writer has retired in disgust at an early age because no re-enforcement of his self-confidence can be found, no encouragement detected anywhere: it is hard to work alone, without the admiration and appreciation of peers and fellow professionals. But *Northanger Abbey*, in addition to its many other interesting facets, contains Jane Austen's private declaration of independence, her determination to write—no matter what. *Northanger Abbey* may attack silly novels, but it is a passionate defence of serious ones. The clarity of its thematic line is marvellous. No matter what direction her private life might take, it suggests, she will always have her work—and she will never give it up. It was a remarkable and a very brave thing for an unmarried, undowried, and utterly unknown young lady to say in the year 1799. But Jane Austen said it—and she meant it, too.

'Oh, that I should live to be called Spinster!'
                    —Lydia Languish (aged 17) in Sheridan's *The Rivals* (1775)

'Jane will be quite an old maid soon, I declare. She is almost three and twenty! Lord, how ashamed I should be of not being married before three and twenty!'
                    —Lydia Bennet in *Pride and Prejudice*

'Mama, the more I know of the world, the more I am convinced that I shall never see a man whom I can really love. I require so much!'
                    —Marianne in *Sense and Sensibility*

'What is there for women but love?'
                    —Barbara Pym, *An Unsuitable Attachment*

'One day in the country is exactly like another.'
                    —Henry Tilney in *Northanger Abbey*

'We live at home, quiet, confined, and our feelings prey upon us.'
                    —Anne Elliot in *Persuasion*

'Young Ladies that have no Money are very much to be pitied!'
                    —Lady Denham in *Sanditon*

CHAPTER 5

The Treacherous Years, 1800-1806

Some time during the month of August 1800 Jane Austen probably completed the brief dramatic version of Richardson's novel *Sir Charles Grandison* on which she had been working irregularly for the past eight or nine years. This would be the last bit of sustained writing she would do for four years—until, in 1804 (in all likelihood), she began 'The Watsons.' The years 1800-1804 were a period of upheaval and unsettlement in her life, and of correspondingly little creativity.

It is well-known that Richardson was her favourite novelist and *Sir Charles Grandison* (7 volumes, 1753-4) her favourite among his novels. Both her brother Henry and her nephew J.E. Austen-Leigh report that her knowledge of Richardson's works—especially *Sir Charles Grandison*—was astoundingly complete. We know that she owned a set of the first edition of *Sir Charles Grandison*, probably a gift from one of her parents, both of whom apparently knew the novel well. There are brief references to Richardson's novel in a few of the Juvenilia. In *Northanger Abbey*, *Sir Charles Grandison* is said to be a favourite of both Catherine Morland and her mother—though Isabella Thorpe, no critic, thinks it unreadable. Charlotte Grandison in Jane Austen's play, as in Richardson's novel, is addicted to non-stop 'raillery.' In this and some other traits she bears some superficial resemblances to Isabella in *Northanger Abbey*; and she (Charlotte) is lectured on her diction in a way that may remind us of some of Henry Tilney's speeches to Catherine on the subject of language.

The play is actually an abridgement of Richardson's novel—abridgements of the gargantuan *Grandison* were popular throughout the eighteenth century—and remains faithful to the spirit of much of Jane Austen's early writing in its tendency toward burlesque and parody (favourite novel or not). In some of these connections the play stands close to *Northanger Abbey*, the last of the three novels

Jane wrote during the 1790s (completed in 1799). Her play, it has been pointed out, illuminates some of Richardson's vulnerable sides: ineptness in handling action, periodic prurience, a tendency to pursue far beyond their interest various strands of his story.

Adaptation of somebody else's work or not, there are a few familiar strains here. One is the related question of marriage and security: Should a woman marry a wealthy man she doesn't like, just to be safe? When Harriet Byron, the heroine of both novel and play, breaks up the (forced) marriage ceremony with the villain Pollexfen, in Jane Austen's version she not only dashes the prayer-book from the clergyman's hand, as in Richardson, but tosses it into the fire too: the added vehemence is the playwright's. Another familiar touch is Jane's insistence on Harriet's advantages of 'mind' as well as 'person' (in this she follows Richardson): Harriet is said in the play to be 'the happy medium between gravity and over-liveliness. She is lively or grave as the occasion requires.' And: 'Her understanding more than makes up for want of fortune.' We know how significant these subjects were for Jane Austen. It is also said of Harriet, interestingly enough, that 'she is too nice about an husband': 'if she do not get a husband now, she never may, for she has refused all the young gentry of the neighbourhood.' 'All' turns out to be three men.

It is tempting to find more autobiography here. Much of the play is taken directly from Richardson's novel; but Jane Austen was selecting ruthlessly—a seven-volume novel reduced to twenty printed pages of dialogue—and we may see, by what is in the play, which themes in Richardson's book interested her most.

The play probably was written for domestic consumption. But the Steventon household, which was soon to break up, never saw it performed so far as we know. The manuscript became submerged for years, only to resurface, for the first time in print, in 1980.

II

In March 1800, while Mrs Leigh Perrot was being tried at Taunton for stealing lace, her nephew Frank Austen, off the coast of Marseilles, captured a French ship laden with corn for the French forces in Egypt without a single man of his own being killed or wounded. For this feat Frank was elevated to the rank of post-captain. Sailing in the Mediterranean, he still had not heard his own good news when he wrote to Cassandra in October. Cassandra, in that month, had gone off to Godmersham again, while Edward and his eldest son visited Steventon. Cassandra remained in Kent until January 1801, staying with Henry and Eliza in London on her way to Godmersham; while in town she dispatched to Jane a pair of pink shoes, some combs, and a cloak. All of this travelling on Cassandra's part gave her sister another opportunity for sustained correspondence —first from Steventon, and later, in November, from Ibthorp, where Jane had gone to visit Martha Lloyd.

In late October and early November 1800 Jane sent her news to Cassandra at Godmersham. She reports that Mrs Martin's circulating library has gone out of business after just two years—this was a time of inflation and rising prices: it was the eighth year of the war with France—and that Frank Austen, writing from Cyprus aboard the *Petterel*, still knew nothing either of his promotion or his prize money. She goes on to describe a recent ball at Basingstoke. She thought her hair 'looked very indifferent; nobody abused it however, & I retired delighted with my success.' All the important families of the neighbourhood were present: but 'There was a scarcity of Men in general, & a still greater scarcity of any that were good for much.' The war was taking its toll on dancing partners. She danced nine of ten dances nonetheless. 'Lady Portsmouth had got a different dress on, & Lady Bolton is much improved by a wig.' Her father, meanwhile, was depressed by lower earnings: his farm cleared only £300 during the past year. 'The Debaries persist in being afflicted at the death of their uncle.' Charles, aboard the *Endymion*, is still awaiting sailing orders. She is reading *Les Veillées du Château*, by Madame de Genlis. Charles, on shore leave at Gosport, has described a local ball there: 'A likely spot enough for the discovery of a Charles: but I am glad to say that he was not of the party, for it was in general a very ungenteel one, & there was hardly a pretty girl in the room.' The flavour, wit, and tone of these letters may perhaps best be demonstrated by quoting a passage such as the following:

> Yesterday was a day of great business with me. Mary drove me all in the rain to Basingstoke, & still more all in the rain back again, because it rained harder; and soon after our return to Dean[e] a sudden invitation & an own postchaise took us to Ash[e] Park, to dine tete a tete with Mr Holder, Mr Gauntlett, & James Digweed; but our tete a tete was cruelly reduced by non-attendance of the two latter.—We had a very quiet evening, I

beleive Mary found it dull, but I thought it very pleasant. To sit
in idleness over a good fire in a well-proportioned room is a
luxurious sensation.—Sometimes we talked & sometimes we
were quite silent; I said two or three amusing things, & M^r
Holder made a few infamous puns.

'To sit in idleness over a good fire in a well-proportioned room is a
luxurious sensation': Jane Austen, now nearly twenty-five, had had
little enough opportunity for such indulgence, but she had not forgotten its advantages. The Mr Holder in question, who had rented Ashe
Park, had made a fortune in the East Indies. The novelist goes on to
tell Cassandra that Lord Portsmouth (the former Lord Lymington)
is to give a ball to celebrate the third anniversary of his marriage. The
Petterel has secured a Turkish ship away from the French—more
prize money for Frank. Another of their father's former pupils, the
Rev Richard Buller, has just married for the second time, and Jane
had wondered whether she would be bombarded with letters full of
sentimental effusions: 'I was afraid he would oppress me by his
felicity & his love for his wife,' but he has written quite a restrained
letter. Only a woman in a peculiarly sensitive state of mind might feel
'oppressed' by news of the married happiness of acquaintances. On
the other hand, she hopes it is true that Edward Taylor—the most
shadowy of her possible early 'suitors'—is to marry his cousin
Charlotte: 'Those beautiful dark Eyes will then adorn another
Generation at least in all their purity.' The 'beautiful dark Eyes' are
the gentleman's; she had never met the lady.
      Martha Lloyd had invited Jane to visit Ibthorp after the
Hurstbourne ball, scheduled for 19 November. 'You are very good in
wishing to see me at Ibthorp so soon, & I am equally good in wishing
to come to you,' the novelist declares. 'I beleive our Merit in that
respect is much upon a par, our Self-denial mutually strong.' She goes
on to invite Martha to come back with her to Steventon at the end of
the month (November 1800). Martha had asked her to bring some
books along. Jane replies: 'You distress me cruelly by your request
about Books; I cannot think of any to bring with me, nor have I any
idea of our wanting them. I come to you to be talked to, not to read
or hear reading. I can do *that* at home; & indeed I am now laying in a
stock of intelligence to pour out on you as *my* share of Conversation.'
Anyway, she adds, Mrs Stent—an elderly and apparently voluble
companion of Martha's, in reduced circumstances—will be present

and babbling on about roosters and hens, so there cannot possibly be any silence at Ibthorp (Mrs Stent undoubtedly is one of the ancestors of Miss Bates in *Emma*). The novelist reports gossip she has heard to the effect that Sir Thomas Williams, the widower of her late cousin Jane Cooper, was about to remarry (he was indeed).

The day after the Portsmouths' ball at Hurstbourne, Jane sent an account of it to Cassandra. 'I beleive I drank too much wine last night,' she declares. 'I know not how else to account for the shaking of my hand today.' She was escorted to the ball by her brother Charles; the *Endymion* was under sailing orders but had not yet departed. She danced nine of twelve dances and only sat down for the other three due to 'the want of a partner.' 'There were very few Beauties,' the novelist reports, '& such as there were, were not very handsome.' A Mrs Blount was the only lady generally admired: 'She appeared exactly as she did in September, with the same broad face, diamond bandeau, white shoes, pink husband, & fat neck.' Also present was a Mrs Warren: 'I was constrained to think [her] a very fine young woman, which I much regret. She has got rid of some part of her child, & danced away with great activity, looking by no means very large.—Her husband is ugly enough; uglier even than her cousin John.' The Debary sisters appeared, '& I was as civil to them as their bad breath would allow me.' Whatever expectations she might have had for this ball clearly were dashed; her disappointment and anger are sublimated in this Swiftian account of it. She was obviously perplexed by the little attention she received: 'Mary said that I looked very well last night . . . my hair was at least tidy.' It wasn't enough. At Ibthorp, meanwhile, Mrs Stent hasn't stopped talking. Sir Thomas Williams's new wife, Miss Emma Wapshire, has been described favourably to her by 'The endless Debaries.' Miss Wapshire, a 'distinguished beauty,' 'is now seven or eight & twenty, and tho' still handsome, less handsome than she has been.—This promises better, than the bloom of seventeen.' Jane says she and Martha will be going back to Steventon in a few days.

And go back they did. When they entered the Rectory, Mrs Austen greeted them in the hall with the news that the family would soon be leaving Steventon and moving to Bath. Jane fainted. She was not a fainter; the emotional disturbance must have been acute. Beneath her celebrated composure she was high-strung. And she was upset. It is significant that for December 1800, though Cassandra remained at Godmersham during the month, there are no letters extant—bearing silent testimony, perhaps, to the novelist's agitated state of mind. Cassandra, as we know, later destroyed the letters she thought too personally revealing; if Jane wrote at all, it must have been in great anguish. In this same month the novelist turned twenty-five; she had lived, during these years, only at Steventon. Did her feelings resemble those of Marianne Dashwood upon leaving Norland—or those of Anne Elliot upon leaving Kellynch? We shall never know. What we do know is that Steventon had been everything to Jane Austen, and she never liked Bath; Anne Elliot, in *Persuasion*, 'persisted in a very determined, though silent, disinclination for Bath.' All Jane's roots were at Steventon. There she could have serene confidence in the stability of her daily life. Suddenly, in two sentences spoken without preamble by her mother, her serenity was exploded. 'Well, girls! it is all settled. We have decided to leave Steventon and go to Bath,' Mrs Austen is supposed to have said to them as they came in the door. The novelist was 'exceedingly unhappy' upon hearing the news, says the author of the *Memoir*, a man not given to exaggeration. There can be no doubt that she was 'unhappy.' Indeed, she was to remain dissatisfied for a good many years. A decade of rootlessness was about to begin; this was a watershed event in her life.

It seems that George Austen, now sixty-nine, had decided to retire, and to pass along to his eldest son James his duties as Rector of Steventon; the living that went with the duties he would retain during his lifetime. Mrs Austen found the house too large for them now and too difficult to run, in inflationary times, on their diminishing income. Her hypochondria, and the habitual presence there of her brother, inclined her towards Bath as a residence. But it is also highly probable that the father and mother thought that their two unmarried daughters were more likely to acquire husbands at Bath than at Steventon—certainly a logical supposition—perhaps in part through the good offices of the rich Leigh Perrots. Cassandra was now twenty-eight, Jane twenty-five; both had a tendency to find the few men they did meet good for little. It was now or never. 'If adventures will not befall a young lady in her own village, she must seek them abroad,' the novelist had written in *Northanger Abbey*. The decision, like many of George Austen's, was reached in a hurry; Jane had no forewarning whatsoever. Consulting no one except his wife, the Rector of Steventon decided to leave his home of the past thirty years. And so the plans were made. From this time forward

Jane Austen saw the world as a less predictable, secure, and comfortable place.

A tradition persists that the Austens decided to move partly to put some distance between their daughters and the Digweed family, still resident at the Steventon Manor House. Jane suggested from time to time that James Digweed was in love with Cassandra; some of the other Austens were certain that Harry Francis Digweed, who was a year or two younger than the novelist, was in love with her. This, however, is only speculation on the part of several early biographers; there isn't a shred of evidence to support it. Indeed, it is fair to point out that such a situation would have constituted a very good reason for the Austens to *remain* at Steventon rather than to leave it, for the Digweed boys would have been good catches. The Digweed theory of the Austens' departure from Steventon is anything but convincing.

By January 1801, though the move to Bath was only months away, Jane was sufficiently reconciled to it to write in a cheerful vein to Cassandra, who remained at Godmersham. The family's plans are taking shape, the novelist writes. 'My Mother looks forward . . . to our keeping two Maids—my father is the only one not in the secret.—We are having a steady Cook, & a young giddy Housemaid, with a sedate middle aged Man, who is to undertake the double office of Husband to the former & sweetheart to the latter. No Children of course to be allowed on either side.' They are undecided as to which part of Bath to settle into: the three leading candidates are Westgate Buildings, Charles Street, and the area around Laura Place and Poulteney Street. She herself prefers Charles Street because it is nearer than the other locations to some good walks. Mrs Austen would like to live in Gay Street; but that neighbourhood, Jane says, is too expensive. Her mother's next choice would be Chapel Row, which opens onto Prince's Street. None of them wants to live too close to the Leigh Perrots in Paragon Buildings: 'we all unite in particular dislike of that part of the Town, & therefore hope to escape.' The novelist liked her uncle but disliked her aunt. Much discussion follows of what is to be taken from Steventon to Bath and what left behind; Jane tells Cassandra that their beds are to be transported to Bath. For the moment, at any rate, she has come to think of Bath as her future home: 'I flatter myself that for little comforts of all kinds, our apartment will be one of the most complete things of the sort all over Bath,' once she gets it fixed up properly. Strains of the old, more relaxed Jane Austen begin to reappear: 'I have now attained the true art of letter-writing, which we are always told is to express on paper exactly what one would say to the same person by word of mouth; I have been talking to you almost as fast as I could the whole of this letter.' Equally characteristic is this comment—about some acquaintances who have benefited financially from the death of a relative: 'I am very glad to hear of the Pearsons' good fortune . . . It brings them a considerable increase of Income, & a better house.' She tells Cassandra that her father plans to have an income of £600 a year in retirement. And she concludes her letter of 3 January 1801 with a statement which both documents her resilience and helps to explain how the Digweed story may have begun:

> I get more & more reconciled to the idea of our removal. We have lived long enough in this Neighbourhood, the Basingstoke Balls are certainly on the decline, there is something interesting in the bustle of going away, & the prospect of spending future summers by the Sea or in Wales is very delightful.—For a time we shall now possess many of the advantages which I have often thought of with Envy in the wives of Sailors or Soldiers.—It must not be generally known however that I am not sacrificing a great deal in quitting the Country—or I can expect to inspire no tenderness, no interest in those we leave behind.

Only a reader utterly devoid of a sense of humour could take any of this seriously.

James Austen, the novelist reports in her next letter, has offered the curacy at Deane to Peter Debary, who has turned it down because 'he wishes to be settled nearer London. A foolish reason! . . . I feel rather indignant that any possible objection should be raised against so valuable a piece of preferment, so delightful a situation!' No doubt James Digweed would take the Deane curacy if Cassandra went along with the house, Jane comments playfully. She has met a Mrs Powlett, who 'was at once expensive & nakedly dress'd.' Mrs Lyford, another friend, 'is so much pleased with the state of widowhood as to be going to put in for being a widow again': she has decided to marry a wealthy man much older than herself. Lord Craven, she says, has installed a mistress at Ashdown Park; this was probably the actress Louisa Brunton. The novelist notes with approval Cassandra's plan to visit London in February before returning to Steventon. Their parents talk of spending summers in Sidmouth once they are installed in

Bath. They are all busy packing up books: there are at least 500 volumes. Unfortunately her pianoforte cannot be transported to Bath and will have to be sold. So will some of her books. She thanks Cassandra for her most recent letter; she would have liked it even better had it cost less to receive. She comments on her sister's announcement that at a recent ball at Chilham she danced four times with a Mr Kemble: 'Why did you dance four dances with so stupid a Man?—why not rather dance two of them with some elegant brother-officer who was struck with your appearance as soon as you entered the room?' The Rectory, she reports, is being redecorated for James and Mary and their family, and much of the furniture sold—she does not think her father will realise more than £200 from the sale, and this includes the 'Brew house.' The debate on where to live in Bath rages on; Cassandra's partiality for Westgate Buildings may win the day, though Laura Place is still a strong candidate. After much persuasion her father has been forced to concede that they must live in 'a comfortable & a creditable looking house.' The women of the neighbourhood have been calling on Mrs Austen to pay their respects and say good-bye; the most recent invasion-force had 'heads full of Bantam-cocks and Galinies' (hens). The Leigh Perrots have invited the Austens to stay with them in Bath while they look for a house, and Jane hopes the stay will not be a long one. She has recently been visited by a friend who, she hopes, will sell 'her black beaver bonnet for the releif of the poor.'

Frank, she reports, is no longer serving in the *Petterel* and is waiting for another ship to be given him: he should be home soon on leave. She hopes that both her Naval brothers will now be promoted—Frank to commander, Charles to first lieutenant. About a neighbour who has recently died, and her successor in the house, Jane writes: 'The Neighbourhood have quite recovered the death of Mrs Rider—so much so, that I think they are rather rejoiced at it now; her things were so very dear! & Mrs Rogers is to be all that is desirable. Not even Death itself can fix the friendship of the World.' The Austens are frantically paying farewell calls everywhere. Old Mrs Knight, Edward's patroness, has been confined to her bed: 'I cannot think so ill of her however in spite of your insinuations, as to suspect her of having lain-in.—I do not think she would be betrayed beyond an *Accident* at the utmost.' This surely borders on bad taste. Of neighbours who have recently been robbed: it 'must be an amusing thing to their acquaintance, & I hope it is as much their pleasure as it seems their avocation to be subjects of general Entertainment.' We are back once again in the realm of sheer maliciousness. The first choice of the family for a residence in Bath has settled on Laura Place. But her mother now has her heart set on Queen's Square, and her uncle—that is, James Leigh Perrot—undoubtedly will take his sister's part. This would suit Jane herself, she tells Cassandra: it would be pleasant to be near Sydney Gardens. She wishes to know whether or not James Digweed has proposed to Cassandra yet. During her most recent visit to Ashe Park, the novelist informs her sister, she found herself shut up in the drawing-room alone with Mr Holder for ten minutes. Despite this 'betrayal . . . into a situation of the utmost cruelty,' no proposal of marriage was made. 'Nothing,' says Jane, 'could prevail on me to move two steps from the door, on the lock of which I kept one hand constantly fixed.' Still, she left Ashe Park 'very cross.' She orders Cassandra to go to the opera in London and 'to lay in a stock of intelligence that may procure me amusement for a twelvemonth to come.' She looks forward to seeing Cassandra: three months of separation constitutes the outer limit of her tolerance.

In February 1801 Jane visited the Bigg Withers at Manydown. While there she wrote to Cassandra, who was staying with Henry and Eliza in Upper Berkeley Street in London. Henry had resigned from the Army and lived in some style with his wife, who had a carriage and a French chef: in these days he seemed mainly devoted to the subject of his own health and had become, like his mother, a terrific hypochondriac. Charles has written to say that the *Endymion* is just off Lisbon, and that Frank is on his way home on leave. Charles is described by the novelist as 'much surprised' by the family's move to Bath, but also as 'reconciled'—though he means to visit 'Steventon once more while Steventon is ours.' They have been to see some neighbours of the Bigg Withers called Dyson: 'The house seemed to have all the comforts of little Children, dirt & litter. Mr Dyson as usual looked wild, & Mrs Dyson as usual looked big.' One notes Jane Austen's linking of little children with dirt and litter; her fondness for children did not increase as she got older.

Cassandra came home shortly after this, and we have no letters for the next several months. The family plan was to go to the Lloyds at Ibthorp in May and from there to Bath. Jane and her mother would go first; Cassandra would follow once a place to live had been found. Their father would pay visits in Kent and London until all was ready in Bath. And so in May 1801 off went the novelist and her mother to the Leigh Perrots in Bath, with whom they stayed while they looked at houses. The month of May was consumed almost entirely in house-hunting. Ultimately they found what they wanted at 4 Sydney Terrace—near those very gardens in which Jane had hoped to walk should they live in this part of town. The house overlooked the pavilion and the trees behind it; the area was sort of the Vauxhall of Bath and lay at the edge of town. Later they were to move to Green Park Buildings.

Cassandra was not to join the family until June, and so during the month of May 1801 we have several letters from Jane at Bath to Cassandra at Ibthorp, where she was visiting the Lloyds, and Kintbury, where she visited the Fowles. These letters are filled with the novelist's latest impressions of the city that was now to be her home, and of the many houses they looked into before settling on the place in Sydney Terrace. She found a great deal to write about; she had not seen the city for two years. By 1801 much of the London smart set had followed the Prince Regent's example and gone to Brighton for its holidays, but the country gentry remained loyal to Bath. To Bath they continued to go, as Cecil says, 'for some urban relaxation and amusement; by night at the theatre or at balls and concerts at the Upper or Lower Assembly Rooms; by day, meeting their friends at the Pump Room, going on expeditions to neighbouring beauty spots, walking the streets to inspect the new fashions at the milliner's or new songs at the music shop or new novels at the bookseller's.'

The journey to Bath, Jane reports, was satisfactory: 'We . . . were exceedingly agreeable as we did not speak above once in three miles.' This may tend to confirm the suggestion, made earlier, that the novelist and her mother were not always comfortable together. There is to be, she complains to Cassandra, only one more major ball at Bath before the 'season' ends and everyone goes off on summer holiday. Bath in warmth and sunlight, she declares, is hardly superior to Bath in rain and mist: 'The first view of Bath in fine weather does not answer my expectations; I think I see more distinctly through rain.' Perhaps rain rather than sunlight more nearly matched her mood. The price of salmon, she says, should go down as soon as the Duchess of York leaves. They have seen several houses: one was rejected because of 'the dampness of the offices'—such things could be mentioned in private correspondence, if not in a novel. At

Steventon the three cows have been sold for 61½ guineas and some new tables for only eleven guineas. Her beloved pianoforte went for eight guineas; she is anxious to hear what she will get for her books. She went to the last ball: 'it was shockingly & inhumanly thin for this place,' and there were too many private parties. Clearly she felt anomalous—as she so often did at Bath. She has met a woman who is absolutely known to be 'an Adultress.' The woman—probably Julia Twysleton, daughter of Lord Saye and Sele—was not specially handsome: 'highly rouged, & looked rather quietly & contentedly silly than anything else.' One man got drunk and was chased around the room by his equally drunken wife before being caught and taken home. They may go to the Assembly Rooms one more time, when she hopes to wear a new white gown she is having made. She has been to a number of dull parties made up chiefly of older people, acquaintances of the Leigh Perrots. She herself has not made any new friends: 'I respect Mrs Chamberlayne for doing her hair well, but cannot feel a more tender sentiment.—Miss Langley is like any other girl with a broad nose & wide mouth, fashionable dress, & exposed bosom.— [Admiral] Stanhope is a gentlemanlike Man, but then his legs are too short, & his tail too long.—Mrs Stanhope could not come; I fancy she had a private appointment with Mr Chamberlayne.' Jane Austen had not lost her sense of humour—nor were her powers of observation and imagination any less acute or her tone less acid. She found the new crowd a very dull bunch indeed.

They have had their eye on a place in Green Park Buildings, she reports some days later, but once again the 'offices' were found to be damp. In fact, they have seen nothing so far but 'putrifying Houses.' Her father, Jane says, will pick Cassandra up at Kintbury on June 1 and bring her to Bath with him. Frank Austen, on shore leave, is staying with them for a short time. She has managed to make a friend of Mrs Chamberlayne, and they regularly walk together. Mrs Austen has a cold and is theoretically staying in—but accepting all invitations that come her way. The Leigh Perrots do their share of entertaining: 'We are to have a tiny party here tonight; I hate tiny parties—they force one into constant exertion.' She refers to matrimony breezily enough: 'I am prevented from setting my black cap at Mr Maitland by his having a wife and ten children.' James Austen has bought her books, valued by the agent at only £70. 'The whole World is in a conspiracy to enrich one part of our family at the expense of another,' she complains bitterly. One reason why in later years she came to dislike Mary Lloyd Austen, James's second wife, may be that Mary lived at Steventon, while Jane herself had been dishinherited of her old home. The novelist says she has met a man who 'is as raffish in his appearance as I would wish every Disciple of [William] Godwin to be.'

The last letter to Cassandra of this month—May 1801—reports that the Chamberlaynes are leaving Bath and thus Jane is without a walking partner. She has spent some time with Miss Holder, who remembers Cassandra as 'being remarkably lively; therefore get ready the proper selection of adverbs, & due scraps of Italian and French.' In answer to an inquiry by Cassandra, the novelist declares that she has been introduced to no interesting new men. She does like Mr Evelyn, but she has seen very little of him despite his promise to take her out for a drive in his phaeton: 'whether it will come to anything must remain with him.—I really beleive he is very harmless.' Her aunt has been trying to think up a pretext for visiting Mr Evelyn but so far has utterly failed in this endeavour: 'She ought to be particularly scrupulous in such matters & she says so herself—but nevertheless. . . .' The sentence is sadly left unfinished. All of this tends to confirm the suspicion that the move to Bath was designed at least in part to put Jane and Cassandra in the way of husbands. The novelist goes on to report the following day that she has been for her ride in Mr Evelyn's phaeton, and that is that. Charles is in town on leave and has received £40 in prize money. He has spent part of it on presents for herself and Cassandra; she is particularly delighted with some handsome gold chains and topaz crosses. Undoubtedly this suggested the amber cross given to Fanny Price by her sailor brother in *Mansfield Park*; being a midshipman rather than an officer, William Price could not afford the gold chain to go with it. The *Endymion* will soon be off again, ferrying troops to Egypt. Mr Evelyn will take them all to the fireworks display several days hence.

Cassandra and her father arrived in Bath on schedule on June 1, and so Jane Austen's letters to her sister came temporarily to an end.

III

Between May 1801 and September 1804 we have no letters at all. We understand what this usually means: the novelist must have gone through some rough patches in her emotional life, and Cassandra destroyed the evidence. Still, we know some of what happened during these nearly three and a half 'dark' years of Jane Austen's life; we can piece together some of the rest. What with the family's movements and (probably) other dislocations in her emotional life, there is no creative work of Jane Austen's at all during this period to scrutinise for signs (she did not begin 'The Watsons' until 1804). In some artists, adversity is a catalyst: the grain of sand in the oyster. In Jane Austen adversity blanketed energy and inspiration; she wrote only when she was relatively content and secure.

The Austens spent the summer of 1801 by the sea—probably either at Newtown or Sidmouth. We are certain, from a letter written by Eliza to her mother Philadelphia, that the family holiday was spent somewhere by the sea in Devonshire. It was during this time that an important but mysterious incident in the novelist's life took place. It is mysterious because so little is known about it and so many second- and third-hand versions of what happened have been given to posterity via family gossip—nieces and nephews and grand-nieces and -nephews reporting what they were told their Aunt Cassandra told their mama or papa. Its importance will at once be obvious.

What is clear is this. While on holiday in Devon the Austen party became intimate with two brothers, a physician resident in Devonshire and his clergyman-brother visiting him there. The clergyman, a youngish, intelligent, charming, and handsome man, found himself greatly attracted to Jane. Indeed, within three weeks he apparently fell in love with her. He seemed to be on the verge of proposing marriage when the holiday came to an end. The Austens and the clergyman planned to meet again soon—probably before the following summer, though there is a tradition that they agreed to take their holidays together again the next year—at which time it was fully expected by the family that the gentleman would propose to Jane, and that she would accept him. He was considered 'worthy' of the novelist's hand in marriage by *both* sisters, exacting judges—of this there is no doubt. The summer ended, and the happy group broke up. Instead of an early reunion with the gentleman, the Austens received soon afterwards, from his brother, notice of his death.

We have, as stated, none of Jane Austen's letters for the next three years. Either Cassandra destroyed the few that may have been written, or she stayed close enough to her disappointed sister during this time to make the writing of letters largely unnecessary. The bitterness of Anne Elliot in *Persuasion* on the subject of happiness dela,ed may be a rare clue to Jane's own bitterness of spirit during the period 1801-4. Her prospects of marriage were few enough; here was another—the best—snuffed out. This time she had *loved*. The man in question may well have died, as tradition has it; or he may, like Tom Lefroy five and a half years earlier, simply have decamped, leaving his brother to pick up the pieces. Cassandra's story to the family would have been the same in either circumstance (she never *named* the man). The novelist reverted to being only another impoverished spinster—and to sitting for the highly imaginative portrait in J.E. Austen-Leigh's *Memoir* of a life of smooth currents unruffled by changes, crises, attachments, or unhappiness.

The family settled in at 4 Sydney Terrace. Mrs Austen had her periodic bouts of invalidism; they led uneventful lives. The house at Bath (still standing) was in a four-storeyed terrace located conveniently opposite the Sydney Gardens, where the novelist must have done a lot of walking. Nearby were shop-lined Pulteney Street and fashionable Laura Place. The Guildhall, the Abbey, and the Pump Rooms were not far away.

In the autumn of 1801 came the sad news from London of the death of Hastings de Feuillide, Eliza's backward little son, aged just fifteen. It was shortly after this, during the temporary Peace of Amiens, that Henry and Eliza went to France to try to reclaim some property belonging to her first husband and narrowly escaped one of Napoleon's dungeons.

In the summer of 1802 the Austens went on holiday either to Teignmouth or Dawlish. In October Jane and Cassandra together visited Godmersham—Edward's seventh child was born in 1801; his eighth would be born in 1803—and from there they went over to Steventon to spend some time with James and Mary and their family. Near the end of 1802 there occurred yet another bizarre incident in the history of Jane Austen's 'love' life.

In November Jane and Cassandra were still at Steventon. While in the neighbourhood they naturally saw many old friends. One house they visited was that of the Bigg Withers at Manydown. On 3 December the two Austen sisters suddenly and without prior warning reappeared at Steventon. They got out of the carriage with the three Bigg sisters, and 'a tender scene of embraces and tears and distressing farewells took place in the hall' at Steventon, as Mary Lloyd Austen is supposed to have described it. The novelist was highly upset and on the verge of tears. Cassandra and Jane, having hurriedly left Manydown, demanded—without further explanation—that James drive them back to Bath the next day, a Saturday. This meant that James would not get back in time to preach at Steventon on the Sunday and a stand-in would have to be found; but the sisters (uncharacteristically) insisted. They wanted to leave the neighbourhood the next day, and they would not under any circumstances wait until the Monday, as their brother suggested.

What had happened was this. Harris Bigg Wither, then just twenty-one and preparing to take orders, had proposed to Jane during the previous evening (2 December 1802). Now just a few weeks short of her twenty-seventh birthday, she had accepted him. Having second thoughts during the night, she changed her mind the next morning, announced that she had done so, and with Cassandra and the Bigg sisters left Manydown quickly and in obvious embarrassment. Jane Austen could not, it appears, play the role of Charlotte Lucas—twenty-seven when she accepts Mr Collins—after all: she could not, that is, marry a man she didn't love simply in order to have an establishment of her own. Materially at least this would have been a good match for her. Her father had little money to leave her; Harris Bigg Wither was in a position to help him in his last years. The lot of penurious spinster was of course not a happy one. 'For a young woman in Jane Austen's financial position,' as Joan Rees comments, 'the opportunity of marriage, motherhood, and eventually becoming the mistress of . . . an establishment [such as] . . . the handsome Manydown house, situated in the part of the country she regarded as home . . . since her girlhood . . . [and] where one day she might be able to offer her sister a comfortable home, was not an offer to be turned down lightly.' Jane was tempted—then vexed by the embarrassment caused on both sides. One critic declares that Cassandra, fearful of losing her sister to another person, watched her flirtations with jealous fear. But years later Jane's niece Caroline offered another explanation.

> I conjecture that the advantages he could offer, and her gratitude for his love, and her long friendship with his family, induced my aunt to decide that she would marry him when he should ask her, but that having accepted him she found she was miserable. To be sure she should not have said 'Yes' overnight; but I have always respected her for her courage in cancelling

that 'Yes' the next morning; all worldly advantages would have been to her, and she was of an age to know this quite well. . . . My aunts had very small fortunes; and on their father's death, they and their mother would be, they were aware, but poorly off. I believe most young women so circumstanced would have gone on trusting to love after marriage.

Many women in the novelist's position would indeed have gone on, trusting to love after marriage if it had not come before; it is at the age of twenty-seven also that Anne Elliot recovers both her old bloom and her lost lover. But for Jane Austen, it was not to be. As Douglas Bush reminds us, 'she had a very high ideal of the love that should unite a husband and wife . . . All her heroines . . . know, in proportion to their maturity, the meaning of ardent love.' In *Sense and Sensibility*, we may recall, Elinor ponders that 'worst and most irremediable of all evils, a connection for life' with the wrong man. Clearly the experience at Sidmouth (or Newtown) in the summer of 1801 had shown the novelist what being in love was like. She knew she was not in love with Harris Bigg Wither—a recluse who stammered and had a mean temper—and was never likely to be. At any rate, two years later that gentleman consoled himself with another lady, one Anne Howe Frith. Cassandra continued from time to time to visit her old friends the Bigg sisters at Manydown, but so far as we know Jane never went to that house again.

During this brief period of peace with France, Frank Austen remained on shore, and half-pay, organising a series of lookouts— mostly Kent fishermen—whose task it was to give the alarm should Napoleon's fleet approach any unprotected part of the coast. While stationed at Ramsgate, Frank met, and later became engaged to, Mary Gibson, whom he married in 1806. Jane and Cassandra (separately) visited her in Ramsgate in 1803, and both liked her immensely—notwithstanding their hope that Frank would marry Martha Lloyd (years later, of course, he did). Also in 1803 James Digweed, who was supposed by the novelist to be in love with her sister, went to the altar with Mary Susannah Lyford, daughter of the lady who, according to Jane, specialised in marrying rich old men and becoming an increasingly wealthy widow.

In this same year the novelist decided on a second attempt at publication. Since Cadell had unceremoniously refused 'First Impressions' in 1797, Jane Austen had not tried the publishers again.

Now she submitted to another house *Northanger Abbey*—still called 'Susan' at this stage of its existence.

Why this manuscript rather than one of the others she had on hand? *Pride and Prejudice* had already been tainted by rejection. The likelihood is that she still was not entirely satisfied with *Sense and Sensibility*, that very difficult book never specially esteemed by the family. But the third novel was topical: Gothic romances remained popular, and 'Susan' was a burlesque of them. So it was 'Susan' that she brought with her on a visit to Henry and Eliza in London in 1803. Henry took over from his father the task of marketing Jane's work. He gave the novel to his man of business, a Mr Seymour, who in turn took it to Crosby and Sons of London and submitted it to them on behalf of the anonymous author. Crosby looked the manuscript over, and after only a brief delay offered to pay £10 for it and to publish it at an early date. We may be certain that the novelist was delighted. Here at last was authorship, at no financial risk to herself—and a half-year's allowance into the bargain. How was she to know that Crosby, after announcing forthcoming publication in the press ('*Susan: A Novel in Two Volumes*'), would decide it was too risky, and sit on the book for years? What made the novel topical also made it a chancey undertaking for the publisher. The Gothic romances 'Susan' satirised were still selling—for Crosby as for other houses—and he had no stomach, as it turned out, for publishing a burlesque of them: they were in part his bread and butter. Why he did not come to this decision in the first place and refuse the manuscript, we shall never know. All of this caused Jane more vexation than a mere rejection could have done. But of course her initial reaction must have been one of great pleasure—a pleasure which faded, as time passed, into increased bitterness and disappointment when the promised publication was put off again and yet again. As we know, after the success of *Emma* she bought 'Susan' back from Crosby through Henry's agent (the publisher having no idea with whom he was actually dealing) and revised it slightly for what turned out to be a posthumous edition. Still, in 1803 the sale and the apparent prospect of early publication must have given the novelist's spirits a brief lift. How brief may be seen when we examine 'The Watsons,' a tale she began to write sometime during the following year (1804).

For the mood of 'The Watsons' is anything but sunny. It is the only piece of fiction we have from Jane Austen's 'dark' years—the years between the production of the two 'trilogies'—and, as well as any letters might have done, it betrays her sense of unfulfilment, unsettlement, and unhappiness. We have surmised that the novelist needed a sense of security and contentment to work comfortably; during the period 1804-5, when 'The Watsons' was written and then abandoned, she could have had a sense of neither of these essential things. Her affairs of the heart had ended in terrible disappointment; 'Susan' still had not appeared—she remained wholly unpublished; she was unhappy and bored in Bath, distracted by city life, and without a quiet, peaceful place in which to work.

A fragment of little over 16,000 words, 'The Watsons,' as Joan Rees has characterised it, is 'a realistic and ironic study of women's place in society'; Southam describes it as a story about a 'distressed heroine in a domestic setting.' In either case we can see that its autobiographical content would inevitably be substantial; it is the product *par excellence*—and the only literary product—of Jane Austen's disappointed, frustrated, uncomfortable middle years. 'The Watsons' was abandoned, for reasons we shall soon come to, in 1805; but what remains of it is interesting and revealing. The manuscript is heavily corrected; the writer obviously had trouble with her story from the start. Nor is there any evidence to indicate that she ever tinkered with it again after that first attempt of 1804-5. It belonged to a period of her life she was only too happy to put entirely behind her. There is no ground whatever for the contention of some that 'The Watsons' was a trial run for *Emma*; the two works belong to different universes.

'The Watsons' is nonetheless a recognisably Jane Austen production. At the centre of it once again are two sisters (Emma and Elizabeth Watson) who are said to be much alike and who are very close. Each loves to dance—though, as in *Sense and Sensibility*, there is a disparaging reference to dancing-parties: the writer refers to the inconvenience and discomfort of moving 'from the quiet warmth of a snug parlour, to the bustle, noise & draughts of air . . . of an Inn.' Jane Austen was now twenty-eight. There are two other Watson sisters, Penelope and Margaret; and between Emma and Elizabeth on the one hand and Margaret and Penelope on the other, there is a good deal of coldness—the coldness of that familiar phenomenon sibling rivalry, a rivalry that becomes specially pronounced when the subject of available single men is broached. For the focus of 'The Watsons,' too, is unmarried women in search of husbands. Indeed, it could well have begun with a slightly revised version of the opening of *Pride and*

Prejudice: 'It is a truth universally acknowledged, that a single woman not in possession of a good fortune, must be in want of a husband.' This is what 'The Watsons' is about. As Elizabeth says, 'I think I could like any good humoured Man with a comfortable Income.' Of Emma Watson, the main character, who is described as having 'a lively Eye, a sweet smile, & an open Countenance,' and an 'expression to make [her] beauty improve on acquaintance,' and who bears a number of resemblances to the novelist herself, Elizabeth declares that she is too 'refined' to make a good match: 'I am afraid it will not be for your happiness,' says Elizabeth of Emma's 'refinement.' Indeed, Emma's demeanour is pointedly 'very unlike the encouraging warmth' given off by most of the women in this story when men are around them. She shrinks 'from the dreadful mortifications of unequal Society,' by which she means the society of people demonstrably richer than herself: 'Hard-hearted prosperity, low-minded Conceit, & wrong-headed folly' seem so often to go together. Says Emma:

> To be so bent on Marriage—to pursue a Man merely for the sake of situation—is a sort of thing that shocks me; I cannot understand it. Poverty is a great Evil, but to a woman of Education & feeling it ought not, it cannot be the greatest.—I would rather be a Teacher at a school (and I can think of nothing worse) than marry a Man I did not like.

Jane Austen, 'a woman of Education & feeling,' would not marry merely for rank, money, or 'situation,' as she proved in the Bigg Wither affair. Emma's words reflect the novelist's horror of one of the usual alternatives awaiting the impecunious unmarried woman in those days—a subject treated more fully in the story of Jane Fairfax in *Emma*.

Emma Watson undoubtedly reflects another facet of her author in her carefully drawn dislike of conceited, careless men like Lord Osborne. She tells Osborne himself that 'there are some circumstances which even *Women* cannot controul.—Female Economy will do a great deal my Lord, but it cannot turn a small income into a large one' (this in answer to Osborne's query as to why she doesn't ride). What a world of bitterness is there! Indeed, Elizabeth addresses to Emma a little homily on the very subject of women's dependence:

you know we must marry.—I could do very well single for my own part—A little Company, & a pleasant Ball now & then, would be enough for me, if one could be young for ever, but my Father cannot provide for us, & it is very bad to grow old & be poor & laughed at.

One cannot be young forever; and to be old and poor and laughed at is the greatest horror of all. It is a situation and a theme with which we are by now amply familiar in Jane Austen's world. No wonder she was tempted at Manydown in 1802. A woman in such a position is largely at the mercy of men, who of course have all the advantages: they have the means, they believe (or at least many of them do, 'The Watsons' proclaims) that 'A woman should never be trusted with money,' and they can take a wife or not, as they choose. A woman can only wait and hope.

In 'The Watsons' men are depicted for the most part as inconstant, unpredictable, capricious, vain, and materialistic. It nonetheless remains 'a hard thing for a woman to stand against the flattering ways of a Man' when he sets himself out to flatter, as Elizabeth says—especially when he can provide all the things a woman lacks in her life. Though husband-hunting is again at the centre of the story, the men here are a sorry lot, absorbed in themselves and in making conquests rather than wives of women.

One of the exceptions to this rule is Mr Howard, a clergyman (possibly drawn from the mystery man of the Devon romance of 1801), whom Emma was slated to marry—despite a proposal from Lord Osborne—at the end of the story, according to Cassandra Austen, had her sister finished writing 'The Watsons.' Elizabeth remarks, 'I cannot help feeling for those that are cross'd in love'; certainly it was in this mood that Jane Austen, absorbed by the very real problem of the single woman growing older and without money, wrote the tale.

There are other characteristic touches. An offhand comment about the care elderly ladies should take in the choice of a second husband probably was inspired by the novelist's acquaintance with Mrs Lyford, the professional widow. It is declared that living 'in the Idleness of a Town' makes one more prone to 'Gossip' than living in the country does—a reflection of the novelist's dislike of Bath. Emma had 'been used to many of the Elegancies of Life' before being forced to move to another, smaller home, which she feels may 'be

open to the ridicule of Richer people'; surely there is again in this
something of Jane Austen, who was so unwillingly transported, at
the age of twenty-five, from a comfortable house in Hampshire to
lodgings in Bath. As Brigid Brophy and others have argued,
the sudden reduction of space in Jane Austen's life—her having
abruptly to get used, in her mature years, to cramped quarters, when
she had grown up in a large house—must have been traumatic, must
have touched her vision of the world. She was born in the manor, and
then ejected from it. 'The change in her home society, & stile of Life
. . . had indeed been striking,' 'The Watsons' declares of Emma;
when things are at their worst, she 'thankfully turn[s] to a book.' The
autobiographical flavour is unmistakable. Our last look at the
heroine is sad indeed:

> she was become of importance to no one, a burden on those,
> whose affection she c^d not expect, an addition in an House,
> already overstocked, surrounded by inferior minds with little
> chance of domestic comfort, & as little hope of future
> support.—It was well for her that she was naturally chearful.

On this dark note 'The Watsons' comes abruptly to an end. We shall
soon see why, beyond her own present mood, Jane Austen had no
inclination to finish it. Certainly it is one of her most sombre
performances; and the next two years (1804-6) were to be among the
saddest of her life. 'The Watsons,' cutting so close to the authorial
bone, ceased to engage her interest: life finally became too unpleasant
to go on with the tale, and she stopped writing altogether—
undoubtedly feeling, like Emma Watson, a 'burden' to others, and
'surrounded by inferior minds with little chance of domestic
comfort, & as little hope of future support.' It is an interesting
fragment—more valuable, perhaps, as an index to the novelist's
mood at this time than as a contribution to English literature. 'The
Watsons' remained unpublished until 1871.

With only a few exceptions the critics have remained relatively
silent about this revealing fragment. Mudrick thinks that in her
treatment of 'husband-hunting,' Jane Austen, by now frantically
impatient with her life, finally let her celebrated irony lapse
altogether. Yasmine Gooneratne comments that 'The Watsons'
shows the novelist 'clinging to her ideals rather than calmly stating
them' in the context of what has come to seem to her 'a hostile society.'

And Walton Litz speaks of the fragment as reflecting the novelist's darkening vision of herself as 'isolated and . . . cut off from all expectation and trapped in an alien world. . . . Her situation is an epitome of the dilemma faced by the free spirit in a limited world.' Which is to say that 'The Watsons' was written in a desperate mood—and abandoned in a mood even more desperate. It articulates as perhaps nothing else can the frustration, despair, and loneliness of Jane Austen's barren middle years.

IV

In 1804 came news that Frank Austen had been given command of the *Leopard*, and then of the *Canopus*. Frank was serving under Nelson in the Mediterranean during the long blockade of French shipping which was to be punctuated by Nelson's death at Trafalgar and the destruction of Napoleon's plans for the invasion of England. Frank fought at Cadiz, but had the bad fortune to miss Trafalgar. Soon after the great victory, however, he met Villeneuve, Admiral of the defeated French fleet, who had been taken prisoner. Frank wrote an account of this to his fiancée Mary Gibson in Ramsgate.

> I was on board the *Euryalus* yesterday and was introduced to the French Admiral Villeneuve, who is a prisoner there. He appears to be about forty-five years of age, of dark complexion, with rather an unmeaning countenance, and has not much the appearance of a gentleman. He is, however, so much of a Frenchman as to bear his misfortunes with cheerfulness.

Shamed by his defeat, Villeneuve killed himself six months later.

In 1804 the Austens spent their holiday, during late summer and early autumn, at Lyme Regis, in company with Henry and Eliza. The Henry Austens went on to Weymouth, taking Cassandra with them; Jane stayed with her parents at Lyme. Her affection for the place can most readily be seen in *Persuasion*: she thought it one of the most beautiful spots on earth, being specially impressed by Pinny and the country around Charmouth. One can still find the spot on the Cobb, as Tennyson did, where Louisa Musgrove fell, and the tiny house at the corner of the pier where the Harvilles lived. The steps leading down to the sea, where Mr Elliot first saw Anne, are also there—as are many of the buildings described in the novel, including Mrs Dean's house, where the Austens lodged during part of their stay: a small, brown house on the Cobb side of the bay.

In September 1804 came news that old Mrs Lloyd was very ill, and Cassandra went to Ibthorp to help Martha nurse her (Mrs Lloyd was to live on until April 1805). We have one letter from Jane at Lyme to Cassandra at Ibthorp—the first letter preserved since May 1801, just before the summer of the mysterious romance and its disastrous aftermath. In it the novelist hopes that Cassandra has survived the stop in Weymouth, which she calls 'altogether a shocking place . . . without recommendation of any kind' despite the partiality of the Royal Family for it, and 'worthy only of being frequented by the inhabitants of Gloucester'—a reference perhaps to the Duke of Gloucester, who was at that time visiting the Royal Family at Weymouth, as all the newspapers were reporting. She describes her bathing in the sea at Lyme and going to the Assembly Rooms there. The lodgings at Lyme are not much to her liking: 'nothing . . . can exceed the inconvenience of the offices, except the general dirtiness of the house & furniture & all its inhabitants.' There was a ball: 'Nobody asked me to dance the first two dances'; the next two she danced with a Mr Crawford, and she might have danced on except for being disconcerted by 'a new odd-looking man who had been eyeing me for some time, and at last, without any introduction, asked me if I meant to dance again.' She thought he must be Irish. She has made a new friend, a Miss Armstrong: 'Like other young ladies she is considerably genteeler than her parents.' Is this another dig at her prickly mother? Miss Armstrong, Jane says, is agreeable, but 'seems to like people rather too easily'—unlike the writer herself, of course.

When the Austens returned to Bath it was not to Sydney Terrace but to 27 Green Park Buildings—on the western side of the park, and nearer the Pump Room for the convenience of Mr Austen, who now had to walk with a cane. In any case the short lease of 4 Sydney Terrace, on which the low rent depended, had expired. So it was at Green Park Buildings, a handsome place with a balcony and a pleasant view of both river and open country, that the Austens received, on Jane's twenty-ninth birthday on 16 December 1804, the tragic news of Anna Lefroy's death after a fall from her horse. And here it was too that on 21 January 1805 George Austen suddenly died after only a two-days' illness. On the 19th he had been unwell, and took to his bed. The next day he got up and breakfasted with the family, feeling better, but soon afterwards began to feel feverish again, and went back to bed. He died the next morning. George Austen was buried on 26 January 1805 in the crypt of St Swithin's, Walcot, the Bath church in which he had been married forty-one years earlier. James and Henry came to Bath for the funeral. Over the final resting-place of Jane Austen's father the following is engraved: 'Under this stone rest the remains of the Rev. George Austen, Rector of Steventon and Dean[e] in Hampshire—who departed this life the 21st of January, 1805, aged 73 years.'

It fell to Jane to inform Frank of their father's death. Since her brother's address was problematical, she wrote to him three times; all three letters survived. 'Our dear Father has closed his virtuous & happy life, in a death almost as free from suffering as his Children could have wished,' she writes in her first letter to Frank. There is, she says, no way to prepare him for this news; a circumstantial account of her father's last days follows. She goes on:

Heavy as is the blow, we can already feel that a thousand comforts remain to us to soften it. Next to that of the consciousness of his worth & constant preparation for another World, is the remembrance of his having suffered, comparatively speaking, nothing. Being quite insensible of his own state, he was spared all the pain of separation, & he went off almost in his Sleep.—My Mother bears the Shock as well as possible; she was quite prepared for it, & feels all the blessing of his being spared a long Illness . . . Adieu my dearest Frank. The loss of such a Parent must be felt, or we should be Brutes—. I wish I could have given you better preparation—but it has been impossible.

One can't help wondering a little at the comment that her mother 'was quite prepared' for her husband's death, especially as it was so sudden. The next day Jane, thinking perhaps that she had addressed the letter to the wrong place, wrote again. Here is part of what she says in the second letter:

Everything I trust and beleive was done for him that was possible!—It has been very sudden!—within twenty four hours of his death he was walking with only the help of a stick, was even reading!—We had however some hours of preparation, & when we understood his recovery to be hopeless, most fervently did we pray for the speedy release which ensued. To have seen him languishing long, struggling for Hours, would have been dreadful! & thank God! we were all spared from it. Except the restlessness & confusion of high Fever, he did not suffer— & he was mercifully spared from knowing that he was about to quit the Objects so beloved, so fondly cherished as his wife & Children ever were.—His tenderness as a Father, who can do justice to?—My Mother is tolerably well; she bears up with great fortitude, but I fear her health must suffer under such a shock . . . The serenity of the Corpse is most delightful!—It preserves the sweet, benevolent smile which always distinguished him.

Again a reference to her mother bearing up rather better than one might expect.

But there can be no doubt about her love for George Austen—'His tenderness as a Father, who can do justice to?'—and these passages have been quoted at length precisely to refute the charge of some commentators that Jane Austen's letters on her father's death are stiff and cold. This is not true. The language of the time certainly tended, often enough, to be stiff and cold on such occasions; the novelist's language is in fact uncharacteristically tender.

One can distinguish between her feelings for her father and those for her mother, always more ambivalent. Since this was the only occasion during her lifetime when Jane Austen was to lose a parent, a further word probably ought to be said here about her relations with her parents. The available evidence suggests that she loved her father, and perhaps felt something less than love for her mother. One ought also to take into account the fact that parents in her novels are often seen as the makers of mistakes. Mrs Hodge reminds us that when Catherine returns home with a broken heart in *Northanger Abbey*, her mother fails to recognise the condition; Mr Bennet gives Lydia fatal *carte blanche* in *Pride and Prejudice*, and Mrs Bennet is a fool; in *Mansfield Park* the mother is so bovine that Sir Thomas Bertram leaves the moral training of his daughters in the hands of Mrs Norris while he is away from home; Mrs Dashwood in *Sense and Sensibility* lacks calmness and prudence at moments of crisis, and Mrs Ferrars seems to have no natural feelings at all; Mr Woodhouse in *Emma* is ridiculously feeble; the older generation in *Persuasion* is treated with the devastating irony it deserves. And yet, despite all this, one can perceive, from the distance of 175 years, only good feeling and affection between Jane Austen and her father. If parents in her novels are often bad parents, they may stand in for her mother alone, with whom her relations were always less easy.

Jane wrote once again to Frank—just a short note informing him that Mrs Austen wished him to have his father's compass. How Charles was informed of his father's death we do not know—nor do we know where Cassandra was during those dog days of January 1805. What we do know is that Jane Austen, buffeted in quick succession by the deaths of a valued friend and a beloved father, and living now in a household of widows and spinsters—Martha Lloyd was to join them this spring after her mother's death—pushed aside the morbid, sordid story she was working on ('The Watsons') and never took it up again. It belonged to too painful a time, and she put it out of her mind.

The immediate problem of George Austen's family was, of course, money: survival. On these and related questions such as where to live, the family—James, Henry, and Edward included—held a meeting. Mrs Austen's income was greatly reduced upon the death of her husband, for his Steventon and Deane livings now devolved automatically upon his son James. The relatively prosperous Mrs Austen was suddenly transformed into an impecunious widow with an income of only £210 a year—part of which derived from interest on the £1,000 Thomas Fowle had bequeathed to Cassandra—and two grown daughters to support. But, as might be expected in so close a family as the Austens, the brothers came to the rescue. Charles's income was still too low to admit of his giving the women any aid, but James, Henry, Frank, and the well-heeled Edward all volunteered their help. James and Henry agreed to add £50 apiece to their mother's annual income; Edward gave £100; Frank also offered £100 a year, but Mrs Austen decided that this was more than he could afford, and agreed to take just £50 from him. Oddly enough, there was no offer of help from her rich brother James Leigh Perrot. Later, his widow did help her sister-in-law. This is particularly ironic in view of the fact that the Austens seem always to have preferred the husband to the wife. At any rate, through the gifts she did receive, Mrs Austen's annual income was raised up to £460, and on this she and Cassandra and Jane—and Martha Lloyd, when she joined them, bringing along her own small income—could be relatively comfortable. They would no longer have two maids and a manservant, but they could still afford one servant, and they would manage to visit their friends from time to time. 'Never were children so good as mine!' Mrs Austen declared of her sons' generosity.

It may well have occurred to the novelist that she was now utterly dependent for her existence upon the open-handedness of others. Even Cassandra had some money of her own, though she had thrown it into the family kitty. Jane alone had nothing.

V

In March 1805 Mrs Austen and her daughters moved to 25 Gay Street, a fashionable part of Bath dotted with elegant but small houses. It was in April that Martha Lloyd, left homeless by her mother's death, joined the threesome, and was grateful to do so. Jane and Cassandra were delighted in their turn to have her come to them, for this meant among other things that they could go off on visits to Godmersham and elsewhere without leaving their mother alone.

Cassandra had once again gone to Ibthorp during Mrs Lloyd's last illness; Jane was keeping out of the way of the Bigg Withers, in all likelihood. We have two letters from April 1805 written by the novelist in Bath to Cassandra at Ibthorp. In the course of these, Jane expresses some surprise that their mother has already resumed her normal round of social visiting. She adds that Mrs Austen complains of a cold and fever, but that her appetite doesn't seem to have been affected by either. 'What request we are in!' the novelist declares—clearly with teeth clenched; the note of disapproval is unmistakable. She reports that she has seen her old friends the Chamberlaynes. But 'what a different set we are now moving in!' she observes sadly. There are reflections on the lack of 'smartness' of some of the people they do regularly see. Was Jane Austen beginning to feel *déclassée*? One suspects so. She hopes Mrs Lloyd isn't too uncomfortable: 'May her end be peaceful & easy, as the Exit we have witnessed!' Next day came a letter from Cassandra announcing the imminent death of Mrs Lloyd. The novelist declares: 'The Nonsense I have been writing . . . seems out of place at such a time; but I will not mind it, it will do you no harm, & nobody else will be attacked by it.' She could hardly know that she herself would 'be attacked by it' years later by critics who saw it as further evidence of her heartlessness: but this is hardly a convincing example. Jane says she has heard from Henry: he is 'most affectionate & kind, as well as entertaining;—there is no merit to him in *that*, he cannot help being amusing.' Cassandra has obviously complained of the voluble Mrs Stent. About the future Miss Bates, Jane replies: 'Poor Mrs Stent! it has been her lot to be always in the way; but we must be merciful, for perhaps in time we may come to be Mrs Stents ourselves, unequal to anything & unwelcome to everybody.' A jolly thought: she was nearing thirty. The novelist reports that she is wearing crape now for her father but going to concerts and dinners whenever possible. She has just been to a gathering at which 'There was a monstrous deal of stupid quizzing, & common-place nonsense talked, but scarcely any wit.' The dark mood continued. She has been accused by her friend Miss Armstrong of a 'change of manners' since they met at Lyme. Jane's reaction to this: 'Unlucky me! that my notice should be of such consequence & my Manners so bad! . . . I shall endeavour as much as possible to keep my Intimacies in their proper place, & prevent their clashing . . . Among so many friends it will be well if I do not get into a scrape.' Obviously she had been charged with coldness, and was finding it (understandably enough) difficult to be sunny and warm. Jane tells of having given the number of their house in Gay Street to an acquaintance so that he might call; she is certain that he made a point of forgetting it as soon as she gave it. Some neighbours have let their house—'so we shall get rid of them.' She and her mother have paid a visit to some aristocratic friends of Charles: the man said his wife was not at home, which was a lie. They have gone out of their way to be friendly to the Leigh Perrots, the novelist says; she and her mother must still have expected some offer of financial aid from James Leigh Perrot. It never came. In response to Cassandra's report that a friend of theirs at Ibthorp had had a fall from his horse: 'I am waiting to know how it happened before I begin pitying him, as I cannot help suspecting it was in consequence of his taking orders.' Here at least is a flash of the old wit, even if the comedy is black.

In June 1805 James and Mary Austen became the parents of another daughter, Caroline—who was to be one of Jane Austen's favourite nieces. In August, with Martha Lloyd now installed in Gay Street, Jane and Cassandra left Bath and paid visits to Godmersham and Goodnestone in Kent. It was the novelist's first departure from the detested Bath in many months, and she must have been glad of the change. Cassandra went first to Goodnestone Farm to see Lady Bridges, the mother of Edward Austen's wife Elizabeth, while Jane went directly to Godmersham. Then they switched places briefly. Several letters survive from this period. In the first of these the novelist recounts a visit to nearby Eastwell. Wherever they go, she reports, Cassandra is asked for: 'I said all I could to lessen your merit.' She, Jane, has had a letter from Frank: 'he is in a great hurry to be married, & I have encouraged him in it'—the reference, of course, is to Mary Gibson, waiting patiently in Ramsgate—where Frank was remembered by all her friends as *the* officer who knelt in Church.' They would be married in June or July 1806 and settle in Southampton. Frank meanwhile was in the West Indies taking part in the victory over the French at St Domingo—where, years earlier, Cassandra's fiancé Thomas Fowle had died. For this action, Frank and his shipmates would later (in 1806) be formally thanked by Parliament.

Jane tells Cassandra that it has cost her only two shillings and twopence to have her hair cut; the hairdresser, who charges the more affluent Elizabeth Austen five shillings for the same work, must '[respect] either our Youth or our poverty.' She has gone into the question of her finances: 'instead of being very rich I am likely to be very poor . . . It is . . . well . . . to prepare you for the sight of a Sister sunk in poverty,' she tells Cassandra. She was worried about not having enough money to tip the servants at Godmersham: such things were always sources of vexation for her. When she did save money, it was often on dress. One of the novelist's nieces some years later noted that her two aunts were not 'accounted very good dressers, and were thought to have taken to garb of middle age unnecessarily soon.' Critics have tended to make a good deal of this; the simple truth was that Jane and Cassandra lacked the means to dress elegantly. Neither *wished* to appear old-maidish before her time.

In her next letters Jane, now at Goodnestone, describes the social goings-on there, and admits to a 'fear of being in the way' of the younger members of the family. She notes of the recent death of the Duke of Gloucester that it 'sets my heart at ease, though it will cause some dozens to ache . . . Must we buy [black] lace, or will ribbon do?'—a rather cold-blooded comment by any standards. She reports that she is reading Thomas Gisborne's *An Enquiry into the Duties of the Female Sex*.

Cassandra and Jane spent part of the autumn of 1805 together at Godmersham and then returned to Bath. We have no letters for the rest of 1805 or for all of 1806, which turned out to be another year of turmoil, upheaval, and change—not all of it bad—in Jane Austen's life. We cannot know exactly what she might have felt on 16 December 1805, the date on which she turned thirty, but probably this was not one of her more hilarious days.

The four ladies continued to live in Bath during the first half of 1806, their last lodgings there being in unfashionable Trim Street; Cassandra particularly detested the Trim Street lodgings. Their dislike of the place accounts for a large part of the joy they all felt—Jane especially—when the decision was made, in June 1806, to leave Bath for good. They would do some visiting over the summer and then settle in with Frank Austen and his new wife in Southampton. Frank and Mary said they would be delighted to set up housekeeping with the four ladies; and Jane and Cassandra and their mother were pleased at the prospect of living, once again, in the near vicinity of the family: not only would Frank be there, but James at Steventon would be nearby. The five years in Bath had been unhappy ones, and as far as Jane was concerned this would be a fortuitous escape from dullness and misery. On 2 July 1806 they left Bath.

They went first to Clifton, at which time Martha Lloyd went off to do some visiting of her own in Harrogate. Cassandra, Jane, and their mother went on to Adlestrop Rectory in Gloucestershire and then to Stoneleigh Abbey in Warwickshire. Mrs Austen has left an interesting account, sent to James and Mary at Steventon, of Stoneleigh Abbey—'this vast house,' as she calls it. She complains that the place is so huge that they are all continuously getting lost in it. On the other hand, she obviously enjoyed finding herself, as she puts it, 'eating fish, venison, and all manner of good things, in a large and noble parlour hung round with family portraits.' She says she had expected to find the place 'very fine' but 'had no idea of its being so beautiful . . . The Avon runs near the house, amidst green meadows, bounded by large and beautiful woods, full of delightful walks'; here, perhaps, is one seed of Sotherton in *Mansfield Park*, if Jane perceived the place in the same way. Mrs Austen goes on to describe a part of the house: 'On the left hand of the hall is the best drawing room, within that a smaller; these rooms are rather gloomy Brown wainscot and dark Crimson furniture; so we never use them but to walk thro' them to the old picture gallery. Behind the small drawing Room is the state Bed Chamber, with a high dark crimson Velvet Bed: an *alarming* apartment just fit for a heroine.' Or a hero: undoubtedly this is the room in which Charles I slept. Mrs Austen's description of the bedroom suggests that she had read 'Susan' (*Northanger Abbey*). She concludes her letter with the report that some friends of the Leighs 'fatigue' and even 'torment' her, but they afford 'Jane many a good laugh'—by no means the first instance in which mother and daughter saw things differently. One of the 'friends' at issue, Lady Saye and Sele, was the mother of the 'adultress' Jane had observed in Bath in 1801 and the sister of a woman who had written a novel called *The Mausoleum of Julia*—about which, apparently, she was fond of talking; no wonder Jane was amused. Lady Saye and Sele, however, was not amused during this visit by her aunt Elizabeth, who insisted on taking her up to her dressing-room and reading sermons to her.

We may note that the Austen ladies felt no sense of inferiority while visiting the ancient ancestral pile; this was the home of the Leighs, mainstays of the Tory gentry, and they regarded themselves just as much Leighs as ever, regardless of their income.

While at Stoneleigh Abbey the three ladies visited the remains of Kenilworth, Warwick Castle, Guy's Cliff, and Combe Abbey. From Stoneleigh they went on to stay with Mrs Austen's nephew the Reverend Edward Cooper and his family at Hamstall Ridware in Staffordshire. Cooper was the brother of the Jane Cooper who years earlier had gone to school with Cassandra and Jane. But this must have been a rather tedious interlude—the novelist is known not to have thought very highly of her cousin's sermons—and it may have been from Hamstall that she and some of the others there went off into Derbyshire for several days and saw Chatsworth. Probably her experience of both Stoneleigh and Chatsworth—assuming she went there—contributed to her portrait of Pemberley when she came to revise *Pride and Prejudice* a few years later.

Frank Austen and Mary Gibson were married late in July 1806, and in August the planned rendezvous took place in Southampton. They all moved into lodgings together while a suitable house was sought. One was finally found at 2 Castle Square. This was a rather curious spot. In the middle of the square the landlord, the third Marquess of Lansdowne—eldest son of the sometime Prime Minister, better known as the Earl of Shelburne—had built a fantastic little castle from which his tenants could view, when they wished, his marchioness emerging in her carriage. This edifice was pulled down when the Marquess died in 1809. But it was certainly there during the latter months of 1806, when the Austens decided to take up housekeeping in Southampton; 1806—and not 1805 or 1807, as some have said—is the correct date of the beginning of their residency in Southampton. They remained in lodgings while the Castle Square house was being readied. Frank, awaiting a new appointment at sea, helped hang curtains, and made book-shelves. Jane's task was planning the garden; she decided on fruit bushes and flowering shrubs. Martha Lloyd had not yet rejoined them, but would do so later.

J.E. Austen-Leigh, the author of the *Memoir* of his aunt—he changed his name from Austen to Austen-Leigh upon inheriting the fortune of old Mrs Leigh Perrot, just as his uncle Edward Austen changed *his* name upon inheriting the Knight fortune—had a lively recollection of his grandmother's home in Southampton, which he was able to visit from time to time from nearby Steventon. He remembers 'a pleasant garden, bounded on one side by the old city walls; the top of this was sufficiently wide to afford a pleasant walk, with an extensive view [of the sea], easily accessible to ladies by steps.' It was apparently a large, old-fashioned, fairly comfortable place.

It is clear, however, that Southampton, like Bath, was not entirely to Jane Austen's taste; she never liked cities. Some found it pleasant. Miss Mitford, who visited Southampton in 1812, was struck by its 'life' and 'gaiety' and noted 'the total absence of the vulgar hurry of business or the chilling apathy of fashion.' The novelist certainly considered it an improvement over the awful Bath; and it did afford her something approximating the old family life she had enjoyed at Steventon, though she still missed the Hampshire countryside. At least Southampton was in her old county, and within easy reach of her old home.

Here, at any rate, she was to live until 1809. The nature and flavour of the Austens' new life at Southampton has been described thus:

> It was not all that different from their old pattern [of living] but quieter, in conformity with their greater age and changed circumstances. They still went in for some mild social life: paid calls, accepted invitations to dine and play cards, even attended an occasional ball at the local Assembly Rooms. But their engagements were fewer and, though they made one or two new friends, they avoided cultivating acquaintances who lived more expensively than they could afford to do . . . More and more [their] chief activities and favourite pleasures were to be found at home.

Frank was soon ordered back to sea as commander of the *St Albans*, and so the Austen ladies were again left alone; Martha Lloyd, visiting in Eversley, rejoined them in February 1807. There were no men: it was difficult to put down roots in such circumstances. Were they going to live in Southampton for the rest of their lives, always having to look forward to Frank's next shore leave? When the Austens finally took possession of the house in Castle Square in March 1807, they were still without a real home.

'Of all respectable professions for young women literature is the most uncertain, the most heartbreaking, and the most dangerous.'
—Trollope, 'Mary Gresley'

Jane Austen . . . seemed to have as shrewd an eye as anyone could who didn't really know what sexual feeling was.
—C. P. Snow, *In Their Wisdom*

'But we must stem the tide of malice, and pour into the wounded bosoms of each other, the balm of sisterly consolation.'
—Mary Bennet in *Pride and Prejudice*

'The sweets of housekeeping in a country village!'
—Mary Crawford in *Mansfield Park*

'We none of us expect to be in smooth water all our days.'
—Mrs. Croft in *Persuasion*

CHAPTER 6

The Light and the Dark, 1807–1810

Jane Austen was lonely and unhappy in Southampton. She was thirty-one, and unpublished. Between January 1807, when her letters resume, until the transfer of the Austen women to Chawton two and a half years later, she and Cassandra took turns visiting Edward's family at Godmersham, and this period provides a rich vein of letters written by the novelist. The retreat to rural Hampshire in 1809 was to give Jane a new interest in life and a renewed sense of equanimity and stability; one of the most important results of this change both of surroundings and mood was a return to her work. Once at Chawton, she took up the writing of fiction for the first time since abandoning 'The Watsons' in 1805.

The letters to Cassandra in January and February 1807—there is then a gap: no letters until June 1808—are a mixed bag of gossip, wit, and complaints. If they seem less light and bright and sparkling than some earlier ones, they are often more philosophical—and more subdued. They show her making a virtue of necessity and attempting to resign herself, at least for the time being, to residence in Southampton.

Jane supposes that Cassandra, who had stopped off on her way to Godmersham to visit Mrs Knight in Canterbury, must have a good deal of gossip to catch up on with Edward's elderly patroness. 'Abuse everybody but me,' she advises. The novelist reports that 'Mrs J. Austen'—Mary Lloyd Austen, who was visiting them in Southampton —has invited her to Steventon, an invitation she means to decline. She brings Cassandra up to date on her correspondence and the servants, emphasising 'the very quiet way in which we live.' Of a recent dinner-guest of theirs who was unable to eat the 'underdone' mutton she served up: 'he was so good-humoured and pleasant that I did not much mind his being starved.' There is discussion of the coming confinement of Mary Gibson Austen (Frank's wife), who was with them.

Jane gives an account of her reading, which this month included Madame de Genlis's *Alphonsine*—she was disgusted by its adulterous theme—and Charlotte Lennox's *Female Quixote*, a burlesque of the novel, written half a century earlier. Charlotte Lennox's book, which Jane was rereading, is said to make 'our evening amusement.' Frank's Mary enjoys it, as she should; James's Mary 'has little pleasure from that or any other book.' Jane disliked Mary Lloyd Austen more and more as the years went by. Her mother, the novelist writes, can think of nothing these days beyond 'the comfortable state of her own finances.' Nor, she notes with some asperity, does 'Mrs J.A.' (Mary Lloyd Austen) 'talk much of poverty now.' James's wife, of course, was the mistress of Jane's old home, as well as much of what was once her father's income. In the present household Jane alone, the letter implies, must worry about money. Some indication of her bitterness of spirit on this subject may be gleaned from the account she gives of a recent call made upon a neighbour:

We found only Mrs Lance at home, and whether she boasts any offspring besides a grand pianoforte did not appear. She was civil and chatty enough, and offered to introduce us to some acquaintance in Southampton, which we gratefully declined.

I suppose they must be acting by the orders of Mr Lance of Netherton in this civility, as there seems no other reason for their coming near us. They will not come often, I dare say. They live in a handsome style and are rich, and she seemed to like to be rich, and we gave her to understand that we were far from being so; she will soon feel therefore that we are not worth her acquaintance.

During February 1807 Cassandra remained at Godmersham primarily to help her sister-in-law Elizabeth through yet another confinement. The novelist's letters to Cassandra consist largely of domestic and family news. Jane's sombre mood continued: 'I see nothing to be glad of,' she tells her sister. Frank and Mary have been doing a good deal of shopping, and miss Cassandra's advice; Jane says playfully that if Cassandra does not return soon 'they shall be as spiteful as possible & chuse everything in the stile most likely to vex you, knives that will not cut, glasses that will not hold, a sofa without a seat, & a Bookcase without shelves.' The garden in Castle Square is coming along: she has asked the gardener to procure syringa and laburnum 'for the sake of Cowper's Line' ('Laburnum, rich/In streaming gold; syringa, iv'ry pure': from *The Task*, vi). Most of the children who come to their lodgings strike her as utterly uninhibited; she recently caught one of them going through her desk: 'What is become of all the Shyness in the World?—Moral as well as Natural Diseases disappear in the progress of time, & new ones take their place.—Shyness & the Sweating Sickness have given way to Confidence & Paralytic complaints.' The same child caught rummaging through her desk managed to make a conquest of the novelist, however, before going home: 'she is a nice, natural, openhearted, affectionate girl, with all the ready civility which one sees in the best Children in the present day;—so unlike anything that I was myself at her age, that I am often all astonishment & shame.' Did Jane Austen think of herself, as a young girl, as being the very opposite of 'openhearted,' 'affectionate,' and 'civil'? So it would seem; and of course the perspective of much of the Juvenilia lends credence to this self-portrait.

The novelist returns almost immediately to a more characteristic tone. On the recent death of an acquaintance: 'I had no idea that anybody liked her, & therefore felt nothing for any Survivor.' The Pearsons, whose daughter Mary Henry Austen jilted shortly before his marriage, have unexpectedly turned up in Southampton—to become 'the only Family in the place whom we cannot visit.' James Austen's eldest son (James Edward) is just starting at Winchester, she reports; she looks forward to his staying with them in Southampton from time to time. She is rereading Sarah Burney's *Clarentine* (1796) and not liking it nearly so well as she remembered liking it before: 'It is full of unnatural conduct & forced difficulties.' Much hard work is being done to get the Castle Square house ready for occupancy the following month (March 1807). The letter ends with an astonishingly bad-tempered account of her brother James:

> I am sorry & angry that his Visits should not give one more pleasure; the company of so good & so clever a Man ought to be gratifying in itself;—but his Chat seems all forced, his Opinions on many points too much copied from his Wife's, & his time here is spent I think in walking about the House & banging the doors, or ringing the bell for a glass of water.

This is more than mere neurasthenia; it is open resentment. James had stepped into their father's place—literally—and obviously Jane

was finding it difficult to accept him in it. Somehow or other this
passage managed to escape the sharp eyes, and the scissors, of
Cassandra. The novelist had just recovered from a bout of whooping-
cough and perhaps was not in the best of spirits. On the demise of a
distant relation who left no part of a considerable fortune to them:
'Such ill-gotten wealth can never prosper!' The Adlestrop estate,
after the death of some Leighs, has been settled very much to the
advantage of the tight-fisted Leigh Perrots. Jane is impatient with her
aunt's accounts of her poor health: 'what can have power to vex her
materially?' She herself, needless to say, was continually so 'vexed.'
They are all looking forward to moving at last into Castle Square:
'We hear that we are envied our House & air by many people, & that
the Garden is the best in the Town.' Praise of the garden would have
been of particular interest to the gardener. Jane reports that she has
bought few things for her own use, and no new clothes. They are now
reading Joseph Baretti's *Journal from London to Genoa* (1762; Baretti
was a friend of Johnson's). They expect Martha Lloyd to rejoin them
shortly. On the question of another marriage for Sir Brook Bridges,
whose wife had died the previous year: 'A Widower with 3 children
has no right to look higher than his daughter's Governess.' Jane adds:
'I am forced to be abusive for want of subject, having really nothing
to say . . . I expect a severe March, a wet April, & a sharp May.—And
with this prophecy I must conclude.'

    She was cross and unhappy: no reader of these letters can reach any
other conclusion. She looked forward to occupying the new house in
Southampton; otherwise there was little going on in her life to
interest her. She was surrounded for the most part by pedestrian
minds; there were no interesting men around; she wasn't working;
she was worrying about money. Her fortunes were at a low ebb, her
mood dark.

II

They moved into the house in Castle Square, but this does not seem
at first to have improved Jane Austen's spirits or stimulated the
interest she normally took in her surroundings. Cassandra and
Martha Lloyd returned to the fold; Mary Gibson Austen was nearing
her confinement. Jane read a good deal, as usual. The failure of either
sister to visit Godmersham between the spring of 1807 and the
summer of 1808 helps explain why we have no letters for over a year.

In the evenings the ladies apparently did a good deal of embroidering, read aloud to one another (in the old Steventon tradition), and sometimes played cards. Brag and Speculation seem to have been their favourite games.

In September 1807 Jane, Cassandra, and their mother visited Chawton Manor House near Alton, Hampshire, which was part of the property Edward had inherited from Mrs Knight and currently let—a visit made at Edward's request. They were not shown Chawton Cottage, nearby but also inhabited. All three women liked the house and grounds very much.

Also in 1807 Charles Austen, except for the unfortunate George the family's last bachelor, was married. His bride was Frances Fitzwilliam Palmer (called Fanny), daughter of the Attorney General of Bermuda. The Austens were to like her when they finally met her four years later. Charles was chiefly engaged during this period in the unpleasant—and certainly unprofitable—duty of enforcing British right of search and seizure on shipping off the Atlantic seaboard of America, one of the chief causes of the War of 1812. His letters home undoubtedly helped provide Jane with some of the West Indian background for the next novel she was to write, *Mansfield Park*—for example, how the worsening relations between America and Britain, and the outbreak of war, would affect Sir Thomas Bertram's property in Antigua. Meanwhile, Frank's wife was safely delivered of a daughter, called Mary Jane. The *St Albans* was on convoy duty around the Cape of Good Hope and returned home in 1808, when Frank and his family went into lodgings in Yarmouth. Mary sometimes accompanied Frank on his cruises, and sometimes stayed at home; Fanny Austen, like Mrs Croft in *Persuasion*, went everywhere her husband went.

The other Mary, James's wife, seems to have continued to irritate the ladies in Castle Square—easily fancying herself slighted, being parsimonious, and full of complaints about lack of funds despite relative prosperity—her husband's annual income was about £1,000. James himself continued to come over from Steventon from time to time, his visits apparently still only a mixed blessing. On his trips from Kent into Hampshire to inspect his property there, Edward would often stop in Southampton to see his mother and sisters.

In the spring of 1808 the Austen ladies visited James and his family at Steventon and the Fowles at Kintbury. Jane went to Godmersham in June 1808. James and his family were there at the same time, and

Jane does not seem to have enjoyed the precedence over her enjoyed by her married sister-in-law. She was there again in the spring of 1809. The first trip to Godmersham was framed by a visit to Henry and Eliza in London on the way there and one to Mrs Knight at White Friars in Canterbury on the way home. Henry was a partner in a banking firm with offices in London and Alton. He and Eliza now lived in a small house at 16 Brompton—or Michael's—Place, currently the site of Egerton Mansions.

There can be no doubt that at some time during this first stay at Godmersham Jane received a proposal of marriage from Elizabeth Austen's brother Edward Bridges, a clergyman four years younger than the thirty-two-year-old novelist. There is some evidence to suggest that after his suit failed with Jane in the summer of 1808, he lay in wait for the elder sister and tried his luck with Cassandra during the autumn, while she was visiting Godmersham. Cassandra also declined the honour. There must have been a few giggles between the sisters on the subject of Edward Bridges—who perhaps sat for the portrait of Captain Benwick in *Persuasion*. At any rate, after her experience with Harris Bigg Wither, the novelist presumably knew more about handling proposals from an eligible young man with whom she was not in love.

In June 1808 Edward Austen was the father of ten children—one recalls Elinor Dashwood's 'I never think of tame and quiet children with any abhorrence'—and Elizabeth was expecting yet again; Cassandra would come down to Godmersham in the autumn, for what turned out to be a long stay, to help nurse her sister-in-law through her eleventh confinement. The various trips into Kent by the sisters ensured an uninterrupted flow of correspondence between them for half a year—from June 1808 until January 1809. These letters are among the novelist's most interesting, the vintage Jane Austen often breaking through.

Jane found much news, local and otherwise, to write about while in Kent. 'Where do I begin? Which of all my important nothings shall I tell you first?' commences the earliest of this group (June 1808; Jane was at Godmersham, Cassandra at Southampton). The novelist describes the carriage-journey undertaken along with the James Austens from London to Godmersham by way of Deptford Hill, Blackheath, Dartford, and Sittingbourne; the trip consumed exactly ten and a half hours, including stops for breakfast and luncheon. She is impressed by the growth and sentience of her eldest niece Fanny,

Edward's daughter, now fifteen; but Elizabeth does not appear to be in very good health. Elizabeth's prosperous kinswoman Louisa Bridges is there, and 'looks remarkably well (legacies are a very wholesome diet).' There is a long discussion of the various strategies proposed for getting her home to Southampton, now that she has arrived at Godmersham; obviously impatient with all this, the novelist remarks that after all 'I shall . . . be glad not to be obliged to be an incumbrance on those who have brought me here.' Aunt Jane was growing more anomalous amidst the two large families of James and Edward; one had always to make special arrangements for her, and she was fully aware of it. The trip to Godmersham had been a mixed blessing. The carriage was crowded—'and it is not to be supposed but that a child of three years of age was fidgety' (one of James's children; probably Caroline). Jane never liked to be cramped—especially by children. At least 'the country,' she says, is still 'very beautiful.' Godmersham itself is pronounced dull: 'I feel rather languid and solitary,' says the novelist, surrounded by brothers and sisters-in-law and their children. No doubt she was reminded often enough, unintentionally and in little ways, that the families of James and Edward were not her families; she was just Aunt Jane. Mary Lloyd Austen is coldly referred to, as in previous letters, by the formal appellation 'Mrs J.A.' They mainly discuss food: 'You know how interesting the purchase of a sponge-cake is to me,' the novelist comments wryly. She reports on a visit to Canterbury and calls made on old Mrs Brydges and Mrs Knight. The latter 'tipped' her, and invited her and 'Mrs J.A.' to meet her relatives the Knatchbulls the following week, an invitation immediately accepted. Mrs Knight's present of money was not taken lightly: it 'will make my circumstances quite easy,' Jane declares. 'I shall reserve half for my Pelisse.' She found sending an elegant thank-you note to Mrs Knight an easy task in her suddenly altered financial position—'for I was rich—& the rich are always respectable, whatever be the stile of their writing.' The dinners at Godmersham are 'very pleasant . . . at the lower end of the Table,' where aunts sit. On the death of an acquaintance: 'Mr Waller is dead I see;—I cannot grieve about it, nor perhaps can his Widow very much.' They have been out picking strawberries—the genesis, perhaps, of an incident in *Emma*. On Cassandra as a correspondent: 'You are very amiable & very clever to write such long letters; every page of yours has more lines than this, & every line more words than the average of mine. I am quite ashamed—but you have certainly more little events than we have.' It seems irrelevant banter, perhaps, but an undercurrent of competitiveness is discernible. Sibling rivalry need not be less powerful in the thirties than in the 'teens. The novelist goes on to condemn her own letters, of which she has grown bored: 'I am sick of myself, & my bad pens.' James, she says, is reading aloud Scott's *Marmion* every evening: she thinks little of it. She refers to a spectacular case of adultery reported in the papers, involving the elopement of a married woman with a nobleman: here is part of the plot of *Mansfield Park*. She is pleased to have more physical space at Godmersham than she had in Henry's house at Brompton. And she refers to a cottage she has seen which might come near to suiting Cassandra, her mother, Martha, and herself—further evidence that the Austen women never considered Southampton their permanent residence, and of their desire eventually to move back into the Hampshire countryside and into a place like that inhabited by the Dashwood sisters and their mother in *Sense and Sensibility*. For such a place they kept their eyes open.

Jane writes that what she needs most in life is 'A Legacy,' which would solve all problems: 'a Legacy is our sovereign good.' She describes an interesting visit to White Friars; apparently she got on well with the Knatchbulls. She and Lady Knatchbull made some calls together in the neighbourhood, including one on a woman 'who luckily was not at home.' 'Mrs. J.A.' assumes that her stepdaughter Anna, who is paying a visit to the household at Southampton, will not answer her letters: 'it must be for the pleasure of fancying it.' James is taking a turn in the pulpit at Godmersham. Jane has come to like old Mrs Knight more and more, and to appreciate her good qualities: 'I cannot help regretting that now, when I feel enough her equal to relish her society, I see so little of . . . [her].' The novelist reports with obvious indignation that Frank's wife 'was thought excessively improved' by 'Mrs J.A.' when the latter saw her in Southampton; as we know, Jane preferred Frank's Mary to James's, though Mary Lloyd Austen was one of her oldest friends. Plans are being made for her to go home in July, but she herself is not being consulted: 'till I have a travelling purse of my own, I must submit to such things.' The dependence upon others of the impecunious unmarried female early in the nineteenth century was widespread. She notes Cassandra's complaint about having to go to the Newbury Races: 'I am withstanding those at Canterbury. Let that strengthen you.'

The last letter of this group (June 1808) acknowledges Cassandra's report of the return of Frank Austen aboard the *St Albans* and the mad dash (at 4 a.m.) of some of the Southampton household down to the Isle of Wight to meet him. She wishes to bring Frank's wife a present: would Cassandra recommend a silver knife or a brooch? (This may remind us of Mary Price's silver knife in *Mansfield Park*.) She will buy either one if she can get it for less than half a guinea. Her niece Caroline (James's daughter) will, she reports, be delighted to get back home to Steventon: 'her Cousins are too much for her.' Apparently so: Caroline never visited Godmersham again, though she lived a long time. On their continuing correspondence—soon to cease, since Jane was returning to Southampton: 'I assure you I am as tired of writing long letters as you can be. What a pity that one should still be so fond of receiving them!' There is a sour note here: apparently Cassandra was a less willing and enthusiastic correspondent than Jane, and had managed to make this clear to her younger sister. Indeed, their intercourse was not one of perfect, unswerving equanimity, as so many commentators have assumed. Of a relation who has made a bad match, the novelist writes: 'There is some comfort to *us* in her misconduct, that we have not a congratulatory Letter to write.' A dig at Cassandra's complaint about her correspondence? Edward, Jane reports, has been a marvellous host: he 'excels in doing the Honours to his visitors, & providing for their amusement.' She has been lecturing James on the good taste of his daughter Anna: 'if he felt, he did not express it.' She always thought that Anna was treated too severely by her father—no doubt blaming Anna's wicked stepmother for this.

All in all, Jane sums up, despite the inconveniences of travel and of living in someone else's house, 'it is pleasant to be among people who know one's connections & care about them.' This must have been felt by her to be a shield against loneliness. She continues to watch for the gift that will finally dissolve all their troubles: 'I do not know where we are to get our Legacy—but we will keep a sharp look-out.' In a sudden burst of ill-temper, and apropos of nothing in particular so far as one knows, she observes acidly: 'When are calculations ever right? . . . Nobody ever feels or acts, suffers or enjoys, as one expects.' She could be moody. Quickly enough she reverts to a more characteristic strain: 'The weather is mended, which I attribute to my writing about it.' And then an upbeat note: 'It will be two years tomorrow since we left Bath for Clifton, with what happy feelings of

Escape!' How she must have hated Bath—and the people there, all of them knowing the story of her aunt's imprisonment and trial. On her impending return to Southampton: 'In another week I shall be at home—& then, my having been at Godmersham will seem like a Dream, as my visit [to London] seems already.' Edward and Elizabeth are giving a luncheon party that day: 'I shall eat Ice & drink French wine, & be above vulgar Economy.' On 9 July 1808 she returned to Southampton—and 'vulgar Economy.'

Late in September the sisters traded places—Jane staying home in Castle Square, Cassandra going off to Kent to attend Elizabeth Austen through another confinement. On 1 October the novelist writes to acknowledge the news Cassandra had sent: Edward's wife, after a long and difficult labour, had given birth to a healthy boy. Elizabeth was having some complications, but is now on the mend. Jane sends her 'best wishes' for Elizabeth and her 'second best' for the infant. The physician Mr Lyford has called, and the novelist has consulted him about 'my complaint.' This was an ear infection; the remedy prescribed was cotton moistened with oil of sweet almonds, and it seemed to do the sufferer some good. Mr Lyford has told her that an acquaintance is pregnant: 'poor Woman! how can she be honestly breeding again?' She hears that one of the Miss Biggs is soon to be married: 'I wish it may be so.' She was not pleased on a recent evening to have some unexpected callers: 'About an hour after your toils on Wednesday ended, ours began;—at seven o'clock, Mrs Harrison, her two daughters & two Visitors, with Mr Debary & his eldest sister walked in; & our Labour was not a great deal shorter than poor Elizabeth's, for it was past eleven before we were delivered.' About some friends who have recently been abroad, Jane makes a snappish comment: 'they do not talk quite freely enough to be agreable—nor can I discover any right they had by Taste or Feeling to go their late Tour.' Fitted by 'taste' and 'feeling' for foreign travel, she herself would never go abroad: she must have known this. Her mother is dissatisfied with the house in Castle Square, and they are thinking of moving—perhaps to Alton, in the Hampshire countryside. Henry Austen, who often visited his bank's branch there, has endorsed their mother's idea. Needless to say, Jane is all for it. There is a hint in this letter that she put Henry up to suggesting the Alton plan to Mrs Austen; she would have had ample time for discussion of this with Henry when she visited her brother and his wife in London during the past spring. In Castle Square they are reading Southey's *Letters of Espriella* (1807; purporting to be letters written from and about England by a young Spaniard at the beginning of the nineteenth century). The novelist thinks little of this work: 'The Man describes well, but is horribly anti-english. He deserves to be the foreigner he assumes.' Martha Lloyd has been away, and Cassandra has been writing to her as well as to Jane. 'You have used me ill, you have been writing to Martha without telling me of it,' Jane complains. 'A letter which I sent her on wednesday to give her information of you, must have been good for nothing.' Again here she betrays some exasperation with her older sister, though the matter is trivial enough and the tone ironic. Jane doesn't miss Martha, she declares: 'I am now got into such a way of being alone that I do not wish even for her.' With both Cassandra and Martha out of the house her only company was her mother, whom she obviously considered no company at all. Nor do visitors cheer her up: 'Everybody who comes to Southampton finds it either their duty or pleasure to call upon us.' Her mood was clearly irritable; she was lonely, restless, and impatient. She is sending biscuits to her nephews at Winchester: James's son James Edward and Edward's eldest boy Edward Jr. had by now been joined there by Edward's second son George. She congratulates Edward, who is celebrating his fortieth birthday. At a recent party she refused to play more than one game of cards, 'for the Stake was three shillings, & I cannot afford to lose that, twice in an even^g.' The hostesses, two sisters, 'were as civil and as silly as usual.' Martha is coming back to Southampton that very day; she looks forward to having '*two* companions.' She sends her love to her niece Fanny—who, she says, she 'could not have supposed . . . would ever . . . [be] so much to me. She is quite after one's own heart' (Fanny was now fifteen). Her ear infection has cleared up: 'it [is] a great blessing to hear again.' A Mr Grays of Alton has sent them a pheasant and a hare: 'is this to entice us to Alton, or to keep us away?' Probably, she muses, it is all the work of Henry. Catherine Bigg, soon to be Mrs Hill, has sent her a brooch—a 'very kind & welcome mark of friendship.'

On 10 October, ten days after the birth of her eleventh child in fifteen years, and worn down by an especially arduous confinement, Elizabeth Austen died. The huge family at Godmersham was suddenly motherless; Cassandra made plans to stay on for several months more. Jane got the bad news both from Cassandra and from Mary Lloyd Austen at Steventon. Edward's 'loss and . . . sufferings seem to make those of every other person nothing,' the novelist writes. Cassandra must have told her that Edward bore the tragedy bravely, for she goes on: 'God be praised! that you can say what you do of him—that he has a religious Mind to bear him up, & a Disposition that will gradually lead him to comfort.' And she declares: 'May the Almighty sustain you all—& keep you my dearest Cassandra well—but for the present I dare say you are equal to anything.' Edward's boys at Winchester were sent to Steventon: 'perhaps it is best for them, as they will have more means of exercise & amusement there than they c^d have with us, but I own myself disappointed by the arrangement;—I should have loved to have them with me at such a time.' Once again Mary Lloyd Austen at Steventon had taken something that Jane felt as a matter of principle belonged to her—in this case custody of her nephews. Henry Austen and Lady Bridges (Elizabeth's mother) both went to Godmersham to do what they could. Jane did not offer to go, though by now Martha Lloyd had returned to Southampton and could have stayed with Mrs Austen. Of Elizabeth, the novelist writes simply and movingly: 'We need not enter into a Panegyric on the Departed—but it is sweet to think of her great worth—of her solid principles, her true devotion, her excellence in every relation of Life. It is also consolatory to reflect on the shortness of the sufferings which led her from this World to a better.' She asks for 'some directions about Mourning.' Cassandra had apparently complained that Fanny was too prostrated by grief to be of any use to her in this crisis. We do not know whether or not at this juncture Cassandra asked Jane to come to Godmersham, but the novelist's reply to her sister's complaint about their niece is as follows:

> Edward's loss is terrible, and must be felt as such, and these are too early days indeed to think of moderation in grief, either in him or his afflicted daughter, but soon we may hope that our dear Fanny's sense of duty to that beloved father will rouse her to exertion. For his sake, and as the most acceptable proof of love to the spirit of her departed mother, she will try to be tranquil and resigned. Does she feel you to be a comfort to her, or is she too much overpowered for anything but solitude?

Surely there is an implied rebuke in the final sentence. But by any reckoning this is a cold response to Cassandra's apparent plea for help. And it may be no accident that Jane Austen was drawn to this particular niece: probably they were alike in many ways. In later years, as Lady Knatchbull, Fanny struck almost everyone who met her as a cold fish—and declared her Aunt Jane common and low-bred.

Especially affected by her mother's death, Cassandra wrote, was the eight-year-old Elizabeth. 'Poor child!' Jane replies. 'One's heart aches for a dejected mind of eight years old.' The phrasing is interesting: could she herself remember being 'dejected' as a little girl? At any rate, she does not suggest that the 'poor child' be sent to her. Instead she asks Cassandra a series of what to modern sensibilities might seem morbid questions: 'I suppose you see the corpse? How does it appear?' The novelist hopes Edward will stay away from the funeral. She is sending Cassandra her mourning clothes. '*I* am to be in bombazeen and crape, according to what we are told is universal *here*,' Jane says. Her mourning will cost her some of her precious income, but 'will not impoverish me . . . I am sure I shall have no occasion *this winter*' for any other new clothes. She is having made a silk mourning bonnet covered with crape. She has written, Jane says, to their cousin Edward Cooper, and she hopes 'he will not send one of his letters of cruel comfort to my poor brother.' She still has some lingering questions about Elizabeth's sudden death. Was the physician in the house at the time? 'Is the seizure at all accounted for?' The novelist reports that Mrs Austen has had a letter from Mary at Steventon asking if she would like to have her grandsons with her in Southampton. 'We decided on their remaining where they were,' Jane says. Undoubtedly Edward 'will do us the justice of believing that in such a decision we sacrificed inclination to what we thought best . . . The poor boys are, perhaps, more comfortable at Steventon than they could be here, but you will understand *my feelings* with respect to it.' The gesture by 'Mrs J.A.' seems to have been important to Jane Austen, and she can now think with equanimity of her nephews at Steventon. So much for her 'I should have loved to have them with me at such a time.' The reference to her (italicised) 'feelings' is a bit cloudy; perhaps she and her mother disagreed yet again—this time on the question of the boys' visit. However, the plain fact is that, all her protestations of concern to the contrary, the novelist did not volunteer to care for any of Edward's children during this crisis period of their lives (and in later years she gave Godmersham a very wide berth indeed). Two of them would come to Southampton for a short visit after their mother's death—sent thence from Steventon by Mary Lloyd Austen—but Jane did not offer to go to any of them. Cassandra, Mary Lloyd Austen, and old Lady Bridges between them played mother to Edward's children until the adolescent Fanny, some time later, assumed the maternal role. One may or may not wish to draw conclusions from this. It is clear that the novelist did not especially like children, and certainly she did not like to be near them; grieving, sniffling children were perhaps a particularly appalling prospect. In principle, in theory, she was all kindness; in practice, something less.

Jane's thoughts, she tells Cassandra, are ever with her at Godmersham—and for a fleeting moment the novelist in her surfaces:

> I see your mournful party in my mind's eye under every varying circumstance of the day; and in the evening especially figure to myself its sad gloom: the efforts to talk, the frequent summons to melancholy orders and cares, and poor Edward, restless in misery, going from one room to the other, and perhaps not seldom upstairs, to see all that remains of his Elizabeth.

Fanny, she declares, must now do her best to mother the household, and this 'consideration [should] elevate and cheer her.' Apparently it did not. As usual, Mrs Austen seemed immune to disaster: 'My mother is not ill.' This stark statement surely betrays resentment at her mother's apparent lack of feeling. It is an interesting psychological fact that people who have difficulty feeling are often the quickest to detect and denounce this identical failing in others.

Whatever the answer, the end was of course the same. On 17 October 1808 Elizabeth Bridges Austen, the mother of eleven children, was laid to rest. All the Austen brothers were to lose their first wives; Edward was the only one who did not remarry.

Five days later Edward Jr. and George, fourteen and thirteen respectively, were sent over to Southampton by Mary Lloyd Austen for a five-day visit on their way back to Winchester. In a letter to Cassandra, Jane reports their safe arrival: 'I never saw them looking better. *They behave extremely* well in every respect, showing quite as much feeling as one wishes to see'—but no more, fortunately. One gets the impression of a sympathetic but rather judgmental aunt. Edward has written describing the funeral of their mother: 'they are both very properly impressed by what has happened.' She finds

George, the younger, 'in a different way as *engaging as Edward.*' They play games: 'bilbocatch, spillikins [jackstraws], paper ships, riddles, conundrums, and cards.' Bilbocatch is a game in which one catches a ball with a cup; Jane Austen was from all accounts a particularly formidable competitor in bilbocatch. They also walk. 'Mrs J.A. had not time to get them more than one suit of clothes'—she means mourning clothes—and some are being made for them in Southampton. The boys have been attentive at evening prayers, but return to conundrums at the earliest opportunity. 'Mrs J.A.' has written a pleasant letter about them, 'which was more than I hoped': obviously the novelist could not see her sister-in-law coping as well with two adolescent boys as she herself was doing.

During the stay of Edward and George at Southampton a letter from Fanny arrived which contained the first suggestion of her father Edward's plan to offer his mother and sisters a place of their own to live in. He would give them a choice between two houses on his property—one in Kent, near Godmersham, the other in Hampshire, at Chawton—near Chawton Manor House, which they had visited in September 1807 at Edward's express invitation. The Austen ladies, who had always considered themselves Hampshire-born and -bred, immediately and enthusiastically chose the house at Chawton. The offer by Edward undoubtedly was made for several reasons: he was grateful for the support and aid of his sisters, both past and to come, in helping to raise his now motherless family; and presumably he thought the women could be better looked after if they lived somewhere on or near his property and closer to him and his family. It turned out to be a fortunate turn of events for all concerned. Among other things, it enabled Jane Austen's nieces and nephews to leave to posterity some detailed accounts of their novelist-aunt and her last years at Chawton. More importantly, it enabled her to write again.

The ladies were delighted. This would bring them closer to family life, which in principle at least they valued, and take them away from city life, which they disliked. Chawton Cottage, as it was called, was not far from Steventon; and it was less than half a mile from Chawton Manor, where Edward and his family, no doubt associating Godmersham with Elizabeth and her tragedy, spent a good deal of time from 1812 onwards. The Chawton Manor House was let until 1812 to John Middleton, a widower whose wife had been a Beckford and a cousin of the author of *Vathek*. William Beckford's sister-in-law Maria Beckford was known to Jane Austen in Chawton, and Jane also knew Beckford's daughters. Frank Austen often borrowed the Chawton Manor House in subsequent years; he and his family later settled in Alton, about a mile from Chawton.

The Austen ladies' desire to return to the Hampshire countryside was well-known in the family; to be on the safe side, the suspicious Jane thought Steventon ought to be kept in the dark about their proposed move until the question was definitively settled. The novelist was a bit vague about the cottage at Chawton. 'What sort of kitchen garden is there?' she asks Cassandra. This particular end to their wanderings would be, Jane feels, the best possible one. The prospect of the move to Chawton put her in a sunnier frame of mind. She notes with amusement the recent announcement in a newspaper of a marriage—'Dr Phillot to Lady Frances St Lawrence. *She* wanted to have a husband I suppose, once in her life, and *he* a Lady Frances.'

In the meantime a letter arrived from Cassandra announcing a 'lengthened stay . . . you cannot suppose I like it,' the novelist says, though it is what she expected. She adds: 'Your close-written letter makes me quite ashamed of my wide lines.' Cassandra always seemed to get more words on a page than Jane could; in days when receiving letters could be an expensive business, this was neither an irrelevant consideration nor an unmixed blessing. Jane is glad to hear that Edward has escaped illness and is slowly returning to his normal activities. She recounts a little 'water party' she had with her two nephews, taking them by the Itchen Ferry up to Northam and then walking home. George now reminds her of Henry instead of Edward, she says. The previous evening she taught them to play Speculation. They are preparing for the boys' return to Winchester. She thinks her mother will agree to the Chawton plan, though at first Mrs Austen apparently was sceptical.

Late in November Frank got shore leave to visit Godmersham, and Jane wrote to tell Cassandra of his coming. She notes with approval that Edward Bridges, who had once proposed to her, is about to marry another lady: 'Marriage is a great Improver,' declares the spinster novelist. 'As to Money, that will come you may be sure, because they cannot do without it.' Henry has reported that there are six bedrooms and a great deal of storage space in the Chawton house—her mother was worried about these things. They expect to keep a manservant there. Of a recent wedding in Southampton in which a woman married her children's tutor: both partners must be 'worthy of Envy,' Jane declares, 'for *she* must be excessively in love, and he mounts from nothing, to a comfortable Home.' Marriage and comfort, as usual, were linked in her mind. They have heard from Mrs Leigh Perrot, whose husband had recently become even richer as a result of the settlement of the Stoneleigh estate. The novelist's comment on her aunt's letter shows her in a rather unflattering light.

> My Aunt says as little as may be on the subject by way of information, & nothing at all by way of satisfaction. She reflects on Mr T. Leigh's dilatoriness, & looks about with great diligence & success for Inconvenience & Evil—among which she ingeniously places the danger of her new Housemaids catching cold on the outside of the Coach, when she goes down to Bath—for a carriage makes her sick.

Of course it must have been irritating to see the rich getting richer while she stayed poor; the subject was not one calculated to bring out the best in Jane Austen, and her comments on the elderly woman reek of pettiness. Things have been quiet in Southampton, she says, since Frank and Mary, after the flying visit to Godmersham, went off again on the *St Albans*. They expect James to visit soon, and, while he is in town, to go one night to a play: 'Martha ought to see the inside of the Theatre once while she lives in Southampton, & I think she will hardly wish to take a second view.'

Cassandra stayed on at Godmersham. Writing to her in December 1808, the novelist quotes Mrs Piozzi's *Letters to and From the Late Samuel Johnson*, and promises to avoid mentioning in *her* letters 'unnecessary stuff.' Jane refers to two ladies who have recently called on them. One 'seems a really agreable Woman—that is, her manners are gentle & she knows a great many of our Connections in West Kent'; these would be the Austens of Broadford and surrounding areas. The other 'lives in the Polygon, & was out when we returned her visit—which are *her* two virtues.' This letter shows unmistakable signs of the novelist's improving humour.

> A larger circle of acquaintance & an increase of amusement is quite in character with our approaching removal.—Yes—I mean to go to as many Balls as possible, that I may have a good

> bargain. Everybody is very much concerned at our going away,
> & everybody is acquainted with Chawton & speaks of it as a
> remarkably pretty village; & everybody knows the House we
> describe.

Jane Austen was looking forward to leaving Southampton with the
same anticipation with which she looked forward to leaving Bath in
1805. Her rekindled interest in dancing is indicative. For the first
time in years she actually attended a ball in Southampton; a partial
description of it is contained in a letter to Cassandra:

> the melancholy part was, to see so many dozen young Women
> standing by without partners, & each of them with two ugly
> naked shoulders!—It was the same room in which we danced 15
> years ago!—I thought it all over—& in spite of the shame of
> being so much older, felt with thankfulness that I was quite as
> happy now as then.

How quickly the novelist could find sympathy for those young ladies
who were *not* dancing! The 'shame' of being older is a reference, of
course, to her unchanged state: spinsterhood. That she was no less
happy, as her thirty-third birthday approached, than she had been in
1792, when, while visiting Southampton, she and Cassandra were
taken dancing by Frank, is a declaration we may well wish to
question—though with the removal to Chawton in the offing, her
spirits certainly were higher than they had been for a long time. Jane
tells Cassandra: 'You will not expect to hear that *I* was asked to
dance—but I was.' Her only partner was a man whose name she never
heard and who couldn't speak a word of English.

In Castle Square these days, she reports, they never dine until five
o'clock; and the Leigh Perrots have settled an allowance of £100 a
year on—the James Austens! Of course Jane had been hoping that
her mother's rich brother would do something for *them*: 'My
Expectations for my Mother do not rise with this Event. We will
allow a little more time, however, before we fly out.' It was further
evidence of the novelist's assertion upon surrendering Steventon to
the James Austens in 1801 that there was a conspiracy afoot 'to enrich
one part of our family at the expence of another.' James Austen's
annual income would now have been around £1,100. Jane notes that
Henry and Eliza are going to Godmersham for Christmas: 'with him

& the Boys, you cannot but have a chearful & at times even a merry Christmas.' It could not be an easy period at Godmersham—the first Christmas without Elizabeth Austen. The novelist declares that she and her mother now expect their household to be settled at Chawton by mid-1809. Meanwhile, she has not been doing much of anything: 'I have two hands . . . that lead a very easy life.' Was she, in a happier frame of mind now, beginning to think of writing again? There is no immediate evidence of this—but four months later she was indeed to rouse herself and inquire of Crosby what he intended doing with 'Susan' (*Northanger Abbey*). Of an acquaintance whose first marriage had been unhappy and who had just married again—this time a love-match—the novelist says: 'I consider everybody as having a right to marry *once* in their lives for love, if they can, and provided she will now leave off having bad headaches and being pathetic, I can allow her, I can *wish* her, to be happy.' Her thoughts continued to run on matrimony. She tells Cassandra that during a recent interview the latter had with Sir Brook Bridges during most of which, according to Cassandra, Sir Brook read the newspaper, he was in fact only pretending to read while 'making up his mind to the deed, and the manner of it. I think you will have a letter from him soon.' Sir Brook Bridges did indeed remarry shortly afterwards, but Cassandra was not his choice; nor did he marry a governess—as Jane had recommended as a prudent course to follow for a widower with three children. James's income of £1,100 a year, 'curate paid,' will allow him to keep three horses instead of one, Jane observes. Charles is reported to be well in Bermuda, staying with his wife's family there, and 'looked up to by everybody in all America.' Early in 1809 his wife Fanny gave birth to a daughter, christened Cassandra.

Edward's seventeenth wedding anniversary would have been on 27 December 1808, and Jane supposes it 'must have been a day of sad remembrance' at Godmersham. She has met a man who 'is so totally deaf that they say he could not hear a cannon, were it fired close to him; having no cannon at hand to make the experiment, I . . . talked to him a little with my fingers'—a reminder that the novelist had learned to speak to the deaf years earlier in order to communicate with her unfortunate brother George. She recommended that the deaf man read Madame de Staël's *Corinna*. Jane also reports that she has recently met several elderly spinsters in Southampton, and that fervently she hopes to be, at their age, neither so 'friendless' nor so 'captious.' Like everyone else, she worried about growing older.

Henry, the novelist says, is anxious about his banking business; banks, like the rest of British commerce, were in an increasingly depressed state as the war with France continued to drag on. She has heard from the Digweeds, who will again be near them when they have gone to Chawton. Mrs Digweed, according to Jane, 'looks forward with great satisfaction to our being her neighbours. I would have her enjoy the idea to the utmost, as I suspect that there will not be much in the reality.' Jane declares she would prefer to be intimate with the Digweeds' bailiff and his wife, who 'are said to be remarkably good sort of people.' This is not good-natured.

The plans for moving to Chawton went forward. They would have a pianoforte again—'as good a one as can be got for thirty guineas, and I will practise country dances, that we may have some amusement for our nephews and nieces, when we have the pleasure of their company.' (In *Persuasion*, Anne Elliot plays country dances for her sisters-in-law at Uppercross.) When they moved from Steventon to Bath, Jane had had to sell her pianoforte (and for only eight guineas; one may gauge the rate of inflation, fueled largely by the war, by noting what, seven and a half years later, she had to pay for the equivalent item): obviously, having one again was symbolically important to her. Her spirits were high; in a few months, thanks to Edward's generosity, they would once again have a spacious home of their own in the Hampshire countryside. And so the year 1808, unlike so many of its predecessors, ended for Jane Austen on a note of high optimism. She was almost merry.

III

Replying to what must have been an accusation of dullness from Cassandra, the novelist informed her (in January 1809) that in fact the ladies in Southampton have been 'doing nothing . . . and I am therefore quite dependent upon the communications of our friends, or my own wits,' for 'matter'; she apologises for past epistolary 'deficiency.' As we have seen, the relationship between the sisters was not always tranquil. Jane goes on to say how delighted she is that a time has been fixed for Cassandra's return to Southampton (mid-February). Frank's ship the *St Albans* is now in Portsmouth but 'may soon be off to help bring home what may remain by this time of our poor army, whose state seems dreadfully critical.' This is a reference to the heavy casualties sustained during the Peninsular Campaign in

Spain by the British army fighting the forces of Napoleon there. In January 1809 Frank Austen was instructed to take charge of the disembarkation of the troops from Coruña after General Sir John Moore's long and terrible retreat in the face of Marshal Soult's superior forces. At the last moment the French attacked and were defeated by Moore's smaller band of desperate men, who suffered great losses in the course of the 'victory.' The survivors were to be brought home. Jane Austen goes on in this letter to repeat rumours she has heard about a possible 'Regency'—that is, that the Prince Regent may act for his mad father George III. 'Unlucky that I should have wasted so much reflection on the subject,' says the novelist, when 'my most political correspondents' (probably Henry and Eliza) 'make no mention of it.' Still, the subject was in the air; and as a matter of fact the future George IV did indeed become Regent during the following year, 1810. Jane Austen's letter of 10 January 1809 should be reread by those who claim that she took no interest in current events and knew nothing about them.

The plans for their removal to Chawton are tentatively fixed, the novelist tells her sister. They will leave on 3 April, and sleep that night either at Alton or Dartford. For a week they will visit friends or relations in Hampshire or Kent, and arrive at Godmersham on 11 April. There they will remain until Edward has the Chawton house ready for them: Jane expects to move into it sometime in May or June (as it turned out, they did not get into it until July). Her niece Fanny has declined Cassandra's invitation to come back to Southampton with her: it is just as well, the novelist declares, for 'we have not the hope of a bed for her.' She is reading *Memoirs of an American Lady* (1808) by Catalina Schuyler, and *Margiana, or Widdrington Tower* (1808) by Mrs Sykes (five volumes). The latter intrigues her: 'We are just going to set off for Northumberland to be shut up in Widdrington Tower, where there must be two or three sets of victims already immured under a very fine villain.' The Gothic romance continued in good health. Henry, she tells Cassandra, is now in a happier frame of mind about his bank. She has sent an edition of *Marmion* to Charles—'very generous in me, I think.' The first edition, in quarto, was priced at thirty-one shillings and sixpence, but several octavo editions appeared in 1808 priced at twelve shillings, and undoubtedly it was an octavo edition that went out to Charles Austen. They have had a report of a ball at Manydown from her niece Anna: 'a smaller thing than I expected, but it seems to have made Anna very happy. At *her* age it would not have done for *me*' (Anna was fifteen). She wishes Cassandra 'many happy returns' on the occasion of her thirty-sixth birthday. Of some relations James and Mary had visited and of whom Mary has written a glowing report: '*Her* praise . . . proves nothing more than [their] being civil and attentive to them.' Mary also 'writes of Anna as improved in person, but gives her no other commendation.' Anna lost her real mother at the age of two, and Jane was always trying to catch Anna's stepmother Mary Lloyd Austen in the act of treating the girl with less affection than she treated her own children. Martha Lloyd is being pursued, Jane claims, by a local clergyman (married). Martha will be away visiting throughout most of March: 'we shall enjoy ourselves the more, when we *can* get a quiet half hour together,' the novelist tells her sister (translation: when, that is, they can get away from Mrs Austen). She is reading two new novels by Sydney Owenson (Lady Morgan) called *Ida of Athens* and *The Wild Irish Girl* (1806). The former 'must be very clever, because it was written as the Authoress says, in three months.' The latter, a best-seller of sorts, looks less promising, Jane thinks—but 'If the warmth of her Language could affect the Body it might be worth reading in this weather.' Mrs Austen has been complaining of her health, but the novelist supposes this is chiefly a result of the unusually cold temperatures. Edward Cooper has published another volume of his sermons (the third) which she likes a little better than its predecessors: but they are all too full of 'Regeneration and Conversion' for her. She complains of hearing little from Frank and Mary in Portsmouth. There will be a ball the following week, but Jane does not expect to dance—even if asked. Of a local woman who incorporated into her wedding ceremony a loud parade: 'To *attract* notice could have been her only wish . . . it announces not *great* sense, and therefore ensures boundless Influence.' In this letter is enclosed a short mock-heroic poem on the virtues of Brag versus those of Speculation (both card games played regularly at Godmersham)—so far as we know the only bit of original composition done by Jane Austen during the Southampton years. The novelist begs her sister not to work too hard at Godmersham: 'remember that Aunt Cassandras are quite as scarce as Miss Beverleys' (a reference to the heroine of *Cecilia*). Her excellent spirits may be inferred from the following bit of fun:

You used me scandalously by not mentioning Ed. Cooper's

(Plate 1)

Front view of the Rectory at Steventon, drawn by Jane Austen's niece Anna Austen Lefroy (c. 1814)

(Plate 2)
Silhouette of Cassandra Austen, the novelist's sister

(Plate 3)

Manydown House in 1833, by G.F. Prosser, where Jane Austen refused a proposal of marriage in 1802

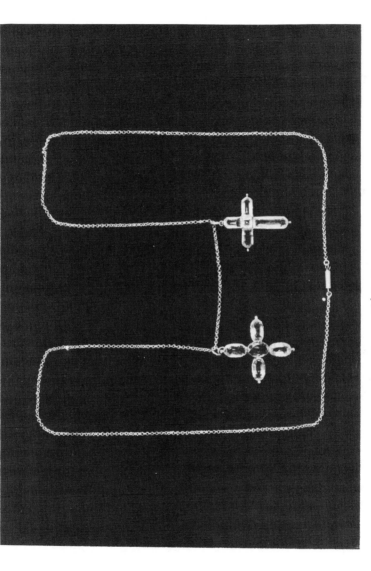

(Plate 4)

The topaz crosses with gold chain given to Jane Austen by her brother Charles in 1801; in *Mansfield Park*, William Price gives a topaz cross to his sister Fanny

(Plate 5)
Chawton Cottage, where Jane Austen lived 1809–17

(Plate 6)
The first page of a letter, dated 11 December 1815, from Jane Austen to the Rev James Stanier Clarke; the novelist tells the Prince Regent's librarian and chaplain that *Emma*, dedicated to the Prince Regent (the future George IV), would shortly be published—and replies to Clarke's advice to write a novel about a clergyman resembling himself

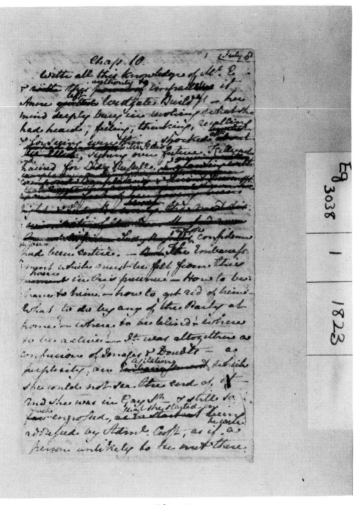

(Plate 7)
Opening of Chapter X, Volume II, of *Persuasion*, later rewritten; first page
of the cancelled chapter, in Jane Austen's hand (July 1816)

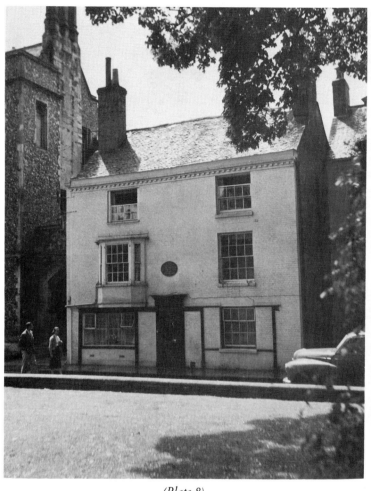

(Plate 8)
No. 8 College Street, Winchester; Jane Austen spent the last two months of
her life here, and died in one of the rooms on the middle storey (July 1817)

sermons;—I tell you everything, and it is unknown the
Mysteries you conceal from me.—And to add to the rest you
persevere in giving a final e to Invalid thereby putting it out of
one's power to suppose Mrs E. Leigh even for a moment, a
veteran Soldier.

Cassandra's latest account of Fanny pleases her: 'I hope she will not
turn good-for-nothing this ever so long.' She notes Cassandra's
admission that she has been showing Jane's letters to Fanny, and that
from time to time the precocious niece takes it upon herself to
comment on her Aunt Jane's style:

> I am gratified by her having pleasure in what I write—but I wish
> the knowledge of my being exposed to her discerning
> Criticism, may not hurt my stile, by inducing too great a
> solicitude. I begin already to weigh my words and sentences
> more than I did, and am looking about for a sentiment, an
> Illustration or a metaphor in every corner of the room. Could
> my Ideas flow as fast as the rain in the Store closet it would be
> charming.

Fanny, perhaps, had wondered at her aunt's plain, unmetaphorical
style of writing in an age of romantic and sentimental excess; here is
Jane Austen's witty response—complete with 'sentiment,' 'illustra-
tion,' and 'metaphor' in its final sentence.

Cassandra reported she was reading Hannah More's *Cœlebs in
Search of a Wife* (1809; just out, and the author's most popular work:
it is interesting to note that Cassandra read Hannah More as she was
published). Jane replies: 'You have by no means raised my curiosity
. . . My disinclination for it . . . is real; I do not like the Evangelicals.'
She goes on to add, somewhat facetiously: 'Of course I shall be
delighted, when I read it, like other people, but till I do I dislike it.'
One of the novelist's contemporaries commented later that she 'had
on all the subjects of enduring religious feeling the deepest and
strongest convictions, but a contact with loud and noisy exponents
of the then popular religious phase made her reticent almost to a
fault.' It would seem that in religious matters Jane was the 'higher'
(i.e., more liberal) of the two sisters; in later years she was to find the
Evangelicals more sympathetic. She hopes their two maidservants
will come with them to Chawton. Then: 'You depend upon finding

all your plants dead, I hope.—They look very ill I understand.—Your silence on the subject of our Ball, makes me suppose your Curiosity too great for words.' Needless to say, an account of the ball follows; she was asked to dance once. Anna has had her hair cut short; her Aunt Jane roundly disapproves. The novelist has told Martha that the (apparently mythical) attachment between Martha and the amorous clergyman, though of course 'immoral, has a decorous air.' Jane is grieved by the news of the death of General Moore in Spain.

In the final letter of this group (30 January 1809)—having heard something from Cassandra, obviously, on the subject of Hannah More—the novelist defends her instinctive dislike of that lady's new book: 'in Cœlebs, there is pedantry & affectation.' She wonders why the author didn't use the name 'Caleb, which has an honest, unpretending sound.' Sir Thomas Williams has apparently retired from the Navy: 'Lucky Man! to have so fair an opportunity of escape.—I hope His wife allows herself to be happy on the occasion, & does not give all her thoughts to being nervous.' Here speaks the sister of two men on active duty in the Navy at a time when Europe was engaged in one of its bloodiest struggles. Edward Cooper's eldest son (Edward Jr.) is going to Rugby. Jane's comment: 'it will be a great change, to become a raw school boy from being a pompous Sermon-Writer, & a domineering Brother.—It will do him good I dare say.' So much for Edward Jr.; the Hamstall Coopers were of course far from being the novelist's favourite cousins, yet she seems to expend here an inordinate amount of vindictive energy upon a small boy. Of their brother Edward's plan to visit Steventon: 'Mrs J. Austen's hospitality is just of the kind to enjoy such a visitor'—she means, of course, a rich one. She criticises the deathbed conversation, as it has been reported in the press, of General Moore, as redolent more of the 'Hero' than the 'Christian.' Sir John is supposed during his last hours in January 1809 to have said nothing about God or the next world but a good deal about how he might be viewed by public opinion in England, and by posterity; considering the circumstances—he was a brave soldier—Jane Austen's attitude is ungenerous. But then we know that often she could be ungenerous. Her mother, the novelist reports, is as strong as ever, despite the usual complaints. She looks forward to hearing Cassandra's account of Chawton: others may be vague about a house, but 'For one's own dear self, one ascertains and remembers everything.' Frank and Mary continue to be silent in Portsmouth: 'We are very patient.'

Surely Jane Austen was in a mood brighter than any she had been in for some years. We also see the novelist, in these letters to her sister, growing alert again to literary matters—always a concomitant of improving spirits in her. In fact, the next extant letter of hers is one addressed to Crosby, inquiring about 'Susan.' We may as well look at this letter now, for it and its successor are the last correspondence we have for the next two years—until April 1811.

On 5 April 1809 the novelist, using the pseudonym of Mrs Ashton Dennis and a return address of the Post Office, Southampton—the departure from that city was put back some days—wrote to Crosby in the following terms:

> In the spring of the year 1803 a MS. Novel in 2 vol. entitled Susan was sold to you by a Gentleman of the name of Seymour, & the purchase money £10 rec^d at the same time. Six years have since passed, & this work of which I am myself the Authoress, has never to the best of my knowledge, appeared in print, tho' an early publication was stipulated for at the time of sale. I can only account for such an extraordinary circumstance by supposing the MS. by some carelessness to have been lost.

If this is indeed the case, declares 'Mrs Ashton Dennis,' she would be happy to supply the publisher with another copy sometime before August (no sooner, since all their effects had been packed up for Chawton, and would not be unpacked there until July). Should Crosby wish for another copy of 'Susan,' however, Mrs Ashton Dennis makes it quite clear that she 'will engage for no farther delay when it comes into your hands.' She asks for a quick answer, as she is leaving Southampton in 'a few days. Should no notice be taken of this address, I shall feel myself at liberty to secure the publication of my work, by applying elsewhere.' Many years had passed since the nervous young author of 'First Impressions' had shyly put her initial literary effort into the hands of her father.

Crosby's answer is dated 8 April:

> We have to acknowledge the receipt of your letter of the 5th inst. It is true that at the time mentioned we purchased of Mr Seymour a MS. novel entitled *Susan* and paid him for it the sum of 10£ for which we have his stamped receipt as a full consideration, but there was not any time stipulated for its

publication, neither are we bound to publish it, Should you or anyone else we shall take proceedings to stop the sale. The MS. shall be yours for the same as we paid for it.

Crosby was still making money from his Gothic and sentimental romances, and was not about to foul his own nest. Jane did not have £10 to spare, and 'Susan' remained where it was. If she was disappointed, frustrated, and angry, who could blame her?

The novelist's only other surviving piece of correspondence from this period is dated 26 July 1809 from Chawton and consists entirely of a poem in couplets of fifty-two lines congratulating Frank on the birth, on 9 July, of a son and heir (his first child was a daughter). Early sections of the poem refer to Frank's own boyhood:

> Thy infant days may he inherit,
> Thy warmth, nay insolence of spirit;—
> We would not with one fault dispense
> To weaken the resemblance.
> . . . His saucy words & fiery ways
> In early Childhood's pettish days,
> In Manhood, shew his Father's mind
> Like him, considerate & kind;
> All Gentleness to those around,
> And eager only not to wound.
>   Then like his Father too, he must,
> To his own former struggles just,
> Feel his Deserts with honest Glow,
> And all his self-improvement know.—
> A native fault may thus give birth
> To the best blessing, conscious Worth.

The poem ends with a complacent account of their own household— they had just settled into their new home:

>   As for ourselves, we're very well;
> As unaffected prose will tell.—
> Cassandra's pen will paint our state,
> The many comforts that await
> Our Chawton home, how much we find
> Already in it, to our mind;
> And how convinced, that when complete

It will all other Houses beat
That ever have been made or mended,
With rooms concise, or rooms distended.

For they were now at Chawton at last; and Jane Austen's thoughts, quite obviously, had turned to literature again.

IV

Between July 1809 and April 1811 no letters of the novelist's are extant. This must largely be because Jane and Cassandra were seldom apart for long during these years. Both lived at Chawton. When Cassandra went up to see Edward's family at the Chawton Manor House, the sisters were only a meadow apart—half a mile—and letters were unnecessary. Cassandra went to Godmersham only for several short visits: we know that Jane did not go there at all between the spring of 1809 and 1813. The less travelling, the fewer letters. During the years 1809-10 the novelist mostly stayed home—and worked. Still, one can piece together much of her life during this period.

On 7 July 1809, Jane, Cassandra, their mother, and Martha Lloyd moved into Chawton Cottage. They had left Southampton in April, visited friends in Great Bookham, and stayed with Edward and his family at Godmersham until the Cottage was ready for them.

Chawton was a small village on the western edge of Alton and about a mile away from its centre, where the branch office of Henry Austen's bank could be found. The road from central Alton to the village of Chawton was lined with trees; as one approached Chawton, thatched cottages came into view, and the Manor House could be seen rising up on a hill to the left. Communication with Edward at Chawton was of course easy; communication with Steventon was by lanes impassable to carriages. James had to come on horseback, while Edward could just walk down the hill from the Manor House.

Chawton stood directly on the Winchester Road, the main artery connecting Portsmouth to London. From Chawton to Hyde Park Corner was less than fifty miles: the journey to London could be made in a day by coach.

Chawton is in the midst of pretty country; there are beech trees everywhere, and the timber generally is heavy. The Manor House half a mile away, full of high, panelled rooms, was on the slope of a hill above the church, surrounded by gardens and meadows and trees, with a commanding view of the valley beneath. The valley was planted mostly with beeches, and called Chawton Park.

Those who haven't seen the 'Cottage' at Chawton shouldn't be misled by its name. It was a large house—as the six bedrooms would imply—which had once been a posting-inn, and thus stood in the centre of the little village. More recently it had been the home of Edward Austen's bailiff, or chief steward. James Edward Austen-Leigh remembered the Cottage well and described it as having 'A good-sized entrance and two sitting-rooms made the length of the house.' A piano stood in the larger of the two parlours, which was that on the left-hand side of the house and looked out on the garden; the original, large drawing-room window, which had opened directly out on the Winchester Road, was blocked up because of noise, and turned into a book-case instead. The garden was large—'part flower, part vegetable, part turfy orchard.' Around the garden ran a thickly planted shrubbery walk of gravel, where the ladies often strolled for exercise and air. As at Southampton, there was a syringa—also hedgerows—along with sweet williams, columbines, and other flowers. There were fruit trees, and a good deal of long grass which had to be mowed regularly. The garden was screened from the noisy road by a high hornbeam hedge planted by Edward to help maintain privacy and quiet within. Mrs Austen gave up the housekeeping entirely to Cassandra and Jane and loved instead to work in the garden at Chawton (almost to the end of her days)—often attired in the green round smock of a labourer when digging the potatoes. But anyone who wanted to could, despite the blocked windows and high hedges,

> get a glimpse of the stir of the great world as manifested in the ever varying traffic of the highroad: coaches and carriages, farm carts and curricles, trotting horsemen and trudging pedestrians, farmers spanking along in their gigs, naval officers on leave cantering up for a spree in the capital and, four or five times in the year, the boys of Winchester School arriving for term or dispersing for the holidays. During pauses in the rattle of the long distance traffic, the scene was gently animated by the dawdling movement of village life.

A good deal of traffic went by at all hours; and Mrs Austen, when she was not working in the garden, apparently was fond of standing at one of the front windows and watching it pass.

The smaller, right-hand parlour was used as a sitting-room, and here, not far from a moulded mantelpiece, Jane Austen placed her mahogany writing-desk. Since this was indeed a sitting-room, any member of the family, or for that matter any visitor, could easily come in without prior warning. Tradition has it that the novelist protected herself from sudden visitations and interruptions when working by allowing the door to this room to creak when opened, thus giving her an opportunity to slip her tiny manuscript paper under a blotting-book before anyone could see what she was doing. Apparently she begged that this door be left untended and unrepaired, and it was. She did not speak to outsiders about her literary activities. To them she seemed to be just another country spinster, living the life such a woman would live.

The Cottage itself was a Georgian, two-storeyed, russet brick building with sash windows and a tiled roof. It stood right on the corner where the road from Gosport intersected the great London-Portsmouth highway. The front door of the Cottage opened inward on a combined hall and dining-room. At the rear of the ground floor were the kitchen and the 'offices'—also a bakehouse and a stable, where later a donkey and a cart would be quartered; they could not afford a carriage. A narrow stairway connected the ground floor to the six bedrooms upstairs.

James Austen's daughter Caroline remembered that, when staying with her grandmother and aunts,

> the awful stillness of night [was] frequently broken by the sound of passing carriages, which seemed sometimes even to shake the bed . . . Everything indoors and *out* was well kept—the house was well furnished, and it was altogether a comfortable and ladylike establishment, tho' I beleive the means which supported it, were but small . . . The house was quite as good as the generality of Parsonage houses then—and much in the same style—the ceilings low and roughly finished —*some* bedrooms very small—*none* very large but in a number sufficient to accommodate inmates, and several guests.

Chawton Cottage still stands, but it has been divested of virtually everything that gave it its particular character in Jane Austen's day.

After the death of Charles Austen's first wife in 1845, the house was divided into tenements for labourers. The shrubbery went untended, and the grounds blended into and became indistinguishable from those of surrounding dwellings. Today one gets little sense of what it must have been like during the years 1809–17, when the novelist lived there.

Jane and Cassandra shared a bedroom, as they always had done. There was no private dressing-room for them, as there had been at Steventon, and fires could not be lit in unoccupied bedrooms awaiting guests; Jane had to work where it was warm and bright, which was downstairs. But the place agreed with her. At Chawton she revised for publication *Sense and Sensibility* and *Pride and Prejudice* (both light revisions, as suggested earlier); composed *Mansfield Park, Emma*, and *Persuasion*; wrote two fragments, *Sanditon* and the 'Plan of A Novel'; and tidied up 'Susan' for publication (posthumously, as *Northanger Abbey*). Between the summer of 1809 and the spring of 1811 she completed the last revisions of *Sense and Sensibility* (published in November 1811—her first book to appear) and *Pride and Prejudice* (published in 1813). In February 1811 she began the first novel she would complete since 1799, when 'Susan' was finished: *Mansfield Park*. So this period from mid-1809 to early 1811 was an important one for Jane Austen. Feeling comfortable and secure for the first time since leaving Steventon, she began to bring out in earnest the series of books that established her reputation as one of the greatest of the English novelists. As it turned out, luckily for her and for posterity, Chawton Cottage was to be her home for the rest of her life.

One important result of the move to Chawton was that for the next eight years the novelist came under the scrutiny of some of her nieces and nephews, several of them already teenagers. Two of these—Anna Austen Lefroy and her half-brother J.E. Austen-Leigh, both children of James Austen—in later years wrote vivid accounts of their aunt. Caroline Austen, another daughter of James—J.E. Austen-Leigh's sister, Anna's half-sister—wrote equally vivid, but not equally accurate, memoirs. Caroline was a good deal younger than the others: there were twelve years between her and Anna, seven between her and James Edward. And she knew her aunt before she was able to form a mature judgment of her; Caroline was just twelve when Jane Austen died. The other niece to whom the novelist was close, Fanny Austen Knight, later Lady Knatchbull, was the same age as Anna, but always more reticent than her cousins about family affairs.

The consensus among Jane Austen's nieces and nephews seems to be that though, in her mid-thirties (the novelist turned thirty-four in December 1809), she had not lost any of her youthful charm or her slim figure or her bright eyes—or the impression she gave of 'health and animation' (according to James Edward)—she deliberately dressed herself, as did Cassandra, in the style of an older woman who no longer went in for fashion or was interested in keeping up with it. Almost always she wore a cap, a badge in those days of middle age. It must be said in Jane Austen's defence that there were no theatres or assembly rooms near Chawton—nothing much to dress up for. If one wanted to take part in the activities of county society—dinners, garden parties, card parties—one needed a carriage; one couldn't arrive in a donkey-cart. And they were poor. So the women kept pretty much to themselves, and dressed accordingly.

Cassandra's famous portrait of her sister makes her look, as one critic puts it, 'plump, prim, and pop-eyed'—by no means beautiful; another example, perhaps, of our old acquaintance sibling rivalry? Caroline Austen declared that her Aunt Jane simply 'was not so handsome as Cassandra.' But Anna Austen Lefroy described Jane Austen thus at this period of the novelist's life:

> The figure tall and slight, but not drooping; well balanced, as was proved by her quick firm step. Her complexion of that rare sort which seems the particular property of light brunettes; a mottled skin, not fair, but perfectly clear and healthy; the fine naturally curling hair, neither light nor dark; the bright hazel eyes to match, and the rather small, but well-shaped, nose.

Anna, who was between her sixteenth and twenty-fourth years during the time Jane Austen lived at Chawton, added that the novelist, though attractive, was not especially handsome. She seemed shy with strangers, though she was animated enough with intimates; at other times, Anna declared, she could be 'very grave,' which fits what we know about her moodiness. Anna, who later married a son of Jane's old friend Mrs Lefroy, was probably the most incisive of the Austen nieces and nephews; her accounts of the novelist are more likely to be trustworthy than those of the adoring but youthful Caroline, the arrogant Fanny, or even those of James Edward, whose *Memoir* of his aunt betrays a pomposity and fastidiousness Jane undoubtedly would have found amusing. But the author of the *Memoir*, who was nineteen when his aunt died, would be a more reliable witness than the enthusiastic but immature Caroline.

Caroline insisted to her dying day that her novelist-aunt never turned her neighbours to ridicule, and 'was as far as possible from being censorious or satirical'—an opinion easily disproved by even the most casual reading of the letters, and in fact specifically contradicted by James Edward, who says in his *Memoir* that at Chawton and elsewhere the neighbours 'often served for her amusement.' Indeed, it was specifically of the Chawton period of Jane Austen's life that Virginia Woolf so shrewdly remarked:

> for my own part, I would rather not find myself alone in the room with her. A sense of meaning withheld, a smile at something unseen, an atmosphere of perfect control and courtesy mixed with something finely satirical, which, were it not directed against things in general rather than against individuals, would be almost malicious, would, so I feel, make it alarming to find her at home.

Even Caroline admitted that her mother suspected that her daughter might be considered by the novelist a nuisance, and warned her privately 'not [to] be troublesome to her aunt' Jane. No similar warning was issued about Aunt Cassandra.

For what it may be worth, Caroline gives an account of the novelist's personal appearance—less flattering, perhaps, than one might expect under the circumstances:

> her's was the first face that I can remember thinking pretty. . . . Her face was rather round than long—she had a bright, but not a pink colour—a clear brown complexion and very good hazle eyes. . . . Her hair, a darkish brown, curled naturally—it was in short curls round her face (for *then* ringlets were *not*). She always wore a cap—Such was the custom with the ladies who were not quite young—at least of a morning but I never saw her without one. . . . I beleive my two Aunts were not accounted very good dressers, and were thought to have taken to the garb of middle age unnecessarily soon.

The ladies kept a maid and a manservant at Chawton, and the servants needed some supervision. Mrs Austen, now seventy, did little but embroider and work in the garden, and Jane and Cassandra did much of the housework themselves. Visitors invariably called Chawton Cottage well-kept and clean. Cassandra was the chief housekeeper and a sort of executive officer; Jane's special charges apparently were keeping up an adequate supply of sugar, tea, spruce-beer, mead, and (home-made) wine. She also prepared breakfast each day. She practised a good deal on the piano, usually before breakfast; perhaps she was clearing her mind for the work she would take up after breakfast. David Cecil has remarked that her musical taste was probably on the lowbrow side; certainly there is little evidence to suggest that she knew she was living in one of the greatest of musical periods, that of Haydn and Mozart and Beethoven. As we have seen, she looked forward to having a pianoforte again so as to be able to play 'country dances' for her nieces and nephews, and concerts bored her. On the other hand—in *Emma* some recently published music arrives along with Jane Fairfax's new piano: it includes work by J.B. Cramer, who was much admired by Beethoven, and some settings of Irish and Scottish melodies which may well be Beethoven's settings, published just about this time. In any case, the novelist's nephew James Edward remembers her playing traditional songs ('The Soldier's Lament,' 'The Yellow Haired Laddie') with spirit and sweetness. So far as we can tell, she never played for anyone outside the family circle. All who knew her during this period testified to her extraordinary manual dexterity—not only on the piano, but in games, in needlework, in folding letters and wrapping parcels, and so on. She wrote a clear, strong hand. It was a cruel irony that the disease which attacked her some years later weakened the nervous system and rendered her decreasingly dexterous.

Jane's time for writing was after breakfast. The other ladies knew what she was up to and left her alone in the little sitting-room. In the early afternoon there would usually be a walk—either in the back garden, or farther afield in Chawton Park, or to the Manor House or elsewhere. There was the occasional shopping trip into Alton. The chief meal of the day, 'dinner,' was served as a rule between three and four-thirty. Afterwards the ladies settled down for an evening of conversation, and sometimes of cards. 'Tea' would have been taken in the drawing-room. Jane Austen's nieces and nephews are agreed that her conversation was amusing and often full of laughter. The last part of the evening was frequently spent reading something aloud; the novelist was said to read with particular dramatic flair—as her father had done.

She also, of course, read a good deal on her own. She reread Richardson, Johnson, Crabbe, Cowper, and Fanny Burney. As always, she read all the new novels she could get hold of—including those of Maria Edgeworth, which she much admired. She also enjoyed, as before, non-fiction—biography, travel, history, memoirs. She read less new poetry—though there are references in her letters and novels to Scott and Byron.

Jane left much of the charitable work in the village to Cassandra: making clothes for the poor, visiting the sick, teaching the uneducated, and so on, never interested her. Caroline Austen recalled that she was on 'friendly, but rather distant terms' with her neighbours. But the novelist listened to Cassandra's accounts of life in the village—and inevitably stored them away for possible future use. There was the occasional trip to London to see Henry and attend plays and operas, and the less occasional trip to see Edward: his family was a bit too large and noisy to suit her, fond as she was of her niece Fanny. Jane's brothers occasionally left a nephew or niece at Chawton Cottage to visit, and their memories of her are invariably interesting. Much as she loved her Aunt Jane, Anna thought her Aunt Cassandra 'the more equably cheerful' of the two sisters— another suggestion of the novelist's moodiness. But Caroline said of her Aunt Jane:

> Her charm to children was great sweetness of manner and she seemed to love you, and you loved her naturally in return. This . . . was what I felt . . . before I was old enough to be amused by her cleverness; but soon came the delight of her playful talk. Everything she could make amusing to a child . . . she would tell us the most delightful stories chiefly of Fairyland, and her Fairies had all characters of their own. The tale was invented, I am sure, at the moment, and was sometimes continued for two or three days . . . . we often had amusements in which my Aunt was very helpful. She was the one to whom we always looked for help. She would furnish us with what we wanted from her wardrobe, and she would often be the entertaining visitor in our make-believe house. She amused us in various ways.

The nieces and nephews are agreed that Jane Austen was inspired more than anything else by her neighbours when she turned to story-telling (the Fairies were just for very little girls). She invented preposterous tales about the doings of her neighbours, especially those she had seen but didn't know well, regaling her listeners with incredible details. 'Her description of the pursuits of Miss Mills and Miss Yates—two young ladies of whom she knew next to nothing'—was an example Caroline Austen remembered. 'They were only on a visit to a near neighbour but their names tempted her into rhyme and on she went!'

Despite this maternal side of the novelist, quite clearly being an aunt was enough for her; there is no sign that she yearned for motherhood:

> However wholeheartedly she seemed as a woman to enter into the life around her, into its joys and sorrows and pleasures and problems, Jane Austen the artist was present at them, a detached invisible figure, observant to gather the fuel that might one day kindle her imaginative spark to flame. Here it was that she differed from most women. The creative impulse which in them fulfilled itself as wife and mother in her fulfilled itself as an artist.

Of course she never had the chance of being a mother; the rest of this seems just, and indeed we can agree with Virginia Woolf that finding Jane Austen 'at home' might well have been a daunting experience for a visitor. Certainly her celebrated 'detachment' remained—indeed, in some ways broadened—as the years went by. On the other hand, the liberating circumstances of Chawton, and the end to any marriage plans she might have been harbouring, freed her to concentrate on her work. This is precisely what she did at Chawton during the years 1809 and 1810.

And yet she continued to keep that work a secret from all but her nearest intimates: her passion for secrecy came close to being a mania—the famous creaking door is just one example of this. She took elaborate pains to conceal from the outside world her true vocation. There is even a story that she threw down on the counter of the Alton library a copy of *Sense and Sensibility*, 'saying she knew it must be utter rubbish from its name.' Her nephew James Edward read her first two published novels before he knew who wrote them.

As J.E. Austen-Leigh, author of the *Memoir* (1870-71) of his aunt, he expressed as eloquently as anyone ever has the extent to which she worked in secrecy, obscurity, and loneliness:

> Jane Austen lived in entire seclusion from the literary world; neither by correspondence, nor by personal intercourse was she known to any contemporary authors. It is probable that she never was in company with any person whose talents or whose celebrity equalled her own; so that her powers never could have been sharpened by collision with superior intellects, nor her imagination aided by their casual suggestions. Whatever she produced was a genuine home-made article. Even during the last two or three years of her life, when her works were rising in the estimation of the public, they did not enlarge the circle of her acquaintance. Few of her readers knew even her name, and none knew more of her than her name. I doubt whether it would be possible to mention any other author of note, whose personal obscurity was so complete . . . A few years ago, a gentleman visiting Winchester Cathedral desired to be shown Miss Austen's grave. The verger, as he pointed it out, asked, 'Pray, sir, can you tell me whether there was anything particular about that lady; so many people want to know where she was buried?' During her life the ignorance of the verger was shared by most people; few knew that 'there was anything particular about that lady.'

Why did she court obscurity so severely? Why this passion for secrecy? Probably there were several causes, all stemming from insecurity, lack of self-confidence. What, after all, had she ever done? Her two attempts to publish had met with rebuffs. The only literary praise or encouragement she had received had come from the closest members of her immediate family—and none of them was a publisher. It is impossible to say how much of a role her unmarried state played—the implied rejection by men—but this too might well have undermined her sense of her own worth. She had been humiliated before: she would not be humiliated again. She would keep her work to herself until she was certain a publisher would take it; and even then, assuming the worst from the critics, she would not place her name on the title-page: she would not put at risk her hard-won tranquility or her privacy. One cannot, of course, 'know' this:

one can only guess what went through her mind. At any rate, that was her plan, and she carried it out.

More and more, as the years went by, she devoted herself to her work. She found she could write comfortably and securely at Chawton; she felt she belonged there, that she would not soon be leaving. As Miss Lascelles has observed, the life at Chawton was specially congenial to the novelist because 'it was a country [life], and she had always been dissatisfied with life in a town, feeling that it had no natural roots.'

During the year 1810, though we have no documentary evidence of this, it may safely be said of Jane Austen that she stayed home and worked hard. She made some changes in *Pride and Prejudice* and perhaps a few more in *Sense and Sensibility*—getting them ready, she hoped, for publication. A good deal of critical discussion has focussed on the question of why *Sense and Sensibility*, of all the novels, should have been the first to be published. Why not *Pride and Prejudice*, the family favourite—and, as 'First Impressions,' the first to be written? The answer seems clear enough. *Pride and Prejudice* was tainted: years ago, in its earlier form, it had been summarily refused by the publisher Cadell. The author was not willing to risk another rejection of something so close to her heart—something so beloved. It was the book her father had taken in hand for her: she would not trust it to the tender mercies of the London market—not quite yet. *Northanger Abbey*, as we know, was not available; as 'Susan,' Crosby still owned it, and legal action had been threatened if she tried to take it elsewhere. *Mansfield Park* was not begun until February 1811, and not finished until 1813. She had no desire to return to 'The Watsons': it belonged to a period of her life too painful to go back to in any form. Actually, then, it should not be surprising that *Sense and Sensibility* was the first to appear; all the other possibilities had in some way been eliminated.

The novelist revised *Sense and Sensibility* late in 1809 and on into 1810. Only later, probably during the latter half of 1810, did she turn her attention to *Pride and Prejudice*—drafted earlier than *Sense and Sensibility* but published, in the event, two years later. And so it was that *Sense and Sensibility*, surely the weakest of her three earliest novels, was the first of them to be sent off into the big world. It was accepted for publication in 1810 or early in 1811, and Jane Austen was reading proofs as early as the spring of 1811. Her career as a publishing novelist had begun. She was thirty-five.

Crawford was waiting for me in the ragged shadows of the trees, turned to face me like a bayed animal. I felt a surge of power. I wanted to call him a son of a bitch, but, in keeping with the times, I settled for cad. 'You cad,' I said, shoving him back a step, 'how dare you come sniffing around here after what you did to Maria Bertram in *Mansfield Park*? It's people like you—corrupt, arbitrary, egocentric—that foment all the lust and heartbreak of the world and challenge the very possibility of happy endings.'

—T. Coraghessan Boyle, 'I Dated Jane Austen' (1979)

She did not care much for babies once they were born.

—Elizabeth Bowen, *To the North*

'What a blessing, that she never had any children! Poor little creatures, how unhappy she would have made them!'

—*Emma*

'To yield readily—easily—to the *persuasion* of a friend is no merit with you.'

'To yield without conviction is no compliment to the understanding of either.'

'You appear to me, Mr Darcy, to allow nothing for the influence of friendship and affection. A regard for the requester would often make one readily yield to a request, without waiting for arguments to reason one into it.'

—*Pride and Prejudice*

Emma, if she thought about her name at all, was reminded not of Jane Austen's heroine but rather of Thomas Hardy's first wife—a person with something unsatisfactory about her.

—Barbara Pym, *A Few Green Leaves*

But Miss Austen has no romance—none at all.

—John Henry Newman

'We all like a play.'

—Charles Musgrove in *Persuasion*

CHAPTER 7

The Years of the Second 'Trilogy,' 1811–1816: *Mansfield Park, Emma, Persuasion*

In 1803 Jane Austen had hopefully brought along on a visit to Henry and Eliza in London the manuscript of 'Susan.' The result of this venture, as we know, had been bitter disappointment. Now, eight years later, having entrusted the manuscript of *Sense and Sensibility* to Henry, who functioned as a sort of literary agent for her, she came to London to correct proofs of what would be her first published novel. In April 1811 she was with Henry and his wife at 64 Sloane Street—in those days part of a pleasant suburb from which one could easily 'walk to London.' Henry's bank was still successful, he remained relatively prosperous, and he and the worldly Eliza, the former French countess, had a large circle of friends. While in London this April, Jane met many people, visited theatres and museums, and accepted most of the social invitations that came to her through her brother and sister-in-law.

The publisher of *Sense and Sensibility*, Thomas Egerton of the Military Library, Whitehall, would not undertake publication at his own risk. Fortunately Jane did not have to hand over any cash to underwrite publication, but she did have to sign an agreement, apparently negotiated by Henry, to reimburse Egerton in case of loss on the book; she began to save money in earnest for this possible eventuality.

As it turned out, *Sense and Sensibility* covered its expenses easily and earned the novelist an additional £140 on its first edition alone; and there was a second edition in 1813 which was to earn Jane Austen substantially more. Of all of her novels only *Pride and Prejudice*, appropriately enough, went into a third edition—two editions in 1813, another in 1817—during her lifetime. The novelist's earnings might have been much greater if she had published with one of the larger houses—Constable, say, or Murray (John Murray eventually did take over the publication of her novels)—more prosperous than

Egerton's; they could have puffed her books more than Egerton did. But we are getting ahead of ourselves.

It is possible that Henry either put up or guaranteed the money for publication of *Sense and Sensibility* without telling his sister, but of that we must remain uncertain. During this period it cost between one and two hundred pounds to bring out the average edition of a two- or three-volume novel. When *Sense and Sensibility* appeared, the title-page declared it to be printed 'for the Author' ('A Lady') by C. Rowarth and published by T. Egerton. Publication at the author's expense was perfectly respectable at the time; Burns, for example, paid for the publication of his first volume of poems. Johnson and Pope often published by 'subscription,' soliciting funds from friends and backers to underwrite their works. As we know, Fanny Burney published *Camilla*, her third novel, by subscription—Jane Austen being one of the subscribers (courtesy of her father); *Camilla* earned more for Miss Burney than either of her two preceding novels. We know enough of Jane's Austen's life, circumstances, and personality to understand why she could never have considered publication by subscription. Few people knew who she was; even fewer knew her as an embryo novelist. Besides the members of her immediate household and her brothers, the only others in on the secret of her authorship in 1811 seem to have been her niece Fanny and old Mrs Knight, who apparently offered some advice about the income and financial affairs of the Dashwoods.

In April 1811, while Jane was in London with Henry and Eliza, Cassandra was at Godmersham on another of her extended sojourns with the large motherless family there; James's daughter Anna was staying with Mrs Austen and Martha Lloyd at Chawton during the absence of the two sisters from home. Unlike so many of the novelist's earlier letters, those written during this period of her life convey an unmistakable sense of buoyancy and satisfaction. At last she was doing what she always hoped to be doing—publishing fiction—and there is here a shade of self-confidence and even of self-satisfaction patently missing from so many of the previous, more querulous, letters. She felt at last, clearly, that she was beginning to fulfil her rightful destiny. A book of hers was soon to be published; she was revising another, and had recently begun an altogether new tale.

Jane gives Cassandra a long account of visits to galleries, calls made and returned—she intended to call on Miss Beckford, but was prevented from doing so by bad weather—and plays seen. 'I am sorry

to tell you,' the novelist writes, 'that I am getting very extravagant &
spending all my Money'—some of it on silk stockings for herself. The
contingency fund for *Sense and Sensibility* was getting off to a slow
start: 'I am really very shocking.' She has been spending Cassandra's
money too, she says, on her sister's order of some new muslin. Henry
and Eliza are giving a musical party in her honour the following week
to which eighty people have been invited. Sixty-six appeared, including
Miss Beckford; the gathering was reported in the social columns of
the *Morning Post*. In the midst of all this gaiety she still had her
sombre moments: 'I am a wretch, to be so occupied with all these
Things, as to seem to have no Thoughts to give to people &
circumstances which really supply a far more lasting interest—the
Society in which You are [Godmersham]—but I do think of you all I
assure you.' She reports that Frank Austen, who had been serving as
Admiral Gambier's flag-captain on the *Caledonia*, has lost this post
due to Gambier's (temporary) disgrace, and is looking out for
another one. Later, in July 1811, he was given command of the
Elephant, in which he served until 1814. Jane plans to visit her friends
the Hills at Streatham during the first week of May on her way back
to Hampshire; Mrs Hill was the former Catherine Bigg, who married
the Rev Herbert Hill, the father-in-law of Southey's daughter. The
novelist had hoped to see Mrs Siddons in several productions, but the
actress has been ill and invisible. She responds to Cassandra's report
that Frank's new child is a son: 'I give you joy of our new nephew, &
hope if he ever comes to be hanged, it will not be till we are too old to
care about it.' Cassandra had obviously inquired about the status of
Sense and Sensibility. Jane declares: 'I am never too busy to think of
[it]. I can no more forget it, than a mother can forget her sucking
child'—and a first-born child at that. She has corrected proof sheets
up to the first appearance of Willoughby, she says (this on 25 April);
she hopes the book will be published in May or June. In fact it was not
advertised until the end of October, and finally appeared in
November; Jane Austen had a few things to learn about publication.
The novelist has noted Mrs Knight's strictures on matters touching
the Dashwoods' income: 'I will get them altered if I can.' She did not
have a chance to do any 'altering' until the second edition of 1813.
Jane adds that Mrs Knight is sure to 'like my Elinor, but [I] cannot
build on any thing else.' She has been told that Charles Austen,
sailing in the *Cleopatra*, should be home soon on leave—but as the
gentleman who conveyed this information to her 'was certainly in

liquor . . . we must not quite depend upon it.' She has seen *The Hypocrite*—Bickerstaffe's adaptation of Cibber's version of Molière's *Tartuffe*—and met an elderly French Count whom Eliza knew in Paris: 'If he w^d but speak in english, *I* would take to him.' They have tried to get hold of a copy of Mary Brunton's *Self-Control*, a best-seller of the season, but failed. The subject of a popular new work of fiction prompts this comment from Jane: 'I . . . am always half afraid of finding a clever novel *too clever*—& of finding my own story and my own people all forestalled.' She has made up a couplet on the fortunes, as reported by Cassandra, of a local acquaintance, one Emma Plumbtree:

> I am in a Dilemma, for want of an Emma,
> Escaped from the Lips, of Henry Gipps.

The novelist congratulates Edward on the postponement in Parliament of the Weald of Kent Canal Bill, passage of which would have been adverse to his landholding interests. 'Between Session and Session/The first Prepossession/May rouse up the Nation,/And the villainous Bill/May be forced to lie still/Against Wicked Men's will. There is poetry for Edward and his Daughter [Fanny].'

Jane paid her visit to Streatham as planned, and by the middle of May was back at Chawton. Cassandra remained at Godmersham. Jane's letters to her in May and June 1811 are informative, but after this there is a gap of seventeen months in the correspondence—until November 1812. The novelist refers sardonically to Mrs Leigh Perrot, who has written to say that drives in her new barouche only give her headaches—'a comfortable proof, I suppose, of the uselessness of the new carriage.' Margaret Beckford, daughter of the author of *Vathek*, has eloped and been married; the story is in the newspapers. Jane was now beginning work on *Mansfield Park*—which, like the story she was now revising, *Pride and Prejudice*, has a spectacular elopement woven into its plot. The garden is blooming, the novelist tells her sister: peonies, pinks, sweet-williams, columbines, syringas, several dozen greengages, and 'a great crop of Orleans plums,' along with an apricot tree just beginning to bear fruit, fir and beech trees and hedges, have made the back garden a miniature paradise. Anna is still with them: Jane thinks it is 'always safest' to keep her away from their neighbours, the dangerous Digweeds. She has discouraged Mrs Knight from giving her a spinning-wheel, as the generous old lady proposed to do: 'I had a great mind to add that if she persisted in giving it, I would spin nothing with it but a rope to hang myself.' Though her needlework was deft, spinning and sewing were not among Jane Austen's favourite pastimes. Cassandra's beloved mulberry trees, she reports, are not doing well: 'I will not say that [they] are dead, but I am afraid that they are not alive.' One notes Jane's tendency to torment Cassandra with dire reports of her favourite plants.

On 16 May, Wellington had defeated Soult at the bloody battle of Albuera—the Peninsular Campaign was still very much in progress—and the novelist's reference to the event comes in another of those seemingly off-hand remarks of the sort that have sometimes caused rage and disgust among unfriendly critics. Jane writes to Cassandra: 'How horrible it is to have so many people killed!—And what a blessing that one cares for none of them!' Surely this is not the same cold-hearted nastiness so prone to crop up in letters of earlier years, but rather an expression of genuine relief that no one they knew, and especially none of their brothers, had been killed. The subject is quickly dropped; the awareness, however, is there. If V.S. Pritchett thinks of Jane Austen as 'a war novelist,' this sort of remark undoubtedly is one reason why. The novelist looks forward eagerly to Cassandra's return to Chawton. Frank and Mary are now living at Cowes while Frank waits for a ship. Henry and a friend came to stay overnight while on a visit to the Great House; Henry's friend admired their trees 'but greived that they should not be turned into money.' Anna is still at Chawton, managing somehow to lead an active social life: she has had, says her Aunt Jane with just a trace of asperity, 'plenty of the miscellaneous, unsettled sort of happiness which seems to suit her best.' They have re-stocked their supply of port and brandy. No one has ever suggested that the Austen ladies were teetotalers. 'We must buy currants for our Wine,' Jane reminds Cassandra. There is a reference to Scott's 'Lady of the Lake' (1810), which the novelist was apparently reading. She has enjoyed eating the strawberries ripening in the garden: 'had *you* been at home, this would have been a pleasure lost.' The old King (George III) is reported to be dying, and their mother, always economical, has ordered mourning—figuring that bombazine would be cheaper before the royal demise than after it. 'If I outlive him it will answer my purpose; if I do not, somebody may mourn for me in it: it will be wanted for one or the other . . . before the moths have eaten it up,'

Mrs Austen declared philosophically. As it turned out, George III lived until 1820 and she herself until 1827. By 1820 there were fewer mourners in the immediate family than the old lady could have foreseen; not only was Jane dead, but so was her eldest brother James. The son of George III was now Regent, as the novelist had predicted two years earlier.

During the summer of 1811 a number of visitors kept the ladies busy (Cassandra came home early in July). Besides Anna and Henry and his friend, Frank and Mary came to stay—as did Charles Austen, back in England after seven years' absence. Charles brought with him his previously unseen wife Fanny and their two young daughters, Harriet and Cassandra. All four apparently made a good impression. The ladies found Charles, though of course looking older, for the most part unchanged, and as amusing as ever. In a letter to her aunt Philadelphia, Cassandra characterises Fanny as a 'very pleasing little woman, she is gentle and amiable in her manners and appears to make him very happy.' Caroline Austen, some years later, described her new aunt on first sight as 'fair and pink with very light hair.'

Henry came again, this time with Eliza, for a stay of two weeks. Whenever she could find a moment amidst all this turmoil, Jane worked away at *Mansfield Park* (much of the final draft, however, was written during the following two years, 1812–13). The novelist kept anticipating news from Egerton—and was continually disappointed. In July and August she seems to have expected *Sense and Sensibility* to be published in September. September came and went, and the book did not appear. Jane must have wondered if she had another Crosby on her hands—and whether *Sense and Sensibility*, like 'Susan,' would turn out to be another buried novel.

II

On 28 September 1811 Jane Austen's niece Fanny recorded in her diary this note: 'Letter from At. Cass. to beg we would not mention that Aunt Jane wrote *Sense and Sensibility*.' At the end of October Egerton finally advertised the novel. The first announcement, appearing on 31 October, described the book simply as 'Sense and Sensibility: a Novel. In three volumes. By a Lady.' The list of new novels in which this notice appeared also contained references to Maria Edgeworth's *Tales of Fashionable Life* and a book by Fanny Burney's half-sister called *Traits of Nature*. *Sense and Sensibility* was published in November—a month before Jane Austen's thirty-sixth birthday—priced at fifteen shillings in boards. The first edition of about 1,000 copies sold out in twenty months. As early as 25 November 1811 Lady Bessborough, sister of the Duchess of Devonshire and mother of Lady Caroline Lamb, was recommending it to Lord Granville Leveson-Gower, her lover. 'Have you read *Sense and Sensibility?*' asks Lady Bessborough. She characterises it as 'A clever novel. They were full of it at Althorpe, and though it ends stupidly I was much amused by it.' If Lady Bessborough was reading Jane Austen, then so was 'Society'—especially the Whig aristocracy, that 'last and glittering representative of the distinctive culture of the eighteenth century.' The book seems to have aroused little interest among the writers of the Romantic movement, who in any case were not, for the most part, enthusiastic novel-readers.

By July 1813, as we have seen, Jane had earned £140 from *Sense and Sensibility*, a figure which ought to be multiplied by at least twenty to give us a present-day equivalent. The financial success of the book was to encourage Egerton, as we shall see, to offer £110 for the copyright of the next book the novelist sent him (*Pride and Prejudice*). She asked for £150, but accepted the lower offer. These figures may be compared with the £30 Fanny Burney got for *Evelina*, the £60 Goldsmith earned from *The Vicar of Wakefield*, and the £100 Maria Edgeworth made from the sale of *Castle Rackrent*. There can be no doubt that, financially at least, *Sense and Sensibility* was an unexpectedly substantial commercial success—long before publication of the second edition in November 1813. *Pride and Prejudice* appeared in January 1813, and though the novel-reading public was not to know Jane Austen's name until after she was dead, it learned very quickly to look forward to each new volume produced by the anonymous 'Lady' who wrote *Sense and Sensibility*—thus the substantial sales of *Pride and Prejudice*, *Mansfield Park*, and *Emma* during the novelist's lifetime.

Sense and Sensibility was advertised three times in the *Morning Chronicle* in November 1811. The first review appeared in February 1812. For reviewers' reactions Jane waited anxiously. Had the reviews been devastating, she might, given her sensitivity and her various insecurities, have published no more, regardless of sales. But the book was well-received by the only two journals which noted it. Except for *Emma*, which was something like a best-seller, the contemporary press, in part because they were published anonymously and in part because little critical attention generally was accorded fiction during this period, devoted scant attention to Jane Austen's novels during her lifetime.

A word should be said about the place of and attitude toward fiction in the early nineteenth century. At the time Jane Austen published her novels—that is, during the second decade of the nineteenth century—women did not attend the universities, as we know. Men did not study English literature as part of any academic curriculum. Fiction was not deemed an important branch of the literary arts, and readers and critics for the most part did not look upon novelists as a literary species likely to add to the world's storehouse of significant art. Fiction was considered a leisurely amusement—'Castle-building,' as Charles Jenner put it in 1770 in *The Placid Man*—and worse, and novelists were rarely esteemed. The novel as serious literature, the novel as written by Aphra Behn, Richardson, Defoe, Fielding, Smollett, Sterne and others, had been replaced by the novel of their imitators, the novel of sentimentality and sensibility, the circulating-library novel. Thus, in 1775, the year of Jane Austen's birth, Sheridan in *The Rivals* has Sir Anthony Absolute tell Mrs Malaprop: 'A circulating library in a town is an ever-green tree of diabolical knowledge!' Three years later, in her preface to *Evelina* (1778), Fanny Burney wrote sorrowfully: 'In the republic of letters, there is no member of such inferior rank, or who is so much disdained by his brethren of the quill, as the humble Novelist . . . among the whole class of writers, perhaps not one can be named of which the votaries are more numerous but less respectable.' Plucking up her courage, however, Miss Burney proceeded to throw down the gauntlet directly at the feet of the critics—as Jane Austen was to do in *Northanger Abbey*, perhaps in part as a result of reading this passage—by declaring that novels had already become too popular to be conveniently banished from the shelves, and that the writing of them 'ought rather to be encouraged than contemned.' The rush to the libraries in the latter half of the eighteenth century both proved Fanny Burney right and continued to provoke anti-fiction diatribes, based to some extent on fears of the effect of democratised reading habits on 'people who had no business reading,' from a number of different sources. As Richard D. Altick reminds us, the appearance of hundreds of 'trashy' novels in the later years of the eighteenth century encouraged this reaction against fiction.

Among the pessimists and optimists alike sprang up a rigid . . . association of the mass reading public with low-grade fiction. This was to have far-reaching consequences during the nineteenth century, for out of it grew the whole vexatious 'fiction question' . . . opposition to fiction on religious and moral principles became a convenient stalking-horse for the other motives which it [became] less politic to avow. This tendency was already marked in the eighteenth century; people who, for social or economic reasons, opposed the expansion of the reading public found it handy to conceal their true purposes by harping on the common reader's notorious preference for the novel.

The campaign against fiction was one of the most strenuous activities of both the Evangelical and the Utilitarian movements in the first third of the nineteenth century (here, perhaps, is one source of Jane's early disdain for the Evangelicals). Both groups regarded all forms of imaginative literature, and especially the novel, with suspicion. Novels were held to be dangerous because they over-excited the imagination of young people; they were linked, like current-day television, to corruption, dissipation, and all sorts of immorality, including adultery and divorce. Imaginative literature was considered frivolous; Bentham excluded it from his ideal republic because it had no practical utility. Random reading was regarded by many as a waste of time; literature, after all, did not teach skills. Various Methodist tracts even argued that it could be proven from Scripture that God specifically forbade the reading of novels; one of the Utilitarian organs announced to its readers that 'Literature is a seducer; we had almost said a harlot.' No wonder lighter literature was often kept out of the libraries; indeed, many of the early Mechanics' Institute libraries allowed within their walls only books on or about the various branches of science. By 1800 novels were so numerous and in such bad repute that respectable journals such as the *Scots* and *Gentlemen's* magazines ceased to notice them at all. The reading public had convincingly demonstrated its size and enthusiasm in the 1790s, when Burke's *Reflections on the Revolution in France* sold in the thousands, Tom Paine's rejoinder in *The Rights of Man* sold in the hundreds of thousands, and the Cheap Repository Tracts of Hannah More and others sold, unbelievably enough, in the millions.

Political and religious controversy provided stimuli for reading in the 'nineties and on into the 'teens when thousands of workingmen subscribed to Cobbett's radical journal, the *Political Register*. Some began to fear that it had been a mistake to teach reading to working-class children in Robert Raikes' Sunday schools. The reading of novels, however, was always considered, by the various Establishments of the time, as the most frivolous and dangerous form of reading for what George Gissing later in the century was to call the 'quarter-educated.' Coleridge, certainly no literary Establishmentarian, nevertheless spoke for many when he asserted in 1808 that 'where the reading of novels prevails as a habit, it occasions in time the entire destruction of the powers of the mind.' As late as 1826 the publisher Constable launched a series of cheap and popular publications that did not include fiction, and two years later the competing Murray's Family Library did the same. Things had changed considerably by 1865, when the founders of the *Fortnightly Review*, described by Anthony Trollope as 'the most serious, the most earnest, the least devoted to amusement, the least flippant, the least jocose' of literary periodicals, decided that their new journal must always contain a novel.

All of this may help explain why, oddly enough, there was hardly any serious criticism of Jane Austen's fiction either during her lifetime or immediately after it. Indeed, attention to her work grew by leaps and bounds only in the second half of the nineteenth century. If the early notices of her novels sound desultory, let us remember how little the novel was taken seriously as a literary form in Jane Austen's day—as she complains so bitterly in *Northanger Abbey*. It was considered more a frivolous amusement for ladies than an art. Thus the curious informality of the first notice of *Sense and Sensibility*, which appeared in the *Critical Review* in February 1812:

> A genteel, well-written novel is as agreeable a lounge as a genteel comedy, from which both amusement and instruction may be derived. *Sense and Sensibility* is one amongst the few, which can claim this fair praise. It is well written; the characters are in genteel life, naturally drawn, and judiciously supported. The incidents are probable, and highly pleasing, and interesting; the conclusion such as the reader must wish it should be, and the whole is just long enough to interest without fatiguing. It reflects honour on the writer, who displays much knowledge of character, and very happily blends a great deal of good sense with the lighter matter of the piece.

This was more than enough to satisfy the hopes and expectations of the *Critical Review*'s writer—and, presumably, the journal's readers.

The only other contemporary notice of the novel appeared in the *British Critic* three months later, in May 1812. The anonymous reviewer complained mildly about the 'perplexity in the genealogy of the first chapter' and confessed to being 'somewhat bewildered among half-sisters, cousins, and so forth,' but he went on to give the novel high (and intelligent) praise:

> We think so favourably of this performance that it is with some reluctance we decline inserting it among our principal articles, but the productions of the press are so continually multiplied, that it requires all our exertions to keep tolerable pace with them . . . The characters are happily delineated and admirably sustained . . . An intimate knowledge of life and of the female character is exemplified in the various personages and incidents which are introduced, and nothing can be more happily pourtrayed than the picture of the elder brother, who required by his dying father, to assist his mother and sisters, first, resolves to give the sisters a thousand pounds a-piece, but after a certain deliberation with himself, and dialogue with his *amiable* wife, persuades himself that a little fish and game occasionally sent, will fulfil the real intentions of his father, and satisfy every obligation of duty. Not less excellent is the picture of the young lady of over exquisite sensibility, who falls immediately and violently in love with a male coquet, without listening to the judicious expostulations of her sensible sister, and believing it impossible for man to be fickle, false, and treacherous. We . . . assure [our readers], that they may peruse these volumes not only with satisfaction, but with real benefits, for they may learn from them, if they please, many sober and salutary maxims for the conduct of life, exemplified in a very pleasing and entertaining narrative.

These were the only formal notices of the novel to appear during Jane Austen's lifetime. Certainly they were encouraging; inevitably she saw them. And that the public was buying up the book she could not help but be aware as she made her final revisions of *Pride and Prejudice* and worked steadily away at *Mansfield Park*.

III

Throughout the rest of 1812 Jane laboured on her new book, getting *Pride and Prejudice* ready for Egerton. In April Edward and his daughter Fanny visited Chawton for three weeks. Old Mrs Knight died later in this year, and Edward now formally adopted the name of the family to which he owed so much—the name which had been borne by every successive owner of the Chawton and Godmersham estates since the sixteenth century. With Mrs Knight's death came a considerable increase in his fortune. In June the novelist and her mother visited their old home at Steventon for a fortnight, and Cassandra later on may have found it necessary to destroy any letters Jane wrote from there, given her feelings about the place and its current mistress. From this time until her death in 1827, Mrs Austen, now seventy-two, chose never again to pass a night away from her home at Chawton; she always said that her last visit had deliberately been paid to her eldest son and the place where she had spent most of her married life.

Her youngest son, meanwhile, had got a ship—the *Namur*, lying at Sheerness; some years later the Victorian writer Douglas Jerrold was to serve as a midshipman in this same vessel. Charles and his wife and children, Cassandra reported to her aunt Philadelphia, were living on board the *Namur*. Their new 'residence,' Cassandra said, 'is so much the cheapest home [they] could have that they are very right to put up with little inconveniences.' She went on to give her aunt news of Edward and his family, and added: 'I hope those young people will not have so much happiness in their youth as to unfit them for the rubs which they must meet afterwards, but with so indulgent a father and so liberal a style of living I am aware there must be some danger of it.' Now nearly forty, Cassandra begins to sound pompous; certainly the warning was an apt one, however, as the character of Fanny Knight (for one) would demonstrate in later years.

In the autumn Edward temporarily moved his large family from Godmersham to the Great House at Chawton for an extended stay, which must have been pleasant for the inhabitants of Chawton Cottage. Among other things, this brought Jane and her eighteen-year-old niece Fanny closer together; the latter continued to be one of the novelist's few literary confidants—'almost another sister,' as Jane described her. Edward had decided he could afford now not to lease the Great House—rather, he would use it for his own pleasure as a second residence.

Anna Austen, James's daughter, was now also eighteen, and she too was close to her novelist-aunt—though she was not let in on the secret of Jane's authorship until the following year, 1813. Still, their intimacy continued to grow throughout 1812, fuelled by frequent visits paid by Anna to Chawton. She and her Aunt Jane, Anna recalled later, usually talked about books:

> It was my amusement during part of a summer visit to the cottage to procure novels from the circulating library at Alton, and after running them over to narrate . . . their stories to Aunt Jane, to her amusement, as she sat over some needlework. . . . We both enjoyed the fun, as did Aunt Cassandra in her quiet way.

The circulating library at Alton, as well as a private local literary society, enabled the novelist in these days to broaden the range of her reading. We find her looking through an *Essay on the Military Policy and Institutions of the British Empire* (1810) by Captain Sir Charles Pasley of the Engineers, and being delighted by a volume of parodies of contemporary and older authors (Scott, Byron, Crabbe and others) called *Rejected Addresses* (1810), by two brothers, James and Horatio Smith—a collection of imaginary addresses to be spoken at the opening of Drury Lane Theatre.

In November 1812 Jane wrote to Martha Lloyd, who was away visiting a sick friend. Edward and several of his daughters have come over from the Great House for a short visit, Jane reports. They were sorry to leave the Cottage: she prefers to think this is because their next stop is Steventon. Edward has now formally changed his name from Austen to Knight: 'I must learn to make a better K.' Edward's fourth son William (now fourteen), on his way to Winchester, will be their next visitor: they expect him to stay a week. Yes, she declares, the quatrain she sent in a previous letter on the subject of a friend of Southampton days, Camilla Wallop, was entirely her own. These lines have now been unearthed, though the original letter is missing:

> Camilla, good humoured and merry and small,
> For a husband, it happened, was at her last stake,
> And having in vain danced at many a ball
> Is now very happy to jump at a Wake.

Mrs Wallop was a widow of advanced years who had just engaged herself to marry the Rev Henry Wake—thus the pun in the last line.

There follows a rather complacent announcement: *Pride and Prejudice* has just been sold.

> Egerton gives £110 for it.—I would rather have had £150, but we could not both be pleased, & I am not at all surprised that he should not chuse to hazard so much.—It's being sold will I hope be a great saving of Trouble to Henry, & therefore must be welcome to me.—The Money is to be paid at the end of the twelvemonth.

The terms, though not all that the novelist had hoped for, represented a tremendous improvement over those negotiated for *Sense and Sensibility*. Neither Jane nor Henry had to put up any money or sign any guarantees this time: the publisher took the full risk upon himself. Egerton obviously wanted to bring out as soon as possible another novel by the author of *Sense and Sensibility* while that book was still the talk of the town. Indeed, *Pride and Prejudice* was to appear with amazing speed—in January 1813, just two months after its purchase. Egerton could be quick when he wished. Though Jane's announcement to Martha is made without fanfare—sandwiched between several paragraphs of local gossip—the novelist must have been delighted by the quick disposal of *Pride and Prejudice*. Within several weeks she would be thirty-seven; now, clearly, she had a vocation. The beloved 'First Impressions,' the family favourite for so many years, was at last going to see the light of day.

The letter to Martha closes with some characteristic phrases. The garrulous Mrs Stent, apparently, was gravely ill; Jane hopes that she 'will not be much longer a distress to anybody.' Of a woman who has just married a local bachelor in the town where Martha is staying: 'Happy Woman! to stand the gaze of a neighbourhood as the Bride of such a pink-faced, simple young Man!'

Cassandra, at Steventon in January and February 1813, was the recipient of some exuberant letters from her sister, who found herself in a very good humour these days. The imminent publication of the most cherished of all her books represented a high point of her life. Her ability, for the first time in nearly fifteen years, to sustain work on a wholly new tale—*Mansfield Park*—also must have buoyed her up.

She is reading, Jane reports, Sir John Carr's *Descriptive Travels in the Southern and Eastern Parts of Spain and the Balearic Isles in the Year 1809* (1811)—which makes it clear 'that there is no Government House in Gibraltar. I must alter it to the Commissioner's.' And so in *Mansfield Park* William Price remarks on the new style of hair-dressing adopted by the ladies at the 'Commissioner's' House in Gibraltar. Jane's failure to explain this tells us that Cassandra was conversant with as much of *Mansfield Park* as had been completed. The novelist says she has had a rather disagreeable drive with some neighbours: '*I* would rather have walked, & no doubt *they* must have wished I had.' They have been to a dinner party during which Miss Benn, a friend of Mary Lloyd Austen's who was staying in the neighbourhood, manoeuvred a place at the table for herself next to Mr Papillon (a distant relation of the Knights), who proceeded to ignore her: 'she had an empty plate, & even asked him to give her some mutton twice without being attended to. . . . There might be design in this, to be sure, on his side; he might think an empty stomach the most favourable for love.' Obviously Jane was in good spirits. There is a reference in this letter to Mrs Grant's round table in *Mansfield Park* and some discussion of the correct placement of players around it for a game of whist. The novelist observed on this evening out how the game was set up—and noted that the group of people there was much less 'agreeable' than those around Mrs Grant's table. She remarks a bit snappishly that a book society at Steventon and Manydown is just now being formed, some time after their own came into being, and sees this as proof of the 'superiority in ours over [their] society, which I have always . . . felt. No emulation of the kind was ever inspired by *their* proceedings.' She was feeling competitive. No one *there* suggested a book society: they were simply copying what had already been done at Alton and Chawton. She says she is trying to get hold of Mrs Anne Grant's *Letters from the Mountains* (1807). She has had a walk with Miss Papillon, the sister of the man being pursued by Miss Benn: '*I* had a very agreeable walk, & if *she* had not, more shame for her, for I was quite as entertaining as she was.' The new note of self-confidence is clear. She is delighted to hear that the weather at Steventon has been worse than the weather at Chawton.

   Pride and Prejudice: A Novel. In three volumes. By the Author of 'Sense and Sensibility' was published in London on 29 January 1813. The first edition of about 1,500 copies was priced at eighteen shillings. The same two journals which had reviewed *Sense and Sensibility* printed notices of the new novel. The *British Critic* called *Pride and Prejudice* 'very far superior to almost all the publications of the kind which have lately come before us.' Elizabeth, Darcy, and Collins are singled out for particular approval. The review concludes: 'we have perused these volumes with much satisfaction and amusement, and entertain very little doubt that their successful circulation will induce the author to similar exertions.' The *Critical Review* declared that every member of the Bennet family 'excites the interest, and very agreeably divides the attention of the reader.' Elizabeth, 'whose archness and sweetness of manner render her a very attractive object,' is compared to Shakespeare's Beatrice, and praised to the skies. 'On the character of Elizabeth,' the reviewer rightly concludes, 'the main interest of the novel depends'—and she is more than up to the task of keeping the reader intrigued: her 'sense and conduct are of a superior order to those of the common heroines of novels.' Each of the main characters is admired in turn. The final paragraph, echoing sentiments expressed in the *British Critic*, must have specially pleased Jane Austen:

> We cannot conclude, without repeating our approbation of this performance, which rises very superior to any novel we have lately met with in the delineation of domestic scenes. Nor is there one character which appears flat, or obtrudes itself upon the notice of the reader with troublesome impertinence. There is not one person in the drama with whom we could readily dispense;—they have all their proper places; and fill their several stations, with great credit to themselves, and much satisfaction to the reader.

Pride and Prejudice quickly made its mark in society. At a dinner party Sheridan remarked that the novel was 'one of the cleverest things he had read.' Warren Hastings, as we know, liked the book immensely. Annabella Milbanke, the future (unhappy) Lady Byron, was impressed by *Pride and Prejudice*, and described it in a letter as 'the fashionable novel' of the season: 'I really think it is the *most probable* [novel] I have ever read,' she commented. This was also the opinion of William Gifford, editor of the influential *Quarterly Review* and a reader for John Murray (Gifford was later instrumental in getting Murray to publish *Emma*). Mary Russell Mitford praised *Pride and Prejudice*, and so did Henry Crabb Robinson, the friend of Wordsworth and Coleridge; the latter said the book kept him up two nights running. The Austen family—those in on the secret—was of course delighted; Charles reported that several of his fellow officers had read the novel and liked it. Only a few found the book too sharp and the writer too satirical, too critical. *Pride and Prejudice* quickly became popular. The first edition was sold out within six months— by July 1813; a second edition appeared in November 1813, and a third in 1817. There is nothing on record to suggest that Egerton ever paid Jane Austen more than the original £110 (there was no royalty arrangement), and it is a singular irony that she earned less from *Pride and Prejudice* than any of her other novels. But with the success of her first two books she had been able to put by £250, a not inconsiderable amount in those days, and certainly much more than she had ever had at any time in her life. She worked tenaciously on *Mansfield Park* throughout the first half of 1813, despite the temptation to slow down, relax, and savour her success. She had momentum now, and an audience. But that audience wanted more, and new material had to be found. 'Susan' was still unavailable, and her first two books had of course been written years earlier. Much labour was required.

On the very day *Pride and Prejudice* was published, we find Jane dispatching a letter to Cassandra. 'I have got my own darling child from London,' the novelist writes exultantly about the arrival at Chawton of three printed copies of this long-time favourite. She is amused by Egerton's price of eighteen shillings: 'He shall ask £1.1 for my two next & £1.8 for my stupidest of all' (Murray was to ask £1.4 for *Emma*, but none of her books was priced as high as £1.8). She reports that they have been reading *Pride and Prejudice* aloud to Miss Benn, who of course knew nothing about its authorship. Jane was delighted to find that the visitor 'was amused . . . she really does seem to admire Elizabeth. I must confess that I think her as delightful a creature as ever appeared in print, and how I shall be able to tolerate those who do not like *her* . . . I do not know.' Here is further proof, should we need it, of the very *personal* way in which Jane viewed Elizabeth Bennet; we have seen how much of the novelist there is in her heroine. Jane complains about some typographical errors and a few obscurities brought about by vague pronoun references, but declares (paraphrasing *Marmion*, vi, 38):

> I do not write for such dull elves
> As have not a great deal of ingenuity themselves.

She worries about the second volume of the novel being too short; in the first edition there were 307 pages in the first volume, 239 in the second, and 323 in the third. She adds: 'I have lop't and crop't so successfully, however, that I imagine [*Pride and Prejudice*] must be rather shorter than [*Sense and Sensibility*] altogether.' It certainly seems so, but in fact Jane was wrong; *Pride and Prejudice* is slightly longer. She goes on to make a celebrated, and highly controversial, remark: 'Now I will try to write of something else, & it shall be a complete change of subject—ordination.' This is a reference to the novel now under way, *Mansfield Park*. That *Mansfield Park*, as it turned out, is not a novel exclusively about 'ordination' need not have puzzled so many for so long. The fact is that Jane had written, in all probability, less than two-thirds of the new book by January 1813. *Mansfield Park* was not completed in its first draft until July of that year, and as late as December the novelist was still rewriting and polishing it. It did not appear until May 1814, which gave her plenty of time for additional revision and alteration. The plain truth is that in January 1813 she obviously had not worked through the book's resolution. 'Ordination' is a theme in the novel. Several of its leading men are clerics, or aspiring ones; Edmund's vocation is discussed at some length—most notably in Volume I, Chapters 9 and 11; the social status of clergymen is made an issue by Mary Crawford; and Edmund's decision to be ordained over her objections is an important statement of his—and the novelist's—values. The remark to Cassandra is that of a writer who has got some of these things down on paper and some of them worked out in her mind, but not as yet seen her way to the end of the book—not yet seen its entire thrust—and thus written of it prematurely and incompletely. *Mansfield Park* is about ordination, but it is about a good many other things as well.

Jane thanks Cassandra for the results of her 'enquiries'—probably about the disposal of clerical livings, a subject about which James, with whom Cassandra was staying, would have known a great deal—and to ask her sister to find out if there are many hedgerows in Northamptonshire. Whether or not a particular geographical area had hedgerows during the period from, roughly, 1750 to 1850, depended on how vigorously Enclosure was being administered there—thus the novelist's question: she wanted to get it right. The answer was no, and she abandoned in *Mansfield Park* any thought of using the device, picked up later in *Persuasion*, of eavesdropping through hedgerows, probably at Sotherton—an excellent example, as Chapman points out, of Jane Austen's 'realistic scruples.' Another would be the fact that nowhere in her books is there a conversation between men alone; having no firsthand knowledge of what might be said in these circumstances, she refused to write such a scene. In *Emma*, Mr Knightley repeats to the heroine certain things he has heard Mr Elton say when speaking in the company of men; but the conversation of men alone is reported only at secondhand in Jane Austen's novels.

Jane tells Cassandra that the nightly readings of *Pride and Prejudice* to Miss Benn have been less successful of late because Mrs Austen has been doing the honours: she reads too quickly, the novelist complains, 'and though she perfectly understands the characters herself, she cannot speak as they ought.' As a witness to so many family theatricals, Jane would have been a rigorous judge. Her mother's inept readings notwithstanding, she herself remained delighted with *Pride and Prejudice*. The famous statement which follows is so obviously ironic that one is astonished by the number of critics who over the years have insisted on taking it seriously:

> The work is rather too light, and bright, and sparkling; it wants shade; it wants to be stretched out here and there with a long chapter of sense, if it could be had; if not, of solemn specious nonsense, about something unconnected with the story; an essay on writing, a critique on Walter Scott, or the history of Buonaparté, or anything that would form a contrast, and bring the reader with increased delight to the playfulness and epigrammitism of the general style. I doubt your quite agreeing with me here. I know your starched notions.

Needless to say, Jane would not have changed a word if she could—and indeed did not do so in subsequent editions. The notion that she regretted any lack of seriousness in the novel is absurd; the phrase 'solemn specious nonsense' and the examples she offers of what the novel *might* have contained make this obvious. Her only genuine complaint concerns a printing error: two speeches inadvertently have been run together into one in the third volume. She also wonders if she has made a mistake in describing the evening meals at Longbourn as 'suppers': 'I suppose it was the remains of Mrs Bennet's old Meryton habits.'

There have been a number of visitors to Chawton, Jane tells

Cassandra—'all of whom my Mother was glad to see, & I very glad to escape'—including Miss Beckford. The novelist mentions a woman who, if she does not marry a particular man, will be considered by Jane 'a Maria' with 'no heart'—clearly a reference, notwithstanding the theories of Dr Chapman, which are a bit ingenious here, to the character of Maria in *Mansfield Park*. The novelist goes on to say that she is delighted with the praise both of Cassandra and of Fanny Knight (as we must now call her) for the printed version of *Pride and Prejudice*. Of Fanny, Jane writes: 'Her liking Darcy & Elizabeth is enough, she might hate all the others if she would.' Three of Edward's boys are dining at Chawton that day on the way down from Winchester. Jane gives Cassandra permission to let Anna in on the secret of her authorship: 'You know that I meant to do it as handsomely as I could.' The second Lady Williams 'has taken to her old tricks of ill-health again, & is sent for a couple of months among her friends. Perhaps she may make *them* sick.' The novelist takes a gratuitous crack at her old friends/enemies the Bigg Withers at Manydown, where Cassandra is about to go on a visit on her way back to Chawton. In 'the Breakfast parlour there,' Jane declares, 'one always sees . . . those enormous great stupid thick quarto volumes . . . Ladies who read those . . . must be acquainted with everything in the world. I detest a quarto.' Such ladies obviously are unable to 'understand a man who condenses his thought into an octavo.' Thus, for example, Pasley's book on the military police in the British Empire, which she enjoyed reading, must be 'too good for their Society' of readers. She pretends to have heard 'complaints . . . from all quarters' about the Manydown Book Society. Another evening's reading of *Pride and Prejudice*, she reports, is required for Miss Benn. She herself is hard at work on *Mansfield Park*.

Cassandra came home in February 1813, and the two sisters were not separated again until May, when Jane went to London. In mid-February the novelist wrote to Martha Lloyd, who was still away from Chawton. There has been a terrible storm, Jane reports, most of which her mother managed to sleep through. Edward's three Winchester sons are spending the night with them on their way back to school. Henry has written from London to say that Eliza is unwell, but they have had no further news of her. Frank and Mary have moved into yet another set of lodgings, this time in Deal: 'I think they must soon have lodged in every house' on the coast, the novelist declares. She thanks Martha for answering her 'enquiries' about

Northamptonshire—again, obviously, in connection with *Mansfield Park*, which is set in that county. The house itself, Sir Thomas Bertram's home, probably is based on Cottesbrooke in Northamptonshire—with whose owner, Sir James Langham, Henry Austen was acquainted. This would be compatible with the statement in the present letter—a statement which has puzzled some scholars—that Martha need not make further 'enquiries' since, Jane says, 'I am sure of getting the intelligence I want from Henry.' Having chosen Cottesbrooke (not Godmersham) as her Mansfield Park and Northamptonshire as her county, the novelist characteristically wished to make all other details of the novel topographically accurate. The letter ends with a reference to the scandalous affairs of the Prince Regent and his wife, the Princess of Wales. From 1806, when a government commission began to look into the conduct of the Princess, up to the present, various improprieties—mostly of a sexual nature—committed both by Caroline herself and by her husband, the future George IV, had been uncovered. In 1814 Princess Caroline left England and went to live in Italy, while the Regent dallied with his current mistress, Lady Oxford. Jane writes vehemently to Martha about the newspaper accounts, stimulated early in 1813 by Caroline's release to the press of a letter she had written to her husband, which he left unanswered, of the couple's carryings-on. The novelist declares that she supports the Princess rather than the Prince 'because she *is* a Woman, & because I hate her Husband.' But, Jane adds, she 'can hardly forgive her for calling herself "attached & affectionate" to a Man whom she must detest,' and for making a friend of Lady Oxford. She concludes that if she 'must give up the Princess' after all, 'I am resolved at least always to think that she would have been respectable, if the Prince had behaved only tolerably by her at first.' But George III's eldest son never 'behaved only tolerably.' As always, Jane Austen in her Hampshire cottage kept up her interest in the news of the nation.

IV

On 25 April 1813 Henry's wife Eliza, who had been ill for some time, died at the age of fifty-one; Madame la Comtesse de Feuillide, to whom 'Love and Freindship' had been dedicated, was no more. Soon after his wife's death Henry went down to Chawton to stay with his mother and sisters and be comforted, and when he returned to London on 20 May, via the Hog's Back, he took with him his favourite sister Jane. She found the views between Guildford and Esher especially beautiful: 'I hope somebody cares for these minutiae,' the novelist told her sister. From Sloane Street Jane wrote to Cassandra at Chawton. In consequence of her mourning, the novelist could not go to the theatre on this short trip (the last week of May), but she found other things to do in town—including helping Henry pack up the Sloane Street house and move to chambers over his bank at 10 Henrietta Street; the changeover to less commodious quarters was not completed until the autumn. Jane reports that while at Guildford she bought a pair of gloves for four shillings—'upon hearing which everybody at Chawton will be hoping and predicting that they cannot be good for anything'—and that the entire trip from Chawton Cottage to London, including stops for lunch and supper, the total distance being forty-nine miles (requiring one change of horses—at Bedfont), took just twelve hours. Martha Lloyd had inherited £1,250 from one of her many ailing friends, and mention of this is made in the letter. The house in Sloane Street is of course sombre, but 'the quietness does me good.' The novelist always preferred peace and quiet to noise and bustle. Attentive readers of her novels and letters have detected in them an interesting dialectic of silence versus clamour. Jane also describes an exhibition of water-colours she and Henry visited at Spring Gardens. One portrait reminded her of 'Mrs Bingley' (Jane Bennet), 'but there was no Mrs Darcy,' unfortunately. 'Mrs Bingley' was dressed in white and green, which the novelist thinks appropriate; had a likeness of Elizabeth been on display, undoubtedly she would be arrayed 'in Yellow.' Probably no portrait of Jane's special favourite is there because 'Mr D. prizes any Picture of her too much to like it . . . exposed to the public eye.—I can imagine he w^d have that sort of feeling—that mixture of Love, Pride, & Delicacy.' Obviously the characters of *Pride and Prejudice*, unlike those of *Sense and Sensibility* and *Northanger Abbey*, remained constantly in her thoughts; nor is there any mention of the persons of *Mansfield Park*, now nearing completion. During her last years members of the family, especially Fanny Knight, were fond of asking Aunt Jane how the people in *Pride and Prejudice*—but not the other books—were getting along, and occasionally the novelist would speculate on the present lives of the Darcys and Bingleys.

Henry and Jane also went to see some paintings by Reynolds at the Great Exhibition of the British Academy in Somerset Place, Pall

Mall. Henry, in the first of many such indiscretions, had divulged the secret of his sister's authorship to Miss Burdett, the sister of the famous Whig radical Sir Francis Burdett. Burdett had married a Miss Coutts, daughter of the equally famous banker; and Henry, as a banker himself, had got to know the family well. Jane tells Cassandra that she is 'rather frightened by hearing that [Miss Burdett] wishes to be introduced to *me*.—If I am a wild Beast, I cannot help it. It is not my own fault.' She was not at this stage pleased by the beginning of her fame; and as the secret of her authorship became less and less a secret in subsequent years, more audiences of this sort would be asked of her—and most of them refused. Henry, the novelist tells Cassandra, is taking his bereavement philosophically, and already looking forward to the time when he can accept invitations again. They plan to return to Chawton via Windsor, Henley, Reading, and Steventon, and Jane is pleased by the prospect of an interesting three-day journey—if not especially by the visit to Steventon. Meanwhile, she and her prosperous brother are taking pleasant drives around town in the warm spring weather: 'I could not but feel that I had naturally small right to be parading about London in a Barouche,' the novelist writes ruefully.

In July, back at Chawton, she completed the first draft of *Mansfield Park*, and between August and December 1813 she was chiefly involved in revising and polishing it for publication; the new book wasn't shown to Henry until the following March. Also in July Edward's family moved over to the Chawton Great House for an extended stay while Godmersham was being re-painted, and there was much visiting back and forth between the two households. Jane became even more intimate during this summer with her niece Fanny, now twenty, who undoubtedly was told something about the new novel. Fanny's diary for this period records some of their frequent meetings: 'Aunt Jane and I had a very interesting conversation'; 'Spent the evening with Aunt Jane'; 'Had leeches for headache. Aunt Jane came and sat with me.' During this summer the family also had to go into mourning for Thomas Leigh of Stoneleigh Abbey, who died at seventy-nine 'the possessor,' the novelist declared, 'of one of the finest Estates in England & of more worthless Nephews and Nieces than any other private Man in the United Kingdoms.' There was some good news: Henry was promoted from Deputy Receiver to Receiver-General for Oxfordshire, with an appropriate increase in income.

Frank, meanwhile, was on convoy duty in the Baltic off Sweden aboard the ship he commanded, the *Elephant*, and during this summer of 1813 Jane addressed an interesting letter to him. She envies him, she says, the opportunity of 'seeing something of a new Country, & one that has been so distinguished as Sweden.' His profession, she declares, must have its pleasures as well as its privations.

> Gustavus-Vasa, & Charles 12th, & Christina, & Linneus—do their ghosts rise up before you?—I have a great respect for former Sweden. So zealous as it was for Protestan[t]ism!—And I have always fancied it more like England than many countries;—& according to the Map, many of the names have a strong resemblance to the English.

Jane Austen always maintained a strong and sympathetic interest in the careers of her sailor-brothers—even, it appears, poring over the maps of their routes and destinations. Certainly she must have known more about Europe and its geography than many have supposed. Her reference to 'former Sweden' shows she was aware that Napoleon's Marshal Bernadotte had become Crown Prince of that country; in 1818 he would become its King Charles XIV.

The letter to Frank reports that Edward's son George, now eighteen, is in his last term at Winchester, and headed for Oxford. Henry is expected soon at the Cottage for a long visit while his new rooms in Henrietta Street are readied for him. He seems, Jane says, to be in a happy state of mind despite his loss:

> Upon the whole his Spirits are very much recovered.—If I may so express myself, his Mind is not a Mind for affliction. He is too Busy, too active, too sanguine.—Sincerely as he was attached to poor Eliza moreover, & excellently as he behaved to her, he was always so used to be away from her at times, that her Loss is not felt as that of many a beloved wife might be, especially when all the circumstances of her long and dreadful Illness are taken into the account. He very long knew that she must die, & it was indeed a release at last.

The Austens seem to have spent a good deal of time explaining away or justifying lack of feeling in one another. Perhaps Henry's emotional coldness was in part what attracted the novelist to him above all her other brothers—just as warm-hearted Edward, fearless Frank, and flamboyant Charles all (obviously) preferred Cassandra to

Jane. Charles's first three daughters were named Cassandra, Harriet, and Elizabeth (his wife's name, remember, was Fanny). It was not until 1825, when Jane had been safely dead for eight years, that he named a daughter (his fourth) after her. It is worth noting that Charles was not the only Austen brother loath to name a daughter after 'Aunt Jane.' Frank's girls were called Mary, Cassandra, Elizabeth, and Catherine. Edward named his daughters Fanny, Elizabeth, Marianne, Louisa, and Cassandra. Anna Austen Lefroy was christened Jane Anna. James did give her Jane's name, but the family never used it. The obvious conclusion is that some of Jane Austen's brothers, despite her strong attachment to them, did not feel so strongly attached to her. This may help illuminate for us, in a silent way, exactly how 'difficult' a character the novelist really was, and how uncongenial some of her brothers may have found her.

But to continue. Charles's daughters Cassandra and Harriet, the novelist informs Frank, stayed with them at the Cottage during the month of June. The elder of the two (Cassandra) was considered by her Aunt Jane to be spoiled and wilful; the novelist reports that she and her sister took the two girls in hand during their visit to Chawton. The two girls taken so severely in hand were all of five and three years old respectively at this time. The younger girl, Harriet, is said to be more 'sweet-tempered.' The five-year-old Cassandra ever afterwards dreaded visits to Chawton Cottage—so roughly, apparently, was she treated by her Aunt Jane. Charles and his family, Jane tells Frank, are now back at Southend. It is in this letter that she complacently mentions the marriage of her former suitor Mr Blackall to Miss Lewis. She goes on to declare proudly 'that every Copy of [*Sense and Sensibility*] is sold and that it has brought me £140 besides the Copyright' (Egerton would soon be recommending a second edition of the novel). With the £110 she received for *Pride and Prejudice*—the copyright, remember, was sold to Egerton—she has 'now therefore written myself into £250—which only makes me long for more.' Speaking of which: 'I have something in hand—which I hope on the credit of [*Pride and Prejudice*, which was being bought up at a prodigious rate] will sell well, tho' not half so entertaining.' It is interesting to note how little a favourite with Jane Austen this most controversial of her novels was from the start. She asks Frank's permission to use in her new book the name of his current ship and those of 'two or three other of your old Ships . . . I *have* done it, but it shall not stay, to make you angry.—They are only just mentioned.'

Frank was not angry; and so in *Mansfield Park* William Price, after escorting his sister Fanny to Portsmouth, is met with the news that his ship the *Elephant* is certain to cruise westward on its forthcoming voyage, and that it has been sighted lying in harbour between the *Endymion* and the *Cleopatra*. This is one of several ways in which Frank Austen's naval career wove its way into British literature. The letter closes in a typically irreverent strain: 'God bless you.—I hope you continue beautiful & brush your hair, but not all off.—We join in an infinity of Love.'

When, in mid-September, Henry ended his visit to Chawton and returned to London, he was accompanied on the journey by his sister Jane. She helped him settle into his new bachelor quarters in Henrietta Street, Covent Garden. From there she went on a rare—and, as it turned out, a last—visit to Edward's family at Godmersham. Here she stayed from late September to early November 1813, still working away at the manuscript of *Mansfield Park*—the later chapters of which impatiently describe, as we shall see, the effects on a neurasthenic nature of a household full of noisy children. During her seven-weeks' absence from Chawton, Jane wrote ten long letters—nine to Cassandra, one to Frank—after which, again, there is a gap in the correspondence (this time just five months, until March 1814).

Jane complains to Cassandra in her first letter from London (15 September 1813) that too many children sat inside the coach with her during the trip to London; she felt crowded. Henry has told Lady Robert Kerr up in Scotland about the authorship of *Pride and Prejudice* 'with as much satisfaction as if it were my wish.' He has also told Warren Hastings, and is sending him a copy of *Sense and Sensibility*. Hastings especially admired Elizabeth in *Pride and Prejudice*—which, the novelist declares, 'is particularly welcome to me.' Edward and Fanny are also in town, and they are all going to see Colman and Garrick's *The Clandestine Marriage* at Covent Garden. The previous night they saw *Don Juan*, 'whom we left in hell at half-past eleven.' They have also been to *Five Hours at Brighton*, by Samuel Beazley, and a musical farce attributed to Millingen, called *The Beehive*. She has been given £5 by 'kind, beautiful Edward.' And she has purchased a cap which, she thinks, resembles Harriet Byron's in *Sir Charles Grandison*. Buying a new gown, Jane noted a change in style: 'to my high amusement . . . the stays now are not made to force the bosom up at all; *that* was a very unbecoming, unnatural fashion. I was really glad to hear that [gowns] are not to be so much off the shoulders as they were.' She has had her hair curled: 'I thought it looked hideous, and longed for a snug cap instead, but my companions silenced me by their admiration.' The novelist reports that she has had 'no pain in my face' since she left Chawton—the first indication, perhaps, of the onset of serious illness. They were all disappointed at not seeing the poet Crabbe at Covent Garden—his wife was sick—when they went to see Kane O'Hara's *Midas*. Some of their circle preferred *Don Juan*, 'and I must say that I have seen nobody on the stage who has been a more interesting character than that compound of cruelty and lust.' Jane is using some of her newly acquired riches to buy material for gowns. She begs Cassandra to accept a portion of it from her as a present; there is no mention of any present for her mother.

The next day the novelist writes again. For once, to her delight, they are staying home in the evening. 'My Eyes are quite tired of Dust and Lamps.' She went out, however, to buy some caps, and they have been besieged by visitors: 'we were hard at it . . . we have not had a q^r of an hour to spare.'

Having gone back with Edward and Fanny to Godmersham for the beginning of a six-weeks' stay, Jane wrote again to Cassandra at Chawton. She repeats her request that her sister not refuse the present from her of a new gown: 'Remember . . . I am very rich.' There is some crowing here. Mary Lloyd Austen has committed another folly of one kind or other: 'How can Mrs J. Austen be so provokingly ill-judging?' She admits that her new wealth has made her 'less indifferent' to 'Elegancies . . . I am still a Cat if I see a Mouse.' She is with her niece Fanny a good deal at Godmersham, and they have become even more intimate (one gathers; this is not stated). The Knatchbulls have visited Godmersham, bringing with them the 'lovely Wadham,' their son—the late Mrs Knight's nephew. 'He seems a very harmless sort of young Man,' Jane writes, with 'nothing to like or dislike in him.' Of an acquaintance in the neighbourhood whom everyone seems to admire: 'I suppose he has quick feelings— but I dare say they will not kill him . . . I set him down as sensible rather than Brilliant—There is nobody Brilliant nowadays.' She quotes a line from James Beattie's *The Hermit* (Beattie was better known as the author of *The Minstrel*, 1771–4): '"'Tis night & the Landscape is lovely no more," but to make amends for that, our visit to the Tyldens is over.' While at the Tyldens she leafed through R.B.

Harraden's *Cantabrigia Depicta: A Series of Engravings* of the Cambridge colleges, a quarto published in 1809. The novelist complains again of facial pain. She is relieved not to have to go to Goodnestone Fair, which is 'likely to be a baddish' one this year; and when the others have gone off to it she appreciates the peace and quiet left behind. 'I am now alone in the Library, Mistress of all I survey,' Jane writes—a reference to Cowper's *Verses on Alexander Selkirk* (1782), which opens with the famous line, 'I am monarch of all I survey.' She and Fanny are reading together John Bigland's *Letters on the Modern History and Political Aspect of Europe* (1804), but finding it slow going. The news of her authorship seems to have reached Brighton, where a Dr Isham (godfather to one of Edward Cooper's children) has been heard to say that he is certain he will like her novel (*Pride and Prejudice*) much more than Fanny Burney's new work (*The Wanderer, or Female Difficulties*, announced for publication in five volumes in 1814). Jane concludes: 'I have this moment seen Mrs Driver driven up to the Kitchen Door. I cannot close with a grander circumstance or greater wit.'

Two days later the novelist wrote to Frank aboard the *Elephant*, responding to a letter recently received from him. Jane tells her brother it was well worth the two shillings and threepence it cost to receive: Frank gives 'so much real intelligence that it is enough to kill one.' Among other things Frank had written of the price of things in Sweden—'our cheapest Butcher's meat is double the price of theirs . . . nothing under 10^d,' the novelist declares—and of Mecklenburg, a fashionable watering-place ('How can people pretend to be fashionable or to bathe out of England!'). She adds, referring to the unusual luxury of her present surroundings: 'But I have no occasion to think of [such things] where I am now; let me shake off vulgar cares & conform to the happy Indifference of East Kent wealth.' Jane describes how every member of Edward's large family was conveyed back to Godmersham and compares it to 'the account of St Paul's shipwreck, when all are said by different means to reach the shore in safety.' She gives a brief account of the visit to London, declaring that *The Clandestine Marriage* was the only piece she really enjoyed: 'the rest were sing-song and trumpery . . . *I* wanted better acting.—There was no Actor worth naming. I beleive the Theatres are thought at a low ebb at present.' The novelist complains that Edward's eldest son (Edward Jr.) 'is no Enthusiast in the beauties of Nature' and seems interested only in field sports, though in other ways he has turned out well enough. He and his brother George—they were now nineteen and eighteen, respectively—go out every morning without fail to hunt or shoot. Jane never had anything good to say of field sports (or billiards, for that matter). There is no real news: 'In this House there is a constant succession of small events, somebody is always going or coming.' Enough 'bustle' for her, at any rate. She thinks little of Edward Bridges' wife: 'the sort of woman who gives me the idea of being determined never to be well' and who revels in illnesses due to 'the consequence they give her.' Jane recollects herself, and adds: 'This is an ill-natured sentiment to send all over the Baltic!' The gentleman had proposed marriage to her in 1808.

In giving her permission to use the names of his ships in her book, Frank must have sent along a warning that by doing so she would be running the risk of destroying her authorial anonymity—for Jane says here:

> I thank you very warmly for your kind consent to my application & the kind hint which followed it.—I was previously aware of what I sh^d be laying myself open to—but the truth is that the Secret has spread so far as to be scarcely the Shadow of a secret now—& that I beleive whenever the 3^d [book] appears, I shall not even attempt to tell Lies about it.—I shall try rather to make all the Money than all the Mystery I can of it.—People shall pay for their knowledge if I can make them.—Henry heard P. & P. warmly praised in Scotland by Lady Robt Kerr and another Lady;—& what does he do in the warmth of his Brotherly vanity & Love, but immediately tell them who wrote it! A Thing once set going in that way—one knows how it spreads!—and he, dear Creature, has set it going so much more than once. I know it is all done from affection & partiality—but at the same time, let me here again express to you & Mary my sense of the *superior* kindness which you have shewn on the occasion, in doing what I wished.—I am trying to harden myself. After all, what a trifle it is in all its Bearings, to the really important points of one's existence even in this World!

Among other things, this interesting passage shows us how truly desirous Jane Austen was of making money by her books—she liked praise, but she liked pewter, too—and of remaining at the same time out of the public eye. She was tired of a lifetime of pinching pennies and dependence on others, yet feared fame almost as much as she coveted financial security. Nevertheless, resentment of her many years of artistic obscurity is also plainly articulated here: 'People shall pay for their knowledge if I can make them.'

During the autumn of 1813 Anna Austen (James's daughter), now twenty, became engaged to a Mr Michael Terry. The engagement was not thought well of by the Austen family, and for various reasons it was soon broken off. Anna then engaged herself to Ben Lefroy, brother of the Rector of Ashe and son of the novelist's dead friend Anna Lefroy. This pleased the family better. In her letter to Frank, however, Jane expresses some reservations. Though Ben is 'sensible, certainly very religious, well connected & with some Independance,' there is, worries Anna's aunt, 'an unfortunate dissimularity of Taste between them . . . he hates company & she is very fond of it;—this, with some queerness of Temper on his side & much unsteadiness on hers, is untoward.' The 'unsteadiness' undoubtedly refers to the quick order in which Mr Terry was secured and dismissed and another found to fill his place. Though Jane was always fond of Anna, she remained a judgmental aunt. The novelist never became as intimate with the impetuous, excitable Anna as with the cooler Fanny Knight.

An interesting postscript concludes this letter to Frank. Jane adds: 'There is to be a 2^d Edition of S & S. Egerton advises it.' The second edition of *Sense and Sensibility* was published in November 1813—like the first edition of the novel at the author's expense, the advantage to her being a large share of the profits should there be any. In fact, to anticipate briefly, it sold extremely well, and Jane Austen's account books show that during 1814 Egerton paid over to her £350 as her share of the profits on the first edition of *Mansfield Park* and the second edition of *Sense and Sensibility*. There is no way of telling how much was paid for each item, since *Mansfield Park*, like *Sense and Sensibility*, was published at the author's expense—Egerton thought less well of it than its predecessors, and worried about its reception. He did not buy the copyright of *Mansfield Park*; indeed, the only one of Jane Austen's three novels offered him of which he did secure the copyright was *Pride and Prejudice*, which he must have seen at once was likely to succeed with the public. As we know, *Pride and Prejudice* went into three editions during the novelist's lifetime. Published in January 1813, the first edition was sold out in July. The second edition appeared quickly enough, since the book belonged to the publisher rather than the author—in November 1813, at the same time as the second edition of *Sense and Sensibility*. Having sold the copyright of *Pride and Prejudice*, Jane made no money from the reprints of her greatest novel, and in fact never earned more from it than the £110 Egerton paid for the copyright. Despite Egerton's misgivings, the first edition of *Mansfield Park* (May 1814; about 1,500 copies) was to sell out completely in six months. Over the question of a second edition of *Mansfield Park* in November 1814 the novelist was to leave Egerton and go to John Murray, who helped her make substantial earnings from *Emma*, the last of her books to appear during her lifetime, though he wound up losing a considerable amount on the second edition of *Mansfield Park*, which failed miserably in 1816. But we are getting ahead of ourselves. The point is that the eventful month of September 1813 ended for Jane on a highly hopeful note.

In October the novelist described for her sister a dinner-party at Godmersham, during which she sat next to a man who 'talked away at a great rate about nothing worth hearing.' An M.P. is coming to stay for a few days: 'If I can, I will get a frank from him & write to you all the sooner.' She now regrets having been so severe, in her letter to Frank, on the subject of the sporting habits of young Edward and George: 'they were both at the Sacrament yesterday. After having much praised or blamed anybody, one is generally sensible of something just the reverse soon afterwards.' The novelist is certain, now that she has written this, that the two young men, who are out hunting, 'will come home & disgust me again by some habit of Luxury or some proof of sporting Mania—unless I keep it off by prediction.' Field sports are used as a negative index in Jane Austen's fiction; as we have seen, she always disliked them—no less when they were thrust under her nose. She has finally managed to obtain a copy of Mary Brunton's *Self-Control*, a best-seller of 1810, '& my opinion is confirmed of its being an excellently-meant, elegantly-written Work, without anything of Nature or Probability in it.' The novelist declares she was 'exceedingly amused' by Cassandra's description of a woman who has the measles: it 'made me laugh heartily.' She has decided that she must someday have a heroine named Charlotte; the heroine of *Sanditon* would be called Charlotte. Cassandra apparently mentioned that she was reading Southey's just-published *Life of Nelson* (1813), for Jane replies: 'I am tired of Lives of Nelson, being that I never read any. I will read this however, if Frank is mentioned in

it.' She complains that Charles, now at Nore, has not visited, though
he keeps promising to do so, nor has Mary Austen (Frank's wife),
who is at Deal—though all of them are together in the same county: it
'seems unnatural—It will not last so for ever I trust.' She goes on: 'I
dined upon Goose yesterday which I hope will secure a good Sale of
my 2^d Edition.' Chapman cites *British Apollo* (1708), I, 74: 'pray tell
me whence/The Custom'd Proverb did commence, /That who eats
Goose on Michael's Day, /Shan't Money lack, his Debts to pay'; Old
Michaelmas Day was 11 October, the date of this letter. Presumably
the novelist refers here to the second edition of *Sense and Sensibility*,
in which she had a continuing financial interest, rather than that of
Pride and Prejudice, in which she did not. She and Fanny, Jane
reports, have developed a passion for 'Tomatas.' She complains of a
visit planned to begin so early 'that I [will not have] time to write as I
would wish'—further evidence that she was still hard at work on the
manuscript of *Mansfield Park*. She invites Cassandra to write again:
'Tell me your sweet little innocent ideas.' This mostly sneering, bad-
tempered letter shows that Jane Austen's moodiness had by no
means abated. Despite some literary success and the satisfaction of
beginning to earn an income, the sharp angularity of her personality
had not been smoothed.

Writing to Cassandra again in October 1813, the novelist declares
her purpose of composing a particularly long letter—this one is about
2,300 words, very long indeed—in case she can get it franked by the
visiting M.P., Mr Lushington, due soon to arrive. She has been on the
dreaded morning visit: 'I never saw so plain a family, five sisters so
very plain! . . . It was stupidish . . . there was a lack of Talk
altogether,' and some friends of the family they were visiting 'only sat
by & looked at us.' Edward Bridges has brought a friend to visit
Godmersham—the latter described by Jane as 'not agreable.—He
certainly is no addition.' They have managed, however, to get rid of
another visitor: 'I did not like *him* either. He talks too much & is
conceited—besides having a vulgarly shaped mouth.' Obviously she
was growing tired of Godmersham. A noticeable change is a reference
to the relief she feels at *not* having to attend a neighbourhood ball: '*I
was very glad to be spared the trouble of dressing & going & being
weary before it was half over.*' The novelist was two months away
from her thirty-eighth birthday, tired and crabby; the old youthful
enthusiasm for dancing had left her altogether.

There follows a celebrated comment: 'Only think of Mrs Holder's being dead!—Poor woman, she has done the only thing in the World she could possibly do, to make one cease to abuse her.' Jane Austen's cold-hearted nastiness had its periods of remission, but it seems always to have been there just beneath the surface, available to be dredged up at certain moments. She was certainly in a snappish mood now. Charles and his family have proposed a visit, she says, at the same time as another family with children: 'The two parties of Children is the chief Evil.' As we know, she was never very fond of children—especially young ones in large groups. The peace and quiet of Godmersham were being destroyed around her. Fanny Price, at Portsmouth in *Mansfield Park*, becomes neurasthenic, shrinking from the sounds of children's raised voices and slamming doors, and is quick to retire to her room with a headache when things are at their noisiest. The novelist was playing this very role now. Like her Fanny, she had come from a quiet, peaceful home to be plunged into a situation in which disorder, noise, and children reigned. No wonder Jane never went back to Godmersham after 1813.

A myth still prevails in some quarters that Jane Austen loved children. We have seen ample evidence to the contrary. Brigid Brophy is surely right to remind us that some of the novelist's 'funniest sarcasms are against babies' and to surmise that 'she held it against [them] that they were not rational. More bitterly still, she held it against mothers that they showed an irrational adoration of their babies.' Christopher Ricks observes that one might 'expect a very great novelist of family life' to have more to say about children than in fact she does, and notes that Jane Austen 'did not minister [in her novels] to the over-estimation of parental and filial love.' From the Juvenilia on we have noted what D.H. Lawrence called Jane Austen's 'apartness.' In her writings she obviously does not think it part of her enterprise, as Ricks says, 'to show what a dutiful and loving relation between adult and child' might be like—a striking omission, surely, in 'a very great novelist of family life.' Jane Austen's novels convey an impatient understanding of spoiled children and of their flatterers, but of little else when it comes to the very young. 'One does not care for girls until they are grown up,' she declared to her niece Anna in 1814. No wonder the Austen nieces and nephews often preferred Aunt Cassandra to Aunt Jane.

We have noted the absence in Jane Austen's novels of many sensible parents; the last books contain, as we shall see, a number of satisfactory *surrogate* parents but few if any admirable real ones.

Surrogate parents, she may have felt, were likely to be the best ones. One critic goes so far as to suggest that Jane Austen's fiction reflects 'her allegiance to childless adulthood.'

But to return to the autumn of 1813. Jane tells Cassandra that she had been looking forward to Charles's visit, but now it can give her little pleasure: it will 'make us such a motley set.' With no Mrs Edward Austen to supervise the enormous household, the domestic burden, of course, fell upon her and her niece Fanny; the novelist was never so well-equipped as Cassandra to deal with these matters. She grows positively abusive about another visitor in the house, who 'does no good to anybody.—I cannot imagine how a Man can have the impudence to come into a Family party for three Days, where he is quite a stranger, unless he knows himself to be agreable on undoubted authority.' Jane supposes that Charles probably 'will be as happy as he can with a cross Child or some such care pressing on him at the time.' She is certain that his difficult daughter Cassandra will 'disappoint me by some immediate disagreableness.' Cassandra was five.

In the beginning Jane Austen welcomed the advent of nieces and nephews; now they had grown too many for her. She anticipates the visit of the next group of them with fear and resentment. Fortunately, the novelist declares, the billiard table at Godmersham draws most of the gentlemen to it after dinner, 'so that my B^r [Edward,] Fanny & I have the Library to ourselves in delightful quiet.' More and more as time went by, 'quiet' was regarded by Jane Austen as an all too rare and increasingly valuable commodity. She goes on to complain that bread now costs two shillings and sixpence. And yet another visitor has come: 'very plain,' is the novelist's verdict. Charles and his family, she goes on to report, have just now arrived, and she is glad to see him—though he timed his coming very badly indeed, and 'It was quite an even^g of confusion.' Some of the superfluous visitors are beginning to take their leave, now that Charles and family have come: 'I shall be glad to have our numbers a little reduced.' She quite likes the M.P., Mr Lushington. This was Stephen Rumbold Lushington, who sat in the House of Commons for nearly thirty years as M.P. first for Rye and then for Canterbury. In later years he served as a privy councillor and became Governor of Madras. He was a year younger than the novelist. He speaks well, she tells Cassandra, and is fond of Milton. 'I am rather in love with him.—I dare say he is ambitious & Insincere.' This may appear

innocuous—unless one reads it to mean, not unreasonably, that the
men Jane Austen has been 'in love with' have had a tendency, as she
sees it, to give her up due to excessive ambition (the desire for
influential wives) or because they had never meant anything by their
attentions in the first place—about which she, trusting fool, was
taken in. Certainly, however read, it appears a bitter comment.
Charles's daughter Cassandra, Jane goes on, looks more and more
like her mother: 'I never knew a wife's family-features have such
undue influence.' This bad-tempered, angry letter ends on another
uncharitable note: 'Now I think I have written you a good sized
Letter & may deserve whatever I get in reply.' The novelist had had
enough of Godmersham, though her visit was scheduled to go on for
another three weeks.

The last of Jane's letters of 1813 (October and November) were
addressed to Cassandra in Henrietta Street, London, where she was
visiting Henry. The novelist says she is doing her best to 'extract . . .
Charles from his wife and children' so that he may have a little sport
while at Godmersham. Cassandra must have passed along a
complaint from Mrs Austen, for Jane says here: 'I suppose my mother
will like to have me write to her. I shall try at least.' But there is no
record of her having done so; she was not in the habit of writing to her
mother. Indeed, the collected edition of Jane Austen's letters does
not list a single letter to her mother written during the course of her
lifetime, though the two women were separated often enough and the
novelist wrote regularly to other members of the family—and to
Martha Lloyd. There are several possible explanations for this.
Perhaps she did write to her mother, and Mrs Austen discarded or
destroyed the letters. Perhaps, again, she did write, the letters were
kept, and Cassandra destroyed them all—certainly an interesting
circumstance in itself, if true. These possibilities strike one as
unlikely, however. Much more likely is that she did not write to her
mother at all. So far as we know—as much as modern scholarship has
been able to tell us—only something between seven and nine letters
written by the novelist (that is, absolutely known to exist at one
time) are missing, and thus unpublished. This means that even if Jane
Austen did address any letters to her mother, the number of them
must have been very small—and this over a lifetime. The novelist's
letters to other members of her family, as well as those to Martha
Lloyd, have in many cases been preserved; yet, to repeat, *not one*
letter to her mother has ever been found, or even listed in any source.

This may lend some credence to the hypothesis that Jane and her mother were not the best of friends. If she did write and Mrs Austen discarded the letters or Cassandra destroyed them, this reading of the relationship between mother and daughter is not materially damaged.

But to return to the novelist's correspondence with her sister in the autumn of 1813. Taking note of the death of the poet Crabbe's wife, Jane writes: 'I have only just been making out from one of his prefaces [that to *The Borough*, 1810] that he . . . was married. It is almost ridiculous . . . I will comfort *him* as well as I can, but I do not undertake to be good to her children. She had better not leave any.' Once again a startling heartlessness is betrayed here. She and Fanny and a few friends are going on a several days' expedition to Fredville and Wrotham to visit some nearby acquaintances. Jane tells Cassandra, somewhat petulantly, that she is 'not at all in a humour for writing; I must write on till I am.' Sir Brook Bridges has arrived at Godmersham with a friend for a visit; she likes the friend better. She plans to leave Godmersham on 13 November, stop briefly in Wrotham, spend some time in London with Henry, and proceed from there with Henry back to Chawton (possibly via Bookham for a short visit). She will be sending this letter by hand along with someone going the next day to Chawton: 'I *had* thought with delight of saving you the postage, but money is dirt.' Cassandra was counting on a visit to Adlestrop in Gloucestershire but had had to give up the idea; and Jane, hoping that her sister isn't too disappointed, misquotes the *Essay on Man*: ' "Whatever is, is best [right]." There has been one infallible Pope in the world.' A crabby reference to the seemingly continuous change in styles of women's clothing follows, ending with the novelist's declaration that 'I do not know and I do not care' about the subject. On Edward Bridges, her former suitor: 'I think the pleasantest part of his married life must be the dinners, and breakfasts, and luncheons, and billiards that he gets . . . at [Godmersham].' So much for him.

Jane gives her sister advice on how to enjoy herself in London: 'be sure to have something odd happen to you, see somebody that you do not expect, meet with some surprise or other . . . . Do something clever.' She has received, she reports, some bad news from Steventon. Anna's fiancé Ben Lefroy has turned down a 'highly eligible' curacy due to his reluctance to take orders. He says, the novelist remarks with some asperity, that 'he has not made up his mind as to taking orders so early, and that, if [James Austen] makes a point of it, he must give up Anna rather than do what he does not approve. He must be maddish. They are going on again at present as before—but it cannot last.' Anna was sent to Chawton to recover her senses. In the event, Ben Lefroy did take orders three years later, and he and Anna were married after all. What is significant here is Jane's impatience with the gentleman because of his indecision. 'Why on earth shouldn't he take orders?' her letter seems to ask: scruples be damned. The clergyman's daughter (and sister) was putting the finishing touches on *Mansfield Park*—a book about 'ordination,' according to her—during the period of this letter. Of course the subject was very much on her mind; and of course she sided with Edmund Bertram rather than Mary Crawford ('A clergyman is nothing') in the novel about to be completed.

Through Cassandra the novelist now conveyed an offer to the still unwell Henry to spend a longer time with him in London if he wished it; feeling better, Henry accompanied Jane back to Chawton during the third week of November, as planned. Edward, in his capacity as a magistrate, had recently visited a local gaol, and taken Jane with him. 'I was gratified—& went through all the feelings which People must go through—I think in visiting such a Building,' the novelist tells her sister. This is extremely perfunctory, and one cannot help wishing for more; but Jane Austen rarely lets her emotions poke through, and indeed the visit to the gaol may not have disturbed her in the least. The Clapham Sect was much interested in prison reform around this time; but she was no Wilberforce (and no Dickens). The weather, she goes on to remark, 'seems to improve. I wish my pen would too.' Surely this signifies more than a desire to write a clever letter to Cassandra; the novelist must have been experiencing some difficulty in completing *Mansfield Park*. Indeed, from the testimony of Edward's daughter Marianne (twelve in 1813), we may surmise that Jane worked on her book in the Godmersham library for several hours almost every day during this autumn.

The novelist tells her sister that she hopes to have Charles and Fanny at Chawton at Christmas, but she is not looking forward to seeing her troublesome little niece Cassandra: they must not, Jane writes hopefully, 'force poor [Cassandra] to stay if she hates it.' The second edition of *Sense and Sensibility* is being advertised now— which, the novelist declares, gives her great pleasure. The next day they are dining with Edward's friends the Wildmans at Chilham Castle (near Godmersham), staying there overnight, and going to a

concert the following day; Jane expects to find more amusement in
the concert than the visit. At Chilham they will meet the Harrisons,
connections of the Lefroys. Jane rehearses for Cassandra a speech she
supposedly plans to make to Mrs Harrison about Ben Lefroy: '"My
dear Mrs Harrison . . . I am afraid the young Man has some of your
Family Madness—& though there often appears to be something of
Madness in Anna too, I think she inherits more of it from her
mother's family [the Mathews] than from ours."' There follows a
patronising comment on Cassandra's letters to her: 'it is really a very
pretty hand now and then . . . . I wish I could get as much into a sheet
of paper.' She has had, she reports, a letter from her mother: Anna is
now at Chawton, and Ben is to visit her there—'an excellent time . . .
now that we, the formidables, are absent.' Just at the moment
Godmersham is blissfully empty, except for her: 'I have five Tables,
Eight & twenty Chairs & two fires all to myself.' As we know, the
novelist never liked to be cramped. Cassandra wrote that Henry's
trusted servant William had decided to retire and leave London,
which he disliked, for the country, which he missed. Jane responds:
'An inclination for the Country is a venial fault.—He has more of
Cowper than of Johnson in him, fonder of Tame Hares & Blank verse
than of the full tide of human Existence at Charing Cross.' Cowper is
full of hares (see notes); the reference to Johnson is taken from
Boswell's *Life* (2 April 1775). She hears, says Jane, that she herself is
'read & admired in Ireland too,' which obviously pleases her. She is
worried about the money Henry has had to advance for the second
edition of *Sense and Sensibility*; in the event, we know, the investment
turned out an excellent one. The novelist informs her sister that she
has met a woman who 'admires Crabbe as she ought.—She is at an age
of reason, ten years older than myself at least.' There follows a
poignant comment about her own age (she would be thirty-eight the
next month): 'as I must leave off being young, I find many Douceurs
in being a sort of Chaperon for I am put on the Sofa near the Fire &
can drink as much wine as I like.' She has cultivated an affection for
Lady Bridges, who was also of the party: 'I liked her, for being in a
hurry to have the Concert over & get away, & for getting away . . . with
a great deal of decision & promptness, not waiting to compliment &
dawdle & fuss.' This is not the first time Jane Austen waxed
impatient at a concert—one recalls how delighted she was at Bath not
to be able to hear any music from their lodgings—nor is her
admiration of a 'no-nonsense' sort of woman surprising. Undoubtedly

there was something of the Lady Bridges type both in her and her sister—'the formidables,' as she characterised Cassandra and herself. She liked Lady Bridges for finding 'me handsomer than she expected, so you see I am not so very bad as you might think.' But the novelist came back to Godmersham from Chilham very tired and wondering how she would get through a ball scheduled to take place a few days before her departure—a far cry from the Jane Austen of earlier years. She was interested now only in what sort of female company she might have 'on the Sofa near the Fire.' These last few letters show her ageing rapidly.

A copy of the second edition of *Sense and Sensibility* has arrived and 'stares me in the face . . . I cannot help hoping that *many* will feel themselves obliged to buy it,' Jane tells Cassandra. 'I shall not mind imagining it a disagreable Duty to them, so long as they do it.' As we know, Jane Austen had more interest in the fate of the second edition of *Sense and Sensibility*, in which she had a financial share, than in that of *Pride and Prejudice*, which Egerton brought out in the same month and about which the author, having no legal status of any kind, was not consulted. It is even possible that Jane never actually saw the second edition of *Pride and Prejudice*; she does not mention seeing it, and there would have been no reason—except a motive of charity or politeness—for Egerton to send her a copy.

'What news!' the novelist writes to Cassandra. Wellington had won the great battle of Vittoria, and the French wars appeared to have been victoriously concluded. On 4 November 1813 both Houses of Parliament declared England 'saved'; writing two days later, Jane Austen had already heard the news from London and was commenting on it in a letter. Again it is interesting to note, in the face of so much speculation to the contrary, how closely she followed current events of national interest. Of a lady the novelist has just met: 'she is altogether a perfect sort of Woman . . . going about with 4 Horses, & nicely dressed.' She snaps at Mr Gipps, whose handing her into a carriage was 'acceptable' only 'for want of a better Man.' Some acquaintances have called: 'They came & they sat & they went.' Jane is sorry to hear that Henry is still unwell but delighted that her nephews Edward and George have reached Oxford safely: about her own family her interest and solicitude, like those of most of us, were likely to be more unvarying.

The novelist left Godmersham at last, never to see it again, on 13 November 1813, and a week later arrived back at her beloved—and

quiet—Chawton. In the following month she turned thirty-eight—
and finally completed her revision of *Mansfield Park*. She rested from
her labours for only a few weeks. On 21 January 1814 she began
another novel, on which she was to work for the next fourteen
months—until 29 March 1815, to be exact. The new book was called
Emma.

V

Mansfield Park is Jane Austen's *Vanity Fair*. Almost everyone in it is
selfish—self-absorbed, self-indulgent, and vain. This helps make it
her most unpleasant novel—and, largely for this reason, her most
controversial. Critics have fallen all over themselves trying to
explain, justify, expound or attack its moral slant. Misreadings of the
book by otherwise sensible men and women are legion: *Mansfield
Park* 'continually and essentially holds up the vicious as admirable,'
says Kingsley Amis. Often we find critics complacently discussing
such things as the expulsion of wit and the scourging of irony in
Mansfield Park; it is frequently felt that Fanny Price is a failure, and
so the novel as a whole must be too. The book is supposed somehow
to be 'different'—not at all, really, Jane Austen's sort of thing, thus
requiring a good deal of explanation. This is nonsense. *Mansfield
Park* is very much of a piece with her other books, and in fact it is one
of the best of them. It is also one of her most autobiographical
volumes. No doubt because of its apparent complexity, more has
been written about it than any of the other works.

Like *Pride and Prejudice*, which preceded it into print by only a
year, *Mansfield Park* is largely about true and false values, right and
wrong ways of looking at things—how to live, in short. 'Selfishness
must always be forgiven you know, because there is no hope for a
cure,' declares Mary Crawford. In this, as in everything else she says
and does, Mary—as well as her brother Henry—is wrong. Like Becky
Sharp—and Milton's Satan—she is more lively and amusing than
many of her fellow players. But, as in Thackeray's novel—and
Milton's poem—the author's moral perspective on false values never
wavers. 'Miss Crawford, in spite of some amiable sensations, and
much personal kindness, had still been Miss Crawford, still shewn a
mind led astray and bewildered, without any suspicion of being so;
darkened, yet fancying itself light,' as the narrator remarks late in the
story; Edmund observes of Mary, ultimately, that she lacks 'the most
valuable knowledge we could any of us acquire—the knowledge of

ourselves.' 'Her mind was entirely self-engrossed,' says the narrator of Mary. It is indicative that when Fanny remarks to Mary that 'One cannot fix one's eyes on the commonest natural production without finding food for rambling fancy,' Mary should reply that she sees 'no wonder in . . . [nature] equal to seeing myself in it.' Henry Crawford, meanwhile, is described as subject to 'cold-blooded vanity'; 'entangled by his own vanity'; a victim of 'the temptation of immediate pleasure'; and 'unused to make any sacrifice to right.' Dr Grant's great fault, it is obvious, is lack of self-knowledge. Everyone at Mansfield is, to quote a well-known passage in the novel, 'shut up, or wholly occupied each with the person . . . dependant [sic] on them . . . for every thing.'

Of course vice is alluring: it is supposed to be. But we perceive Mary as odious throughout. She and her brother may be more interesting than Fanny Price and Edmund Bertram—more fun at a dinner-party—but we know that immorality can be more seductive and fascinating than virtue. And certainly it is easier often enough to mock propriety than attempt to understand it, as Stuart Tave, in what is perhaps the best essay on *Mansfield Park*, has said. He goes on to remind us that what the Crawfords really represent is 'liveliness without life'; they are foils to the less 'lively,' but more virtuous, protagonists. That virtue may be duller than vice need not require us to be vicious. Jane Austen hints at something like this in the final chapter of the novel: 'the public punishment of disgrace . . . is . . . not one of the barriers which society gives to virtue. In this world, the penalty is less equal than could be wished.'

Mansfield Park is not nearly as complicated a book as so many have thought. Fanny Price, looking on and listening, 'not unamused to observe the selfishness which, more or less disguised, seemed to govern them all, and wondering how it would end,' stands in for the novelist here. True, the light and bright and sparkling Elizabeth Bennet has gone away. Too much time has passed; the writer cannot possibly be the same person. Her view of things, inevitably, is different from what it was in the relatively cheerful 1790s. But Fanny Price is as much a part of Jane Austen's personality as Elizabeth Bennet; and it is this, perhaps, that many critics have not wanted to see or admit. A few have recognised that *Mansfield Park* is no 'sport' among the books. 'Can we doubt that [Fanny's] is Jane Austen's own position, that even when the self is alone and unsupported by human example of approval, it must still imperatively act in accordance with what is right, must still support what is valid in its moral inheritance?', Alistair M. Duckworth asks. For Jane Austen, as for Johnson, 'there can be no stability of life, no certainty of conduct, without principles of action,' Tave reminds us. It is always Fanny who sees what the others are up to when they themselves do not understand their own actions. It is she who has the strength of character here—dull or not. 'The novel . . . is designed to vindicate Fanny Price and the values for which she stands,' as Bernard J. Paris rightly says. Fanny's 'judgment may be quite . . . safely trusted,' Edmund declares. We needn't love her in order to see that her moral perspective is the most strictly focused one in *Mansfield Park*. 'If you are against me, I ought to distrust myself,' Edmund remarks to Fanny over the business of the theatricals. Indeed he should. Later he tells his father: 'Fanny is the only one who has judged rightly throughout, who has been consistent.'

Those who believe that 'there is no discernible irony hedging off what [the characters] say from what their author is apparently saying' are surely wrong. And because so many readers have felt this way, the point here about the consistency and clarity of the novel's moral slant must be all the more emphatically made. Nor is *Mansfield Park* in any way a falling off from the high standard set by preceding volumes. John Henry Newman, incidentally, is known to have read this book once a year 'to preserve his style.'

Let us consider the autobiographical resonances of a novel said so often to be uncharacteristic of its author.

Fanny Price has a sailor brother who, after some impatient delay, is promoted through family connections—and who, as we have seen, brings her a present of jewellery; Charles Austen is the obvious model here. Like Charles, William Price loves to dance. William tends to write long, chatty letters to Fanny; of course Frank and Charles wrote to Jane, but not as often as she'd have liked—so there may be some wish-fulfilment here. 'I cannot rate so very highly the love or good nature of a brother, who will not give himself the trouble of writing any thing worth reading, to his sisters, when they are separated,' Fanny declares. William is also more generous about distributing his prize-money to his relations than either of Jane Austen's sailor brothers ever was: the unspoken reproach may be inferred. Much is said in this book about the advantages 'for a lad who, before he was twenty, had gone through . . . bodily hardships and given . . . proofs of mind. The glory of heroism, of usefulness, of exertion, of endurance' is extolled in *Mansfield Park*. And there is, as we have seen, the use in the novel of the names of several of Frank Austen's ships. Mr Price's description, in Volume III, Chapter 7, of exactly how the *Thrush* lies in harbour at Spithead is so technical and nautically exact that we may be certain it was drafted for Jane Austen by her brother Frank, who was staying at Chawton when this section of *Mansfield Park* was written.

Between the sisters, Maria and Julia, there is sibling rivalry in love matters more spectacular than in any of the works we have previously encountered—with the possible exception of the youthful 'Three Sisters.' The love between siblings, *Mansfield Park* pointedly reminds us, which is 'sometimes almost every thing, is at others worse than nothing.'

Also we have one mother here, Lady Bertram, who is selfishly heartless, and uninterested in her children—and indeed in everything which does not directly concern herself; and another, Mrs Price, who virtually ignores a grown-up daughter. Can this be a coincidence? While there may be little of Mrs Austen in Lady Bertram, the fact remains that in refusing to 'go into public with her daughters' and being 'too indolent even to accept a mother's gratification in witnessing their success and enjoyment at the expense of any personal trouble,' Lady Bertram undoubtedly recapitulates the reclusive side of Mrs Austen, who became disinclined while still a healthy woman to leave home for any reason. Of Lady Bertram it is said: 'Every thing that a considerate parent *ought* to feel was advanced for her use; and every thing that an affectionate mother *must* feel in promoting her children's enjoyment, was attributed to her nature'—falsely, of course, for she feels nothing. The phrasing here is vivid, and possibly reflects an aspect of Jane Austen's view of her mother. Lady Bertram's 'playing at being frightened' in emergencies may represent Mrs Austen's lifelong hypochondria, which always annoyed her novelist-daughter. The mortification of Fanny at her mother's indifference to her is described by the novelist with equally striking vividness: 'She had probably alienated Love by the helplessness and fretfulness of a fearful temper, or been unreasonable in wanting a larger share than any one among so many could deserve.' The last part of this statement sounds distinctly personal; the Austens, like the Prices, were a large family, and, possibly, there was not enough time for a busy mother laden with household cares to tend to all the needs and desires of a younger daughter. Mrs Price's 'heart and her time

were . . . quite full; she had neither leisure nor affection to bestow on
Fanny. Her daughters never had been much to her. She was fond of
her sons . . . her time was given chiefly to her house and her servants.'
The Austens, remember, had six boys and two girls, and throughout
her early and middle years Mrs Austen would have been chiefly
concerned with household management. Nor can there be any doubt
that she doted on her sons. In *Mansfield Park* Fanny reflects bitterly
that her mother had 'no curiosity to know her better, no desire of her
friendship, and no inclination for her company.' Should we still fail to
get the point, the novel makes it plain for us: 'Mothers certainly have
not yet got quite the right way of managing their daughters . . . To be
neglected before one's time, must be very vexatious . . . [it is] entirely
the mother's fault.' Probably Jane Austen was 'neglected before [her]
time' by her mother; it goes far to explain her hostile nature as an
adolescent, her lifelong penchant for satire, and the number of silly
and insipid mothers who populate her books. We have seen other
instances of her impatience with and resentment of her mother; here,
these things are articulated in sublimated ways, but without much
artifice.

And it must be equally clear, though critics do not notice this, that
Fanny's aunt Norris is a highly unflattering likeness of Mrs Leigh
Perrot. Mrs Norris is a tight-fisted aunt who torments a saintly
niece—and steals. Of course Mrs Leigh Perrot was exonerated of the
shoplifting charge. But we have seen how angry the Austen women
were when, after George Austen died and during subsequent years,
the Leigh Perrots refused to help any member of the family except
the already comfortable James Austen. Since James Leigh Perrot was
Mrs Austen's brother, and since he was perceived as affectionate and
likeable, his wife was blamed by the Austens for parsimoniousness—
though, as we have seen, she was to be more generous to the Austen
family than her husband. That Mrs Norris is a malicious portrait of
the resented aunt of the Austens is obvious. Mrs Norris, on two
occasions, steals baize from Mansfield Park; eventually the whole
curtain bought for the theatrical is secreted away in her own house.
After the ball at Mansfield she makes off with 'all the supernumerary
jellies.' It has been said of Mrs Leigh Perrot that she 'had an invincible
propensity to theft' and that the Austen family knew it. True or
not—Mrs Leigh Perrot was never convicted of anything—a malicious
mind could easily link her with stealing things. Jane Austen must
have been thinking of her when she created Mrs Norris. As for Mrs

Norris's impoverished nieces in Portsmouth—Mrs Price's verdict on her sister undoubtedly reflects the feelings of Mrs Leigh Perrot's nieces at Bath, Southampton, and Chawton: 'Aunt Norris lives too far off, to think of such little people as you.'

Other aspects of autobiography are patent here. Into every one of her novels Jane Austen throws at least one ball, much in the manner in which Trollope was to introduce a fox-hunt into almost every book. Inevitably, what interests a writer will find its way into the fiction. Fanny's enjoyment of dancing may remind us of the novelist's years earlier. 'Such an evening of pleasure before her . . . she began to dress for it with much of the happy flutter which belongs to a ball.' Afterwards, creeping up to bed, Fanny is still 'feverish with hopes and fears, soup and negus, sore-footed and fatigued, restless and agitated, yet feeling, in spite of every thing, that a ball was indeed delightful.'

Like Jane Austen, Fanny becomes a subscriber to a circulating library—'amazed at being any thing *in propria persona*, amazed . . . to be a renter, a chuser of books!' Like the novelist, Fanny abhors 'improvements' made by gardeners and architects (it is indicative that Henry Crawford is said to be 'a capital improver') who tear up avenues of trees, remove walks, and fabricate ruins to recreate the 'natural' through a synthetic impression—an extension of a similar theme running through *Sense and Sensibility* and *Northanger Abbey*.

In this connection, *Mansfield Park* betrays further Jane Austen's love of nature, her dislike of urban life, and her growing neurasthenia and distaste for 'society.' 'We do not look in great cities for our best morality,' Edmund declares; it might be one of the novel's epigraphs. Even the quality of sunshine is said to be 'a totally different thing in a town and in the country.' In Portsmouth, 'its power was only . . . a stifling, sickly glare, serving to bring forward stains and dirt that might otherwise have slept. There was neither health nor gaiety in sun-shine in a town.' Fanny in Portsmouth—losing, as she observes, the glories of a garden in spring—sits 'in a blaze of oppressive heat, in a cloud of moving dust.' In the country it is a different matter altogether:

> Fanny spoke her feelings. 'Here's harmony!' said she, 'Here's repose! Here's what may leave all painting and all music behind, and what poetry can only attempt to describe. Here's what may tranquillize every care, and lift the heart to rapture! When I look out on such a night as this, I feel as if there could be neither

wickedness nor sorrow in the world; and there certainly would
be less of both if the sublimity of Nature were more attended
to, and people were carried more out of themselves by
contemplating such a scene.'

Thus Fanny at Mansfield. The emphasis here is on the tranquillising
of care; in the city, 'care' is stimulated rather than 'tranquillised.'
When Fanny returns home to Mansfield from Portsmouth, 'Her eye
fell every where on lawns and plantations of the freshest green; and
the trees, though not fully clothed, were in that delightful state, when
farther beauty is known to be at hand, and when, while much is
actually given to the sight, more yet remains for the imagination.'
Here is another indication that Jane Austen preferred nature
untouched by 'improvers,' who left little to the 'imagination.'

Fanny's love of nature is underscored by her hatred of noise and
disorder; and the Portsmouth chapters of *Mansfield Park* show the
novelist's neurasthenia growing by leaps and bounds—undoubtedly stimulated by her hatred of Godmersham, where we know she
spent nearly two months revising the novel. As her letters of the time
show, she grew impatient to be gone from that house, where a
continuous stream of visitors and an oversupply of children, as in the
Price household in Portsmouth, provided a constant uproar and
made life miserable for anyone who valued peace and quiet. In
Portsmouth the Price boys run around and slam doors until Fanny's
'temples ached'; she is said to be 'stunned' by the noise. 'The living in
incessant noise was to a frame and temper, delicate and nervous like
Fanny's, an evil which no superadded elegance or harmony could have
entirely atoned for. It was the greatest misery of all.' Here, certainly,
is the neurasthenic novelist at Godmersham, a place she never liked.
It is no accident that Fanny at Portsmouth, subjected to 'closeness
and noise . . . confinement, bad air, bad smells,' thinks of Cowper's
line, 'With what intense desire she wants her home' (*Tirocinium: or,
A Review of Schools*, 565). The 'ceaseless tumult of her present
abode,' where 'every body was noisy, every voice was loud,' where
'the doors were in constant banging, the stairs were never at rest,
nothing was done without a clatter, nobody sat still, and nobody
could command attention when they spoke,' must be Jane Austen at
Godmersham (or possibly in Ilchester), unheard and 'wanting her
home.' The account of the effects on a sensitive nature of noise and
chaos cannot be wholly invented. *Mansfield Park* gives us a

magnificent picture of the novelist's personality in her late thirties. In this way it may be seen as less a 'sport' among the novels than a most characteristic and revealing performance.

Other elements of autobiography should be mentioned. There may well be a carry-over of the traumatic Bigg Wither affair in the story of Fanny Price and Henry Crawford. Her abrupt refusal of him elicits from her family surprise and some resentment. Sir Thomas petulantly declares that 'The advantage or disadvantage of your family—of your parents—of your brothers and sisters—never seems to have held a moment's share in your thoughts'; and he refers to Fanny's behaviour in this crisis as 'a wild fit of folly, throwing away . . . such an opportunity of being settled in life, eligibly, honourably, nobly settled, as will, probably, never occur to you again.' Something like this may well have been said to the novelist by a member of her family when she turned down Harris Bigg Wither, seen by the Austens and their connections as a respectable, pleasant, prosperous man who, among other things, would have provided Jane with a large house in Hampshire and a comfortable income—at a time when she had nothing of her own, no means whatever of 'being settled in life.' Certainly we cannot know if her mother or sister or aunt or a brother or anyone else spoke to her in this vein. But it is abundantly clear, from evidence only recently come to light, that Cassandra tried to persuade Jane to alter the ending of *Mansfield Park* to allow Henry Crawford to marry Fanny Price. Apparently feeling that Fanny should indeed be well 'settled in life,' Cassandra argued the matter gamely; Jane stood firm and would not allow it. Probably Cassandra's influence is responsible for the assertion late in the novel, by way of mitigation, that if Crawford had 'been satisfied with the conquest of one amiable woman's affections,' and had he 'persevered,' Fanny must have given way to him eventually. In the event, Fanny of course is seen to be right in her resistance to Crawford. Her judgment never misleads her; 'for the purity of her intentions she could answer.' She understands 'how wretched, and how unpardonable, how hopeless and how wicked it was, to marry without affection.' The sorely tempted novelist may well have felt something like this during that awful, unforgettable night at Manydown, in the course of which she changed her mind about marriage. After all, as Fanny declares, a woman is not *required* to love a man, 'let him be ever so generally agreeable. Let him have all the perfections in the world . . . a man [need not] be acceptable to every woman he may happen to like himself'—which is as passionate a defence as we are likely to find anywhere of Jane Austen's rejections of the men who, during her lifetime, offered to marry her.

The marriage question is of course at the centre of *Mansfield Park*, as it is in the other books. 'There certainly are not so many men of large fortune in the world, as there are pretty women to deserve them,' the narrator complains in the novel's opening paragraph. And yet marriage as an institution is attacked here with special vehemence —perhaps in part for the very reason of the personal applications involved. Maria is said to be 'prepared for matrimony by an hatred of home, restraint, and tranquillity; by the misery of disappointed affection, and contempt of the man she was to marry.' Mary Crawford tells Mrs Grant that 'Every body is taken in . . . in marriage . . . it is, of all transactions, the one in which people expect most from others, and are least honest themselves . . . it is a manœuvring business.' Jane Austen undoubtedly felt 'taken in' by men on several occasions—early on by Tom Lefroy, perhaps; the mysterious clergyman who courted her in Devon may have escaped at the last moment through means other than death; both Edward Taylor and Edward Bridges seemed to be smitten with her, yet with astonishing rapidity found other ladies to love; and there was Harris Bigg Wither, who on one evening appeared to be someone she might like to marry, and by the next morning, after much reflection, turned out to be someone quite different.

None of this need diminish the role of marriage in giving a woman consequence. *Mansfield Park* provides a series of glimpses into the novelist's resentful perspective during the years leading up to her literary success and recognition. The most usual complaint is lack of personal consequence among others—which must have been especially galling to an intelligent and sensitive woman in her thirties who had had her chances to marry, after all, but had found marriage 'a manœuvring business' and had eschewed it, thus being required to accord precedence, as a matter of form, to married women, no matter who they were. One recalls Jane Austen's annoyance, during her 1808 visit to Godmersham, at having to give way in company to her married sister-in-law and old acquaintance Mary Lloyd Austen. We can see the novelist's distress and impatience in Fanny's feeling that she 'can never be important to any one'; in her inevitable knowledge, according to the narrator of *Mansfield Park*, of 'the pains of tyranny, of ridicule, of neglect,' and of often seeing her desires 'misunderstood' or 'disregarded, and her comprehension under-valued'; in Mrs Norris's declaration to Fanny that 'wherever you are, you must be the lowest and last'; in Fanny's being 'unused to have her pleasure consulted' on any matter; and in the description of her at one point as being 'dependent, helpless, friendless, neglected, forgotten.' In all of this there must be a touch of the novelist's own sensibility, though outwardly Fanny is not much like her author. But that word 'neglect' echoes and re-echoes through the book. And, as we have seen, Fanny's values are almost always Jane Austen's.

'To be in the centre of . . . a [family] circle, loved by . . . many . . . to feel affection without fear or restraint, to feel herself the equal of those who surrounded her, to be at peace'—these are the things Fanny cherishes, as the novelist surely did. Away from Chawton—in 'society,' among strangers—Jane could not be secure of them. 'A well-disposed young woman, who did not marry for love, was in general but the more attached to her own family,' *Mansfield Park* tells us. Outside the family circle she was more likely to lack 'consequence,' certainly; and 'To be neglected before one's time' is 'very vexatious,' as we know. Thus Fanny's sexual jealousy of all the acknowledged beauties in the novel; the sight of Mary Crawford fills her 'full of jealousy and agitation.' The 'necessity of self-denial and humility' and 'the advantages of early hardship and discipline,' of 'the consciousness of being born to struggle and endure'—a phrase later stolen by Charlotte Brontë for use in *Jane Eyre*, despite her avowed dislike of Jane Austen's work—are insisted upon instead. And it is precisely these qualities which Maria Bertram and Mary Crawford, so successful with men, conspicuously lack.

Another characteristic and recognisable touch here is the double vision we encounter on questions of security, comfort, and luxury. While it is better to have these things than not to have them, it is also seen to be ridiculous to measure all life, to tote people up, purely on the basis of wealth. The attack on materialism goes on, but it is tempered in *Mansfield Park* by some sober thought. 'A large income is the best recipé for happiness I ever heard of,' Mary declares. 'It is every body's duty to do as well for themselves as they can.' And: 'Varnish and gilding hide many stains.' Still, the moral price paid for personal comfort must not be too high; the price Mary pays is too high, and the result is loss of happiness. Jane Austen attacks the subversive side of Mary with special emphasis. 'A poor honourable is no catch,' she makes Mary say; and Fanny comments that Mary 'had only learnt to think nothing of consequence but money.' Mary's friend Mrs Fraser 'could not do otherwise than accept [her husband], for he was rich, and she had nothing.' This is marriage merely as a stepping-stone to luxury. 'Every thing is to be got with money,' says Miss Crawford: it is one of the bitterest comments in the novel. Almost everyone in *Mansfield Park* is rated by others on the basis of how much he or she has, or can get. Fanny alone seems immune to most of these influences: 'she likes to go her own way . . . she does not like to be dictated to . . . she certainly has a little spirit of secrecy, and independence.' As we know, the novelist fiercely protected her own independence—no doubt wistfully wishing at times that she didn't need to do so.

We may see something of the Austen sisters in the amusing account of the Owen sisters, about whom Mary comments: 'Their father is a clergyman and their brother is a clergyman, and they are all clergymen together.' And that familiarly malicious, heartless side of Jane Austen surely is in evidence when, after relating how little Lady Bertram has to write letters about until the near-fatal illness of her elder son, the novelist comments acidly that 'Lady Bertram's hour of good luck came' and that Tom's ordeal 'was of a nature to promise occupation for the pen for many days to come.' This is the novelist herself—the Jane Austen of the letters—speaking, and not Lady Bertram. William Price, ravenous for promotion, is portrayed as impatiently looking forward to the death of the officer immediately superior to him on the *Thrush*. And the novelist is certainly hard on poor Dr Grant at the end of the book. 'To complete the picture of good' facing Edmund and Fanny, the narrator comments, 'the acquisition of Mansfield living by the death of Dr Grant'—due to overeating—'occurred just after they had been married long enough to begin to want an increase in income.' There is no irony here.

Two most controversial aspects of *Mansfield Park*, traditionally, have been the theme of 'ordination,' which we have touched upon in passing, and the business of the theatricals—and 'acting' in general. In fact there need be little confusion about either of these matters. Jane Austen treats them here with clarity and precision, and in a highly characteristic way.

Though obviously the novel, in its final form, turned out not to be exclusively about 'ordination' after all, attitudes toward the church, both as an institution and as a profession, are indeed central to the story.

We should never forget that Jane Austen was the daughter of a clergyman, and the sister—as it turned out—of two others. She grew up in a household in which it was taken for granted that the profession of clergyman was an important and useful one—one which society could not do without, especially in times of moral laxness. She herself was always a believing Christian, though rarely an aggressive one.

One critic, arguing that the Christianity of *Mansfield Park* is ardent, sees Fanny as the very embodiment of Christianity itself. While it may be tempting for others—once again—to take the side of the vivacious and irreverent Miss Crawford, who makes fun of clergymen, against Edmund and Fanny, who are sometimes pompous and didactic on the subject of religion, one cannot for a moment suspect Jane Austen in *Mansfield Park* of any animus against the church. Mary Crawford's famous 'A clergyman is nothing' (in terms of social distinction, she means; Eliza de Feuillide is supposed to have said something of the sort to James Austen many years earlier, when he proposed marriage to her) touches off a debate in the novel on the merits of the profession.

Mary: 'A clergyman has nothing to do but to be slovenly and selfish—read the newspaper, watch the weather, and quarrel with his wife. His curate does all the work, and the business of his own life is to dine.'

Edmund: 'It is impossible that your own observation can have given you much knowledge of the clergy. You can have been personally acquainted with very few of a set of men you condemn so conclusively.'

Mary: 'I speak what appears to me the general opinion; and where an opinion is general, it is usually correct.'

Edmund: 'Where any body of educated men, of whatever denomination, are condemned indiscriminately, there must be a deficiency of information, or . . . of something else.'

Edmund rightly surmises that Mary has got her 'information' from the example and the dinner-table conversation of the worldly Dr Grant. Certainly the novelist has no defence for *his* sort of clergymen—or any pity either, as we have seen. But the novel does take up the cudgels for the profession. 'It is not in fine preaching only that a good clergyman will be useful in his parish and his neighbourhood,' Edmund declares. His 'private character' and 'general conduct' provide an example for his neighbours. It is for this reason that he himself plans to live in Thornton Lacey rather than permit a curate to 'do all the work.' 'Human nature needs more lessons than a weekly sermon can convey,' as Sir Thomas puts it. If the clergyman 'does not live among his parishioners and prove himself by constant attention their well-wisher and friend, he does very little either for their good or his own.' A man of social consequence himself, Sir Thomas is not blind to the importance of the profession, and encourages Edmund in his clerical career. The assertion of self-improvement when a clergyman does his proper duty is also taken up by Fanny, who makes a little speech on the subject:

> A man—a sensible man like Dr Grant, cannot be in the habit of teaching others their duty every week, cannot go to church twice every Sunday and preach such very good sermons in so good a manner as he does, without being the better for it himself. It must make him think, and I have no doubt that he oftener endeavours to restrain himself than he would if he had been any thing but a clergyman.

The question, then, turns not so much on 'ordination' as on attitudes toward the profession of clergyman. It is no surprise that the immoral characters in the novel have no use for the church, while the virtuous ones—dull or not—defend it, with Jane Austen's unwavering blessing.

While the question of the theatricals has been endlessly debated, it is a much simpler matter than many readers have thought. For Jane Austen there is inherently nothing wrong with putting on plays, or acting in them. We have seen that the novelist, from the time she was a young girl, loved the drama. Early on she relished the family theatricals at Steventon, and later the professional theatre in London. All her life she was a dedicated theatre-goer—sometimes attending the theatre every night when she was in the metropolis. As she makes Charles Musgrove declare in *Persuasion*, 'We all love a play.' The point here is that putting on theatricals at Mansfield Park is not in itself an evil thing. In this particular instance the occasion is used in selfish ways by several people; the situation of some of the principal characters simply makes it wrong to perform a play like *Lovers' Vows*. For these reasons, rather than for any generic ones, the theatricals can be condemned. That is to say, an activity which may be perfectly acceptable in life, may be used thematically in fiction for negative purposes. As Edmund says later of the time of the theatricals, 'we were all wrong together.'

There were at least four adaptations of Kotzbue's *Natural Son*, originally published in Germany in 1791. In England it appeared under the title of *Lovers' Vows*, and enjoyed a great vogue between 1798 and 1802. Interior evidence, as Chapman says, suggests that the characters in *Mansfield Park* are using the fifth edition of Mrs Inchbald's text of the play. *Lovers' Vows* was reprinted again and again; in 1799, for example, a twelfth edition was announced. Between 1798 and 1802 *Lovers' Vows* had successful runs at Covent Garden, Bath, the Haymarket, and Drury Lane. It was popular into the 1830s; Nathaniel Hawthorne saw a production of it in Salem, Massachusetts, in 1820. Between 1801 and 1805 it was performed six times at the Theatre Royal in Bath; since Jane Austen resided in Bath during these years, it is very likely indeed that she saw it there. The point is that the play's concern with adultery, elopement, and an abandoned wife and its attack on the conventions of contemporary marriage and its exaltation instead of feeling and impulse, render it spectacularly inappropriate to the characters in *Mansfield Park* as they are placed at the time rehearsals of *Lovers' Vows* are going forward. Clearly it is dangerous for Maria to play a fallen—or falling—woman, illicitly seduced. Rushworth is cast as a foolish suitor, Mary as a free-thinking 'modern' girl (Hazlitt remarked that the role of Amelia in this play was about as far as any contemporary actress was prepared to go; no wonder Edmund is horrified), and Yates as an advocate of elopement. Slated to portray a lovelorn clergyman, Edmund argues that 'the man who chooses the profession' of clergyman 'is, perhaps, one of the last who would wish to represent it on the stage'—especially when the character is presented unsympathetically. Surely a main ground of Jane Austen's disapproval is that the actors are playing exaggerated versions of themselves rather than really 'acting'—to which in fact she had no objection. In *Persuasion*, a fashionable evening party is pronounced invariably to be a less interesting and instructive experience than a night spent at the theatre, where—unlike real life—hypocrisy and insincerity are confined to the stage. Those who prefer parties to plays are that novel's most insipid characters. One might recall Jane's impatient declaration after seeing *The Clandestine Marriage* in London the previous year: '*I* wanted better acting.—There was no Actor worth naming.' Later in this same year, of another play in town, she would remark: 'Acting seldom satisfies me.' No other serious reason for her disapprobation of the theatricals can exist— except, perhaps, the alteration of the house in the absence of its master. Indeed, the theme of 'My father's house' is resonant.

Surely Fanny's private opinion of the goings-on once again is that of the novelist. Reading through the play, Fanny is astonished 'that it could be chosen in the present instance.' Its 'situation' and its 'language' are thought by her to be unfit for 'a private Theatre,' for 'home representation.' This is undoubtedly true; and anyone who reads both *Mansfield Park* and *Lovers' Vows* will immediately understand the grounds of objection. As a follower of the fortunes of the Prince Regent and his wife, Jane Austen knew of the extraordinary condition of manners and morals at the Saxon court and within the House of Brunswick in these days; inevitably she would have been suspicious of any play emanating from Germany. Needless to say, there is no blanket condemnation in *Mansfield Park* of the theatre or of acting. Indeed, the novel refers enthusiastically to 'a love of the theatre' and 'an itch for acting . . . among young people' as being 'general' and beyond reproach. It is only this play, in these circumstances, that is objectionable. Otherwise, it is clear, Edmund would feel differently. 'Nobody loves a play better than you do, or can have gone much farther to see one,' Julia reminds him. Tom Bertram 'can conceive no greater harm or danger to any of us in conversing in the elegant written language of some respectable author than in chattering in words of our own'—sentiments in which, quite clearly, the novelist would concur. Tom goes on to remind the family that Sir Thomas (like George Austen) has always been fond of promoting 'the exercise of talent in young people . . . for any thing of the acting, spouting, reciting kind . . . he has always a decided taste. I am sure he encouraged it in us as boys'—as, of course, Jane Austen's father encouraged such activities at Steventon. Indeed, the tradition of family readings in the evening persisted long after his death, as we have seen. It is indicative that Sir Thomas, upon his unexpected return to the house, does not condemn the theatricals outright, but merely inquires *which play* is being rehearsed; and that Fanny, so stunned by the choice of *Lovers' Vows*, always takes great pleasure in hearing 'good reading . . . To *good* reading . . . she had long been used'—like Marianne Dashwood in *Sense and Sensibility*. The fact that Henry Crawford reads skilfully and is also a villain hardly constitutes grounds for arguing that Jane Austen hated acting and actors. Being glib and articulate, Henry reads well. What is called into question by his suspect glibness—his capital acting, his good reading, his propensity for 'fine' preaching before fashionable London congregations—is his *professional* (clerical) commitment. Mary Crawford is a brilliant conversationalist, while Fanny is not; does this mean that the novelist preferred dull conversation to lively? We know she loved good conversation. We are supposed, as readers, to retain our moral judgment despite any number of provocations to waver. Certainly Jane Austen's perspective never wavers. One should see *Mansfield Park* not so much as a falling off from *Pride and Prejudice* as simply a book in a different vein. They are different works and tell different stories by different means. Neither is any more 'characteristic' of Jane Austen than the other: she is equally the author of both.

There is, finally, another botched ending here. Once again, in working out the novel's conclusion, Jane Austen uses summary rather than dramatic scene. Again she cannot bear, it seems, to show us her characters' happiness. That goes on offstage; her interest is chiefly in their struggles.

In *Mansfield Park*'s last chapter we have another noisy authorial intrusion into the story, another retreat into cold third-person summary, and a happy resolution glimpsed only from afar. 'Let other pens dwell on guilt and misery. I quit such odious subjects as soon as I can, impatient to restore every body, not greatly in fault themselves, to tolerable comfort, and to have done with all the rest.' It may be tempting to see this as irony—as, that is, another burlesque of the novel in less capable hands, this time the focus being the diet of poetic justice indiscriminately handed round at the end. But Jane Austen's 'impatience'—and 'impatient' clearly is the key word in the passage just quoted—to have done with her story, once she has got everybody where she wants them, shows up too often in her fiction to be so easily passed over. As in the other novels, she cannot bring herself to write a final love scene. Darcy and Elizabeth, Edward and Elinor, Henry and Catherine, all come to a final understanding out of our hearing. And so here: 'I . . . intreat every body to believe that exactly at the time when it was quite natural that it should be so, and not a week earlier, Edmund did cease to care about Miss Crawford, and became as anxious to marry Fanny, as Fanny herself could desire.' We have been waiting all through the novel for this to happen; when it finally does we are not allowed to see it, or Fanny's joy, at firsthand.

Somewhat self-consciously, Jane Austen offers a reason why she has written such an ending: 'Let no one presume to give the feelings of a young woman on receiving the assurance of that affection of which she has scarcely allowed herself to entertain a hope.' Why not? Is it because the novelist never played such a scene herself, or had these 'feelings'—and thus forbears to write about them? As we know, she always disliked trying to describe things of which she had no knowledge. Surely by now, at thirty-eight, she had realised that she would never play such a scene herself; perhaps, then, it was too painful for her to invent one.

The mood of *Mansfield Park* is more sombre than that of the first three novels—though *Sense and Sensibility* runs it a close race. Now middle-aged and disappointed, Jane Austen was finding it harder to be sunny. Her anger, for example, embraces Maria Bertram, who is not forgiven at the end of *Mansfield Park*, as Lydia Bennet was in *Pride and Prejudice* for a similar offence (Maria, of course, is much the guiltier of the two). The passage of time, the novelist tells us at the end of *Mansfield Park*, often undermines and revises 'the plans and decisions of mortals, for their own instruction, and their neighbours' entertainment.' No longer is detachment from the spectacle of life—seeing others as 'entertainment' for oneself—treated ironically, as it was in *Pride and Prejudice*. For Jane Austen, detachment had become less a peril to be avoided than a state of existence with which to become reconciled.

Fanny, when depressed, reflects that 'there is nothing like employment, active, indispensable employment, for relieving sorrow. Employment . . . may dispel melancholy.' And so Jane Austen found 'employment' in writing, and kept on writing to 'dispel melancholy.' Hers was indeed—the Austen family's memoirs notwithstanding— often a melancholy disposition.

VI

Throughout February 1814 at Chawton the novelist was making her beginning on *Emma*, which she continued to work on for the next thirteen months. In this month, Henry came to visit his mother and sisters; when he returned to London at the beginning of March, Jane went with him on a literary mission. During the journey to Henrietta Street, delayed by snowstorms and broken by an overnight stay at Cobham with breakfast at Kingston, Jane's brother and agent was introduced to her new tale. The novelist began to read *Mansfield Park* to him when they arrived at Bentley Green, just west of Farnham, and had got as far as the marriage of Mrs Rushworth before they reached London. From this point on Henry read the manuscript, brought along to be shown to Egerton, on his own; the general idea that Henry Austen never saw *Mansfield Park* until it was in proof is incorrect. While Henry was reading *Mansfield Park* with delight, Jane was thoroughly enjoying E.S. Barrett's *The Heroine, or, Adventures of a Fair Romance Reader* (1813), a burlesque of Mrs Radcliffe's fiction.

From London, Jane reported to Cassandra that 'Henry's approbation [of *Mansfield Park*] . . . is even equal to my wishes. He says it is very different from the other two, but does not appear to think it at all inferior.' 'Different' but not 'inferior' was a shrewd judgment of the new book. The novelist confesses to thinking the first half of *Mansfield Park* 'the most entertaining part.' Henry, she says, specially likes Mrs Norris and Lady Bertram as characters. And he admires Henry Crawford 'properly, as a clever, pleasant man'—not, she means, improperly: Henry was not for a moment taken in by him. A measure of Henry's 'understanding,' Jane says, is that he 'likes Fanny'.

By March 1814 Wellington had crossed the Spanish border and was working his way north toward Paris as the allied armies closed in on Napoleon from the east. Jane tells Cassandra that peace is expected in the English capital. Her new novel, meanwhile, was going well: she was working on *Emma* at a new table placed for her by Henry in the front room. After some trouble they managed to get tickets for *The Merchant of Venice*, with Kean as Shylock, at Drury Lane: 'There are no good places to be got at Drury Lane for the next fortnight.' Wyndham Knatchbull, Jane reports, has been invited to visit them: 'if he is cruel enough to consent, somebody must be contrived to meet him.' She probably had hopes in this direction for her niece Fanny, who would soon be in London; she wasn't far wrong. Knatchbull was the second son of Sir Edward Knatchbull, the eighth of that name; Fanny Knight eventually would become the second wife of Wyndham's more prosperous elder brother, the ninth baronet.

Jane makes an ill-natured reference to her least favourite niece Cassandra, Charles's daughter, who was visiting Chawton in her aunt's absence and sleeping in Jane's bed in the room the novelist shared with her sister. 'I hope,' says Jane Austen, that 'she [finds] my

Bed comfortable . . . and has not filled it with fleas.' Once earned, Jane's dislike was unyielding, even for a small child and near relation. That another Cassandra was sleeping in her bed and taking the place close to her sister inevitably did not improve the novelist's opinion of the unfortunate girl. Her attitude toward one of her most famous literary contemporaries, meanwhile, may be gauged from the well-known statement about his just-published poem: 'I have read the Corsair, mended my petticoat, & have nothing else to do' (5 March 1814). So much for Byron. Edward and Fanny had now arrived in Henrietta Street, and the four went to Drury Lane together. They enjoyed Kean. 'I cannot imagine better acting . . . it appeared to me as if there were no fault in him anywhere,' says the woman suspected of having written into the book about to go to press at that moment a general condemnation of the entire profession of acting. Jane complains that Kean's 'part was too short,' the other actors inferior, and the play itself 'heavy.'

At this time there was a national bereavement of sorts. Six weeks of mourning had been declared for the Queen's brother, the late Duke of Mecklenburg-Strelitz. The novelist responded by wearing brown, and trimming her dresses with black satin ribbon twisted into the shape of roses instead of the usual plain double plaits. 'Ribbon trimmings are all the fashion,' she informs Cassandra. She was now looking forward to her next publication, which her brother was just finishing. The happy author found he liked it 'better & better.' Now just short of the end, Jane reports, Henry defies 'anybody to say whether [Henry Crawford] would be reformed, or would forget Fanny in a fortnight.' She looks forward to the visit of Cassandra to London two weeks hence; Martha Lloyd would stay with their mother at Chawton. The novelist complains of a rise in the cost of tea. It has been snowing hard: 'What is to become of us?' They have tickets to see *The Devil to Pay*, a farce by Charles Coffey which greatly amused Jane, and an opera, *Artaxerxes*, at Covent Garden—probably in the version by Thomas Arne, whose English libretto was a translation of an old Italian text by Metastasio. Typically, the novelist found the opera 'very tiresome.' They have been urged to see Charles Dibdin's *The Farmer's Wife*, but 'I have had enough for the present'—perhaps another sign of flagging energies; still, they went.

Cassandra was to arrive in London for a short visit during the third week in March, and then their party would break up. Edward and Fanny would return to Godmersham, taking Henry with them for the Easter holidays. With Martha Lloyd continuing to stand guard at Chawton during April, Cassandra would visit the Leighs at Adlestrop, and Jane the Hills at Streatham—at this time a country village south of London. The novelist would be back home at Chawton in May, the month in which Egerton was now scheduled to bring out *Mansfield Park*. Clearly, Henry had acted for her with dispatch.

Writing to Cassandra for the last time before their reunion in London, Jane declares that they all disliked *The Farmer's Wife* ('a Musical thing in 3 Acts') and left before it was over—though she admits that she is not a reliable judge of singing. As for her mother having a cold, as Cassandra had reported—well, she has one too, probably worse. Let us see, the novelist writes, 'between us which can get rid of it first'—an apparently guileless statement, but a telling one when viewed in the context of the generally unfriendly feelings for her mother to which we have been witness. They have tickets, during Cassandra's visit to London, to see 'Young in Richard' at Covent Garden. She refers in this letter to her niece Cassandra as 'your little companion'—as if, that is, she herself and the little girl were not connected. Cassandra was bringing her niece to London with her. Charles Austen, whom Jane did not see on this visit, though it was several weeks long, was staying with his wife's family in Keppel Street. The little girl was to be delivered there 'immediately'—that is, without a stop in Henrietta Street—Jane Austen grimly proclaims.

And what of *Mansfield Park*? The novelist tells her sister that Henry's approbation did not lessen toward the end of the book. 'He found the last half of the last volume *extremely interesting*.' Perhaps she had been worried about the book's last section. Equally likely, since we know that Cassandra had suggested that Henry Crawford marry Fanny Price, is that Cassandra had criticised the ending as written—and that Jane was driving home the contrary opinion here, in italics. The letter ends with another unfriendly reference to her mother. Mrs Austen apparently had complained that Jane, before leaving for London, neglected to pay some grocery bills, for which the household at Chawton was now being dunned. The novelist declares that her mother had forgotten to give her the money to pay the bills—'and *my* funds will not supply enough.' Had the old lady decided that her successful novelist-daughter was now rich enough to take over the household expenses at Chawton, or at least share them? The italics again seem significant. Certainly, if the suggestion was ever made, Jane never agreed to it; her mother was still drawing a comfortable income from her sons, while her own fortune was closely tied to the sales of her books. Whatever the case, it is clear that their relationship remained an uneasy one.

Jane continued to move about southern England. After her visit to the Hills at Streatham in April, she returned to Chawton. Her literary career continued to flourish. *Mansfield Park: A Novel. In three volumes. By the Author of 'Sense and Sensibility', and 'Pride and Prejudice'* was published by Egerton in May 1814 at eighteen shillings —the same price as *Pride and Prejudice*, though *Mansfield Park* is longer by a quarter. It was announced in the *Morning Chronicle* on the 23rd and again on the 27th; in June a number of the novelist's friends and relations were already reading it. The first (badly printed) edition was 1,500 copies. John Murray afterwards 'expressed astonishment that so small an edition of such a novel should have been sent into the world.' It was sold out by November, though the book, astonishingly enough, did not receive so much as a single contemporary review, and seems to have made less of an impression on the reading public than *Pride and Prejudice*. While it is well known that Jane Austen was flattered and pleased by Scott's review of *Emma* in the *Quarterly* the following year, it is not well known that she was incensed by the omission in it of any mention of *Mansfield Park*. The novelist wrote in 1816 to John Murray, who was then her publisher: 'I cannot be but sorry that so clever a man as the Reviewer of *Emma* should consider [*Mansfield Park*] as unworthy of being noticed.' Still, *Mansfield Park* was widely, and for the most part favourably, read.

No doubt somewhat dubious of the success of a tale so different from its immediate predecessor, Egerton had offered, and Henry had advised Jane to accept, publication on the same terms as *Sense and Sensibility*—that is, on commission at the author's expense. The sale of the first edition satisfied everyone, though Jane was annoyed by the many printing errors. We do not know exactly how much *Mansfield Park* earned for her. But, as Mrs Hodge reminds us, when John Murray later on offered £450 for the combined copyrights of *Sense and Sensibility*, *Mansfield Park*, and *Emma*, he was told by Henry Austen that this was less than the total amount the novelist had made on *Mansfield Park* and the second edition of *Sense and Sensibility*. Henry may have been exaggerating, or mistaken; in the account of her literary earnings Jane Austen made not long before her death she put down the figure of £350 as the amount she had received to date on *Mansfield Park* and the second edition of *Sense and Sensibility*. We may look forward here to complete the early publishing history of Jane Austen's most controversial novel. When Egerton hesitated over a second edition of *Mansfield Park*, the novelist accepted Murray's offer to take the book over. Murray's records show that *Emma* and the second edition of *Mansfield Park*, both of which he brought out from Albemarle Street, were published at the author's expense, with ten percent commission going to the publisher. While *Emma*, as we shall see, made a profit, the second edition of *Mansfield Park* lost a little more than £182. Eventually, after the novelist's death, this second edition did clear nearly £119. In 1821 Murray remaindered his unsold copies of the book. Later, Cassandra and Henry sold the copyright of all the novels except *Pride and Prejudice* (owned by Egerton) to Richard Bentley for £250.

Perhaps because no critical attention whatsoever was paid to *Mansfield Park*, Jane set about methodically collecting opinions from her family and friends of her third published novel. These opinions have been preserved. While reactions varied more than they had for *Pride and Prejudice*, they were generally gratifying to the author. Most of the family—Cassandra, Mrs Austen, Frank, Charles, Edward's two eldest sons—preferred *Pride and Prejudice* to *Mansfield Park*, though many of them preferred *Mansfield Park* to *Sense and Sensibility*. Some readers—mostly outside the family—did place *Mansfield Park* first among the three books. Anna Austen liked *Mansfield Park* better than *Pride and Prejudice*, but preferred *Sense and Sensibility* to either. Martha Lloyd hated Mrs Norris. Mrs Austen, on the other hand, enjoyed Mrs Norris—but found Fanny 'insipid.' This could not have improved relations between mother and daughter.

Late in June 1814, while Cassandra went to London to stay with Henry, and Martha Lloyd again stood guard over Mrs Austen, Jane paid a fortnight's visit to the Cookes in the village of Bookham in Surrey. There is a Randall's Road, and a church with a monument in it to a certain Mr Knightley, in the nearby village of Leatherhead. Bookham itself is not far from Box Hill—where, three years later, Keats would finish *Endymion*; and it was strawberry time. Jane, remember, was hard at work on *Emma* now.

The novelist did not sit still. From mid-July to mid-August she was back at Chawton. In August, Henry, who was still Receiver-General for Oxfordshire, moved from his rooms in Henrietta Street to a house at 23 Hans Place, and his favourite sister came up to London, in a crowded public coach, to assist him. Jane stayed several weeks, and returned to Chawton early in September. The frequent separation of the sisters during this summer of 1814 gave rise to more correspondence between them. Also productive of letters written by Jane Austen during this period was her niece Anna's attempt at a novel, called 'Which Is the Heroine?', the first instalments of which were sent to Jane in March 1814. Anna, seeking advice and encouragement, continued to dispatch her work in segments to her novelist-aunt, who responded with long, detailed answers, and general advice about fiction-writing—especially interesting in light of the fact that much of the rest of this time was devoted by Jane Austen to the writing of one of her greatest novels.

'Which Is the Heroine?' was never finished. It was laid aside by Anna, and ultimately burned by her. In later years Anna Austen Lefroy remarked that after her aunt's death she could not bear to look at the manuscript.

Between the end of May and the end of September 1814—by which time the shocking news had arrived of the death, at Nore, of Charles Austen's wife Fanny after the birth of her fourth child; Charles's 'difficult' daughter Cassandra was packed off to stay with her aunts at Chawton—Jane Austen wrote letters to three correspondents: Anna, Cassandra, and Martha Lloyd.

In a letter to Anna, Jane suggests that characters in novels be neither too good nor too bad, and issues a warning about exactitude in dialogue. She also presses her niece for more 'scenes'—though she doesn't use this word—and less third-person description. Writing to Cassandra in London, the novelist reports that Fanny Knight, who was staying at Chawton with a party from Godmersham, had taken their mother out of the way for several hours, which has given her an opportunity to write. She could work with Cassandra in the room with her, but not her mother. The Cookes at Bookham admire *Mansfield Park* greatly—'especially the manner in which I treat the clergy.' She warns Cassandra not to be trampled in London. Peace was being celebrated, and the Russian Tsar and the Prussian King were in town with vast trains; the Prince Regent was being hissed everywhere by supporters of his wife, Princess Caroline. All of these things, the letter makes clear, were known to Jane Austen in her country village; as always, she kept up with current events. The novelist tells Cassandra that Mrs Austen's firewood has been delivered—but, through some error, no kindling: 'She must therefore buy some.' This seemingly gratuitous remark may suggest that arguments over financial responsibility for household expenses were still going on between mother and daughter. Jane has, she says, called upon two sisters in the neighbourhood, each of whom is certain she is the original of Fanny Price. Little sympathy is spared by the novelist for the Duke and Duchess of Rutland, whose son, the Marquess of Granby, had just died: 'I hope, if it please Heaven there should be another son, they will have better sponsors and less parade.'

In August, Jane wrote again to Anna about 'Which Is the Heroine?' 'Enthusiasm,' the novelist declares, would have been a better title; it may have been dropped because Madame de Genlis used it some years earlier. She corrects Anna on some details of names and places—showing, once again, how carefully she herself paid attention to such matters, and how important she thought it was to do so in fiction. 'There is no such Title as Desborough—either among the Dukes, Marquisses, Earls, Viscounts or Barons,' Jane Austen informs her niece; a peerage under the title of Desborough was created in 1905. Again there are minute factual corrections— 'They must be *two* days going from Dawlish to Bath; They are nearly 100 miles apart'—and, this time, more insistence on economy of expression. The novelist discusses the questions of who might and might not be introduced to whom among families in a small town and how such forms of introduction ought to take place. 'A Country Surgeon . . . would not be introduced to Men of . . . rank,' she remarks. Jane suggests omitting something which 'to those who are acquainted with [*Pride and Prejudice*] . . . will seem an Imitation.' And she concludes by advising Anna not to write about things she is not acquainted with at firsthand: 'you had better not leave England. Let the Portmans go to Ireland, but as you know nothing of the Manners there, you had better not go with them. You will be in danger of giving false representations. Stick to Bath. . . . There you will be quite at home.' As a writer of fiction, Jane Austen abhorred 'false representations': fiction should be as 'true' as possible.

In August 1814 the novelist was again in London, staying with Henry at his new house in Hans Place. She gives Cassandra an account of her journey to town in a public coach, which also contained several children: she was pleased to arrive and be picked up by 'a nice large cool dirty Hackney Coach.' She likes the house in Hans Place; it is comfortable, and its garden 'is quite a Love.' But the

journey tired her out, Jane admits. She hopes and suspects that
Henry will soon marry again. Early in September, still in London but
scheduled to return to Chawton the very next day, the novelist wrote
to Martha Lloyd, who was visiting friends in Bath while Cassandra
looked after Mrs Austen. Martha had just come into a small legacy—a
circumstance always interesting to Jane Austen: 'It gave me very
great pleasure to hear that your money was paid, it must have been a
circumstance to increase every enjoyment you can have had.' The
power of money to bring comfort and ease of mind—'to increase
every enjoyment'—was a subject close to the novelist's heart, as we
know. No doubt, Jane declares, the place is much changed: 'How
many alterations you must perceive in Bath! and how many People
and Things gone by, must be recurring to you!' She has had a quiet
but pleasant visit in London: 'two or three *very* little Dinner-parties
at home, some delightful drives in the Curricle, and quiet Tea-
drinkings.' There follows an interesting comment on contemporary
fashions in women's clothing:

> I am amused by the present style of female dress; the coloured
> petticoats with braces over the white Spencers [a close-fitting
> jacket or bodice] and enormous Bonnets upon the full stretch,
> are quite entertaining. It seems to me a more marked *change*
> than one has lately seen.—Long sleeves appear universal, even
> as *Dress*, the Waists short, and as far as I have been able to
> judge, the Bosom covered . . . Petticoats short, and generally,
> tho' not always, flounced.—The broad-straps belonging to the
> Gown or Boddice, which cross the front of the Waist, over
> white, have a very pretty effect I think.

Jane Austen had her eye on international affairs as well as fashions.
Henry and his friends, she tells Martha, think there will be another
war with America, which would be ruinous for England. An unusual
note of religious chauvinism creeps in here: 'If we *are* to be ruined, it
cannot be helped—but I place my hope of better things on a claim to
the protection of Heaven, as a Religious Nation, a Nation in spite of
much Evil improving in Religion, which I cannot beleive the
Americans to possess.' On a brighter note—she is to see Egerton
before she leaves town, and looks forward to getting an account of
the sales of her books. She has been to some exhibitions, and was
pleased to be able to view Benjamin West's painting of Christ's

rejection by the Elders—'the first representation of our Saviour which ever at all contented me.' But she misses the country; 'The language of London is flat.' As always, she tired quickly of city life. She reports the news that Mrs Charles Austen has just been delivered of a girl.

Back at Chawton, Jane resumed her correspondence with her niece Anna, telling her she had been 'much amused' and entertained by the latest instalment of 'Which Is the Heroine?' The novelist goes on to preach a sermon on the necessity of providing reasons for characters in fiction to do things, and on making them act in a consistent way. 'Nothing can be very *broad*,' Jane Austen declares; subtlety, care, and motivation are all required. There is more advice about who might visit whom and under what circumstances—though Jane also warns here against overburdening the reader with superfluous information: 'I hope when you have written a great deal more you will be equal to scratching out some of the past,' she says. The more Anna can 'curtail'—Henry James might have said 'foreshorten'—the better.

Obviously Jane was taking a genuine interest in the work of her niece; she sends detailed, specific criticism. Her letter to Anna contains one of her most well-known pronouncements:

> You are now collecting your People delightfully, getting them exactly into such a spot as is the delight of my life;—3 or 4 Families in a Country Village is the very thing to work on—& I hope you will write a great deal more, & make full use of them while they are so very favourably arranged. You are but *now* coming to the heart & beauty of your book; till the heroine grows up, the fun must be imperfect.

It hardly needs saying that Jane Austen's own novels do not always limit themselves to '3 or 4 Families in a Country Village,' though some have argued that they do. Certainly such situations as the one she describes here 'delighted' her as a reader and writer of novels. And this is the relatively uncomplicated subject she recommends the young and inexperienced girl to cut her teeth on as a novice teller of tales. Her own books go way beyond these modest boundaries, as every reader of them must know; this celebrated comment has to be considered in its context. The phrase 'till the heroine grows up, the fun must be imperfect,' is an interesting one. All of Jane Austen's novels, in one way or another, trace the development, chronological and moral, of their heroines, and clearly this too was one of the 'delights' of her writing life. Indeed, she goes on to declare in this same letter that 'One does not care for girls till they are grown up.' A sweeping statement; given what we know about Jane's attitudes toward children, it must be seen as a characteristic one, touching life as well as art.

The last two paragraphs of this letter were appended the following week, after news was received of the death of Jane Austen's sister-in-law. One languid sentence is devoted to the tragic and sudden death of Charles's young wife—referred to only as 'this sad Event.' The 'sad event' left Charles, now thirty-six, the widower-father of three young girls. Her mother, says Jane—and this is wholly in character—'does not seem the worse now for the shock.' And then the novelist goes immediately on to invite her niece to send more of her work whenever it may be ready—a cold-blooded performance, surely. One recalls that during her fortnight in London the previous month Jane did not see Charles or his wife, though they were staying nearby. Very likely some sort of coolness had developed between the novelist and her youngest brother—perhaps over her treatment of Charles's eldest daughter Cassandra. In the present instance, as when Edward's wife Elizabeth died years earlier, there is on record no offer by Jane Austen to go to the suddenly motherless family—though she did pay them a visit several months later—or of their asking her to come to them.

Throughout the autumn of 1814, Jane continued to read segments of 'Which Is the Heroine?' as they were presented to her, and to send advice to the young author. We find her emphasising, yet again, the central importance of making characters in fiction believable: 'a few hints' are often enough to do this, she says. Reference is made to 'a handsome, amiable, unexceptionable Young Man (such as do not abound in real Life) desperately in love.' There is playfulness here—but also, certainly, an undertone of bitterness and regret. It was a complaint Jane Austen made all of her life. She wishes Anna would not use the phrase '"vortex of Dissipation." I do not object to the Thing, but I cannot bear the expression;—it is such thorough novel slang—and so old, that I dare say Adam met with it in the first novel he opened.' Jane thinks Anna's story wants more incident—though she cautions against anything 'Improbable' or unsubtle. She approves, she says, of Anna's showing her work to Ben Lefroy, to whom she was now engaged. Apparently in reply to a query from Anna about *Waverley*, which had just been published anonymously and become the talk of the literary season, Jane Austen writes:

> Walter Scott has no business to write novels, especially good
> ones.—It is not fair.—He has Fame and Profit enough as a
> Poet, and should not be taking the bread out of other people's
> mouths.—I do not like him, & do not mean to like Waverley if I
> can help it—but fear I must . . . I have made up my mind to like
> no Novels really, but Miss Edgeworth's, Yours & my own.

She had guessed the authorship immediately. Despite the tongue-in-
cheek tone, clearly Jane Austen, no less interested in 'Fame and
Profit' than anyone else who has ever written novels, was miffed that
Scott had chosen to take the fiction-reading public by storm at the
same time that one of her own books had been published—at her own
expense, and on commission.

She concludes with news of some Chawton neighbours:

> The Webbs are really gone. When I saw the Waggons at the
> door, & thought of all the trouble they must have in moving, I
> began to reproach myself for not having liked them better—but
> since the Waggons have disappeared, my Conscience has been
> closed again—& I am excessively glad they are gone.

So much for the Webbs.

Anna continued to enjoy her engagement to Ben Lefroy. On
8 November 1814, now twenty-one, she married him from Steventon
Rectory. Though Chawton and Steventon were only sixteen miles
apart, the Austen ladies did not attend the wedding. At her new home
in Hendon, Anna Austen Lefroy continued to work on 'Which Is the
Heroine?' and send extracts to her aunt for comment and advice.

During this period of her life Jane Austen was very much on the go.
She visited Henry again in London later in November, calling on the
newlyweds in Hendon on the way. While in London she finally went
to see Charles and his girls, and conferred with Egerton. She returned
home early in December; saw her thirty-ninth birthday at Chawton;
and after Christmas, together with Cassandra, went off to visit her
friends Mrs Heathcote and Miss Bigg at Winchester, and James
Austen and his family at Steventon.

Fanny Knight, now also twenty-one, was at this time—November
1814—thinking seriously of engaging herself to a modest, pious,
humourless, scholarly, intelligent, kindly character by the name of
John Plumtre, the brother of a friend of hers. For a while Fanny
thought herself in love with Plumtre and worried that the gentleman

might not care for her. As the affair progressed, Fanny's doubts grew. In mid-November, however, Plumtre declared himself in love with her, and made a formal proposal. Immediately Fanny sent off an urgent appeal to her Aunt Jane expressing fears and reservations and asking for advice.

This was a busy time at Chawton, and the novelist obviously felt hemmed in. Frank and his wife were visiting; so was Edward. Charles's devastated father-in-law had come to fetch his grand-daughter Cassandra. Martha Lloyd was on her way back from Bath. *Emma* was nearing its end. The novelist was soon to go to London. Now, in addition, she had to assume the role of marriage counsellor to a motherless girl who—ominously—promised to take whatever advice she offered. 'You frighten me out of my wits' by making such assertions, Jane wrote to Fanny.

Despite the many distractions—her work on *Emma* not least of them—the novelist found time to offer counsel, even copiously, on the subject of marriage. This correspondence is especially interesting. Jane begins by declaring that she had to wait until Aunt Cassandra was out of the way—these communications were to be kept secret even from her. The novelist says plainly that Fanny cannot really be in love if Mr Plumtre does not stir deep feelings in her. She touches on the phenomenon we have come to know as mediated desire: 'What strange creatures we are!—It seems as if your being secure of him . . . had made you Indifferent,' Jane writes. 'How shall we account for it?' She goes on: 'Fanny, your mistake has been one that thousands of women fall into. He was the *first* young Man who attached himself to you. That was the charm, & most powerful it is.' Here, perhaps, speaks the voice of experience; no doubt she was recalling Tom Lefroy. If only, says Jane Austen, Fanny could direct herself back into love with Mr Plumtre—he seems in many ways so admirably suited to her. The novelist makes a revealing statement:

> There *are* such beings in the World perhaps, one in a Thousand, as the Creature You and I should think perfection, where Grace & Spirit are united to Worth, where Manners are equal to the Heart & Understanding, but such a person may not come in your way, or if he does, he may not be the eldest son of a Man of Fortune, the Brother of your particular friend, & belonging to your own County. Think of all this Fanny. Mr J.P. has advantages which do not often meet in one person.

Again the voice of experience speaks—for hadn't she herself been tempted, in almost identical circumstances, by the suit of Harris Bigg Wither? Fanny had complained that Plumtre was too retiring and quiet, and inclined toward Evangelicalism. Jane writes:

> His only fault indeed seems Modesty. If he were less modest, he would be more agreable, speak louder & look Impudenter;—and is it not a fine Character of which Modesty is the only defect? . . . And as to there being any objections . . . from the danger of his becoming . . . Evangelical, I cannot admit *that*. I am by no means convinced that we ought not all to be Evangelicals, & am at least persuaded that they who are so from Reason and Feeling, must be happiest & safest.

As she got older her religious views grew more conservative (January 1809: 'I do not like the Evangelicals'). The novelist goes on to advise Fanny not to worry too much about the gentleman's lack of wit: 'Wisdom is better than Wit, & in the long run will certainly have the laugh on her side.' Those who believe that *Pride and Prejudice* is somehow more characteristic of its author than *Mansfield Park* should be made to reread this passage.

By this time in her life Jane Austen had given a good deal of thought to the question of love—and been disappointed. The letter articulates her fear that her niece's fastidiousness might render her as lonely as her aunt had been. Having come down so decidedly on the side of safety and dullness, however, the novelist could not resist a parting shot which in effect explodes the argument she had been at such pains to construct. Fanny must under no circumstances accept John Plumtre, Jane declares, unless she really loves him: 'Anything is to be preferred or endured rather than marrying without Affection; and if his deficiencies of Manner . . . strike you more than all his good qualities . . . give him up at once.' The lady who had agonised over the offer of Harris Bigg Wither speaks again here. Should Fanny's lover be refused he will suffer for a while, but he will recover: 'it is no creed of mine . . . that such sort of Disappointments kill anybody.' Her own past suitors married elsewhere; she herself had suffered 'Disappointments,' and lived.

In the event, Fanny did give up John Plumtre, though she had lingering regrets for a number of years. In 1820, at age twenty-seven, she married Sir Edward Knatchbull—shortly after the gentleman inherited his title. In later years, Sir Edward would oppose Corn Law reform and Catholic emancipation. Given that cold, judgmental quality in Fanny—it was she who, in later years, described her aunts as somewhat common and not well-bred—one might consider that Mr Plumtre had a narrow escape.

Jane's letter to her niece was not entirely concerned with the problem of Fanny's future. The novelist comments too on letters she has received from Anna Lefroy. Since her marriage, Jane tells Fanny, Anna's communications 'have been very sensible & satisfactory, with no *parade* of happiness, which I liked them the better for.—I have often known young married Women write in a way I did not like, in that respect.' Let us have no *parade* of happiness, by all means.

Jane Austen's publishing career continued to keep her happily occupied. Henry has been urging her, she informs Fanny, to come to London and negotiate with Egerton the terms of the second edition of *Mansfield Park*. She cannot leave Chawton for some days owing to the various claims on her time and the presence of visitors, but she is not indifferent to the matter: 'I am very greedy & want to make the most of it.' Fanny need not concern herself with money matters; she herself hasn't that luxury. As we know, the novelist's desire to earn as much as she could from her books was always quite uncomplicated.

Writing to her other grown-up niece, Jane commands Anna to 'make everybody at Hendon admire Mansfield Park' in advance of her visit to the newlyweds. After leaving the Lefroys and going on to London, the novelist wrote from town that they had been to the theatre and seen *Isabella, or the Fatal Marriage*—Garrick's adaptation of Southerne's 1694 tragedy, *The Fatal Marriage, or the Innocent Adultery*. Jane Austen was disappointed: 'Acting seldom satisfies me. I took two Pocket handkerchiefs, but had very little occasion for either.' As we know, she admired good acting, and was an exacting critic. She is going, Jane reports, to visit Charles's little girls in Keppel Street. What she says next may tell us in part why her niece Cassandra often got on her nerves. When, while at Chawton, she heard of Anna's wedding, little Cassandra 'asked a thousand questions, in her usual way—What he said to you? & what you said to him?' Providing such answers obviously was not among Jane Austen's favourite activities.

Writing again to Fanny, this time about her visit to Anna and Ben, the novelist strikes an astonishing note:

I was rather sorry to hear that she *is* to have an Instrument; it seems throwing money away. They will wish the 24 [guineas] in the shape of Sheets & Towels six months hence;—and as to her playing, it never can be anything.—Her purple Pelisse rather surprised me.—I thought we had known all Paraphernalia of that sort. I do not mean to blame her, it looked very well & I dare say she wanted it. I suspect nothing worse than it's being got in secret, & not owned to anybody.—She is capable of that you know.—I received a very kind note from her yesterday, to ask me to come again & stay a night with them; I cannot do it, but I was pleased to find that she had the *power* of doing so right a thing. My going was to give them *both* Pleasure very properly.

What can we say of the woman who wrote this? It is patronising, condescending, and disloyal. It plainly shows the preference of the aunt for the cool, calculating, undemonstrative niece over the impulsive, warm-hearted, emotional one. But it also betrays heartlessness, priggishness, and above all mean-spiritedness—attacking as it does the few pleasures available to the newly married girl living with her husband's family in a place she had hardly seen before. It denigrates her taste and her talents—in the firm belief, obviously, that Anna's first cousin will be pleased to receive such declarations. And it was dispatched as the novelist was also sending friendly messages from London to Hendon. Here, perhaps, is the worst moment in Jane Austen's letters.

Having disposed of poor Anna, the novelist enters into another long discussion of Fanny's relations with John Plumtre—and comes down once and for all against the engagement.

When I consider how few young Men you have yet seen much of—how capable you are (yes, I do still think you *very* capable) of being really in love—and how full of temptation the next 6 or 7 years of your Life will probably be—(it is the very period of Life for the *strongest* attachments to be formed)—I cannot wish you with your present very cool feelings to devote yourself in honour to him. It is very true that you never may attach another Man, his equal altogether, but if that other Man has the power of attaching you *more*, he will be in your eyes the most perfect.

Again experience speaks here. The shadowy summer romance in Devon years earlier, so far as we know the strongest attachment of Jane Austen's life, occurred when she was in her mid-twenties—a time of one's life when, she tells Fanny, such things are most likely to happen to one. What she could not know was that Fanny's 'present very cool feelings' would be chronic rather than temporary.

Jane offers her niece another reason for not marrying Mr Plumtre—a more practical one. 'Years may pass, before he is Independant.—You like him well enough to marry, but not well enough to wait' (here is an early hint of a theme of *Persuasion*). Again the importance of material comfort is insisted upon. Above all, the novelist declares, 'nothing can be compared to the misery of being bound *without* Love . . . *That* is a Punishment which you do *not* deserve.' Here, at least, we can read her advice to a niece without wincing.

Jane goes on to speak of other things. She gives Fanny an account of her visit to Charles and his daughters. Harriet (aged four) sat in her lap, '& seemed as gentle and affectionate as ever, & as pretty.' Fanny (aged two) talks too much (!), but may be the loveliest of the three in time. 'That puss Cassy, did not shew more pleasure in seeing me than her Sisters, but I expected no better;—she does not shine in the tender feelings.' Jane Austen was quick enough to identify lack of tenderness when she thought she had found it in another—even a six-year-old niece who had no reason to be pleased to see her.

Jane concludes with some news of *Mansfield Park*. They are going that very day (30 November 1814) to see Egerton, she tells Fanny, to settle the question of a second edition. It is not as easy as it should be to make money from writing: 'People are more ready to borrow & praise, than to buy,' she complains. She adds: 'tho' I like praise as well as anybody, I like what Edward calls *Pewter* too.' In a sense, money is love. In the event, as we know, Egerton's hesitation over another edition of *Mansfield Park* was to drive Jane Austen into the waiting arms of the famous John Murray, the publisher of Byron among others.

During the last month of the year the novelist wrote several notes to Anna. She acknowledges receipt of the next instalment of 'Which Is the Heroine?', and remarks: 'I *do* think you get on very fast. I wish other people of my acquaintance could compose as rapidly.' Perhaps the unsatisfactory interview with Egerton had dampened her spirits and delayed the completion of *Emma*. As usual, she was having trouble with endings. Of an acquaintance recently married, Jane remarks: 'I have never seen it in the Papers. And one may as well be single, if the Wedding is not to be in print.' For a woman, not only to marry, but to be *known* to be married, is important. She is reading the just-published *Rosanne, or A Father's Labour*, by Laetitia Matilda Hawkins: 'very good and clever, but tedious.' The novel is sound on 'serious subjects' but deficient in humour and thus 'absurd' on 'lighter topics.' Apparently in reply to the information that one of Anna's acquaintances wishes her novels contained more incident, Jane Austen replies that she will write a book, in imitation of Mary Brunton's *Self-Control*, in which her heroine 'shall not merely be wafted down an American river in a boat by herself, she shall cross the Atlantic in the same way, & never stop till she reaches [Gravesend].'

The visit to London came to an end in January 1815, and Jane went off on visits to Winchester and Steventon. She was back at Chawton in March when, on the 10th, the newspapers announced an event which electrified Europe, and would have been especially unsettling to a family with two of its men in the Navy: Napoleon had escaped from his island exile, and landed in France. On the 23rd it was reported that Louis XVIII had fled Paris; war seemed imminent again. Six days later, on 29 March 1815, Jane Austen finished *Emma*.

VII

Written in fourteen months between January 1814 and March 1815, the new novel was completed more quickly than any of Jane Austen's previous books—though *Persuasion* would take her just twelve months to write. Negotiations over the publication of *Emma* as well as some other extracurricular matters, rather than any extended revision of the novel, were to prevent it from being published for another nine months. But there can be no doubt that *Emma* had reached its final form by the end of March 1815. It was announced in the *Morning Chronicle* for 21, 22, and 23 December 1815 as 'by the Author of *Pride and Prejudice*'; it was also mentioned in the *Observer* for 10 December as forthcoming. *Emma* did indeed appear in December 1815, though its title-page is dated 1816. The publisher, Murray—who would also bring out the second edition of *Mansfield Park* in 1816—printed 2,000 copies of *Emma*, and sold 1,250 within twelve months; still, no second edition of *Emma* was published until 1833. The price of the first edition was twenty-one shillings in boards. A few thousand words longer than *Mansfield Park*, *Emma* is Jane Austen's longest novel.

There are a good many autobiographical strains here—references to things in the author's own life—though *Emma* remains no more directly autobiographical than any of the other novels, despite the speculations of much modern criticism. Indeed, in being, like *Northanger Abbey*, the story of a woman led astray by her imagination, *Emma* is if anything perhaps less directly autobiographical than most of the other books. Still, a great many of *Emma*'s judgments and standards coincide with those of Jane Austen. Mudrick tells us that 'This time the author is in her novel and never out of it'—not an unjust assessment by any means.

Mrs Goddard's school—'a real, honest, old-fashioned Boarding-school, where a reasonable quantity of accomplishments were sold at a reasonable price, and where girls might be sent to be out of the way and to scramble themselves into a little education, without any danger of coming back prodigies'—bears some resemblance to the Abbey School at Reading, where Jane and Cassandra went as children. Like Mrs Latournelle, the easy-going Mrs Goddard takes a relaxed view of female education and imposes upon her students a highly elastic schedule. Surrey is the setting here, and Highbury, as we have seen, bears some resemblance to Bookham in Surrey, which Jane Austen knew well and had recently visited. The Austen family, like some of the characters in *Emma*, was fond of making up charades to stump each other; one of Jane's was composed on a banknote—and perhaps for this reason has survived:

> You may be on my first by the side of a stream,
> And my second compose to the nymph you adore,
> But if, when you've none of my whole, her esteem
> And affection diminish, think of her no more.

We know that Martha Lloyd's friend Mrs Stent may have sat for the portrait of Miss Bates. In October 1813, when Jane was staying at Godmersham and visiting acquaintances in Canterbury, the party called upon an elderly Mrs Miles and her unmarried daughter; the latter, Jane reported in a letter, a great talker, 'provided us with plenty to laugh at. She undertook *in three words* to give us the history of Mrs Scudamore's reconciliation, and then talked on about it for half an hour, using such odd expressions, and so foolishly minute, that I could hardly keep my countenance.' Here, obviously, is another candidate for Miss Bates. The description of Miss Bates given in the novel, incidentally—unlikely as it may seem—could also be a piece of wistful, ironic self-portraiture: 'Her youth had passed without distinction, and her middle of life was devoted to the care of a failing mother, and the endeavour to make a small income go as far as possible.'

Mr Weston, like Jane's brother Henry, 'had satisfied an active, cheerful mind and social temper by entering into the militia of his county.' Mrs Austen appears in various disguises in the novel. Mrs Churchill's hypochondria was probably suggested to the novelist by her mother's. *Emma* declares that hypochrondria can be justified in one way only: 'The event [Mrs Churchill's death] acquitted her of all the fancifulness and all the selfishness of imaginary complaints.' Mr Woodhouse, meanwhile, is probably a male version of Mrs Austen, though no one has noticed this before. Like Jane's mother, he hates to go anywhere; and his hypochrondriacal ways could well be a burlesque of those of Mrs Austen. He is said to suffer from 'habits of gentle selfishness.' Emma's deceased parent is described (by Mr Knightley) as having been 'the only person able to cope with her'—Emma, he means. Mr Woodhouse remembers his wife as being much more clever than he, with a better memory—which also neatly fits the role-reversal theory if we wish to see Jane Austen's parents as in some way models for Emma's. Mr Woodhouse is said to be 'no companion' for his daughter. 'He could not meet her in conversation, rational or playful.' Emma tells Mr Knightley that 'Nobody, who has not been in the interior of a family, can say what the difficulties of any individual of that family may be.' This, to say the least, is suggestive.

Again here we have the bad-parents theme. Mr Woodhouse is a spectacularly feeble parent. Mr Weston is a non-existent one: he has simply given his child away (to the Churchills). Similarly, the Bateses gave Jane Fairfax to the Campbells.

Emma Woodhouse lives in a place which 'afforded her no equals' and so suffers from 'intellectual solitude'; this must certainly have been true of Jane Austen. Indeed, Emma at home, surrounded by her usual companions and 'the quiet prosings of three . . . women,' finds that 'every evening so spent, was . . . long.' The novelist's restlessness is reflected in her protagonist's feeling that she is often 'doing more than she wished, and less than she ought,' and in her fear 'of falling in with the second and third rate of Highbury, who were calling . . . for ever.' Jane Fairfax's 'Oh! . . . the comfort of being sometimes alone!' is Jane Austen speaking in her own voice—very much in the vein of Fanny Price at Portsmouth. One of Emma's great bugbears, we are told, is 'a crowd in a little room.' Indeed, the neurasthenia theme, as so often before connected with children, is very much present here once again. Isabella's children at Hartfield, when 'variously dispersed and disposed of, produced a noise and confusion' said to be nerve-wracking. John Knightley's long speech in Volume I, Chapter 13 on the virtues of staying home and the discomforts and inconveniences of travelling even short distances, may reflect an increasing conviction of the novelist's as she grew older.

Emma's advice to Harriet on the subject of Robert Martin's proposal of marriage is identical with that given by Jane Austen to her niece Fanny in November and December 1814 in connection with the suit of John Plumtre. Emma tells Harriet: 'If a woman *doubts* as to whether she should accept a man or not, she certainly ought to refuse him. If she can hesitate as to "Yes," she ought to say "No" directly. It is not a state to be safely entered into with doubtful feelings, with half a heart.' As we know, Jane was speaking here, at least in part, from experience. Emma, who has a tendency to laugh at Mr Knightley's 'speeches' on the subject of her connection with Harriet, often finds she has to 'run away to indulge the inclination'— something the novelist did from time to time to avoid embarrassing others.

Jane and Cassandra surely had their ups and downs over the years, but when they were close the sisterly relationship must have resembled that described between Emma and Mrs Weston:

> there was not a creature in this world to whom she spoke with such unreserve; not any one, to whom she related with such conviction of being listened to and understood, of being always interesting and always intelligible, the little affairs, arrangements, perplexities and pleasures of her . . . [life]. She could tell nothing . . . in which Mrs Weston had not a lively concern; and half an hour's uninterrupted communication of all those little matters on which the daily happiness of private life depends, was one of the first gratifications of each.

Except for her sister, Jane Austen never had in real life the sort of friend she gives Emma here—someone to whom 'all those little matters on which the daily happiness of private life depends' could be communicated. 'Oh! the blessing of a female correspondent, when one is really interested in the absent!' The words are Frank Churchill's, the sentiments Jane Austen's—and her female correspondent, of course, her sister.

Again we have here the mandatory ball, with dancing described in loving terms. Like Jane Austen, Emma does some of her best thinking in the garden shrubbery. This heroine also loves nature, and hates 'improvements.' The book portrays as well the novelist's lifelong horror of governess-ing—and emphasises the importance of an income if an unmarried woman is to avoid this awful fate. Jane Fairfax actually suffers a physical collapse (in Volume III, Chapter 9) at the prospect of going out and becoming a governess. What is called in *Emma* the 'governess-trade'—as in 'slave-trade'—is said to demand retirement 'from all the pleasures of life, of rational intercourse, equal society, peace and hope,' and to substitute for these things 'penance and mortification for ever.' 'If you are for a genteel easy profession, bind yourself seven years as an apprentice to turn a cutler's wheel,' Goldsmith's *The Vicar of Wakefield* (1766) recommends, 'but avoid a school by any means.'

Money carries its usual significance. Having it or not makes the difference between the whole person and the maimed—a characteristic theme. Emma is struck by 'the contrast between Mrs Churchill's importance in the world, and Jane Fairfax's . . . one was every thing, the other nothing—and she sat musing on the difference of woman's destiny'—no doubt also a favourite theme of many of Jane Austen's reveries. About people in Jane Fairfax's position, the novelist has Emma quote *Romeo and Juliet* (V, i, 72): 'The world is not their friend, nor the world's law.' One additional (and familiar) reason is offered for avoiding at all costs the 'governess-trade.' 'If other children are at all like what I remember to have been myself,' Emma declares, no governess's salary could be sufficiently ample—yet another of the novelist's references to herself as a 'difficult' child, perhaps.

On questions of marriage and 'tenderness,' *Emma* strikes some recognisable notes. Mrs Weston's marriage, it is said, will make her 'secure of a comfortable provision.' On the other hand, as Emma declares—and here *Emma* restates a theme of *Mansfield Park*—'A woman is not to marry a man merely because she is asked, or because he is attached to her.' The novelist takes some pleasure in expanding on this theme: 'it is always incomprehensible to a man that a woman should ever refuse an offer of marriage. A man always imagines a woman to be ready for anybody who asks her.' Jane wasn't, and neither is Emma. In an apparently good-natured exchange with Mr Knightley, the heroine makes a bitter comment of the sort we might associate with the earlier novels, especially *Northanger Abbey*:

> till it appears that men are much more philosophic on the subject of beauty than they are generally supposed; till they do fall in love with well-informed minds instead of handsome faces, a girl, with such loveliness as Harriet, has a certainty of being admired and sought after, of having the power of choosing from among many. . . . I am very much mistaken if [men] in general would not think such beauty . . . the highest [claim] a woman could possess . . . I know that such a girl as Harriet is exactly what every man delights in—what at once bewitches his senses and satisfies his judgment. Oh! Harriet may pick and choose.

Emma's assessment of Harriet's qualities may be inflated, but the complaint is the same: men are not interested in 'well-informed minds'—only in things superficial. Jane Austen grumbles about this in book after book. It smacks both of disillusionment and special pleading.

Volume I, Chapter 10 takes up the marriage question directly when Harriet asks Emma why she has never married—'so charming as you are!' Emma replies that she 'must find other people charming—one other person at least,' before marrying. Indeed, she 'must see somebody very superior to any one I have seen yet, to be tempted.' Some undiluted autobiography, perhaps? At this stage in Emma's life she 'would rather not be tempted. I cannot really change for the better.' Marriage could only be a change for the worse. She adds: 'I have none of the usual inducements of women to marry. Were I to fall in love . . . it would be a different thing! but I have never been in love; it is not my way, or my nature. . . . And, without love, I am sure I should be a fool to change such a situation as mine.' Like Jane Austen herself in 1813–14, Emma no longer has any need of 'fortune,' 'employment,' or 'consequence,' as she says here. If any of this is even remotely autobiographical, we may be excused for thinking that Jane Austen might never have been in love—that it was not her 'way,' or in her 'nature,' as the passage above has it, to be in love with anyone. She may have been a woman incapable of love.

Harriet asks Emma if she is not afraid of being an old maid. The reply, which might have been different a few years earlier, is that a *poor* old maid may be an object of contempt according to contemporary perspectives, 'but a single woman, of good fortune, is always respectable.' This makes a nice companion-piece to the famous opening of *Pride and Prejudice*: fifteen years later, it is Jane Austen's declaration of independence. Feeling herself now a woman of consequence, she will not take a back seat to anyone simply because she is unmarried. Thus the fun made in *Emma*, at the expense primarily of Mrs Elton, of the question of precedence—the convention of married women having precedence at social gatherings over unmarried ones. The satire takes its point from the fact that the married woman in question here, Mrs Elton, for whom precedence is terribly important, is vulgar and insipid—while the unmarried woman, Emma, who according to the rules must come after Mrs Elton, is intelligent and cultured, if sometimes impercipient. It is one of the conventions of the time Jane Austen attacks with vehemence. 'Mine is an active, busy mind, with a great many independent resources,' Emma tells Harriet; she does not need a marriage to prop her up. The novelist always hated the convention of unmarried ladies being least and last, an attitude we have noted both in her private life and in her fiction.

Nor is Emma, in her unmarried state, without objects upon which to lavish affection; again Jane Austen's heroine speaks a passage of pure autobiography (one must change 'a sister' to 'brothers'):

> I shall be very well off, with all the children of a sister I love so much, to care about. There will be enough of them, in all probability, to supply every sort of sensation that declining life can need. There will be enough for every hope and every fear; and though my attachment to none can equal that of a parent, it suits my ideas of comfort better than what is warmer and blinder. My nephews and nieces!—I shall often have a niece with me.

'What is warmer and blinder' does not make Emma comfortable so much as what is more detached, more distant. If Emma is at all like her author, one may reasonably conclude that Jane Austen's maternal and amorous interests were tepid, at least in her thirties. Mr Knightley puts it bluntly (and accusingly) to Emma that 'There is safety in reserve, but no attraction.' Surely Jane Austen understood 'safety in reserve.' While liking Mr Weston, Emma finds herself put off by his 'open-heartedness'—an unusual ground of objection. At one point in *Emma* the heroine questions the advantages of what she calls 'tenderness of heart' and the 'warmth' of 'an affectionate, open manner.' As for 'tenderness of heart'—'I have it not,' she concludes. These things are again redolent of autobiography. Nonetheless, there is an autumnal tone of regret in the last view we are given of the happy Harriet, whom Emma finds herself envying for having 'created so steady and persevering an affection in . . . a man' (Robert Martin).

Throughout *Emma* the *tempers* of people (the word is used again and again)—Jane Fairfax, Harriet Smith, John Knightley, Frank Churchill, Mr Weston, and the others—are a preoccupation of the novelist. *Emma* is by far the most psychological of the novels, that book of Jane Austen's in which, more than anywhere else in her work, the human mind is so often caught in the process of thinking. It is possible that the novelist became more interested in her own 'temper' as time went on—equally so that she was consciously pushing her work into a more sophisticated realm. In *Emma* the dialogue brilliantly follows the associative processes of the thinking mind. This makes it one of the most 'scenic,' in Jamesian terms, of Jane Austen's novels, and may help to explain why it is such a favourite of modern readers. Surely Virginia Woolf was right to suggest that Jane Austen, had she lived another twenty years, would be considered now a foreruner of James and Proust. The wonderful scene in Volume III, Chapter 5 in which Mr Knightley watches the others play a game—he is 'so placed as to see them all; and it was his object to see as much as he could, with as little apparent observation'—reminds one of the famous scene in *The Golden Bowl* in which Maggie watches the others playing bridge, momentarily oblivious to her presence. Indeed, in having almost complete freedom of action, Emma resembles many of the heroines of James—her position leaving her free to act out her wilful errors, and take the consequences.

Whether or not for these reasons *Emma* is Jane Austen's greatest novel, as many have argued, is a moot point. By any definition it is a great book—psychologically deep, full of humour and suspense, beautifully written, and brilliantly plotted. Jane Austen's plots are often underrated. Here, on the surface at least, the story is simply that of a single year in a Surrey village; we do not go, in *Emma*, to London, Portsmouth, or Bath. Indeed, *Emma* is the only heroine who does not take even one overnight trip into new surroundings. Despite this relative lack of movement, *Emma* ranks with *Pride and Prejudice* as among the most skilfully plotted novels in English. We are kept guessing, while the three major movements of the novel—Emma's collisions with the Messrs. Elton, Churchill, and Knightley—continue to reveal the characters to us and Emma's character to herself. In showing us how to think, *Emma*, like Jane Austen's other great works, also shows us how to live, and in so doing it draws us in completely. As Julia Prewitt Brown has written, the great pleasure of reading *Emma* 'comes from our willing immersion in the everyday concerns and relationships of this world. . . . The novel's very self-absorption makes it . . . wonderful. It is a world that believes in itself entirely, and hypnotized, we too believe.'

This need not suggest that *Emma* is inferior to the other novels in wit or humour; one can sparkle and yet be deep. The first paragraph of Volume II, Chapter 4, may remind us both of the ironic opening of *Pride and Prejudice* and the caustic nature of some of the novelist's letters: 'Human nature is so well disposed towards those who are in interesting situations, that a young person, who either marries or dies, is sure of being kindly spoken of.' Mr Elton at one point finds himself surrounded by 'the woman he had just married, the woman he had wanted to marry, and the woman whom he had been expected to marry.' Mr Woodhouse worries about Emma's health while Mr Knightley is proposing to her in the garden: 'Could he have seen the heart, he would have cared very little for the lungs.' Some of the wit, as usual, borders on the malicious—such as Emma's famous jibe at the expense of Miss Bates during the expedition to Box Hill, and her uncharitable parody, in Volume II, Chapter 8, of that lady's usual mode of speech.

A major theme of *Emma* concerns the role of fancy—equated here with 'whims' and dreams; Emma is said to be 'a great dreamer'—in human affairs. Emma's over-active imagination is responsible for much of the muddling of personal relationships in the novel, which comes down heavily on the side of 'sense'—Mr Knightley's 'short, decided answers,' for example—over 'sensibility.' Emma's great fault, in the words of the novel, is that she will not allow in herself 'a subjection of the fancy to the understanding,' as she should, since 'fancy' is seen here as the enemy of 'understanding.' She is, unfortunately, 'an imaginist'—'creating' what she 'sees,' to cite the well-known phrase from Cowper's *The Task* (1784–5) quoted in *Emma* to describe the heroine's characteristic ratiocinative processes. Near the end of her last major work, *The Italian* (1797), Mrs Radcliffe wrote:

> what ardent imagination ever was contented to trust plain reasoning, or to the evidence of the senses? It may not willingly confine itself to the dull truths of this earth, but, eager to expand its faculties, to fill its capacity, and to experience its own peculiar delights, soars after new wonders into a world of its own!

The Italian ties overly developed imaginative faculties to the credulity and superstition that made possible both the Inquisition and popular acceptance of it. In the course of Jane Austen's story, Emma is asked to 'thoroughly understand her own heart' (again, *understanding* is emphasised) and to 'persuade herself' that in 'fancying' she had been 'acting to the contrary' of 'understanding'— that she has been, in fact, 'entirely under a delusion, totally ignorant,' subject to what are called here the 'errors of imagination.' Mrs Radcliffe felt that she could count on the 'fancy' of her readers—that their delight in flights of imagination would keep them turning her pages. As in *Northanger Abbey*, Jane Austen wishes to show what dangers may entrap that sort of sensibility which delights in 'romance'—whether in fiction, or in life. *Emma* is a powerful plea for the subjection of the imaginative faculties to the rational ones. Of all Jane Austen's novels, it is perhaps the most deeply rooted in eighteenth-century rationalism, though this is not the usual critical verdict.

The attack on romance lies alongside a passionate plea for clarity and openness in human affairs. Robert Martin is praised for always speaking 'to the purpose; open, straight forward, and very well judging'; Mr Knightley for doing 'nothing mysteriously.' Mr Knightley is said on several occasions to love an 'open temper'— which sometimes makes him impatient with Jane Fairfax, and causes him to dislike the shifty Frank Churchill from the first. 'Plain dealing [is] always best,' the novel declares. 'Suspense' about a person's motives is 'abhorred.' Frank is ultimately condemned for having 'none of that upright integrity, that strict adherence to truth and principle, that disdain of trick and littleness, which a man should display in every transaction of his life.' Was the novelist recalling the times she had been deceived or disappointed by devious men, and is Frank Churchill the manifestation of this? Perhaps. 'Seldom, very seldom,' the narrator comments sadly, 'does complete truth belong to any human disclosure; seldom can it happen that something is not a little disguised, or a little mistaken.' In the Fairfax-Churchill relationship, what is condemned is *intrigue*. 'Mystery; finesse—how they pervert the understanding!' declares Mr Knightley. He adds: 'does not every thing serve to prove more and more the beauty of truth and sincerity in all our dealings with each other?' It is one of the novel's paramount themes. 'Oh! if you knew how much I love every thing that is decided and open!' remarks the chastened Emma, at one time an arch-plotter herself. In the penultimate chapter she is relieved to find that 'The disguise, equivocation, mystery, so hateful to her to practise, might soon be over.' And so at the end she can 'look forward to giving [Mr Knightley] that full and perfect confidence which her disposition was most ready to welcome as a duty.'

Emma learns not only to subject fancy to understanding but also to prevent understanding from being diverted by mystery and finesse into the clandestine manipulation of others for selfish ends. These themes are closely related; surely they illuminate a major strand of the novelist's thought during these years—a carry-over, perhaps, from the attack in *Northanger Abbey* on 'spying' and lack of openness with one's neighbours. Emma's verdict in the Fairfax-Churchill affair—'What has it been but a system of hypocrisy and deceit,—espionage, and treachery?—To come among us with professions of openness and simplicity; and such a league in secret to judge us all!'—reminds us, as *Northanger Abbey* does, that 'spying,' 'espionage,' is both anti-social and immoral; and it underlines the belief that men and women must learn to live together openly and honestly. Whether the repetition of this interesting theme suggests paranoid tendencies in the novelist is a nice question: certainly Jane Austen, in her books at least, was concerned by and sensitive to the 'espionage' of others.

Though one of Jane Austen's most 'dramatic' novels, *Emma* suffers from a familiar defect: the retreat by the novelist at crucial moments from the 'scenic' mode into detached, third-person summary. Thus Mr Elton's proposal to Emma during the carriage-ride home from the Westons, which could have been a splendid dramatic moment, is described in a laconic third-person voice rather than rendered dramatically. Thus Emma's confession to Harriet of

her mistake in regard to the state of Mr Elton's affections is related by
the narrator rather than portrayed dramatically; a 'scene' is needed
here, yet all we get is high emotion viewed from a distance, as if it were
going on in another room. And Jane Austen retreats once again at the
single most important moment in the book: Mr Knightley's proposal
of marriage to Emma, and her acceptance of him. All we get is this:
'What did she say?—Just what she ought, of course. A lady always
does.' In this fashion the event towards which the whole novel
has been leading is disposed of. Again the writer avoids the
direct depiction of strong feelings; again the ending disappoints.
Emma later relates both to her father and Mrs Weston the story
of her betrothal to Mr Knightley, but in both instances the
same dreary technique is used: we are *told* what passed, but not
shown.

Yet again one feels compelled to ask—is this because Jane Austen
never played such scenes herself? Perhaps. There is at least one
uncharacteristic though amusing lapse from the factual in *Emma*
(Volume I, Chapter 18), and the novelist's brother Edward, who
knew about such things, caught it immediately. 'I should like to
know, Jane,' he asked his sister, 'where you get those apple trees of
yours that blossom in July?'

VIII

The year 1815 was one of Jane Austen's most fertile, creative periods.
She worked very hard—so hard in fact that between January and
August she had virtually no time for letter-writing; not one letter, at
any rate, survives from this period. She travelled little if at all during
these months. Indeed, her very immobility helps account for the
paucity of documentary information available for this time of her life.
We do know, however, that she completed the final draft of *Emma*
on 29 March 1815, and began *Persuasion* four months later—on
8 August, to be exact. She would take just a year to write this book, her
last completed novel.

Spring and summer 1815 was an interesting time in the outside
world too. Napoleon, having escaped from Elba, caused the powers
allied against him to raise three-quarters of a million troops to finish
him off once and for all. 'The occupants of the house on the busy
Southampton road must have been intensely aware of the build-up of
men and material in Flanders,' as Mrs Hodge suggests. Napoleon was

defeated at Waterloo in Belgium in June. By July he was on his way to his final exile at St Helena.

Frank Austen was at Chawton, but Charles was on duty in the Mediterranean, where Napoleon's brother-in-law Murat—who had taken the title King of Naples—was causing trouble to the Allies. Charles Austen was recalled to northern Europe for this last war against Napoleon. In May 1815, before leaving his station in Palermo, Charles wrote to his sister about her growing fame:

> Books became the subject of conversation, and I praised 'Waverley' highly, when a young man present observed that nothing had come out for years to be compared with 'Pride and Prejudice', 'Sense and Sensibility,' &c. As I am sure you must be anxious to know the name of the person of so much taste, I shall tell you it is Fox, a nephew of the late Charles James Fox . . . That you may not be too much elated at this morsel of praise, I shall add that he did not appear to like 'Mansfield Park', so well as the first two, in which, however, I believe he is singular.

This young fan of the novelist's was the son of Lord Holland, whose wife used to read Jane Austen's novels aloud to her husband when his gout was bad.

Closer to home, Anna and Ben Lefroy left Hendon for Hampshire and moved into an old farmhouse converted into a private dwelling and called Wyards. It was on the Basingstoke road just outside Alton, and within walking distance of Chawton. On 29 September 1815, when Jane Austen wrote to her now-pregnant niece in her new home, she must have been working away at the early chapters of *Persuasion*. She tells Anna that she would have visited her by now had not her (un-favourite) niece Cassandra preferred to go to the Alton Fair instead —and that doubtless some day Anna's child 'may revenge the insult' by preferring to see the Alton Fair rather than her cousin Cassandra. Jane also informs Anna that during the first week of October, Henry is expected at Chawton in order to conduct her to London for a visit.

On 4 October the novelist went up to London with her brother, primarily to conduct negotiations for the publication of *Emma* with John Murray. Egerton's decision in November 1814 not to reissue *Mansfield Park* had determined her to change publishers. The visit to Hans Place was to prove longer than she intended, however—for

Henry fell ill with an attack of bilious fever, and Jane stayed on to nurse him. She was to remain in London until December.

On 17 October she wrote a long letter to Cassandra. She describes Murray as 'a rogue of course, but a civil one.' He has offered £450 for *Emma*, Jane reports, but wants the copyrights of *Sense and Sensibility* and *Mansfield Park* thrown in as well. This means that Murray in fact was giving only about £150 for the copyright to *Emma*—much less than the novelist expected. 'It will end in my publishing for myself I daresay,' Jane tells Cassandra.

Murray liked *Emma*: 'He sends more praise . . . than I expected.' Murray's reader, William Gifford, editor of the *Quarterly Review*, had written to the publisher: 'Of *Emma* I have nothing but good to say. I was sure of the writer before you mentioned her.' He appended an interesting aside: 'I have for the first time looked into *Pride and Prejudice* and it is really a very pretty thing. No dark passages; no secret chambers; no wind-howlings in long galleries; no drops of blood upon a rusty dagger—things that should now be left to ladies' maids and sentimental washerwomen.' Gifford offered to help Jane Austen revise *Emma* and correct proofs of the novel—an offer which was summarily refused.

Henry Austen's response to Murray's offer for *Emma* has been preserved:

> Your official opinion of the merits of *Emma* is very valuable and satisfactory . . . the quantum of your commendation rather exceeds than falls short of the author's expectation and my own. The terms you offer are so very inferior to what we had expected that I am apprehensive of having made some great error in my arithmetical calculation . . . the sum offered by you for the copyright of *Sense and Sensibility*, *Mansfield Park*, and *Emma* is not equal to the money which my sister actually cleared by one very moderate edition of *Mansfield Park* . . . and a still smaller one of *Sense and Sensibility*.

As it turned out, Jane kept the copyrights of *Sense and Sensibility*, *Mansfield Park*, and *Emma*. *Emma* and the second edition of *Mansfield Park* were brought out by Murray at the novelist's expense, with a ten-percent commission going to the publisher. The results, as Mrs Hodge points out, might be said to justify Murray's caution:

The figures for 1816 show that *Emma* made a profit of £221 6s. 4d. (that is after deduction of the expenses of publication and the publisher's commission), but at about the same time the second edition of *Mansfield Park* made a loss of £182 8s. 3d. Logically enough, the loss on the second book was set against the profit on the first, and in her summary of her earnings Jane Austen refers to £38 18s. for the first profits of *Emma*.

By 1820 the posthumous edition of *Northanger Abbey and Persuasion* had cleared nearly £496, while *Emma* netted more than £372, and the second edition of *Mansfield Park* ultimately earned a profit of nearly £119. Murray remaindered them all in 1821. Jane Austen earned less than £700 from her books during her lifetime. As Mrs Hodge reminds us, Constable offered Scott £1,000 for *Marmion* (1808) sight unseen, and Longman offered Thomas Moore £3,000 for *Lalla Rookh* (1817) before the poet had written a line. Perhaps more to the point, Maria Edgeworth's novels usually earned her, on average, profits in the neighbourhood of £1,500–2,000 apiece.

During the negotiations with Murray, Henry Austen remained at home in Hans Place, suffering acutely from bilious fever. With her brother in bed, Jane found herself dining tête-à-tête one night with Mr Seymour, Henry's business agent. Jane calls this a 'comical consequence' of Henry's absence, and Chapman and others have speculated that Mr Seymour had at some time proposed marriage to the novelist; nothing else, alas, is known of this affair. Jane tells Cassandra only that she alternates between nursing Henry and 'working or writing' in a back room. And so some of *Persuasion* was composed piecemeal in Knightsbridge.

Henry's condition finally alarmed her enough to call in a well-respected physician from the corner (number 62) of Sloane Street: Charles Thomas Haden, aged just twenty-nine. Haden, who was to introduce English medicine to the stethoscope, happened to be friendly with several members of the Prince Regent's household, and one of the Prince's personal physicians was also called in as a consultant. To her astonishment, Haden informed Jane during one of his visits to Hans Place that the Prince was an admirer of her works, and kept a set of them in each of his residences. By now the 'secret' of her authorship must have been an open one in some circles—especially those within shouting distance of the loquacious Henry.

The novelist's meeting with the royal physicians at her brother's bedside was to have further consequences. But before any of them could occur, Henry's health took a decisive turn for the worse, and Jane became seriously alarmed. She summoned James and Cassandra from Hampshire and Edward and Fanny from Godmersham. She also wrote a 'preparatory letter' to the Leigh Perrots at Scarlets. During the last week of October 1815, as members of the family gathered at Hans Place, Henry Austen's life was in danger. Jane and Cassandra nursed him assiduously. Gradually he began to recover. Previous writers on Jane Austen have speculated that this onerous nursing chore undermined her own health; there is no evidence of this. On 30 October Jane wrote to her niece Caroline to let her know of Henry's improvement, and to acknowledge receipt of some stories Caroline had written (around this time, inevitably perhaps, Caroline's brother James Edward, now near the end of his time at Winchester, began a novel). Jane reminds Caroline that the birth of her half-sister Anna's child, named Jemima, has significantly altered her, Caroline's, status: 'Now that you are become an Aunt, you are a person of some consequence & must excite great Interest whatever you do. I have always maintained the importance of Aunts as much as possible.'

She was also corresponding with Murray. She asked him to call on her to discuss business, now that he had the manuscript of *Emma* in hand—and she thanked him for sending Henry a copy of Scott's *Field of Waterloo*. A few weeks later we find the novelist complaining to Murray about printers' delays—hardly justified, since he brought the book out less than three months after receiving the manuscript. The brief delay apparently was due to a shortage of paper occasioned by the recent conclusion of the European wars. We also find her asking him an astonishing question—something in the nature of a bombshell, actually: 'Is it likely that the printers will be influenced to greater dispatch and punctuality by knowing that the work is to be dedicated, by permission, to the Prince Regent?'

The dedication of *Emma* had come about in this way. Haden had informed his fellow physicians in the service of the Prince Regent, as well as the Prince's librarian and domestic chaplain, the Rev James Stanier Clarke, that he had met the author of *Pride and Prejudice*, and saw her regularly at the bedside of her brother. The future George IV was duly informed, and asked Clarke to call upon the novelist and show her every attention. Clarke came to see her in Hans Place, bearing an invitation. Would Jane like to see Carlton House, a royal residence? She would. The visit to Carlton House duly took place on 13 November 1815, Clarke escorting the novelist on a tour which, on the Prince's instructions, included the library and other apartments. During the visit to Carlton House, Clarke apparently told Jane that she was free to dedicate her next novel, or for that matter any future work, to the Prince Regent—should she wish to do so. 'Here,' as F.B. Pinion tells us, 'was a dilemma: Jane disapproved of the Prince Regent very strongly. . . . She had no intention of accepting the offer . . . until she was advised that the wish was tantamount to a command.'

Before the matter of the dedication was absolutely settled there was a brief tussle. Jane Austen, who had always considered Princess Caroline badly treated by her libertine husband, tried to wriggle off the hook. Two days after the visit to Carlton House she wrote to Clarke. Had she understood him correctly—did he mean to say that she was 'at liberty to dedicate any future work to HRH. the P.R. without the necessity of any solicitation on my part'—or had she perhaps misunderstood him altogether? She wanted 'to be quite certain of what was intended' and to know 'whether it is incumbent on me to shew my sense of the Honour, by inscribing the Work now in the Press, to H.R.H.' She wished, she said, to appear neither 'Presumptuous' nor 'Ungrateful.' She also desired to avoid 'the Honour.' But it was all too true: Clarke left her in no doubt as to her duty. It was not *'incumbent'* (his italics) on her to dedicate her forthcoming work to the Prince—'but if you wish to do the Regent that honour either now or at any future period, I am happy to send you that permission which need not require any more trouble or solicitation on your Part.' Here was the answer, plain and simple; and thus *Emma*, of all English novels, was dedicated to George IV, of all English monarchs, 'By His Royal Highness's Permission, Most Respectfully,' by 'His Royal Highness's Dutiful and Obedient Humble Servant, the Author'—Jane having been told by Murray what to say. The novelist arranged with her publisher to have royal presentation copies specially bound in scarlet with the Prince of Wales's feathers on the spine.

The rest of Clarke's letter (16 November 1815) must have convinced Jane that Mr Collins had come to life. He gives her much pompous praise, singling out *Mansfield Park* for special honours, and comments on her 'Genius' and her 'Principles': 'in every new work your mind seems to increase its energy and powers of discrimination.'

This being the case, he would venture to suggest a subject for her next novel. Why not write the life of an English clergyman, 'Fond of, & entirely engaged in Literature,' who divides 'his time between the metropolis & the Country'—there follows Mr Clarke's own itinerary for the next several weeks; in fact, why not write a book about himself? He would send her a volume of his sermons.

The novelist took a month to answer this bizarre letter. In the meantime she brought her sister up to date on various matters. Murray had lent her a number of books, and been most kind. Obviously she had grown attached to Haden: 'Tomorrow Mr Haden is to dine with us.—There's Happiness!—We really grow so fond of Mr Haden that I do not know what to expect.' She may have been 'expecting' something from Mr Haden—who, however, following the usual line pursued by Jane Austen's potential lovers, proceeded to marry another lady soon afterwards. She could give Cassandra good news of their brother: Henry was much better. Some female acquaintances have offered 'to drink tea with us tomorrow . . . here is an end of our extreme felicity in our Dinner-Guest [Haden].—I am heartily sorry they are coming! It will be an Even^g spoilt. . . . Another little Disappointment.' She is sending Cassandra £5 'for fear you should be distressed for little money.' This is an interesting turnaround; obviously the novelist was gaining some satisfaction from her new solvency. The printer's boys, she reports, are constantly bringing and returning proofs of *Emma*; she has seen most of the first and third volumes now, and a little of the second—the date was 24 November 1815. She and Haden have been discussing music: he believes that anyone non-musical 'is fit for every sort of Wickedness. I ventured to assert a little on the other side.' No doubt Haden's reference was to serious music; the novelist's response would have been very much in character.

Throughout the last week of November, Jane continued to read proofs of *Emma* and answer the printer's queries on the spot, which of course was conducive to rapid production. Her first inclination, she informed Cassandra, was *not* to dedicate *Emma* to the Prince Regent, but she had been 'obliged to do it.' Mr Haden has come to dinner again, bringing 'good Manners & clever conversation. . . . Mr H. dines here again tomorrow.' He is now reading *Mansfield Park*, she reports, and prefers it to *Pride and Prejudice*. Recently they have not been 'plagued' by visitors, but as it is 'a fine bright Sunday' she fears some will come. Obviously 'visitors' were no longer to the novelist's taste—except a favoured one or two. We may recall Emma's horror of 'visitors'—especially of the second- and third-rate variety. Jane says she plans to be back at Chawton during the third week of December. Henry continues to improve. 'We are glad the Mama's cold has not been worse'; Mrs Austen was having another of her little illnesses. Jane tells Cassandra that Henry has been considering an absence from town due to the impending failure of his banking business: by then the failure was seen as inevitable. Still, she remains cheerful—in part, perhaps, because Mr Haden has again come to dine: 'I need not say that our Even^g was agreable.' She takes some trouble to deal with a misapprehension of, and a suggestion of disapproval from, Cassandra. The favoured Mr Haden is not just an apothecary: 'he is a Haden, nothing but a Haden, a sort of wonderful nondescript creature on two legs, something between a Man & an Angel—but without the least spice of an Apothecary.—He is perhaps the only Person *not* an Apothecary hereabouts.' This sounds like a woman in love. She must have known that the younger man would find a younger wife; and perhaps the bitterness of the early chapters of *Persuasion*, then being written at Hans Place, take their tone in part from the novelist's certainty—in Anne Elliot, who is in her twenties, it is no more than a fear—that time has passed her by, the bloom of youth being too far gone ever again to attract a man. Now approaching her fortieth birthday, Jane Austen was ten years older than Haden. In any case, she admired him, and was quick to let her sister know that here was no ordinary tradesman—as surgeons in those days were classed. Haden at the time was physician to the Brompton Dispensary, a signal honour for so young a man.

A disquisition on the uselessness of music-masters follows. Largely self-taught, and lowbrow in her musical taste, Jane Austen had little use for professional teachers of music.

Cassandra had written that their mother disliked the unseasonably warm weather; Jane's response is entirely in character.

> I am sorry my Mother has been suffering, & am afraid this exquisite weather is too good to agree with her.—*I* enjoy it all over me, from top to toe, from right to left, Longitudinally, Perpendicularly, Diagonally;—& I cannot but selfishly hope we are to have it last till Christmas;—nice, unwholesome, Unseasonable, relaxing, close, muggy weather!

The novelist seems to be revelling here in the very weather which is making her mother ill. Certainly she herself does not write like a woman indisposed in any way—and this just seventeen months before her death.

Henry, she reports, now has to go to his office every day to sign papers—apparently in preparation for the impending bankruptcy. 'By Manœvring & good luck' they 'have foiled' the attempts of some would-be guests to visit—'& we saw nobody but our Precious [Haden], & Mr Tilson,' one of Henry's banking partners.

There is a story that about this time during Jane's stay in London, Henry was approached by a nobleman who was giving an evening-party and wished the novelist to attend. Among the guests would be Madame de Staël, who had expressed a desire to meet Miss Jane Austen. Would she come? She would not; she disliked the idea of going into public *as an author*. The story was told later by Henry, and may or may not be true.

On 11 December the novelist finally replied to J.S. Clarke's letter of the previous month. She told him that the Prince Regent, by arrangement with Murray, was to have his copy of *Emma* three days before the official publication date. She goes on:

> My greatest anxiety at present is that this fourth work should not disgrace what was good in the others. But on this point I will do myself the justice to declare that, whatever may be my wishes for its success, I am very strongly haunted with the idea that to those readers who have preferred 'Pride and Prejudice' it will appear inferior in wit, and to those who have preferred 'Mansfield Park' very inferior in good sense.

As usual, *Sense and Sensibility* is not mentioned. She concludes by declaring herself unequal to the sort of clerical portraiture suggested by Clarke:

> I am quite honoured by your thinking me capable of drawing such a clergyman as you gave the sketch of. . . . But I assure you I am *not*. The comic part of the character I might be equal to, but not the good, the enthusiastic, the literary. Such a man's conversation must at times be on subjects of science and philosophy, of which I know nothing; or at least be occasionally abundant in quotations and allusions which a woman who, like

me, knows only her own mother tongue, and has read very little in that, would be totally without the power of giving. A classical education, or at any rate a very extensive acquaintance with English literature, ancient and modern, appears to me quite indispensable for the person who would do any justice to your clergyman; and I think I may boast myself to be, with all possible vanity, the most unlearned and uninformed female who ever dared to be an authoress.

There is much to interest here: the disinclination to deal with unfamiliar subject-matter; the low rating of her education; and of course the amused tact with which the man is fended off. But the egregious Clarke remained undaunted. Replying a few days later, he attempted to propitiate the novelist by telling her how much her praises were being 'sounded as they ought to be' by the 'Lord Egremonts at Petworth,' adding that he 'very much admired' *Emma* himself—though having 'read only a few Pages.' He went on:

Do let us have an English Clergyman after *your* fancy—much novelty may be introduced—shew dear Madam what good would be done if Tythes were taken away entirely, and describe him burying his own mother—as I did—because the High Priest of the Parish in which she died—did not pay her remains the respect he ought to do. I have never recovered the Shock. Carry your Clergyman to Sea as the Friend of some distinguished Naval Character about a Court—you can then bring foreward like Le Sage many interesting Scenes of Character & Interest.

Jane Austen did not answer this letter. Clarke, however, was to be heard from again—and, by his gratuitous advice, to provide the genesis for her last burlesque, the 'Plan of a Novel, according to hints from various quarters' (1816), written during the following winter and spring.

Emma was published on the novelist's fortieth birthday—16 December 1815. Perhaps Jane hoped it would be a lucky date. This was the last work of hers to appear during her lifetime. As soon as it was in print, Henry Austen bought back from Crosby, for £10, the manuscript of 'Susan' (*Northanger Abbey*); only then did he tell the astonished publisher that it had been written by the author of *Pride and Prejudice*.

The novelist returned home to see the old year out at Chawton.
The year 1815 had been a productive one. *Emma* had been completed
and published, and *Persuasion* begun. 'Susan' was back in her hands.
In addition, in 1815 *Raison et Sensibilité, ou les Deux Manîeres
d'Aimer. Traduit librement par Mme. Isabelle de Montolieu* had
appeared in Paris. In the next year *Le Parc de Mansfield, ou Les Trois
Cousines*, and *La Nouvelle Emma, ou les Caractères Anglais du Siècle*
were brought out in France. And *Emma* was published in Philadelphia
in 1816.

One of those to whom a presentation copy of *Emma* was sent was
the Countess of Morley, a lady of some literary capacity who had
conveyed to the novelist warm appreciations of her earlier works;
another was Maria Edgeworth, whose books Jane Austen admired.
The Countess responded promptly: 'I am already become intimate in
the Woodhouse family, & feel that they will not amuse & interest me
less than the Bennetts, Bertrams, Noriss & all their admirable
predecessors.—I *can* give them no higher praise.' Jane's modest reply
suggests that the trepidation she felt on the subject of *Emma*'s
popularity, articulated in the letter to Clarke some weeks earlier,
had not abated: 'In my present state of doubt as to her reception in
the World, it is particularly gratifying to me to receive so early an
assurance of your Ladyship's approbation.—It encourages me to
depend on the same share of general good opinion which *Emma*'s
Predecessors have experienced, & to believe that I have not yet—as
almost every Writer of Fancy does sooner or later—overwritten
myself.' It is just as well that the novelist did not see the letter Miss
Edgeworth wrote to her brother on the subject of *Emma*:

> There was no story in it, except that Miss Emma found that the
> man whom she designed for Harriet's lover was an admirer of
> her own—& he was affronted by being refused by Emma &
> Harriet wore the willow—and *smooth, thin water-gruel* is
> according to Emma's father's opinion a very good thing & it is
> very difficult to make a cook understand what you mean by
> *smooth thin water-gruel*!

Another presentation copy was sent to Anna Lefroy, Jane Austen
commenting that she was certain Anna was as eager to see her *Emma*
as she was to see Anna's Jemima, now nearly three months old. Jane's
books were her children. In this letter, written at the end of

December 1815, she comments that the new novel now 'has been read by all' at Chawton.

And so she waited, in January and February 1816, for the world's verdict on her latest offspring. Had she 'overwritten' herself? Now in the midst of *Persuasion*, she must have desired some sort of critical reaction to its predecessor. At first there was a deafening silence, due in part to Murray's failure to publicise the book; Jane may well have begun to think that *Emma*, like *Mansfield Park* before it, would not be reviewed at all. With this possibility in mind, she began, during the winter of 1816, to collect and transcribe opinions of *Emma*—as she had done for *Mansfield Park*—from among her circle, and beyond it, whenever the information was available. The number of opinions she gathered was swelled by the two visits she and Cassandra paid together early in the new year—one to their friends Mrs Heathcote and her sister Miss Bigg, who were living in Winchester, and the other to the James Austens at Steventon. Caroline Austen, eleven now, was especially taken with her Aunt Jane, as her published reminiscences show. Much of the rest of the winter months was devoted, at Chawton, to the writing of *Persuasion*.

From the list Jane compiled of reactions to *Emma*, we learn that Cassandra liked it better than *Pride and Prejudice* 'but not so well as M.P.'; Frank Austen preferred it to all the other novels 'on account of it's peculiar air of Nature throughout'; and Charles Austen also placed it first among her novels. Francis Jeffrey of the *Edinburgh Review* was said to have been kept up reading *Emma* three nights running. The majority view in the family circle, however, was against the new book. Fanny Knight 'could not bear' the heroine, while her father ranked *Emma* below *Sense and Sensibility* and *Pride and Prejudice* (but above *Mansfield Park*); the James Austens thought it the least successful of the four published novels; Mrs Austen liked it better than *Mansfield Park*, but still preferred *Pride and Prejudice*; Martha Lloyd placed it below both *Pride and Prejudice* and *Mansfield Park*; the Leigh Perrots wrote diplomatically that 'Darcy & Elizabeth had spoilt them for anything else.' Mrs Digweed declared that 'if she had not known the Author, she could hardly have got through it'; another friend wrote that her husband disliked *Emma* so much she dared not repeat his opinion. Ben Lefroy thought *Emma* lacked 'Incident,' and 'Did not like the Heroine so well as any of the others.' Anna ranked it, with *Sense and Sensibility*, below the other novels, though she confessed to preferring Emma to all the other heroines. At Kintbury, old Mr Fowle 'read only the first & last Chapters, because he had heard it was not interesting.'

This initial, lukewarm reception was to be repeated, in a finer tone, in much of the published criticism of the novel. Reviews did appear at last between March and September 1816. The *Literary Panorama* found itself unable to take *Emma* seriously, complaining that 'the gentlemen are rather unequal to what gentlemen should be.' The *Monthly Review* labelled the novel 'harmless amusement' and 'scarcely . . . a composition.' The *British Critic* had 'little to find fault with'; generously, it termed *Emma* 'inoffensive.' In another patronising piece, the *Gentleman's Magazine* began by quoting Horace's 'Dulce est desipere in loco'—it is pleasant to indulge in trifles—and concluded by remarking that *Emma* could claim pre-eminence in an inferior species of composition: 'It is amusing, if not instructive, and has no tendency to deteriorate the heart.'

Some kind words were said along the way, but this was the critical tone taken in 1816 toward one of the very greatest of English novels. The day was saved for Jane by—of all people—Sir Walter Scott. Scott had been invited by Murray, who was also the proprietor of the *Quarterly Review*, to review *Emma* there. In March 1816—though the number is dated October 1815—a long essay by him on Jane Austen's work, which also touched upon the state of the novel at the time, duly appeared. Of all commentaries on her work known to Jane, this piece by Scott was by far her favourite—though his failure to mention *Mansfield Park* in it dismayed and disappointed her. Scott's review in the *Quarterly* was detailed, thoughtful, and influential; the same journal was to demolish Keats's contemporary reputation two years later. This was the only occasion during Jane Austen's lifetime on which her work received, from an intellect equivalent to her own and in a prominent place, the careful and incisive attention it deserved.

According to Scott, *Emma* proclaims 'a knowledge of the human heart, with the power and resolution to bring that knowledge to the service of honour and virtue.' He praises its author for moving the purview of the novel from 'romance' to 'ordinary life,' 'real life,' and suggests, shrewdly, that the writer may well be 'the first . . . of a new class.' The novelist's great strength, he says here, is 'the art of copying from nature as she really exists in the common walks of life, and presenting to the reader . . . a correct and striking representation of that which is daily taking place around him.' Scott declares that the author of *Emma*—not named, of course; at this time he may well not have known who it was—keeps close to 'common incidents, and to such characters who occupy the ordinary walks of life.' In doing so the writer 'has produced sketches of such spirit and originality' that the reader is as 'excited' as he would be by a more 'romantic' treatment. He rates Jane Austen higher than Maria Edgeworth: she is said to 'stand almost alone' in depicting 'the middling classes of society.' The narrative of all her novels, Scott says, 'is composed of such common occurrences as may have fallen under the observation of most folks'; and her

> dramatis personæ conduct themselves upon the motives and principles which the readers may recognize as ruling their own and that of most of their acquaintances. The kind of moral, also, which these novels inculcate, applies equally to the paths of common life.

Scott then goes back to discuss and praise *Sense and Sensibility* and *Pride and Prejudice*. *Emma*, he says, provides less 'story' than the earlier works, yet holds the reader's attention nonetheless. Interestingly enough, he makes a comparison later critics were also to make when reviewing the novels of Jane Austen's admiring disciple George Eliot: 'The author's knowledge of the world, and the peculiar tact with which . . . characters that the reader cannot fail to recognize [are presented], reminds us something of the merits of the Flemish school of painting.' Scott also praises the way in which, in *Emma*, 'the characters of the speakers evolve themselves with dramatic effect.' Reading a novel by this writer, Scott concludes, affords one 'a pleasure nearly allied with the experience of [one's] own social habits.'

Scott was perhaps the first of Jane Austen's readers to see both her pursuit of a new kind of 'realism'—the word was not to enter the English vocabulary, from across the Channel, until the 1840s—largely domestic, and her penchant for using what later would be called the dramatic method in her pursuit of it. His essay was unsigned, but its authorship was widely known; Jane must have drawn great strength from this to go on with her work in the face of *Emma*'s generally lukewarm reception. *Persuasion* directly mentions Scott (and Byron too) several times.

Meanwhile all was not well with the novelist's brothers. In February, Charles's ship the *Phoenix* was wrecked in a gale off

Smyrna. He survived, but this would have been a setback to his naval career. And Austen, Maunde, and Tilson had closed the doors of their establishment; on 23 March 1816 Henry Austen was officially declared bankrupt. The collapse of the Alton bank (patronised largely by farmers), which the London firm had backed, was a factor. A fall in the price of wheat precipitated a dramatic reduction in the value of farming stock. A number of farmers and small businessmen were ruined. England had by no means recovered from the exhausting years of war, and Henry and his partners were among the latest victims. Both Edward Knight and James Leigh Perrot, who had signed notes for Henry, suffered financial losses—£20,000 and £10,000, respectively. Jane, fortunately, had just £13 in the Henrietta Street bank—a portion of the profits of the first edition of *Mansfield Park*—and lost no more than that.

The resilient Henry decided immediately to take orders and start life over again as a clergyman. He was ordained five months later, in August, surprising the local bishop with his knowledge of the Greek Testament. He became a preacher of the evangelical school, known for his eloquence; for years he filled the relatively humble role of perpetual curate at Bentley, near Alton. After some time he married a Miss Eleanor Jackson, who survived him.

Jane's mood in these circumstances was understandably cheerless. 'Our Pond is brimfull & our roads are dirty & our walls are damp, & we sit wishing every bad day may be the last,' she wrote to her niece Caroline. 'Another week perhaps may see us shrinking & shivering under a dry East Wind.'

The Prince Regent's librarian and chaplain wrote to her from the Pavilion at Brighton at the end of March to thank her, officially, 'for the handsome copy' of *Emma*. 'Lord St Helens and many of the nobility, who have been staying here, paid you the just tribute of their praise' for her 'last excellent novel,' J.S. Clarke reported. Once again, however, he went too far. He had just become, he announced, both chaplain and private secretary to Prince Leopold of Cobourg, who was visiting the Prince Regent at Brighton. 'Perhaps when you again appear in print you may chuse to dedicate your volumes to Prince Leopold,' Clarke suggested. 'Any historical romance, illustrative of the history of the august House of Cobourg, would just now be very interesting.'

This episode has always amused Jane Austen's students. It has never been said in Clarke's defence that a historical novel about the

Cobourgs probably would have sold very well indeed at this moment in history—'just now,' as Clarke says. Leopold was in England not merely on a casual visit to the Prince Regent; he was there to negotiate his marriage, which took place two months later, to Princess Charlotte, the heiress-apparent to the throne. Leopold's sister was the mother of Queen Victoria; he himself was the uncle of Victoria's future consort, and later became the first King of the Belgians. The proposal by the Regent's chaplain was in fact not so absurd as it has often seemed to modern readers.

Still, it was not Jane's cup of tea; it was, in fact, another presumptuous piece of interference. The novelist decided that she had had enough suggestions from Clarke, and that only a polite but proper snubbing would shut him up. She proceeded to administer it—in part as follows:

> You are very kind in your hints as to the sort of composition which might recommend me at present, and I am fully sensible that an historical romance, founded on the House of Saxe Cobourg, might be much more to the purpose of profit or popularity than such pictures of domestic life in country villages as I deal in. But I could no more write a romance than an epic poem. I could not sit seriously down to write a serious romance under any other motive than to save my life; and if it were indispensable for me to keep it up and never relax into laughing at myself or other people, I am sure I should be hung before I had finished the first chapter. No, I must keep to my own style and go on in my own way; and though I may never succeed again in that, I am convinced that I should totally fail in any other.

Clarke's badgering at least provoked the novelist to a serious estimate of her literary capabilities and limitations—and perhaps it is therefore unfortunate, though understandable, that he did not venture to write to her again.

What is chiefly interesting here is Jane Austen's continuing animus against 'romance' in any form (even 'serious'; even when it is likely to be popular and profitable); the necessary ingredient, as she sees it, of laughter 'at myself or other people' in what she does; and the restatement of her commitment in her work to the depiction of 'domestic life in country villages.'

A letter from the novelist to Murray dated the same day as the letter to Clarke complains of Scott's omission of *Mansfield Park* from the *Quarterly Review* essay: 'I cannot but be sorry that so clever a man . . . should consider it as unworthy of being noticed.' Her querulous mood is made clear by her account of Clarke's letter. The Prince has thanked her, she tells Murray, 'for the *handsome* copy I sent him of "Emma." Whatever he may think of *my* share of the work, yours seems to have been quite right.'

When Jane felt alienated she often retreated into burlesque and parody, and it was probably around this time—late winter/early spring 1816; the dating cannot be exact—that, returning to an earlier vein, she wrote out her comic 'Plan of a Novel.' The revision of 'Susan' for publication as *Northanger Abbey* may also date in part from this period, though some rewriting certainly occurred later; Jane had to change her heroine's name, and thus the title—in the intervening years since the book was first drafted an anonymous novel called *Susan* had appeared. The 'Plan of a Novel' and *Northanger Abbey* both make fun of the melodrama, the cardboard characters, the stylistic extravagances, and the improbabilities of romantic fiction. By way of mocking parody, Jane Austen offers, in the 'Plan of a Novel,' to draw 'pictures of perfection' in 'thorough novel slang.'

The 'Plan of a Novel, according to hints from various quarters,' is several pages of burlesque, with marginalia identifying the 'quarters' from which some of the 'various hints' have come. The story is to be about a faultless clergyman living in the country with an equally faultless daughter, who has 'dark eyes & plump cheeks' (Austen family traits). Much of the story is to be taken up by the clergyman's relating to his daughter the history of his life—a history which bears a number of similarities to that of the Prince Regent's domestic chaplain. Indeed, there will be a passage on 'the Benefits to result from Tythes being done away, & [the clergyman's] having buried his own Mother . . . in consequence of the High Priest of the Parish in which she died, refusing to pay her Remains the respect due them.' The clergyman is described as 'an Enthusiast in Literature'—Clarke's characterisation of himself. The remainder of the tale is to be taken up by the story of the daughter's pursuit by an 'unprincipled & heartless young Man, desperately in love' with her, who chases her and her father around the world—thus giving the writer an opportunity to 'exhibit a wide variety of Characters,' in the manner of Le Sage. Just as the father and daughter are to be 'unexceptionable' in every respect, so the 'Wicked' characters 'will be completely depraved & infamous, hardly a resemblance of Humanity left in them.' The heroine is to have marriage proposed to her, by perfect young men in love, wherever she goes. Her efforts to avoid the villains, evade her suitors, protect her father, and support them both, are to wear her 'down to a Skeleton, & now & then [starve her] to death.' She is nonetheless at the same time 'to be in the most elegant Society & living in high style.' Finally, exhausted by their adventures, 'the poor Father . . . throws himself on the Ground, & after 4 or 5 hours of tender advice & parental Admonition to his miserable Child, expires in a fine burst of Literary Enthusiasm, intermingled with Invectives again[st] Holder's of Tythes.' The heroine 'crawls back' to her former home, having 'at least 20 narrow escapes' along the way, and ultimately finds a happy ending with the right man.

Mr Clarke, so 'set upon literary immortality,' as Southam aptly puts it, would have been mortified to see his intimations taken so literally; Jane adopted his various proposals as the nucleus of her burlesque, transcribing suggestions almost verbatim from his letters. The result is cruelly hilarious. It is a blanket condemnation not only of romantic fiction but of 'the contemporary practice,' as Southam observes in the only extensive critical discussion of the 'Plan' we have, 'of using fiction as a vehicle for political and philosophical propaganda . . . or as a means of moral and educational improvement.' Jane Austen objected to this 'practice' even in novels of such favourites of hers as Maria Edgeworth and Scott. Like much of the Juvenilia, the 'Plan of a Novel' is both comedy and criticism. It expresses Jane's contempt for much popular fiction and stresses her preference as a novelist to present 'the subject-matter of observed and familiar life with naturalness and probability' and 'an essential fidelity to common experience'—precisely the qualities for which Scott praised her so extravagantly in his *Quarterly Review* essay.

Family matters also occupied Jane Austen during the spring of 1816. In April, Henry visited Chawton and Godmersham, and Elizabeth Leigh, Cassandra's godmother, died. 'The death of a person of her advanced age, so fit to die and by her own feelings so *ready* to die, is not to be regretted,' Jane wrote, rather bluntly, to her niece Caroline. Miss Leigh left £20 to Mrs Austen. 'Your Grandmama is not *quite* well,' the novelist adds here. 'She seldom gets through the 24 hours without some pain in her head.' The exasperated tone is familiar. Sending along with the letter something made for Caroline by the less favoured niece Cassandra, Jane refers to the enclosure as '*this*—whatever it may be.' She hopes Caroline and her father will come to Chawton for the Alton Fair. 'We are almost ashamed to include your Mama in the invitation, or to ask *her* to be at the trouble of a long ride for so few days as we shall be having disengaged,' Jane concludes. 'We do not like to *invite* her to come on wednesday, to be turned out of the house on Monday.' The coolness between the novelist and Mary Lloyd Austen persisted. When Mary fell seriously ill in June of an unnamed malady, no one at Chawton offered to help nurse her at Steventon. But then, as we shall see, the women at Chawton, especially Jane, had other things on their minds.

In May there was a round of visiting. Edward and Fanny came from Godmersham to stay at Chawton for a few days. Shortly after this, Jane and Cassandra went together to Cheltenham for three weeks. It is possible that Jane's ill health dates from this month, for Cheltenham was known for its spa, its 'waters'—Jane, of course, disliked Bath. On the way home they visited the Fowles at Kintbury, who found the novelist in a fatalistic mood, and left on record the impression that she was looking sick and tired. She 'went over the old places, and recalled the old recollections associated with them, in a very particular manner . . . as if she never expected to see them again,' the Fowles said later. On the way back to Chawton, the sisters stopped off at Steventon.

In June, as Jane was nearing the end of *Persuasion*, Frank and Mary Austen visited Chawton with their two daughters; when they departed for London a few days later, they took Cassandra and Martha Lloyd with them and left one daughter behind. Jane found herself closeted with her mother and a nine-year-old niece. It was perhaps in part this combination of events, along with her increasing physical discomfort and the tenseness she was feeling about the conclusion of *Persuasion*, which brought upon the novelist what she termed an attack of bilious fever. She complained of back pains.

July 1816—before the London party returned to Chawton—was a quiet month. Early in July, Jane wrote to James's son James Edward, now eighteen and home at Steventon, a graduate of Winchester and soon to enter Oxford. Her subdued mood is reflected in comments about the weather: 'I begin to think it will never be fine again . . . Oh! it rains again; it beats against the window.' The traffic passing in front of the Cottage informed her that Winchester had broken up for the term: 'We saw a countless number of Postchaises full of Boys pass by yesterday morn^g—full of future Heroes, Legislators, Fools, and Villains.' She adds: 'You have never thanked me for my last letter. . . . I cannot bear not to be thanked.' She has been out riding, she reports, in the donkey-cart usually reserved for her mother—an indication that she was beginning to find walking difficult. A few days later she wrote to Caroline, who had sent her another story. She found it amusing, the novelist told her niece: 'I am particularly glad to find you so much alive upon any topic of such absurdity, as the usual description of a Heroine's father.' Obviously Caroline's first efforts, like her aunt's, were in the parodic vein. Caroline's brother James Edward was staying at Chawton for a few days. 'He has not lost one good quality or good Look, & is only altered in being improved by being some months older than when we saw him last,' Jane Austen remarks of her first biographer. 'He is getting very near our own age, for *we* do not grow older, of course.'

Persuasion was completed a few days later, at least in its first draft. What happened next is told—in part inaccurately, as we shall see—in James Edward's *Memoir* of his aunt:

> The book had been brought to an end in July; and the re-engagement of the hero and heroine effected in a totally different manner in a scene laid at Admiral Croft's lodgings. But her performance did not satisfy her. She thought it tame and flat, and was desirous of producing something better. This weighed upon her mind—the more so, probably, on account of the weak state of her health; so that one night she retired to rest in very low spirits. But such depression was little in accordance with her nature, and was soon shaken off. The next morning she awoke to more cheerful views and brighter inspirations; the sense of power revived; and imagination resumed its course. She cancelled the condemned chapter, and wrote two others, entirely different, in its stead. The result is that we possess the visit of the Musgrove party to Bath; the crowded and animated scenes at the White Hart Hotel; and the charming conversation between Captain Harville and Anne Elliot, overheard by Captain Wentworth, by which the two faithful lovers were at last led to understand each other's feelings. The tenth and eleventh chapters [of the second volume] of *Persuasion*, then, rather than the actual winding-up of the story, contain the

latest of her printed compositions [*Sanditon* had not yet been published when this was written]—her last contribution to the entertainment of the public. Perhaps it may be thought that she has seldom written anything more brilliant; and that, independent of the original manner in which the *dénouement* is brought about, the pictures of Charles Musgrove's good-natured boyishness and of his wife's jealous selfishness would have been incomplete without these finishing strokes. The cancelled chapter exists in manuscript. It is certainly inferior to the two which were substituted for it; but it was such as some writers and some readers might have been contented with; and it contained touches which scarcely any other hand could have given, the suppression of which may be almost a matter of regret.

The 'suppression' was brought to an end in the second edition of the *Memoir* (1871); and the cancelled chapter was reprinted in Chapman's edition of the novels (1923).

Some of what James Edward says here is not quite right, however. About a quarter of the original tenth chapter of Volume II of *Persuasion* was retained virtually verbatim in the new eleventh chapter, and another chapter, the original eleventh chapter, was put into the completed work as Chapter 12 with only a few changes in wording, as Southam has shown. Dissatisfied with the version of the ending completed on 18 July 1816—the original tenth chapter was begun on 8 July, tentatively finished on 16 July, then hauled out again for revision, as Jane Austen's own notes on the manuscript show—the novelist rewrote most of the tenth chapter and, as indicated, used some of the rest of the original material in a new draft of the book's last two chapters. This last revision was completed on 6 August. It is possible, as Susan Morgan has suggested, that *Persuasion*, like *Sanditon*, was titled posthumously; there is a tradition that as late as March 1817 Jane and Cassandra were debating the merits of 'The Elliots' as a title.

The completion of *Persuasion* was an important moment in the novelist's career. The ending as revised renders the climactic love scene more dramatically—with less authorial detachment—than in the previous books. For the only time in the novels the lovers, at the end, resolve their situation at least in part within our hearing. Hitherto, as Marghanita Laski observes, Jane Austen 'had avoided the direct confrontation of lovers at moments of love as she had avoided ever showing us men without the company of women.' Here, through 'conscious art,' 'a triumph of rethinking won through trial and error,' as Southam puts it, 'she was constructing a dramatic and emotional climax'; and so finally we get an ending which more nearly satisfies, both thematically and artistically. It had been the novelist's custom, as we have seen, 'to conclude her stories ironically, with a hasty and deliberately undramatic settlement of events,' as Southam says. She started to do this yet again in the original ending of *Persuasion*—then changed her mind and rewrote it. The rewritten section comprises her last *finished* writing, as Pinion observes, 'and includes the most moving, and perhaps the most artistic, scene in all her works.' Southam calls the new ending 'a passage of extraordinary beauty, unequalled in her other works.'

Perhaps. The fact is that even the new ending embraces a good deal—too much—of summary rather than 'scene.' Jane Austen never entirely escaped her instinct to withdraw at such moments. Still, there is a kind of artistic integrity in this. To the end, the novelist would not write about what she did not know at first-hand.

Because of the various changes in the first draft, she was obliged to make a fair copy of the original tenth and eleventh chapters of the second volume. Thus the original (cancelled) tenth chapter was preserved—the only fragment to have survived from the writing of the novels. For once, we have both Jane Austen's first and second thoughts about an important piece of work. In general the ending of the novel, including the last paragraph of the final version, is heavily corrected. On this and related points in connection with the revision of *Persuasion* one can do no better than refer the interested reader to Southam's study of the manuscripts and Chapman's edition of the novels.

IX

'I consider everybody as having a right to marry *once* in their lives for love, if they can,' Jane Austen wrote to her sister in December 1808. *Persuasion* takes up this argument, and broadens it. It is the novelist's greatest plea for letting love run its natural course—though the old anti-romantic strain is also very much in evidence here.

The argument, as so often in Jane Austen's novels, illuminates true and false ways of *seeing*—true and false moral values. Once again it provides a lesson in how to live: should one, it asks, live as Anne Elliot lives, or as her father and elder sister live. It is in deciding such matters as these that the greatness of *Persuasion* lies. In distinguishing accurate from inaccurate perception, the novel draws our attention to the story of Anne's love for Frederick Wentworth (that most elusive of Jane Austen's heroes), Anne's determination 'to marry . . . for love,' the delay in doing so due to the unworthy values of a well-meaning friend and guardian, and Anne's final realisation of the desired state—a state which eluded the novelist to the end of her days, but which could hardly have long been far from the centre of her attention, or out of her thoughts.

Lady Russell has an overblown 'value for rank and consequence' which has 'blinded her . . . to the faults' of those who possess them. Because of her social prejudices she misjudges both Wentworth and William Elliot, Anne's two suitors, and gives bad advice. Anne ultimately sees that Lady Russell 'had been unfairly influenced by appearances in each,' unable to see below surfaces. At the end of the novel, Lady Russell admits that she has 'been completely wrong.' The narrator comments: 'There is a quickness of perception in some, a nicety in the discernment of character, a natural penetration . . . which no experience in others can equal, and Lady Russell had been less gifted in this part of understanding than her young friend'—that is, Anne.

In the tradition of Wickham, Willoughby, and Henry Crawford, William Elliot is a plausible villain whose chief concern is 'To do the best for himself.' His manners and appearance are good. No one understands his true nature until the end, though Anne is never entirely easy about him.

Wentworth comes back from sea persuaded that Anne's character is still as 'yielding and indecisive' as it had been eight years earlier, when they had been in love, he had proposed to her, and Lady Russell had advised Anne to reject him. He recalls at first only that she had 'deserted and disappointed' him, and 'shewn a feebleness of character in doing so'—'which his own . . . confident temper could not endure.' Being weak and timid, Anne had yielded to 'over-persuasion.' At first he perceives no change in the relationship between the two ladies, assumes that Anne is as much under the sway of the older woman as before, and so renews his suit only after much time is wasted. As Wentworth finally sees, a good deal of 'separation and suffering might have been spared' had he not been 'too proud to ask again. I did not understand you,' he tells Anne. 'I shut my eyes, and would not understand you.'

The shutting of one's eyes to the true nature of others is a theme very much at the novel's core. *Persuasion* argues for the virtues of intelligent personal insight and against the attempts of people, out of pride in their own powers of discernment, to influence the actions of others. A theme of *Emma* is thus repeated. But here the villain of the novel very particularly is 'persuasion' itself; the word is used in various forms more than twenty times. Wentworth complains to Anne, at the end, of 'the indelible, immovable impression of what persuasion had . . . done.' Anne's reply is indicative: though she had been wrong to yield to Lady Russell's persuasion, it was 'persuasion exerted on the side of safety, not of risk.' Even now, seeing how uninformed Lady Russell's advice was, she concludes that she 'was perfectly right' in having taken it, though Lady Russell 'erred.' She should never presume to give such advice in such circumstances herself; but at the same time Lady Russell stood to her then *in loco parentis*, and to have defied her would have made her (Anne) suffer 'in my conscience.' The novel argues that people should not attempt to influence others in this way, even from the best of motives —both because the adviser's judgment may be faulty, and because the advisee may be positioned so as to be forced to take the advice given, whatever its quality. Such had been the case here. Anne, seeing more clearly than the older woman, had felt duty-bound nonetheless to be advised by her. It was an impossible situation; no happy conclusion *could* become possible until she was older, and Wentworth swallowed his pride and tried again.

Anne's ultimate assessment of the matter surely is Jane Austen's:

> she felt that were any young person, in similar circumstances, to apply to her for counsel, they would never receive any of such certain immediate wretchedness, such uncertain future good.— She was persuaded that under every disadvantage of disapprobation at home, and every anxiety attending his profession, all their probable fears, delays and disappointments, she should yet have been a happier woman in maintaining the engagement, than she had been in the sacrifice of it . . . How eloquent could Anne Elliot have been,—how eloquent, at least, were her wishes on the side of early warm attachment, and a cheerful confidence in futurity, against that over-anxious caution which

seems to insult exertion and distrust Providence!—She had
been forced into prudence in her youth, she learned romance as
she grew older—the natural sequel of an unnatural beginning.

In fact a 'young person, in similar circumstances' to Anne's when
younger, *had* recently 'applied' to Jane Austen 'for counsel'—her
niece Fanny. The novelist, we recall, had squirmed; she had suggested
patience, but worried that her advice might drive Fanny to 'that over-
anxious caution' which is condemned here. The autobiographical
resonance is unmistakable. Even more to the point—the famous final
sentence of this passage sounds distinctly personal: one recalls the
near-misses of Jane Austen's early years. The recommendation of
'early warm attachment' and that against 'over-anxious caution' is a
poignant reminder of the novelist's own loneliness. 'She had been
forced into prudence in youth'—surely a reference to the 'early warm
attachment' between herself and Tom Lefroy so unceremoniously
put an end to by supposedly wiser heads. *Persuasion* finally asks us to
trust our own considered judgment, to avoid the undue influence of
others, and to look beneath the surfaces of things and people to find
the truth. The message of the last book is the same as that of the
first.

The emphasis on personal feeling does not suggest that Jane
Austen was suddenly converted, between *Emma* and *Persuasion*, to
any form of 'romanticism,' though some have thought so. *Persuasion*
is often written of as if it had been composed under the influence of
the Romantic poets. This is not so—indeed, something like the
reverse is the case.

The novel argues for *seeing*, for rational perception, as over against
mere blind instinct. *Persuasion*, in fact, continues the attack mounted
in *Emma* on overly imaginative ways of looking at things. During the
walk to Winthrop, as the romantic Louisa Musgrove declares that
she would rather be overturned in a carriage driven by a man she loves
'than driven safely by anybody else,' Anne is roused from thoughts of
autumn to see 'the ploughs at work, and the fresh-made path [which]
spoke the farmer, counteracting the sweets of poetical dependence
and meaning to have spring again.' It is during this walk that
Wentworth makes to Louisa a speech about the virtues of the
hazlenut—possibly a comic result of Jane Austen's reading of
Wordsworth (e.g., 'The Thorn'). Life goes on. Though Anne does
not always take her own advice, we are told, she speaks to Captain

Benwick persuasively indeed about the necessity of interspersing his reading of Romantic poetry—Scott and Byron are mentioned—with 'a larger allowance of prose'; the 'best moralists' are recommended, especially their letters and memoirs. Poetry, Anne observes, can be 'seldom safely enjoyed' by those who enjoy it too much: 'the strong feelings which alone could estimate it truly, were the very feelings which ought to taste it but sparingly.' It is no coincidence that after a general conversation about Scott and Byron—Byron's 'dark blue seas' have just been mentioned—Louisa, in an excess of romantic sentiment at Lyme, jumps on her head. Here is the fruit of excessive romanticism.

Other familiar themes abound. Like *Emma*, *Persuasion* argues that 'There is always something offensive in the details of cunning. The manœuvres of selfishness and duplicity must ever be revolting.' Like *Emma*, Anne prizes 'the frank, the open-hearted, the eager character beyond all others.' She feels she can depend more upon the 'sincerity of those who sometimes looked or said a careless or a hasty thing, than of those whose presence of mind never varied, whose tongue never slipped.' Fashionable evening parties, which encourage hypocritical and insincere behaviour and conversation, are pronounced inferior to evenings spent at the theatre, where such behaviour is confined to the stage. Sir Walter Elliot and his eldest daughter, representatives in this novel of the 'heartless elegance' of 'society,' prefer 'the elegant stupidity of private parties' to the theatre, a state of things Anne finds 'stagnating.' As the irrepressible Charles Musgrove declares, 'What's an evening party? Never worth remembering'; 'I know you love a play . . . We all love a play.' His wife, like other silly women in Jane Austen's books, is preoccupied with questions of rank and precedence.

The novel also manages to get in a characteristic swipe or two at contemporary methods of female education. The Musgrove sisters, who went to school to acquire 'the usual stock of accomplishments,' live, 'like thousands of other young ladies. . . to be fashionable, happy, and merry,' and seem incapable of serious thought. Anne speaks eloquently to Captain Harville of the advantage men have over women in argument: 'Education has been theirs. . . .the pen has been in their hands.'

Other characteristic themes, touching on autobiography, are observable here. *Persuasion* suggests that underneath 'the smooth surface of family-union . . . there may be nothing durable beneath.'

The 'family-piece' describing the Musgroves at Christmas emphasises noise, chaos, and disorder; the unruly Musgrove children are probably drawn from those of Frank and Charles Austen. The fact that the novel seethes with naval officers (Croft, Wentworth, Harville, Benwick)—and that all of them are treated sympathetically, as over against some of their land-bound compatriots—is not surprising in a book written by the sister of two career Navy men. *Persuasion* goes out of its way, perhaps as a sort of family joke, to laud the profession. Navy men are described as 'well to deal with,' and 'desirable tenants.' Sailors are termed liberal, 'neat and careful in all their ways . . . Sailors work hard enough for their comforts.' They are pointedly said to make possible, through the exercise of their profession, 'all the comforts and all the privileges which any home can give.' The impulsive Louisa expounds on the 'friendliness,' 'brother-liness,' 'openness,' and 'uprightness' of sailors, 'protesting that she was convinced of [their] having more worth and warmth than any set of men in England; that they only knew how to live.' Knowing 'how to live' is of paramount importance, of course. The account Jane Austen gives of the accommodations for women available on board various kinds of ships must have been sketched out for her by her brother Frank, who was at Chawton during much of the time *Persuasion* was written (Anne 'had been accused of supposing sailors to be living on board without any thing to eat, or any cook . . . or any servant . . . or any knife and fork'). Though he does not resemble Captain Harville in character, Frank Austen is like him in being handy around the house.

One of the less successful sailors mentioned in the novel is the late Dick Musgrove, and here Jane's fangs show through in undisguised sharpness. It turns out to be one of her most heartless performances.

> the Musgroves had had the ill fortune of a very troublesome, hopeless son; and the good fortune to lose him before he reached his twentieth year . . . he had been sent to sea, because he was stupid and unmanageable on shore . . . he had been very little cared for at any time by his family, though quite as much as he deserved; seldom heard of, and scarcely at all regretted when the intelligence of his death abroad had worked its way to Uppercross. . . . He had, in fact, though his sisters were . . . doing all they could for him, by calling him 'poor Richard,' been nothing better than a thick-headed, unfeeling, unprofitable

> Dick Musgrove, who had never done any thing to entitle him-
> self to more than the abbreviation of his name, living or dead.

This is gratuitously harsh, shockingly cruel and malicious. When Mrs
Musgrove speaks tenderly of her dead son, Anne 'suppressed a
smile'—but Jane Austen seems incapable of doing so. The narrator
points out that Mrs Musgrove is fat, and that fat people look silly
when attempting to express 'tenderness and sentiment'; her retro-
spective grief is referred to as 'large fat sighings over the destiny of a
son, whom nobody alive had cared for.' The 'conjunction' of 'a large
bulky figure' with 'mental sorrow' is termed 'unbecoming'; 'taste
cannot tolerate' it: 'ridicule' only is possible.

There is really nothing to say about this except to observe that
only a woman deficient in feeling and, yes, 'taste,' could have written
it. Some critics have told us that Jane Austen might have excised all
of this had she had more time to polish *Persuasion*. But she went on to
start another novel without touching this passage, while carefully
revising some other sections of *Persuasion*, as we know. She stands
revealed, personally, in the most unflattering light here.

As we come closer to home we may note that we have in *Persuasion*
a good deal of sibling rivalry and alienation once again. Anne dislikes
Elizabeth, who takes every opportunity to slight her younger sister.
Mary competes shamelessly with both Anne and Elizabeth for
attention. Even Henrietta and Louisa Musgrove enter into a brief
competition of sorts for the affections of Captain Wentworth.

Again we have a 'bad parents' theme, and another substitute
mother: Lady Russell takes up, albeit less successfully, the role played
by Mrs Weston in *Emma*. As in *Emma*, the sensible parent is long
dead, while the silly one lives on. It should not be necessary to
catalogue the sins of Sir Walter Elliot as a father. Charles and Mary
Musgrove seem incapable of keeping their offspring in order; the
result is yet another group of noisy, annoying children. Mary even
observes at one point that she is 'more unfit than any body else' to
attend her sick child. The senior Musgroves, on the other hand, are
praised as good parents. Almost alone among the parents in Jane
Austen's novels, 'They do every thing to confer happiness' upon
their children: 'What a blessing to young people to be in such hands!'
This sounds nostalgic. Unlike Anne's family, the senior Musgroves
are 'free from all those ambitious feelings which have led to so much
misconduct and misery.' Their 'heartiness,' 'warmth,' and 'sincerity'

delight Anne 'the more, from the sad want of such blessings at home.'
The vividness of the language may invite us to wonder, yet again, how
happy—and how traumatic—Jane Austen's childhood really was.

The novel has a number of other personal connections. The date of
Mary's marriage is given as 16 December 1810—Jane Austen's thirty-
fifth birthday. Wentworth is said to have been made a commander 'in
consequence of the action off St Domingo,' where Cassandra's fiancé
Thomas Fowle met his end. In Volume I, Chapter 10 of *Persuasion*
Anne overhears Wentworth and Louisa among some hedgerows—a
scene postponed from *Mansfield Park*, when Jane discovered that
there were no hedgerows in Northamptonshire. The novelist visited
Lyme in 1804 and found it beautiful; her letters mention such other
sites alluded to in *Persuasion* as Charmouth and Pinny, and
undoubtedly much of the novel's physical description of the area is
taken from personal recollection. The 'small house, near the foot of
an old pier,' with such small rooms, where the Harvilles live, may be
modelled on the place—Mrs Dean's house, on the Cobb side of the
bay—in which the Austens stayed during part of their visit to Lyme
Regis. Gowland's lotion, so heartily recommended by Sir Walter
Elliot, was fashionable around this time at Bath for facial and skin
complaints, as Chapman's notes to *Persuasion* remind us. Anne
disapproves of 'Sunday-travelling'; this would mesh with Jane
Austen's growing evangelicalism during her last years. Similarly,
Anne's attitude toward non-sabbatarian travel—'I have travelled so
little, that every fresh place would be interesting to me'—must reflect
the novelist's. And Anne Elliot becomes, ultimately, Anne
Wentworth—the name of a connection of Jane Austen's through her
Leigh forebears. The earlier Anne was the second wife of the second
Baron Leigh of Stoneleigh and the daughter of the first Earl of
Strafford, the unfortunate minister of Charles I. The Strafford
Wentworths were ancestors of the Earls Fitzwilliam—a name
prominent in *Pride and Prejudice*. Jane Austen's 'family' plays a more
prominent part in her novels than is generally known; she always
preferred familiar to unfamiliar names, whether of people or of ships.

Elizabeth Jenkins has observed that autobiographical elements in
Persuasion tend to be overstressed. It is quite true that, contrary to
the general belief, this is not one of Jane Austen's most autobiographical performances. As Miss Jenkins points out, Anne Elliot
could not have written *Pride and Prejudice*. Jane Austen was later to
speak of the heroine of *Persuasion*, who was never a personal

favourite of hers, in somewhat disparaging terms: 'too good,' she called her. Certainly Anne is at times a prig. She always behaves perfectly, and, having made a mistake eight years earlier, has nothing left to learn. However—as Tave says—though nobody hears or sees much of Anne, it is nonetheless she who is at the centre of the novel. Probably she is no more—or less—'Jane Austen' than any of the other heroines.

Still, there are interesting autobiographical resonances, as in all of the novels.

Anne is described as a woman possessing 'an elegance of mind and sweetness of character, which must have placed her high with any people of real understanding'; but her family, lacking 'real under-standing,' does not give her her due: she 'was nobody. . . only Anne.' She would have liked 'the power of representing to them all what they were about'—a pretty good summary of exactly what Jane Austen does in her novels. Anne 'had been a very pretty girl, but her bloom had vanished' in her mid-twenties, and now she is 'faded'; 'the years . . . had destroyed her youth and bloom.' The 'art of knowing [her] own nothingness beyond [her] own circle, was become necessary for her.' Nor has she any use for the 'heartless elegance' of so-called social superiors; Lady Dalrymple and her daughter, for example, to Anne 'were nothing.' Her 'idea of good company,' as she says, 'is the company of clever, well-informed people, who have a great deal of conversation.' Unfortunately, only rarely can she have this. 'Jane Austen seems in her last novel to have lost faith in manners,' as Duckworth suggests. Most women, Anne tells Captain Harville, 'live at home, quiet, confined, and our feelings prey upon us.' She plays the piano—her favourite pieces are country dances. 'She knew that when she played she was giving pleasure only to herself; but this was no new sensation . . . she had never, since . . . the loss of her dear mother, known the happiness of being listened to, or encouraged by any just appreciation or real taste.' One might again substitute 'father' for 'mother' here. We may also be reminded of Jane's musical taste, and her early-morning stints at the piano—a fixture of her daily Chawton schedule. A woman who feels surrounded by inferior minds, whose early bloom has been wasted in loneliness, who prefers good con-versation to good breeding, who lives 'at home, quiet, confined' and prey to her own 'feelings,' who plays country dances on the piano, and misses the appreciation and approval of a deceased parent—surely there is something of the novelist in such a character as this.

There are other things. Like her author, Anne hates Bath—and yet is forced to live there for awhile. Anne does 'not think [Bath] agreed with her.' She had gone there after her mother's death—the Austens moved to Bath shortly before George Austen died—and spent some distressing months in the city. So did the novelist. Anne finds Bath too wet, too noisy, too fast, and too urban. 'She persisted in a very determined . . . disinclination for Bath,' from the moment of first seeing it from afar 'smoking in rain'; one recalls Jane's complaints, years earlier, about the dampness of the city, and how much in general she disliked it.

Anne's antipathy to Bath, like the novelist's, is part of a general partiality for country life. Going into a city is described in *Persuasion* neurasthenically: 'the dash of other carriages, the heavy rumble of carts and drays, the hawking of newsmen, muffin-men and milk-men, and the ceaseless clink of pattens [wooden shoes]' assault Anne's senses. She resents 'the littlenesses of a town.' Instead she prefers 'her own dear country,' where one of her chief pleasures is walking. Again—there must be something of Jane Austen in such a character as this.

There are, finally, some more tenuous, but no less interesting, personal resonances here. At the age of nineteen Anne Elliot had fallen in love with a man who had no present means of supporting her—'no hopes of attaining affluence,' as *Persuasion* puts it. They were separated by their guardians; the gentleman left the country to seek his fortune. One is inevitably reminded, it is worth pointing out again, of Jane's 'early warm attachment' to Tom Lefroy—who, like Captain Wentworth (as described in the novel), ultimately satisfied all his own 'sanguine expectations' and 'confidence' and became 'prosperous' and 'distinguished.' The novelist's account of the effect on Anne's life of this blighted romance could well apply to her own feelings after the Lefroy affair—or, for that matter, after the more shadowy summer romance in Devon some years later:

> A few months had seen the beginning and the end of their acquaintance; but, not with a few months ended Anne's share of suffering from it. Her attachment and regrets had, for a long time, clouded every enjoyment of youth; and an early loss of bloom and spirits had been their lasting effect . . . No second attachment, the only thoroughly natural, happy, and sufficient cure, at her time of life, had been possible to the nice tone of her

mind, the fastidiousness of her taste, in the small limits of the society around. . . . She had been solicited, when about two-and-twenty, to change her name, by the young man, who not long afterwards found a more willing mind in her younger sister.

Again here it is suggested that the affections of men are too easily transferable—and not as long-lasting as those of women. 'All the privilege I claim for my own sex . . . is that of loving longest, when existence or when hope is gone,' Anne declares to Captain Harville. There is an unmistakable personal application here; the novelist is airing private disappointments. The 'small limits of the society around' Jane Austen undoubtedly hindered her marriage prospects; while 'the nice tone of her mind, the fastidiousness of her taste'—as she declared often enough herself—rendered her immune to the charms of all but the most exceptional of men, men such as she had little chance of meeting in a country village. Later Anne is proposed to again. 'It is something for a woman to be assured, in her eight-and-twentieth year, that she has not lost one charm of earlier youth,' Jane Austen writes. The tone is exultant; could she be thinking of some of her own more recent adventures—that with Haden the previous year (Jane was thirty-nine); or Edward Bridges' proposal (Jane was thirty-two); or the Bigg Wither affair (Jane was twenty-six)?

Persuasion is the same length as *Northanger Abbey*; they are Jane Austen's shortest books. The two novels were published together posthumously as a four-volume set, along with Henry Austen's 'Biographical Notice,' in December 1817—though the title-page bore the date 1818—just five months after the novelist's death.

Consistent to the last, the critics greeted the new volumes with almost universal silence. Only two contemporary reviews appeared.

In March 1818 the *British Critic*, the first journal to use Jane Austen's name in print, declared that her novels 'display a degree of excellence that has not been often surpassed.' The reviewer goes on to describe her deficient 'imagination' and 'invention': everything in her books is so 'obviously . . . drawn exclusively from experience.' Everyone in the novels is of 'the middle size.' But her 'fidelity' to real life makes her characters seem real to us: 'we instantly recognize among some of our acquaintance, the sort of persons she intends to signify, as accurately as if we heard their voices . . . Her merit consists altogether in her remarkable talent for observation' and her avoidance of extremes. 'In recording the customs and manners of commonplace people in the commonplace intercourse of life,' according to this reviewer, fresh from a reading of *Northanger Abbey*, Jane Austen 'never dips her pen in satire. . . . This is the result of that good sense which seems ever to keep complete possession over all the other qualities of [her] mind . . . she sees every thing just as it is'—in which her alleged 'want of imagination' is useful rather than otherwise, preventing 'exaggeration.' There is some carping at the 'improbabilities' of *Northanger Abbey*, but it is recommended as 'one of the very best of Miss Austen's productions.' The notice concludes with this account of *Persuasion*:

> With respect to the second of the novels, which the present publication contains, it will be necessary to say but little. It is in every respect a much less fortunate performance than that which we have just been considering [*Northanger Abbey*]. It is manifestly the work of the same mind, and contains parts of very great merit; among them, however, we certainly should not number its *moral*, which seems to be, that young people should always marry according to their own inclinations and upon their own judgment; for that if in consequence of listening to grave counsels, they defer their marriage, till they have wherewith to live upon, they will be laying the foundation for years of misery, such as only the heroes and heroines of novels can reasonably hope ever to see the end of.

The writer must have skipped over the passage in which Anne Elliot declares that she was right to take Lady Russell's advice, regardless of its intelligence and its consequences, because of their relative positions and of what was due to the older woman in such a situation. In any case, here begins the long tradition of critical undervaluation of *Persuasion*—a tradition reversed only in recent years.

Two months after this review appeared, *Blackwood's Edinburgh Magazine* for May 1818 described *Northanger Abbey* as 'lively' and *Persuasion* as 'pathetic.' They are quite as good as Jane Austen's preceding works, the article declares, but 'as stories they are nothing in themselves.' The anonymous writer nonetheless believed that Jane Austen's novels in the main possess 'a higher claim to popular estimation than . . . they have yet attained. They have fallen, indeed, upon an age whose taste can only be gratified with the highest seasoned food.' The piece goes on to assert that Jane Austen 'will be one of the most popular of English novelists'—if one can accept her 'certain limited range,' her 'narrow walk,' as constituting a claim to serious consideration. The long roll-call of assessments of Jane Austen's work as somehow 'narrow' or 'limited' may be said to begin here. *Blackwood's* critic says:

> She never operates among deep interests, uncommon characters, or vehement passions. The singular merit of her writings is, that we could conceive, without the slightest strain of imagination, any one of her fictions to be realized in any town or village in England, (for it is only English manners that she paints,) that we think we are reading the history of people whom we have seen thousands of times, and that with all this perfect commonness, both of incident and character, perhaps not one of her characters is to be found in any other book, portrayed at least in so lively and interesting a manner.

This patronising charge of 'commonness' was to dog Jane Austen's posthumous reputation for years—until, in the middle of the nineteenth century, G.H. Lewes, George Eliot and others perceived her mimetic genius as productive of the highest form of 'realism' rather than as anything second-rate. The cry about the absence in Jane Austen's novels of 'vehement passions' was taken up by Charlotte Brontë, Mark Twain and others, and became another critical commonplace which, to this day, may be found in some accounts of the novelist's work.

'I do not pretend to set people right, but I do see that they are often wrong.'
— Mary Crawford in *Mansfield Park*

'You must give me leave to judge for myself, and pay me the compliment of believing what I say.'
— Elizabeth Bennet in *Pride and Prejudice*

'I shall often have a niece with me.'
— Emma in *Emma*

The comic mask so often has a tragic face underneath it.
— Francis Iles, *Before the Fact*

'An Author, whether good or bad . . . is an Animal whom every body is privileged to attack; For though All are not able to write books, all conceive themselves able to judge them . . . to enter the lists of literature is wilfully to expose yourself to the arrows of neglect, ridicule, envy, and disappointment. Whether you write well or ill, be assured that you will not escape from blame.'
— Matthew Lewis, *The Monk* (1794)

I have not tried to prove anything, but only to paint my picture well and to set it in a good light.
— André Gide

CHAPTER 8

Waiting for Death, 1816–1817

The last ten months of Jane Austen's life were full of contradictions. She was her usual brilliant self; she was sulky and quiet. She was all kindness; she couldn't be bothered with others. She wrote; she couldn't write. She walked; she couldn't walk. She was up; she was down. Illness put into relief both the sunshine and the shadows of a complex personality; it also illuminated the softness and the magnanimity of which she was capable—and, in the midst of appalling suffering, her courage, and her serene, unshakable faith.

In September 1816, Cassandra took Mary Lloyd Austen, who had not yet fully recovered her health, and Mary's daughter Caroline, to Cheltenham for several weeks, where Mary tried the recuperative power of the waters. On the way they stopped at Kintbury to pick up Mary Jane Fowle, who joined the party and went on with them to the spa.

Writing to Cassandra from Chawton, Jane reports that her old beau Mr Seymour—Henry's man of business—'is either married or on the point of being married' to another lady. Henry himself is preparing to take orders. Their nephew James Edward is now at Chawton, writing a novel: 'it is extremely clever; written with great ease and spirit'—she only hopes he can keep it going in the same vein. 'Tell Caroline,' she adds, 'that I think it is hardly fair upon her & myself, to have him take up the Novel Line.' They will all—except her mother, of course, who does not go out—be dining with the Digweeds at Alton: neither the host nor the hostess is expected to 'add much to our wit.' She is astonished by Cassandra's account of their expenses at Cheltenham: 'Three Guineas a week for such lodgings!' The landlady must be charging extra because they are staying in the High Street. Cassandra wrote that Cheltenham had been more pleasant when she and Jane were there in the spring.

Undoubtedly the spa 'is to be preferred in May,' the novelist replied. She was to go back there again in May 1817. Jane acknowledges receipt of the ladies' plan for returning from Cheltenham; Caroline would accompany her aunt to Chawton. Some friends staying with Edward at Godmersham have just heard of the death of 'a rich old friend & cousin' by whose demise they will benefit, Jane reports— 'So, there is a happy end' of their visit. Frank's wife Mary is pregnant again, and she 'seldom either looks or appears quite well.—Little Embryo is troublesome I suppose.' The dinner with the Digweeds passed off pleasantly: 'Children well-behaved,' so the evening was tolerable. They played 'Charades & other Games,' as in the old days. Then everyone walked back to Chawton in the moonlight, and it was quite 'beautiful.' The novelist must have been in satisfactory health to be able to take such a walk—from Alton to Chawton—in September 1816. The back pains of which she complained had lessened. Indeed, she refers to herself in these terms: 'my Back has given me scarcely any pain for many days.—I have an idea that agitation does it as much harm as fatigue.' It was the thought of Cassandra's going away that made her ill, she thinks. A local physician is coming to call: 'I am nursing myself up now into as beautiful a state as I can.' Mrs Frank Austen's parents are planning to visit Chawton later in the month: 'there is too much reason to fear they will stay above a week.' She reports that one Sir Thomas Miller has died: 'I treat you with a dead Baronet in almost every Letter.' Certainly Jane's spirits and humour seem unimpaired; these letters of September 1816 have the old vigour and wit.

The novelist urges Cassandra to meet more people in Cheltenham and to write to her about them: 'I am quite weary of your knowing nobody.' Mrs Digweed's maid has a lover, and is being sacked. The cook is also being let go: she 'is guilty only of being unequal to anything.' Their brother Edward is just back from Paris, 'thinking of the French as one could wish, disappointed in everything.' Another acquaintance returned from France reports that the country, with Waterloo behind it and the monarchy restored, is 'a scene of general Poverty & Misery,—no Money, no Trade—nothing to be got but by the Innkeepers.' There is mention here of friends at Bridlington, which has sometimes been assumed to be the model for Sanditon. Ben Lefroy's brother has been visiting them at Chawton: 'I enjoyed Edward's company very much . . . & yet I was not sorry' to see him go, Jane says. 'It had been a busy week, & I wanted a few days quiet, &

exemption from the Thought & contrivances which any sort of company gives.' She is finding housekeeping, in Cassandra's absence, exhausting: 'I often wonder how *you* can find time for what you do, in addition to the care of the House.' She cannot help wondering how Mrs West—Jane West (1758-1852), author of *Alicia de Lacy, an Historical Romance* (1814) and other works—'c^d have written such books & collected so many hard words, with all her family cares.' Jane adds, quite candidly: 'Composition seems to me Impossible, with a head full of Joints of Mutton & doses of rhubarb.' There is a shortage of honey this year: 'Bad news for us.—We must husband our present stock of Mead.' Their cousin Mr Cooper has sent yet another volume of his sermons, which the novelist likes no better than its predecessors: 'they are fuller of Regeneration & Conversion than ever—with the addition of his zeal in the cause of the Bible society.'

These (4 and 8 September 1816) were the last letters Jane Austen was to write to her sister Cassandra during an interesting correspondence stretching back to the year 1796—more than twenty years. The two women were not separated again until the novelist's death ten months later.

The rest of the autumn at Chawton was largely taken up with a steady stream of visitors, and Jane, who found it 'impossible' both to compose and to deal with matters of mutton and rhubarb, wrote nothing further—except some letters in December—until the following January, so far as we know. Cassandra, with Caroline, returned to Chawton at the end of September. Around this time or early in October, Charles Austen, along with his daughters, came to visit his mother and sisters. The Gibsons, Frank's in-laws, remained at Chawton for some time, as Jane had feared. Henry was still there in November, preparing for his ordination. Charles and his girls stayed on during the autumn months. No other documentary information has survived concerning this period of Jane Austen's life. Undoubtedly she was burdened with domestic chores.

Henry was ordained in December, and went to live at Bentley, near Alton. Jane's nephew James Edward, in this same month, left Winchester for good. On her forty-first (and last) birthday—16 December 1816—the novelist wrote to him, at Steventon, a long congratulatory letter. One of the most charming epistles Jane Austen ever dispatched to any correspondent, it begins thus:

One reason for my writing to you now, is that I may have the pleasure of directing to you *Esqre*.—I give you joy of having left Winchester.—Now you may own, how miserable you were there; now, it will gradually all come out—your Crimes & your Miseries—how often you went up by the Mail to London & threw away Fifty Guineas at a Tavern, & how often you were on the point of hanging yourself—restrained only, as some illnatured aspersion upon poor old Winton [probably a reference to the fifth earl] has it, by the want of a Tree within some miles of the City.

James Edward's uncles Henry and Charles, she says, are with them now at Chawton, and both are in excellent health and spirits.

And they are each . . . so agreable in their different way, & harmonize so well, that their visit is thorough enjoyment.— Uncle Henry writes very superior Sermons.—You and I must try to get hold of one or two, & put them into our Novels; it would be a fine help to a volume; and we could make our Heroine read it aloud of a Sunday Evening, just as well as Isabella Wardour in the Antiquary, is made to read the History of the Hartz Demon in the ruins of St. Ruth—though I beleive, upon recollection, Lovell is the Reader.—By the bye, my dear Edward, I am quite concerned for the loss your Mother mentions in her Letter; two Chapters & a half to be missing is monstrous! It is well that *I* have not been at Steventon lately, & therefore cannot be suspected of purloining them;—two strong twigs & a half towards a Nest of my own, would have been something.—I do not think however that any theft of that sort would be really very useful to me. What should I do with your strong, manly, spirited Sketches, full of Variety and Glow?— How could I possibly join them on to the little bit (two Inches wide) of Ivory on which I work with so fine a Brush, as produces little effect after much labour?

The famous last sentence of this passage has sometimes been perversely taken as an admission by Jane Austen that her scope was narrow, her range limited. It is in fact only a little piece of modesty and probably of irony, suggesting that her sort of fiction is perhaps less flamboyant, more subtle, than much contemporary popular

fiction—such as Scott's *The Antiquary*, published in this very year
(1816). What an undisciplined and inexperienced eighteen-year-old
boy might compose, says his aunt as tactfully as possible, would
necessarily belong to a different *genre* altogether. Again the novelist
acknowledges her tendency to work with great dedication on the
smallest, most minute aspect of every book so as to render everything
in it as finished, as polished, as possible. It is an admission of
perfectionism, not of limitation: as she once said, an artist cannot do
anything slovenly. It may also be worth pointing out in this
connection that for many years at Chawton Jane Austen's little ivory
date book, with the day of the week incised minutely at the bottom of
each of the tiny ivory slivers, hung on the wall within her reach. It
measured about two inches. Important engagements for each day of
the week could be written on it in ink, and then washed off. The
novelist's reference to two inches of ivory, always taken meta-
phorically, may in fact be more literal than anyone has thought. In
any case, as an artist she is in no sense a miniaturist.

The difficulty she now faced in getting any of her own work done
may be glimpsed in the wistful reference to her nephew's lost
chapters: 'two strong twigs & a half towards a Nest of my own, would
have been something.' And Jane goes on here to touch on her health.
Revealingly, she is now unable to walk to Alton and back, by moonlight or otherwise—'the walk is beyond my strength (though I am
otherwise very well) & this is not a Season for Donkey Carriages,'
being December. The letter to James Edward goes on to quote a play
well-known to the novelist when she was a girl living at Steventon—
Hannah Cowley's *Which is the Man?*; there was nothing wrong with
Jane Austen's memory, certainly. She also reports that her mother is
anxious to receive some back rent owing from a defaulting tenant;
money seems to have been very much on Mrs Austen's mind during
these years. The letter ends as spiritedly as it began: 'Adieu
Amiable!—I hope Caroline [his sister] behaves well to you.'

During this Christmas season at Chawton, Jane dispatched two
other letters, both brief. Towards the end of December she wrote to
thank Anna Lefroy for the gift of a turkey, commenting that 'Such
Highmindedness is almost more than [her mother] can bear.' Rarely,
even now, could she mention her mother without a hint of asperity or
ridicule. Early in January 1817 the novelist sent a letter, in which
every word is written backwards, to her niece Cassandra, wishing her
both a happy new year and a happy birthday (she was nine; Jane

pretended to think she was three). Her uncle Frank, the novelist told little Cassandra, was learning Latin. Peacetime could be wearisome for sailors.

Such energy, eloquence, and playfulness in her letters suggest that during the winter of 1816–17 Jane Austen was not yet feeling seriously ill.

II

During the latter part of January 1817 the novelist addressed two letters to her niece Caroline. James Edward had again been visiting, and they kept him at Chawton as long as they could—somewhat to the annoyance of his half-sister Anna Lefroy, who wished to entertain him at Wyards. 'We have used Anna as ill as we would,' Jane writes, 'but it is a Vile World, we are all for Self & I expected no better for any of us. But though *Better* is not to be expected, *Butter* may'—and some local news follows. They have been enjoying the young man's novel. As for what Caroline (aged eleven) has sent her—Jane's advice is to be exact in description, even of the most apparently trivial matters, and to leave in the reader's mind no suspicion of absurdity.

Charles Austen was still staying with them, and suffering now from rheumatism. '*I* feel myself getting stronger than I was half a year ago, & so can perfectly well walk to Alton, *or* back again, without the slightest fatigue that I hope to be able to do both when Summer comes,' the novelist declares. She has just spent several days with Frank and Mary and their family: though of course she 'cannot help liking them & even loving them,' the children 'are sometimes very noisy & not under such Order as they ought & easily might' be. Those Musgrove children again. Though feeling better than she had a few months ago, Jane Austen remained sensitive to noise, and believed, as always, in keeping children 'under . . . Order.'

The other letter to Caroline is very brief. It reports that Charles's daughter Harriet is ill; that they are all in mourning for the death of a distant relative, Mrs Motley Austen—'we thought it necessary to array ourselves in our old Black Gowns, because there is a line of Connection with the family'; and that, reading Caroline's latest story, her aunt Jane has come to the conclusion that 'You have some eccentric Tastes . . . as to Heroes & Heroines.'

On 24 January, three days before she began her last sustained stint of fiction-writing, Jane dispatched a letter to her old friend Alethea

Bigg of Manydown, staying at present with her sister Mrs Hill at Streatham. 'I think it is time there should be a little writing between us,' the novelist begins, 'though I believe the epistolary debt is on *your* side.' She reports that she herself has 'certainly gained strength through the winter and am not far from being well; and I think I understand my own case now so much better than I did, as to be able by care to keep off any serious return of illness. I am more & more convinced that *bile* is at the bottom of all I have suffered, which makes it easy to know how to treat myself.' The treatment in question is not specified. Her mother, says Jane, perseveres in her determination not to leave home: 'our donkeys are necessarily having so long a run of luxurious idleness that I suppose we shall find they have forgotten much of their education when we use them again.' She is a little uneasy about Anna's husband Ben, now the father of two children: 'I wish [he] were ordained & all the family in a comfortable Parsonage house.' Henry, whom she calls 'Our own new clergyman,' is coming soon to Chawton, and they will all 'be very glad when [their] first hearing [of him] is over. It will be a nervous hour for our pew, though we hear that he acquits himself with as much ease and collectedness, as if he had been used to it all his life.'

There follows an interesting reference to Southey, Mr Hill's son-in-law and the present poet-laureate (the laureateship, accepted by Southey in 1813, had first been offered to Scott):

> We have been reading the 'Poet's Pilgrimage to Waterloo,' and generally with much approbation. Nothing will please all the world, you know; but parts of it suit me better than much that he has written before. The opening—the *proem* I believe he calls it—is very beautiful. Poor man! one cannot but grieve for the loss of a son so fondly described. Has he at all recovered [from] it? What do Mr. and Mrs. Hill know of his present state?

Such curiosity was natural. Southey had lost his eldest child Herbert in April 1816; the *proem* to the poem contains an affectionate description of the boy.

Jane concludes with a typical sentiment. She hopes their letters from abroad are satisfactory. 'They would not be satisfactory to *me*, I confess, unless they breathed a strong spirit of regret for not being in England.' 'The real object of this letter,' she adds in a postscript, is to get from her friend a recipé for 'some excellent orange wine' they remember having at Manydown; the novelist had not gone back there since the Bigg Wither affair of 1802.

On 27 January 1817 Jane Austen began the work that was eventually called *Sanditon*, the writing of which was to be broken off on 18 March due to her poor health. What we have is only a first draft, and heavily corrected. Twelve chapters were completed between January and March; there are no paragraph divisions, and much is abbreviated—the whole thing, it has been said, conveying 'the air of being written fast to keep pace with the speed of composition'—as if, that is, the writer, puffing and breathless, couldn't get it all down fast enough. This suggests both mental vivacity and physical decline; and such terms indeed seem applicable to Jane Austen during these early months of 1817, for from February on her illness, which had been in remission for some time, attacked her again with renewed vigour.

During the composition of *Sanditon* she kept up her correspondence with her nieces, in February and March writing two long letters to Fanny Knight (now twenty-three) at Godmersham and a shorter one to Caroline Austen at Steventon.

The novelist was in her light and bright and sparkling mood as she addressed Fanny:

> You are the delight of my Life . . . You are worth your weight in Gold, or even in the new Silver Coinage . . . You are the Paragon of all that is Silly & Sensible, common-place & eccentric, Sad & Lively, Provoking & Interesting.—Who can keep pace with the fluctuations of your Fancy, the Capprizios of your Taste, the Contradictions of your Feelings? . . . It is very, very gratifying to me to know you so intimately. You can hardly think what a pleasure it is to me, to have such thorough pictures of your Heart.—Oh! what a loss it will be when you are married. You are too agreable in your single state, too agreable as a Neice. I shall hate you when your delicious play of Mind is all settled down into conjugal & maternal affections . . . Do not imagine that I have any real objection . . . I only do not like you sh^d marry anybody. And yet I do wish you to marry very much, because I know you will never be happy till you are; but the loss of a Fanny Knight will never be made up to me.

Jane Austen's ambivalent feelings during her last months on the subject of matrimony are articulated here—humorously, but, one feels, firmly too. It is also worth noticing that the letter, dated 20 February, was written only eight days after the new silver coinage was proclaimed on 12 February 1817 (replacing a debased currency); as always, the novelist kept herself well-informed.

She writes briefly of her health. 'I am almost entirely cured of my rheumatism; just a little pain in my knee now and then, to make me remember what it was, & keep on flannel.—Aunt Cassandra nursed me so beautifully!' As to John Plumtre, Fanny's old suitor, her aunt writes: 'Why should you be living in dread of his marrying somebody else?—(Yet, how natural!).' Jane Austen knew well enough what it felt like to hear of men marrying elsewhere who had once come courting her. She goes on to warn Fanny, in accents which may remind us of the advice given by Darcy and Miss Bingley to Bingley in *Pride and Prejudice* relative to the Bennet family, against a possible marriage to another suitor, Mr Wildman: 'Think of his Principles, think of his Father's objections, of want of Money, of a coarse Mother, of Brothers & Sisters like Horses, of sheets sewn across.' In the autumn of 1813, while at Godmersham, the novelist had spent two days and a night with Edward's friends the Wildmans at Chilham Castle, and found the visit tiring and dull. Clearly, the Wildmans were not her favourite family. Still, what was social satire two decades earlier would appear to be offered as earnest advice now. Despite the warnings of *Persuasion* about 'persuasion' in romantic matters, Jane Austen sounds alarmingly like her own Lady Russell here.

Fanny's brothers Henry and William, now nineteen and eighteen respectively, were staying at Chawton at the time, and Jane is full of their praises. "We are very comfortable together—that is, we can answer for *ourselves*.' The italics are suggestive; was Grandmama, perhaps, not quite so cordial? The novelist notes that Fanny is 'well stocked' with 'Scandal & Gossip'; and that people are now dancing '*Quadrilles*,' which she thinks 'very inferior to the Cotillions of my own day.' A catty comment about Anna—not for the first time in a letter from Jane to her favourite niece—follows. Anna has recently been at Chawton, looking 'so innocent, as if she had never had a wicked Thought in her Life—which yet one has some reason to suppose she must have had . . . if one remember the events of her girlish days'—undoubtedly a reference to Anna's abortive engagement to Michael Terry a few years earlier. No longer a girl, Anna was now twenty-three, and the mother of two daughters. Jane Austen could be censorious (and disloyal) behind the backs of those with whom she was apparently intimate; we have seen this in her correspondence before.

Avoid 'irrecoverably [attaching yourself] to one Person!' Jane exhorts Fanny at the end of this letter. She begs her niece neither to love, nor to think herself in love.

> Sweet Fanny, beleive no such thing of yourself.—Spread no such malicious slander upon your Understanding, within the Precincts of your Imagination.—Do not speak ill of your Sense, merely for the Gratification of your Fancy.—Yours is Sense, which deserves more honourable Treatment.—You are *not* in love. . . . You have never been really in love.

It is interesting to see the novelist yet again exalting 'Sense' over 'Fancy.' At the end of her life she seems to have had moments when, half hysterically, she considered 'love' an hallucinatory disorder.

Three weeks later we find the novelist acknowledging another letter from Fanny—and offering some familiar sentiments on the suit of the ubiquitous Mr Wildman: 'By your description he can*not* be in love with you, however he may try at it.' Of the flirtatious airs of a friend of Fanny's: 'Who can understand a young Lady?' Of the inconvenient demise of a neighbour of the Knights: "Poor Mrs. . . . Milles, that she should die on a wrong day at last, after being about it so long! . . . I hope her . . . Spirit . . . was not conscious of the division and disappointment she was occasioning'; apparently the heinous crime which constituted Mrs Milles' last earthly act was the breaking up of an agreeable party at Goodnestone. Mrs Milles left behind her an impoverished, unmarried sister-in-law. Jane comments: 'Single Women have a dreadful propensity to being poor—which is one strong argument in favour of Matrimony.' Here is a theme of every one of her books articulated in a single sentence.

The novelist persists in her matrimonial warnings: 'Do not be in a hurry'; when the right man comes along he 'will so completely attach you, that you will feel you never really loved before.' Like Anne Elliot's passionate speech to Captain Harville on the constancy of woman's love, this declaration has the ring of personal experience and conviction. But the tone of voice is Lady Russell's now, not Anne Elliot's.

The novelist reports the news of Mrs Frank Austen's imminent confinement, adding that Mary 'is by no means remarkably Large for *her.'* Anna, she says, has declared that her elder daughter Jemima 'has a very irritable bad Temper . . . I hope as Anna is so early sensible of it's defects, that she will give Jemima's disposition the early & steady attention it must require.' Jane believed that the disposition of a child at least in part must be a reflection and a result of the amount of parental attention it received. Clearly the subject interested her.

It is in this letter to Fanny that she discloses her present publication plans. 'Miss Catherine [*Northanger Abbey*] is put upon the Shelve for the present, and I do not know that she will ever come out; but I have a something ready for Publication, which may perhaps appear a twelvemonth hence. It is short, about the length of Catherine.' What this tells us is that the revision of 'Susan' was long over with, but—for the moment, at least—the tale was out of circulation; Jane had simply put it away. It also suggests that whatever further revisions she may have had in mind for *Persuasion*, if any, were minimal; it is characterised here—and in a subsequent letter—as 'ready for Publication.'

She goes on to give an account of the present state of her health:

> I am got tolerably well again, quite equal to walking about & enjoying the Air; and by sitting down & resting a good while between my Walks, I get exercise enough. I have a scheme however for accomplishing more, as the weather grows springlike. I mean to take to riding the Donkey. It will be more independant & less troublesome than the use of the carriage, & I shall be able to go about with A^t Cassandra in her walks to Alton and Wyards.

The days of long walks were over now. It was the donkey or nothing.

Another passage demonstrates Jane Austen's tendency to keep herself informed of current events. 'If I were the Duchess of Richmond,' she writes, 'I should be very miserable about my son's choice. What can be expected from a Paget, born & brought up in the centre of conjugal Infidelity & Divorces?—I will *not* be interested about Lady Caroline. I abhor all the race of Pagets.' As Mrs Hodge reminds us, the novelist must have known something of Henry William Paget, Lord Uxbridge and later Marquess of Anglesey, whose liaison with the Duke of Wellington's sister-in-law had made it difficult for the two men to serve together in the Army. By the time of Waterloo, two divorces and two marriages had turned Mrs

Wellesley into Lady Uxbridge. At Waterloo, where her husband
bravely commanded Wellington's cavalry, relations between the two
men apparently remained cool. History reports this desultory
exchange between them. 'By God,' said Uxbridge, looking down,
'I've lost my leg.' 'Have you, by God,' said Wellington, and rode on.
Wellington's laconic nature, it must be stressed, was proverbial, and
the story is one of many which may illustrate this rather than any real
'coolness' between him and another man. He once mentioned seeing
a rat inside a brandy bottle. A brash young subaltern remarked that it
must have been a very large bottle. 'It was a damned small bottle,'
came the reply. Subaltern: 'Then it must have been a very small rat.'
Wellington: 'It was a damned large rat.'

The novelist's letter to Fanny ends with a reference to Charles's
daughter Harriet. The seven-year-old child was still ill, and the case
was thought to be grave. 'I hope Heaven in its mercy will take her
soon,' says her aunt Jane. Harriet lived until 1865.

On 14 March the novelist wrote to Caroline. She presses her niece
to urge her brother James Edward to go on with his novel: 'In that he
will find his true fame & his true wealth.' James Edward took orders,
inherited a fortune from his great-aunt Mrs Leigh Perrot, and never
finished his novel. 'I have just rec^d nearly nearly twenty pounds
myself on the 2^d Edit: of S&S—which gives me this fine flow of
Literary Ardour,' Jane says. This was the last royalty payment she
would receive; during her lifetime her literary earnings totalled
approximately £670. 'Fine flow of Literary Ardour' or not, just four
days later, on 18 March 1817, Jane Austen stopped writing the tale
she was engaged on—Sanditon—and, except for half a dozen
(surviving) letters composed over the next four months, laid down
her pen forever.

III

At 25,000 words, Sanditon—which the novelist intended to call 'The
Brothers,' and which was given the title by which it has come down to
us by Henry Austen—is about one-quarter as long as Northanger
Abbey or Persuasion. Critics in the main have tended to ignore it;
only a few have discussed it at any length or taken it seriously, and
many of these—most notably E.M. Forster—have dismissed it as the
last gasp of a dying woman. But 'there is no evidence here of mental
fatigue or loss of ideas,' as Joan Rees observes—or that the novelist's

art had 'reached the end of its trajectory,' as Alistair Duckworth rightly says—quite the contrary. Brian Southam calls it 'the most vigorous of all Jane Austen's writing. There is not the least sign of fatigue in its style, invention, or design.' He goes on, in both of his long essays on the fragment, to emphasise the similarities (and the differences) between *Sanditon* and the rest of the fiction.

Even in its unfinished form—the MS did not have a contemporary editor to regularise spelling and punctuation or smooth out diction—*Sanditon* recognisably is a Jane Austen performance. At the centre of it, as so often in her stories, is the question of appearance and reality, true and false moral values, accurate and inaccurate ways of *seeing*. Before she encounters them, *Sanditon*'s heroine, Charlotte Heywood—the novelist, remember, once said she had always wanted to have a heroine named Charlotte—is told a great many things about Sanditon and its inhabitants. Like Elizabeth Bennet, she must discover the truth of what she has been told—the actual nature of things and people in the world she inhabits—for and by herself. What she hears about Lady Denham, and how she ultimately perceives her, is only one case in point. Southam is surely right to suggest that *Sanditon* could well have been sub-titled 'Delusion and Reality.'

Sanditon is also a familiar performance in its savage attack on 'improvers' and 'developers,' and in its anti-urban bias. Could any breed of man be more calculated to incur the wrath of a Jane Austen than that which seeks to turn unspoiled countryside into urban sprawl? Anticipating such later nineteenth-century attacks on 'developers' and their new methods of 'advertising' as those contained in Gissing's *Demos* and *In the Year of Jubilee*, Jane Austen in *Sanditon* condemns those who feel the need to bring 'civilization' to country villages. Here is part of her description of what Lady Denham and her partner Mr Parker have done to Sanditon:

> A very few years ago . . . it had been a quiet Village of no pretensions; but some natural advantages in its position & some accidental circumstances having suggested to [Mr. Parker], & the other principal Land Holder [Lady Denham], the probability of it's becoming a profitable Speculation, they had engaged in it, & planned & built, & praised & puffed, & raised it to a something of young Renown.

Marilyn Butler has written brilliantly of this theme in *Sanditon*:

the point is Sanditon's perversion from its earlier natural role as fishing village and agricultural community, a place where children are born and vegetable gardens flourish. Its new smart terraces are an artificial engraftment, created by an over-sophisticated society's obsession with its bodily health, and by the economic opportunism of characters like Mr. Parker and Lady Denham. The people who flock to Sanditon are of the type of gentry Jane Austen always censures: urban, rootless, irresponsible, self-indulgent.

Everyone in such places, the novelist declares here, must '"move in a circle",—to the prevalence of which rototory Motion, is perhaps to be attributed the Giddiness & false steps of many.' The 'society' of fashionable towns—its evening parties, its gossip—she always regarded with abhorrence.

Like Bath, Brighton, and Cheltenham, Sanditon is a spa. It may be modelled on Worthing, then a new development; there are references in Jane Austen's letters of 1805 to a proposed visit to Worthing— along with a cryptic reference to a competing visit to Sandling, in Kent. The latter name inevitably is suggestive. So are Sandgate and Sandwich (also in Kent). Whatever its original, Sanditon caters primarily to invalids. Indeed, 'Never was there a place more palpably designed by Nature for the resort of the Invalid—the very Spot which Thousands seemed in need of,' declares Mr Parker. *Sanditon* extends this theme to satirise hypochondria. We know that Jane suffered at close quarters from her mother's hypochrondria during much of her adult life; in all likelihood she worked off some of the results of that particular form of suffering in the character of Mr Woodhouse in *Emma*, as we have seen. Here the attack on hypochondriacs is less gentle, and less subtle.

The sea and air of Sanditon are said to be 'a match for every Disorder ... They were anti-spasmodic, anti-pulmonary, anti-sceptic, anti-bilious & anti-rheumatic.' The fragment bulges with invalids and hypochondriacs of various species—one of them cannot eat toast without huge amounts of butter; otherwise it acts on his stomach like a nutmeg-grater—each of whom is able to demonstrate astonishing strength and blinding energy on selected (and usually private and selfish) occasions. Mr Parker's description of his sister Susan shows Jane Austen writing in a vein approaching something like black comedy:

She has been suffering much from the Headache and Six
Leaches a day for 10 days together releived so little that we
thought it right to change our measures—and being convinced
on examination that much of the Evil lay in her Gum, I
persuaded her to attack the disorder there. She has accordingly
had 3 Teeth drawn, & is decidedly better, but her Nerves are a
good deal deranged. She can only speak in a whisper—and
fainted away twice this morning on poor Arthur's trying to
suppress a cough.

Charlotte sees the Parkers and their relations for what they are:

It was impossible for Charlotte not to suspect a good deal of
fancy in such an extraordinary state of health.—Disorders &
Recoveries so very much out of the common way, seemed more
like the amusement of eager Minds in want of employment than
of actual afflictions & releif. The Parkers, were no doubt a
family of Imagination & quick feelings . . . . an unfortunate
turn for Medecine, especially quack Medecine, had given them
an early tendency at various times, to various Disorders;—the
rest of their sufferings was from Fancy, the love of Distinction
& the love of the Wonderful.

'There was Vanity in all they did, as well as in all they endured,'
Charlotte concludes.

Here, as elsewhere in her work, Jane Austen attacks 'quick
feelings' and 'the love of the Wonderful'—overactive 'Fancy' and
'Imagination'; this is yet another instance—the last—of her lifelong
commentary on the dangers of 'romance' and the excesses of
sentimentality.

Coming into Willingden, Mr Parker sees a cottage 'romantically
situated among wood on a high Eminence at some little Distance,'
and waxes fanciful about it; later he discovers that it is inhabited by
Mr Heywood's shepherd and three old ladies. Sir Edward Denham,
one of Jane Austen's most brilliant creations, speaks of nature as if
he were a Romantic poet on temporary leave from a lunatic
asylum:

He began, in a tone of great Taste & Feeling, to talk of the Sea
& the Sea shore—& ran with Energy through all the usual

Phrases employed in praise of their Sublimity, & descriptive of the *undescribable* Emotions they excite in the Mind of Sensibility.—The terrific Grandeur of the Ocean in a Storm, its glassy surface in a calm, it's Gulls & its Samphire [a maritime plant; but Denham may be remembering the hackneyed 'Dover cliffs' scene in *King Lear*, III, vi, where the word occurs: 'gathering samphire, dreadful trade'], & the deep fathoms of it's Abysses, it's quick vicissitudes, it's direful Deceptions, it's Mariners tempting it in Sunshine & overwhelmed by the sudden Tempest. All were eagerly & fluently touched.

Surely the novelist had been reading the *Lyrical Ballads*—or Byron. When Sir Edward goes on to speak extravagantly of Burns, the following colloquy takes pleace between himself and Charlotte:

Sir Edward: 'Burns is always on fire.—His soul was the Altar in which lovely Woman sat enshrined, his Spirit truly breathed the immortal Incence which is her Due.'

Charlotte: 'I have read several of Burn's [*sic*] poems with great delight . . . but I am not poetic enough to separate a Man's Poetry entirely from his Character;—& poor Burns's known Irregularities greatly interrupt my enjoyment of his Lines.—I have difficulty in depending on the *Truth* of his feelings as a Lover. I have not faith in the *sincerity* of the affections of a Man of his Description. He felt & he wrote & he forgot.'

Sir Edward: 'Oh! no no. . . . He was all ardour & Truth!—His Genius & his Susceptibilities might lead him into some Aberrations—But who is perfect?—It were Hyper-criticism, it were Pseudo-philosophy to expect from the soul of high toned Genius, the grovellings of a common mind.—The Coruscations of Talent . . . are perhaps incompatible with some of the prosaic Decencies of Life.'

Besides indicating that the novelist had adopted the standard early nineteenth-century view of Burns (which was also Wordsworth's) as a man of genius but of irregular habits and undependable temperament—amply documented in Currie's 'Life,' appended to the first edition of the poet's works published in 1800 and in several subsequent editions thereafter—this exchange may be seen in many ways as characteristic of Jane Austen. It is all there—man's tendency to 'forget' before woman does, as *Persuasion* suggests; the belief in '*Truth*' and '*sincerity*' as the cornerstones of art (rather than 'Sensibility'); the conviction that the artist is no less obligated than the ordinary mortal to lead an exemplary life.

Charlotte ultimately discovers Sir Edward to be 'downright silly .... why he sh^d talk so much Nonsense, unless he could do no better, was unintelligible.—He seemed very sentimental, very full of some Feelings or other, & very much addicted to all the newest-fashioned hard words—had not a very clear Brain she presumed, & talked a good deal by rote.'

In fact, Sir Edward has been driven nearly mad by his reading of sentimental and Romantic literature. Written on the heels of *Persuasion*, which also takes an anti-Romantic line, as we have seen, *Sanditon* gives another clear indication of what Jane Austen thought of sentimental literature and its readers. We have encountered this perspective before—not only in *Persuasion*, but also in *Emma*, more forcefully in *Northanger Abbey* and *Sense and Sensibility*, in the Juvenilia and even in the letters (March 1814: 'I have read the Corsair, mended my petticoat, & have nothing else to do'). Sir Edward's taste in novels is described in particular detail and with obvious relish; it provides a good example of the age's predilection for the sort of 'highly seasoned' fiction referred to by *Blackwood's* the following year in its review of the posthumous volume. Sir Edward says:

The Novels which I approve are such as display Human Nature with Grandeur—such as shew her in the Sublimities of intense Feeling—such as exhibit the progress of strong Passion from the first Germ of incipient Susceptibility to the utmost Energies of Reason half-dethroned,—where we see the strong spark of Woman's Captivations elicit such Fire in the Soul of Man as leads him—(though at the risk of some Aberration from the strict line of Primitive Obligations)—to hazard all, dare all, atcheive all, to obtain her.—Such are the Works which I peruse with delight, & I hope I may say, with amelioration. They hold forth the most splendid Portraitures of high Conceptions, Unbounded Views, illimitable Ardour, indomptible [*sic*] Decision—and even when the Event is mainly anti-prosperous to the high-toned Machinations of the prime Character, the potent, pervading Hero of the Story, it leaves us full of Generous Emotions for him;—our Hearts are paralized—. T'were Pseudo-Philosophy to assert that we do not feel more enwraped by the brilliancy of his Career, than by the tranquil &

morbid Virtues of any opposing Character. Our approbation
of the Latter is but Eleemosynary [charitable].—These are the
Novels which enlarge the primitive Capabilities of the Heart,
& which it cannot impugn the Sense or be any Dereliction of
the character, of the most anti-peurile Man, to be conversant
with.

Here is Jane Austen's version of How Not To Do It—a definition of
the kind of novel she had spent a lifetime working to expunge from
public taste, described in language which, one feels, she found equally
repugnant. 'If I understand you aright,' Charlotte replies, succinctly,
to this long speech, 'our taste in Novels is not at all the same.'
    The author of *Sense and Sensibility* and *Northanger Abbey* goes on
in her own voice to attack the literary taste of Sir Edward
Denham:

> The Truth was that Sir Edw: whom circumstances had
> confined very much to one spot had read more sentimental
> Novels than agreed with him. His fancy had been early caught
> by all the impassioned, & most exceptionable parts of
> Richardsons [*sic*]; & such Authors as have since appeared to
> tread in Richardson's steps, so far as Man's determined pursuit
> of Woman in defiance of every opposition of feeling &
> convenience is concerned, had since occupied the greater part
> of his literary hours, & formed his Character.—With a
> perversity of Judgement, which must be attributed to his not
> having by Nature a very strong head, the Graces, the Spirit, the
> Sagacity, & the Perseverance, of the Villain of the Story
> outweighed all his absurdities & all his Atrocities with Sir
> Edward. With him, such Conduct was Genius, Fire &
> Feeling.—It interested & inflamed him; & he was always more
> anxious for its Success & mourned over its Discomfitures with
> more Tenderness than c^d ever have been contemplated by the
> Authors.

Thus Jane Austen continues the assault, begun years earlier in the
Juvenilia, on inept imitators of her favourite Richardson, who turn
out nothing but false sentiment. As in her preceding works, the
excesses of 'fancy' are specially singled out for excoriation, and
associated with lack of insight.

The novelist's attack on sentimental and Romantic fiction concludes here with a hilarious account of the results, morally speaking, of Sir Edward's reading of trashy novels. They have not made him merely fanciful; they have made him deranged.

> Sir Edw:'s great object in life was to be seductive.—With such personal advantages as he knew himself to possess, & such Talents as he did also give himself credit for, he regarded it as his Duty.—He felt that he was formed to be a dangerous Man—quite in the line of the Lovelaces.—The very name of Sir Edward he thought, carried some degree of fascination with it.—To be generally gallant & assiduous about the fair, to make fine speeches to every pretty Girl, was but the inferior part of the Character he had to play.

Looking around for someone appropriate to seduce and carry off with him, Sir Edward settles on Clara Brereton: 'Her Situation in every way called for it. She was . . . young, lovely & dependant.' Even Charlotte—'perhaps . . . owing to her having just issued from a Circulating Library'—sees Clara as, in every way, 'a complete Heroine . . . She seemed placed . . . on purpose to be ill-used. Such Poverty & Dependance joined to such Beauty & Merit seemed to leave no choice in the business.' Making allowances for the novelist's irony, one might conclude that Sir Edward's disease could be contagious—especially among the users of circulating libraries. Sir Edward has in mind no ordinary escapade: he wishes to do something spectacular in the seduction line—'to strike out something new, to exceed those who had gone before him.' He has a problem, however: he cannot afford anything extravagant. 'Prudence,' Jane Austen comments here, 'obliged him to prefer the quietest sort of ruin & disgrace . . . to the more renowned.' Poor Sir Edward: *quiet* ruin and disgrace do not coincide with his concept of duty in these circumstances.

Well: here is no ordinary seducer; here is no Wickham, no Willoughby, no William Elliot. Instead, here is a deeply interesting and amusing psychological study of a type; here is one of Jane Austen's most superb human portraits. Her marvellous account of the character of Sir Edward Denham even by itself must make us bitterly regret the catastrophic illness which put a stop to the writing of *Sanditon*. It promised to be one of her greatest achievements; her critics and students ignore it at their peril. Elizabeth Jenkins is one of the few readers of *Sanditon* to see the true significance of Sir Edward Denham:

> The character breaks new ground; because though Willoughby had a very ugly story in his past, and Wickham thought nothing of eloping with a girl who threw herself at his head, and Henry Crawford was so loose-living that he couldn't resist an affair even in circumstances when it was bound to cost him the engagement he was really anxious to secure; Edward Denham, the young man who had read too many novels and fancied himself as a Lovelace, approached the matter from a different angle, and his attitude is defined with an outspokenness unprecedented even in Jane Austen's workmanlike frankness, and with an almost weary cynicism.

Sir Edward is not the only character in *Sanditon* lacking a true education. There is yet another attack here on inept female 'education' and the false values it may implant. The Miss Beauforts, for example, are 'very accomplished & Ignorant,' their intellectual efforts being expended chiefly on matters of dress—'the object of all' they do being 'to captivate some Man of much better fortune than their own.' The connection between false values, insufficient education, and plain cupidity is centred chiefly in the character of Lady Denham, another portrait one regrets Jane Austen left unfinished. Lady Denham's 'faults,' it is said, 'may be entirely imputed to her want of Education.' She is surrounded by people whose sole object is to get their hands on her money; her sole object is to keep them from succeeding. Lady Denham's idea of what constitutes Sanditon's greatest need is revealing:

> And if we c^d but get a young Heiress to [Sanditon]! But Heiresses are monstrous scarce! I do not think we have had an Heiress here, or even a Co—since Sanditon has been a public place. Families come after Families, but as far as I can learn, it is not one in an hundred of them that have any real Property, Landed or Funded.—An Income perhaps, but no Property. Clergymen may be, or Lawyers from Town, or Half pay officers, or Widows with only a Jointure. And what good can such people do anybody?

This might comfortably fit into one of the early pieces: Jane Austen had come full circle from the Juvenilia. If in *Sanditon* she had been planning to go more deeply into the human psyche than ever before, this last work, had it been completed, might have been her most savagely cynical performance.

As might be expected, there are also one or two autobiographical resonances here. Charlotte's parents are pointedly praised for doing as much as they can, in the small village in which the Heywoods live, to enable their daughters to come in the way of husbands. After all, as *Sanditon* observes, 'young Ladies that have no Money are very much to be pitied!'—husbands must be found for them. Though her intelligence and her powers of discernment are acute, Charlotte, so long as we know her, manages to avoid overt censoriousness. She sees much, but says little—though, as *Sanditon* roundly declares, 'There is a someone in most families privileged by superior abilities or spirits to say anything.' Surely we hear the voice of the novelist here.

No account of *Sanditon* was given out until 1871. In the second edition of his *Memoir*, J.E. Austen-Leigh provided a description of what he called the 'last work,' and quoted some things from it. The whole did not see the light of day until 1925, when it was published in Chapman's edition of the *Minor Works*. To this day, in a sense, *Sanditon* has yet to be reviewed.

IV

What made Jane Austen stop writing *Sanditon?* It began 'in her usual firm and neat hand,' the *Memoir* informs us, 'but some of the latter pages were first traced in pencil—probably, when she was too ill to sit long at a desk—and afterwards written over in ink.'

The disease that killed her was, quite simply, tuberculosis. But it was tuberculosis of a relatively uncommon kind, attacking as it did not the lungs—as in the case of Keats, to take just one contemporary example—but the adrenal glands. Consumption of the adrenal glands had no name in 1817, though later one form of it would be called Addison's Disease. In our day, thanks to the introduction of the drug cortisone in the early 1950s, Addison's Disease has ceased to be a fatal illness; the syndrome it represented is now known simply as adrenal cortex insufficiency, treatable with cortisone. Among other things cortisone prevents the blotchy pigmentation of exposed areas of the skin typical of Addison's Disease and helps control secretions of the pituitary gland. This disease, in other words, is no longer life-threatening—as it was, for example, for John F. Kennedy as recently as the late 1940s.

Jane Austen died of miliary tuberculosis of the adrenal cortex. Adrenal insufficiency may be due to tuberculosis, or simple atrophy. Its onset usually does occur between the ages of thirty and fifty (the novelist was forty-one); periods of remission, in which the disease seems to have disappeared, are not uncommon. In Jane Austen's day, before Thomas Addison came along, in 1849, to give miliary tuberculosis of the suprarenal capsules a label, this form of consumption was nameless, mysterious, and inexorably fatal—usually within a year, since there was no satisfactory treatment of it. Adrenal tuberculosis impared the excretion of the adrenal glands, reducing the patient's immunity to illness. It brought on weakness and exhaustion as a result of reduced appetite and consequent loss of weight, usually resulting in pernicious anemia. It often caused the skin in exposed areas of the body, such as the face, to turn brown and black in places. It caused the sufferer's temperature to fluctuate between fever and subnormal readings. It brought on back pain, but usually very little other pain—until the end. Low blood pressure, a fast heart-rate, anorexia, nausea, vomiting, and occasional epigastric pain (due to gastro-intestinal upset) and bowel disturbances were also typical of adrenal tuberculosis in its untreatable form.

At one time or another during the last year or so of her life, as her letters and the testimony of others demonstrate, the novelist suffered from all of these symptoms. While some attempts have been made to show that she was afflicted with Hodgkin's Disease, this can hardly have been possible. Hodgkin's Disease, a form of cancer, involves enlargement of the lymph glands, usually in the neck first but at any site in the body (there is no evidence of anything like this during Jane Austen's last illness); enlargement of the spleen; and pruritus. Other features of Hodgkin's Disease include progressive weakness and loss of weight, often with a low-grade fever; back pain; and, sometimes, changes in skin pigmentation. It is these last items that have led some to suspect Hodgkin's Disease as the cause of the novelist's death. But Hodgkin's Disease does not cause *discolouration* of skin pigmentation, as does adrenal consumption. When there is adrenal insufficiency, skin discolouration is due to the excess of a hormone which stimulates the pigment-forming melanocytes, the production of which is checked in our day by giving fludrocortisone. The modern treatment, replacing the secretion of the adrenal glands, can now effectively control what was then an inevitably fatal disease but which in the twentieth century is far less common than in Jane Austen's time due to the dramatic fall in the incidence of tuberculosis. For there can be no doubt that the novelist, like so many of her contemporaries, fell victim to that ubiquitous disease.

As we shall see, changes in facial pigmentation were, for Jane Austen, among the most distressing aspects of her last illness; she herself comments on this in letters to several correspondents. 'There is no disease other than [Addison's],' Sir Zachary Cope has written, 'that could present a face that was "black and white" and at the same time give rise to the other symptoms' we know the novelist suffered from. Sir Zachary does not sufficiently emphasise tuberculosis as the primary cause of Jane Austen's death; and he does not consider the possibility of vitiligo—perhaps because this is a relatively common skin condition which can be associated with a number of diseases, among them Addison's. The novelist used the phrase—a 'black and white' appearance—to describe her face. And she was only inter-mittently feverish, which would be compatible with many compli-cations of miliary tuberculosis. Hodgkin's Disease would have caused a more continuous low-grade fever, as well as other complications easily discernible to the sufferer, especially an obser-vant one. If the lymph glands in her neck, for example, had become enlarged, Jane undoubtedly would have noted this, and the phenomenon could hardly have remained unmentioned in her last letters—many of which describe in detail her physical condition.

The diagnosis of Addison's Disease has been summarised by Cope in his well-known medical account of the novelist's final months.

> Here . . . we have the story of an illness . . . beginning with an insidious languor and a pain in the back, progressing steadily yet with definite periods of intermission, and attended by critical attacks of faintness and gastro-intestinal disturbance, yet unaccompanied by any noticeable pain anywhere. . . . During the intermission, the intelligence was acute and the appetite good. The end came in one of the crises in which faintness was a very noticeable feature.
>
> No doubt many of the above symptoms might be accounted for by a number of conditions, but there are very few diseases which could account for them all . . . Addison's disease is

usually . . . due to tuberculosis of the suprarenal capsules, and
it is likely that it was so in Jane Austen's case. The disease ran
its course rapidly, indicating an active pathological process that
might well account for any fever. Pain in the back has been
noted in Addison's disease by several observers.

Acute adrenal insufficiency—tuberculosis of the adrenal cortex—
consumption of the suprarenal bodies or capsules—this is what
brought the novelist to her untimely end. Had she lived 135 years
later, her condition probably could have been controlled by taking
twenty-five milligrams of cortisone a day, as John Kennedy did in the
1950s, and she might have enjoyed a normal life-span and gone on
writing, no doubt with increasing confidence and fame. Without
modern drugs she was destined to be destroyed, at forty-one, by the
progressive anemia brought on by the disease from which she
suffered.

So the last four months of the novelist's life were inevitably
difficult ones. We know that she cut short her walks, and then
abandoned them altogether, getting fresh air by occasional rides on
one of the donkeys—for which a special saddle was made. Later, she
had to give up this form of exercise and became instead a passenger in
the family donkey-cart. Ultimately she ceased going out altogether.
Inside the house she found herself having to lie down for longer
periods of time; sitting up became an ordeal. The author of the
Memoir gives us this picture of Jane Austen at Chawton during her
final illness.

> The sitting-room contained only one sofa, which was frequently
> occupied by her mother, who was more than seventy years
> old. Jane would never use it, even in her mother's absence;
> but she contrived a sort of couch for herself with two or
> three chairs, and was pleased to say that this arrangement
> was more comfortable to her than a real sofa. Her reasons for
> this might have been left to be guessed, but for the importunities
> of a little niece, which obliged her to explain that if she herself
> had shown any inclination to use the sofa, her mother might
> have scrupled being on it so much as was good for her.

This may have been genuine concern for her mother's comfort—or a
disinclination to put herself under an obligation to a parent with

whom she had never had an easy relationship, and whose hypochondriacal ways had annoyed her for years.

As she wasted away, Jane spent more and more time in bed and less
and less in the sitting-room. When she was well enough to sit up, she
sometimes used the opportunity to compose letters. Five days after
she put *Sanditon* aside we find her writing to Fanny Knight—and
three days after that, to Caroline Austen. What these letters (late
March 1817) have in common is the admission—for the first time
without much attempt at qualification—that the writer is not well.

Fanny had asked her suitor Mr Wildman, who certainly was not in
on the family secret, what he thought of her aunt's books; having
received an honest but unflattering reply, she proceeded to report it
to the novelist. He must have 'a Brain . . . very different from mine,'
Jane replies. 'He & I should not in the least agree . . . in our ideas of
Novels and Heroines;—pictures of perfection as you know make me
sick & wicked.' Mr Wildman, it appears, preferred 'perfect' girls as
novel-heroines. Nevertheless, she respects him 'for wishing to think
well of all young Ladies; it shews an amiable & a delicate Mind.' She
herself, of course, always preferred 'realism.' The novelist repeats to
her niece the fact that she now has 'another ready for publication'
(*Persuasion*—described again as 'ready'): 'You will not like it, so you
need not be impatient. You may *perhaps* like the Heroine, as she is
almost too good for me.' Here, perhaps, is an acknowledgement of
that aspect of Anne Elliot—righteousness, bordering at times on
priggishness—which has put off some readers; as we have seen, Anne
was not one of Jane Austen's favourites among her heroines. Henry,
Jane adds, as yet 'knows nothing' of the new book.

The novelist turns to the subject of her health. It is one of the most
detailed statements on the subject she ever put into words:

> I certainly have not been well for many weeks, and about a week
> ago I was very poorly, I have had a good deal of fever at times &
> indifferent nights, but am considerably better now, & recover-
> ing my Looks a little, which have been bad enough, black &
> white & every wrong colour. I must not depend upon being
> ever very blooming again. Sickness is a dangerous Indulgence at
> my time of Life.

When a girl and a young lady, her brilliant complexion had been one
of the things people noticed about her. Despite the wry humour of

the last sentence quoted above, she tells Fanny that she has been 'languid & dull & very bad company' lately. Jane goes on: 'I wish I may be more agreable.' She does not 'venture to Church' any more, she reports.

The novelist informs her niece that James Leigh Perrot is dying at Scarlets (five days after this letter was written, he was dead). Her mother, waiting for further news of her brother, 'sits brooding over Evils which cannot be remedied & Conduct impossible to be understood'—probably a reference to some slight, real or imagined, of which Mrs Austen considered her brother or his wife guilty; perhaps she was wishing that relations between them had been more cordial. Jane also reports that Charles's daughter Harriet is out of danger. Anna Lefroy is pregnant yet again. She 'has not a chance to escape,' the novelist comments. 'Poor Animal, she will be worn out before she is thirty.—I am very sorry for her.—Mrs Clement too is in that way again. I am quite tired of so many Children.—Mrs Benn has a 13th.' Children, as we know, were not her favourite species. Henry, she tells Fanny, finds London a 'hateful place' to visit now that he has got used to country living again: 'he is always depressed by the idea of' going back to town. She has taken a donkey-ride, Cassandra and her nephew James Edward walking by her side. 'A^t Cassandra is such an excellent Nurse, so assiduous & unwearied!' It was her last letter to Fanny.

The last to Caroline praises the girl's improved composition, and predicts that she will soon be writing 'a very pretty hand.' Jane says she enjoyed her ride on the donkey, and hopes to do it again. But she has not been feeling well—'I have still a tendency to Rheumatism . . . I am a poor Honey at present. I will be better when you can come & see us.'

On 28 March 1817 James Leigh Perrot died. His will proved to be a terrible disappointment to the women at Chawton. His various houses and estates, plus £10,000, were bequeathed to his wife and her heirs. The remainder of his property was left in trust to his eldest nephew James Austen—who would die two years later—the income going to Mrs Leigh Perrot during her lifetime. On Mrs Leigh Perrot's death—which did not occur until 1836—the trust was to cease: £6,000 was to go to James Austen (it went to his eldest son, James Edward), and the remainder to be shared equally among the other Austen nieces and nephews. The will provided legacies of £1,000 to each of James Austen's brothers and sisters—excluding George—

who should survive their aunt; all of the Austen children except James and Jane lived long enough to receive these legacies. Mrs Austen, Mr Leigh Perrot's sister, was not mentioned in the will, which had been made in 1811. Perhaps her brother expected to outlive her. He was younger than she by some years; and in any case Mrs Austen was a woman who habitually claimed that she was at death's door. She had cried wolf once too often. Eventually the chief beneficiary of this considerable estate was James's son James Edward, who became the residual legatee under the will of Mrs Leigh Perrot. She subsequently granted allowances to several members of the family—something her husband had never done.

At any rate, not a penny went to Chawton under this will, and the ladies there felt the blow. Jane Austen had feared poverty all of her life. 'Legacies are a very wholesome diet,' she had written to Cassandra, at a less desperate time, in 1808. 'It is very bad to grow old & be poor & laughed at,' says 'The Watsons.' Now that she was in poor health, her failure to secure a legacy, especially when one might so easily have been given, induced a moment of panic. Suddenly feeling helpless, she implored Cassandra—who, along with Frank, James, and Mary Lloyd Austen, had gone to Scarlets to attend the funeral and help console Mrs Leigh Perrot—to come home as quickly as she could. Her spirits improved as soon as Cassandra was again safely in the house.

Writing to her brother Charles on 6 April, the novelist admitted that she had been upset by recent events: 'I have really been too unwell the last fortnight to write anything that was not absolutely necessary.' She went on, in pitiful terms, to describe her present state:

> I have been suffering from a Bilious attack, attended with a good deal of fever. A few days ago my complaint appeared removed, but I am ashamed to say that the shock of my Uncle's Will brought on relapse, & I was so ill on Friday & thought myself so likely to be worse that I could not but press for Cassandra's returning with Frank after the Funeral last night, which she of course did, & either her return, or my having seen [her medical attendant], or my Disorder's chusing to go away, have made me better this morning. I live upstairs however for the present & am coddled. I am the only one of the Legatees who has been so silly, but a weak Body must excuse weak Nerves.

Consumptives, of course, are notoriously prone to nervous complaints, their condition often being ruled by their state of mind. 'Living upstairs' is a euphemism for staying in bed rather than sitting up; Jane must have been quite weak now. Their mother, she tells Charles, has taken her brother's 'forgetfulness of *her* extremely well;—her expectations for herself were never beyond the extreme of moderation,' though she wishes her brother had left something outright to her children. There is a kind word here for Mrs Leigh Perrot: 'My Aunt felt the value of Cassandras company so fully, & was so very kind to her, & is poor Woman! so miserable . . . that we feel more regard for her than we ever did before.' This is charitable; resentment or anger would have been understandable in the circumstances. The letter ends pathetically: 'God bless you all. Conclude me to be going on well, if you hear nothing to the contrary . . . Tell dear Harriet that whenever she wants me in her service again, she must send a Hackney Chariot all the way for me, for I am not strong enough to travel any other way. . . . I have forgotten to take a proper-edged [i.e., mourning] sheet of Paper.' There is no farewell to little Cassandra. On the outside of this letter is written, in Charles Austen's hand: 'My last letter from dearest Jane.'

Shortly after this the novelist received a note from her clergyman cousin Edward Cooper, like the rest of them excluded from his uncle's will—a circumstance, he says, he 'certainly never seriously anticipated.' He obligingly describes the prayers he said for his uncle during his final illness, and comments that he looks forward to meeting him 'in another world, where mis-apprehension, mis-judgment, and mis-representation will have no place.' Unless Jane's sense of humour had deserted her altogether—an unlikely eventuality —she must have been amused by this Collins-like outburst, which went unanswered.

Caroline had planned to spend a few days at Chawton while her parents were at Scarlets. She discovered, however, that her 'Aunt Jane [had become] too ill to have me in the house,' and she went instead to Wyards and stayed with Anna and Ben Lefroy. Caroline and Anna walked over to Chawton one day in April to see their ailing aunt; here is Caroline's account of the visit, written long afterwards:

> She was then keeping her room, but said she would see us, and we went up to her. She was in her dressing-gown, and was sitting quite like an invalid in an arm-chair, but she got up and

kindly greeted us, and then, pointing to seats which had been
arranged for us by the fire, she said 'There is a chair for the
married lady, and a little stool for you, Caroline.' It is strange,
but those trifling words were the last of hers that I can
remember, for I retain no recollection of what was said by
anyone in the conversation that ensued. I was struck by the
alteration in herself. She was very pale, her voice was weak and
low, and there was about her a general appearance of debility
and suffering; but I have been told that she never had much
acute pain. She was not equal to the exertion of talking to us,
and our visit to the sick room was a very short one, Aunt
Cassandra soon taking us away. I do not suppose we stayed a
quarter of an hour; and I never saw Aunt Jane again.

V

On 27 April Jane Austen, the issue of wills now very much present to
her, sat down and wrote out her own. It is a brief and simple
document:

> I JANE AUSTEN of the Parish of Chawton do by this my last
> Will and Testament give and bequeath to my dearest sister
> Cassandra Eliz'th every thing of which I may die possessed or
> which may hereafter be due to me subject to the payment of my
> funeral expenses and to a legacy of £50 to my brother Henry
> and £50 to Mde Bijion which I request may be paid as soon as
> convenient and I appoint my said dear sister EXECUTRIX of
> this my last Will and testament
> JANE AUSTEN April 27; 1817

Madame Bigeon was the French maid of Henry's late wife Eliza; she
kept house for him after her mistress's death and had lost her meagre
savings in his bankruptcy. A later memorandum by the novelist
bequeathed a gold chain—perhaps that given her by Charles—to her
god-daughter Louisa Knight, the ninth of Edward's eleven children,
who was thirteen in 1817, and a lock of her hair to Fanny. Jane
Austen's signature was not witnessed; its validity had to be sworn to
after her death. Mrs Austen, one notices, is not mentioned. In those
days it was unusual for a woman to act as executrix of a will; the

novelist was departing from tradition in not naming one of her brothers. Edward or Henry would have been a logical choice.

Several weeks later new and more alarming symptoms began to appear; in mid-May the local doctor advised Jane to call in a more experienced man. Giles King Lyford, surgeon-in-ordinary at the county hospital in Winchester—and probably, as Marghanita Laski suggests, a nephew of John Lyford of Basingstoke, who had attended the Austens in their Steventon days—was called in for consultation. A man of considerable professional reputation—'in whom great London practitioners expressed confidence,' according to the *Memoir*—Lyford and his treatments (unspecified) seemed to do the novelist some good; as he was based in Winchester, it was decided that at the end of the month Jane would go there, and place herself under his care. A tradition persists that Lyford knew she was dying the moment he looked at her.

Two days before her removal to Winchester, the novelist wrote from Chawton to Anne Sharp, who had at one time been a governess at Godmersham, and had recently inquired about her health. It is a long letter—the last Jane Austen wrote that could be described as more than perfunctory. In it the novelist acknowledges that she has 'been very ill indeed' with 'an attack of my sad complaint'—an attack described as 'the most severe I ever had,' which 'reduced me very low.' She has been in bed more or less continuously for the past five weeks, she reports (this on 22 May 1817), with only occasional 'removals to a Sopha.' Now, she says, she is getting well again—'slowly recovering my strength. . . . I can sit up in my bed & employ myself, as I am proving to you at this present moment.' She could leave her bed if she wanted to, Jane declares, only that 'the [prone] posture is thought good for me.' She goes on: 'How to do justice to the kindness of all my family during this illness, is quite beyond me!' Each of her brothers has been 'affectionate' and 'anxious.' 'Words must fail me in any attempt to describe what a Nurse [Cassandra] has been to me.' Again there is no mention of her mother.

The letter continues. 'I have so many alleviations & comforts to bless the Almighty for!—My head was always clear, & I had scarcely any pain; my cheif sufferings were from the feverish nights, weakness and Languor.' She writes of her illness as if it is passing, or has passed; indeed, she declares, Lyford's treatments have 'gradually removed the Evil.' She is going to Winchester with Cassandra 'for some weeks' to give her physician a chance to re-establish her health fully. 'I am now really a very genteel, portable sort of Invalid,' she remarks. Lodgings have been secured for them in Winchester by their friend Mrs Heathcote—formerly Elizabeth Bigg of Manydown—who lives there, and the two sisters are to make the sixteen-mile journey in James Austen's carriage, which will be sent over from Steventon. The persistence of the novelist's dislike of Mary Lloyd Austen is clear from the comment which follows: 'Now, that's a sort of thing which Mrs J. Austen does in the kindest manner!—But still she is in the main *not* a liberal-minded Woman, & as to this reversionary Property's amending that part of her Character, expect it not my dear Anne; —too late, too late in the day;—& besides, the Property [Mrs Leigh Perrot's] may not be theirs these ten years.' This is only the final expression of a resentment, in part financially motivated, which Jane had harboured toward her sister-in-law for many years. That James Austen's immediate family, rather than his sisters, was to benefit so largely from the estate of the Leigh Perrots could not have improved matters between the two ladies.

Frank's wife, Jane reports, is the mother of another child. She 'has had a much shorter confinement than I have—with a Baby to produce into the bargain. We were put to bed nearly at the same time.' She apologises to Miss Sharp for writing so much of her health: 'with all the Egotism of an Invalid I write only of myself.' She tells her correspondent to address future letters to Chawton: 'the communication between the two places will be frequent.' Her mother, she adds as a sort of afterthought, 'suffered much for me when I was at the worst, but is tolerably well' now. Mrs Austen had made yet another quick recovery. Martha Lloyd 'has been all kindness. In short, if I live to be an old Woman, I must expect to wish I had died now; blessed in the tenderness of such a Family, & before I had survived either them or their affection.' She concludes: 'the Providence of God has restored me—& may I be more fit to appear before him when I *am* summoned, than I sh^d have been now!'

As late as six weeks before her death, Jane Austen apparently believed she was going to recover—there is more here than the emptiness of a false hearty optimism. The letter to Anne Sharp is remarkable for its clarity, eloquence, humility, warmth, and wit. The novelist's sense of humour had not deserted her.

On 24 May, on a rainy morning, the carriage from Steventon duly arrived at Chawton. With their brother Henry and Edward Knight's nineteen-year-old son William riding one on each side of the carriage,

the two sisters, leaving Martha Lloyd with Mrs Austen, were
conveyed through the downpour to their lodgings in College Street,
Winchester, a quiet cul-de-sac of small houses adjacent to the grey
medieval buildings of the school—'and within hearing,' Cecil
reminds us, 'of the drowsy chimes of the great cathedral and the
clamorous daws circling its towers, which, two years later, were to
echo so hauntingly in the ears of the youthful Keats.' They occupied
apartments on the middle floor of Mrs David's three-storey house.
Their bow-windowed drawing-room looked out over the garden, on
the opposite side of the lane, of the Headmaster of Winchester
College. Their friend Mrs Heathcote lived nearby in the Close. Her
son, the future Sir William Heathcote, was a student at the school—
as was Edward's fifth son Charles, now fourteen. The Heathcotes,
according to the *Memoir*, 'did all they could to promote [the sisters']
comfort, during that sad sojourn in Winchester, both by their
society, and by supplying those little conveniences in which a
lodging-house was likely to be deficient.' Mrs Heathcote's sister
Alethea, Jane and Cassandra's particular friend, unfortunately was
away in Switzerland. The novelist bore the journey well, for a time at
least felt better, and continued hopeful of a full recovery.

Winchester, say the novelist's great-nephews in *Life and Letters of
Jane Austen* (1913), was a place 'which all good Hampshire people'
must venerate as 'their county town; a veneration shared by a good
many Englishmen outside the limits of the county.' The famous
cathedral—which was to be Jane Austen's final resting-place—in that
day as in this drew visitors from all over the Kingdom.

At the end of May, Jane wrote two last letters. The first of these
was to her nephew James Edward. In it she reports that she continues
'to get better.' Neither her 'handwriting . . . nor my face have yet
recovered their proper beauty, but in other respects I am gaining
strength very fast.' She is now out of bed all day, though confined to
the sofa. 'I eat my meals . . . in a rational way, & can employ myself,
and walk from one room to another. Mr Lyford says he will cure me.'
Whether she believed him or not we shall never know. Their lodgings
are comfortable. Henry, William Knight, and Mrs Heathcote see
them regularly. Her brother Charles and William Heathcote are
coming to visit them. Her nephew Charles Knight, in the college
infirmary, hopes to call on them soon. The letter ends poignantly: 'God
bless you my dear Edward. If ever you are ill, may you be as tenderly
nursed as I have been, may the same Blessed alleviations of anxious,

sympathising friends be yours, & may you possess—as I dare say you will—the greatest blessing of all, in the consciousness of not being unworthy of their Love. *I could not feel this.*'

Jane Austen's last known letter, by a singular irony, was the first to be published; Henry quoted from it in the 'Biographical Notice' he appended to the posthumous *Northanger Abbey and Persuasion* as an example of his sister's state of mind near the end of her life. The recipient is not known, but probably the letter was addressed to Henry himself. In it Jane repeats that her physician 'talks of making me quite well. I live chiefly on the sofa, but am allowed to walk from one room to the other.' She has gone out once in a sedan-chair, hopes to do it again, and expects to 'be promoted to a wheel-chair as the weather serves.' As for Cassandra, her 'tender, watchful, indefatigable nurse'—'what I owe to her, and to the anxious affection of all my beloved family on this occasion, I can only cry over it, and pray to God to bless them more and more.'

The next section of this letter—touching 'with just and gentle animadversion on a subject of domestic disappointment,' as Henry puts it—was suppressed by him; probably there was an allusion to the Leigh Perrot property, or to the James Austens, or possibly to her mother—who, needless to say, did not traverse the sixteen miles to Winchester to see her daughter during the novelist's final illness. The letter, as printed by Henry, concludes: 'But I am getting too near complaint. It has been the appointment of God, however secondary causes may have operated.' The 'it' is more likely to have been the 'subject of domestic disappointment' censored by Henry than her illness, which at the end of May 1817 she still seemed to believe, or at least hoped, she was conquering.

At Chawton, meanwhile, Mrs Austen was looking forward optimistically to Jane's recovery. During June she wrote twice to Anna Lefroy. Their 'accounts from Winchester are very good,' she reports. 'Mr Lyford says he thinks better of her than he has ever done, though he must still consider her in a precarious state.' Her great-nephew Charles Knight, finally released from the Winchester infirmary, has been to see his aunt Jane, 'and says she looks better and seem'd very cheerful.'

Cassandra, however, was less sanguine. She dismissed the nurse they had hired, and summoned Mary Lloyd Austen to Winchester. Mary—characterised, remember, by Jane as '*not* a liberal-minded woman'—was felt by Cassandra to be the one person she could count on to help her efficiently in this emergency. Jane's unloved sister-in-law spent much of the next six weeks in Winchester. Mary saw at once the true state of things, and wrote frankly to her husband at Steventon; from this time onward it was impossible for the family to entertain any further illusions about the true state of the novelist's health. Thus we find James Austen writing in a more realistic vein to his son James Edward at Oxford in mid-June:

> I must tell you that we can no longer flatter ourselves with the last hope of having your dear valuable Aunt Jane restored to us. The symptoms which returned after the first four or five days at Winchester, have never subsided, and Mr. Lyford has candidly told us that her case is desperate. I need not say what a melancholy gloom this has cast over us all. Your Grandmamma has suffered much, but her affliction can be nothing to Cassandra's. She will indeed be to be pitied. It is some consolation to know that our poor invalid has hitherto felt no very severe pain—which is rather an extraordinary circumstance in her complaint. I saw her [two days ago] and found her much altered, but composed and cheerful. She is well aware of her situation. Your Mother . . . returns not till all is over—how soon that may be we cannot say—Lyford said he saw no signs of immediate dissolution, but added that with such a pulse it was impossible for any person to last long, and indeed no one can wish it—an easy departure from this to a better world is all that we can pray for . . . prepare yourself for what the next letter *may* announce.

'She is well aware of her situation': a month before she died, then, the novelist could no longer entertain any further hope of recovery. This, in addition to her deteriorating condition, may well be why she wrote no letters in June and July 1817—though she did compose scraps and morsels of other things, as we shall see. Caroline Austen, to whom her father's letter to her brother was shown at some stage, scrawled across the bottom of it: 'I now feel as if I had never loved and valued her enough.' Mrs Austen, as her son declares here, may well have 'suffered much'—but, characteristically, recovered quickly from her suffering. A few days after the novelist's death, we find her mother writing to Anna Lefroy: 'I am certainly in a good deal of affliction, but trust God will support me . . . I hope her sufferings were not severe—they were not long . . . Cassandra . . . is in great affliction, but bears it like a Christian.' So much for Jane.

'Here and there, human nature may be great in times of trial,' Jane Austen makes the invalid Mrs Smith say in *Persuasion*, 'but generally speaking it is its weakness and not its strength that appears in a sick-chamber; it is selfishness and impatience rather than generosity and fortitude, that one hears of.' The novelist's last month in the world, lived in full knowledge of imminent death, would appear to be characterised by 'generosity and fortitude' rather than 'selfishness and impatience,' insofar as any determination of this is possible. J.E. Austen-Leigh has said that while Jane was 'fully aware' of her danger, she was 'not appalled by it.' Her two clergyman brothers, James and Henry, remained close at hand, and apparently the novelist gained some comfort from the religious consolation they were able to offer. In accordance with her wishes, the brothers conducted a sacramental service of Holy Communion while she was still strong enough to follow it with full attention. According to Henry's 'Biographical Notice,' Jane 'retained her faculties, her memory, her fancy, her temper, and her affections—warm, clear, and unimpaired to the last.' He adds that she continued to love all 'her fellow-creatures' to the last too—which would have been highly uncharacteristic indeed, as perhaps we now can see for ourselves. She did, however, regret her past unkindnesses to Mary Lloyd Austen, who so assiduously helped Cassandra nurse her during the final weeks. Tradition has it that one day, when she felt she might be near her end, Jane said to her sister-in-law: 'You have always been a kind sister to me, Mary.' Perhaps she wished she had been an equally kind sister to 'Mrs. J.A.'

Through the end of June and into the month of July 1817, the novelist sat or lay looking out of the bow-window of the house in College Street, waiting for death. While she could hold a pen or a pencil, she continued to write. In the second week of July her con-dition took a significant turn for the worse; Mr Lyford declared that she had not long to live. Apparently she received the news calmly. Indeed, just two days before her death she composed some light verse, titled 'Written at Winchester on Tuesday the 15th July 1817'—St Swithin's Day, traditionally the day of the Winchester races:

> When Winchester races first took their beginning
> It is said the good people forgot their old Saint

> Not applying at all for the leave of St Swithin
> And that William of Wykham's approval was faint

A few days later the author of these lines would be lying in a tomb near that of William of Wykeham.

One may safely presume that a woman who could, in what she knew to be her final days, quite deliberately write 'doggerel verse of abominable scansion' about the Winchester races (as one critic characterises them) had not even then altogether lost her sense of humour. Again one recalls Mrs Smith in *Persuasion*—about whom, sometime during the preceding year, Jane Austen had written this remarkably prophetic passage:

> Her accommodations were limited to a noisy parlour, and a dark bed-room behind, with no possibility of moving from one to the other without assistance. . . . Yet, in spite of all this, Anne had reason to believe that she had moments only of languor and depression, to hours of occupation and enjoyment. How could it be?—She . . . finally determined that this was not a case of fortitude or of resignation only.—A submissive spirit might be patient, a strong understanding would imply resolution, but here was something more; here was that elasticity of mind, that disposition to be comforted, that power of turning readily from evil to good, and of finding employment which carried her out of herself, which was from Nature alone. It was the choicest gift of Heaven.

One cannot help feeling that the novelist understood such a disposition so well because she possessed one very much like it. A tough-minded woman, she did not bend or bow easily under affliction. She did not do so now. Here indeed 'was something more'—not only 'elasticity of mind,' but enormous strength too.

On Thursday morning, 17 July 1817, a letter arrived from Fanny Knight. Cassandra unsealed it and gave it to Jane to read. They cheerfully discussed its contents. After lunch Cassandra left College Street to do some shopping. Returning, she found that the novelist had had an attack of severe faintness. It seemed to pass off—long enough, at any rate, for Jane to tell Cassandra about it, and to describe her symptoms. The sisters were still talking quietly as the clock struck six. Before another hour had passed an even severer attack overcame the sufferer, bringing with it this time a period of unprecedentedly acute pain. The novelist characterised the pain as not fixed in any particular place; she said she could not describe her suffering in words, and that this time it was almost beyond endurance. For the first time, Jane Austen's composure began to falter, and she cried out for death. Mr Lyford was called in, gave her something to help her doze, and promised to return. According to Henry, his sister's last voluntary speech conveyed thanks to her medical attendant. What little remains of the story has been told in the opening chapter.

From 7 p.m. on 17 July until she died the next morning at 4.30 a.m. in the arms of her sister, Jane Austen, after praying for death, lay apparently insensible. What thoughts, if any, may have raced through the fading light of her mind we of course shall never know. Did she, perhaps, dream of Chawton, its paths and gardens, and wonder how her mother might greet the news of her death? Did she recall that wonderful moonlit walk she took from Alton to Chawton the previous autumn—when, for the last time, she seemed to possess all her strength? Did her thoughts stray back to that tumultuous trip to London in the autumn of 1815 and her intimacy with Mr Haden, or to her last visit to Godmersham, those evenings in the library there where she finished *Mansfield Park*, and her acquaintance with the M.P. Mr Lushington—with whom, she declared, she was 'rather in love'? Did she remember the arrival of her 'favourite child' *Pride and Prejudice* from London in 1813, or the excitement of holding her very first publication in her hands in 1811, or the years of 'exile' in Southampton and Bath which preceded that first success? Did she recall the awful night at Manydown when she changed her mind about marriage, or the exhilaration and then the disappointment of that heartbreaking summer in Devon? Did she think of any of the other men who populated her world and seemed to like her—Henry's friend Mr. Seymour, Edward Bridges, the Mr Evelyn who was so nice to her in Bath, Harry Francis Digweed, Mr Holder of Ashe Park, Samuel Blackall, Edward Taylor? Did she dream of that vibrant autumn of 1800, when she danced her feet off at the Basingstoke ball, and again at Hurstbourne; or Lady Dorchester's ball at Kempshott at Christmastime two years earlier, when she stood up for all twenty dances? Did her thoughts wander back to Steventon, its shrubbery and its country walks, her friendship with another Anna Lefroy, bittersweet memories of a boy named Tom who had first touched her heart? Perhaps she remembered her father's evening readings, the theatricals put on by her brothers, her own first youthful compositions, and the welcome laughter and admiration of the family when she read them her tale of Elizabeth Bennet. How would her brothers and their children respond to the news of her death; how would her sister take it? Surely some portion of her last earthly thoughts must have been of Cassandra, with whom she had always shared everything; Cassandra, who seemed always to be there, as she was now; Cassandra in whose arms she lay cradled; Cassandra; Cassandra.

Notes on the Pictures

Frontispiece Portrait of Jane Austen from the 1870 *Memoir* by James Edward Austen-Leigh; photograph by J. Butler-Kearney, by permission of the Jane Austen Memorial Trust and the National Portrait Gallery, London

1. Front view of Steventon Rectory, by Anna Austen Lefroy; photograph by J. Butler-Kearney, by permission of the Jane Austen Memorial Trust

2. Silhouette of Cassandra Austen; photograph by J. Butler-Kearney, by permission of the Jane Austen Memorial Trust

3. Manydown House, by G.F. Prosser; by permission of the Hampshire County Library

4. Topaz crosses given to Jane Austen by her brother Charles; the cross consisting of five opal stones (on the right) has been identified by George H. Tucker; photograph by J. Butler-Kearney, by permission of the Jane Austen Memorial Trust

5. Chawton Cottage; by permission of the British Tourist Authority

6. First page of a letter from Jane Austen to the Rev James Stanier Clarke; photograph by J. Butler-Kearney, by permission of the Jane Austen Memorial Trust

7. Opening of the cancelled chapter of *Persuasion*; by permission of The British Library

8. No. 8 College Steet, Winchester; by permission of the British Tourist Authority

Frequently Cited Works

Items mentioned once are given full citation in Notes. Those cited more than once are referred to in abbreviated form, as indicated below:

Brown	Julia Prewitt Brown, *Jane Austen's Novels: Social Change and Literary Form* (Cambridge, Mass., and London, 1979)
Bush	Douglas Bush, *Jane Austen* (New York, 1975)
Butler (I)	Marilyn Butler, *Jane Austen and the War of Ideas* (Oxford, 1975)
Butler (II)	Marilyn Butler, *Romantics, Rebels, and Reactionaries: English Literature and Its Background 1760–1830* (Oxford and New York, 1982)
Cecil	David Cecil, *A Portrait of Jane Austen* (London, 1978)
Chapman	R.W. Chapman, *Jane Austen: Facts and Problems* (Oxford, 1948)
Craik	W.A. Craik, *Jane Austen: The Six Novels* (London, 1965)
Critical Heritage	*Jane Austen: The Critical Heritage*, ed. B.C. Southam (London and New York, 1968)
Duckworth	Alistair M. Duckworth, *The Improvement of the Estate: A Study of Jane Austen's Novels* (Baltimore and London, 1971)
Gillie	Christopher Gillie, *A Preface to Jane Austen* (London, 1974)

Gooneratne	Yasmine Gooneratne, *Jane Austen* (London and New York, 1970)
Grandison	*Jane Austen's 'Sir Charles Grandison,'* ed. Brian Southam, Foreword by David Cecil (Oxford and New York, 1980; 1981)
Halperin	John Halperin (ed.), *Jane Austen: Bicentenary Essays* (Cambridge, London and New York, 1975)
Hodge	Jane Aiken Hodge, *The Double Life of Jane Austen* (London, 1972)
Ives	Sidney Ives, *The Trial of Mrs Leigh Perrot* (Boston, 1980)
Jenkins	Elizabeth Jenkins, *Jane Austen* (London, 1938; 1949)
Kennedy	Margaret Kennedy, *Jane Austen* (London, 1950)
Lascelles	Mary Lascelles, *Jane Austen and Her Art* (London, 1939)
Laski	Marghanita Laski, *Jane Austen and Her World* (London, 1969; rev. ed., 1975)
Letters	*Jane Austen's Letters to Her Sister Cassandra and Others*, ed. R.W. Chapman (London and New York, 1932; rev. ed., 1952; repr. 1959)
Life and Letters	William and Richard Arthur Austen-Leigh, *Jane Austen: Her Life and Letters* (London, 1913)
Litz	A. Walton Litz, *Jane Austen: A Study of Her Artistic Development* (New York, 1965)
Mansell	Darrel Mansell, *The Novels of Jane Austen: An Interpretation* (London and New York, 1973)
Memoir	J.E. Austen-Leigh, *A Memoir of Jane Austen* (London, 1870; 1871)
Morgan	Susan Morgan, *In the Meantime: Character and Perception in Jane Austen's Fiction* (Chicago and London, 1980)

Mudrick — Marvin Mudrick, *Jane Austen: Irony as Defense and Discovery* (Princeton, N.J., 1952; Berkeley, Los Angeles, and London, 1968)

Odmark — John Odmark, *An Understanding of Jane Austen's Novels* (Oxford, 1981)

Pinion — F.B. Pinion, *A Jane Austen Companion: A Critical Survey and Reference Book* (London, 1975; rev. ed., 1976)

Plumb — J.H. Plumb, *Georgian Delights* (Boston, 1980)

Rees — Joan Rees, *Jane Austen: Woman and Writer* (London and New York, 1976)

Smithers — David Waldron Smithers, *Jane Austen in Kent* (Westerham, Kent, 1981)

'Some Notes on Background' — Elizabeth Jenkins, Address given at the Annual General Meeting of the Jane Austen Society (Report for the Year 1980)

Southam — B.C. Southam, *Jane Austen's Literary Manuscripts: A Study of the Novelist's Development through the Surviving Papers* (Oxford, 1964)

Tave — Stuart M. Tave, *Some Words of Jane Austen* (Chicago and London, 1973)

Watt — Ian Watt (ed.), *Jane Austen: A Collection of Critical Essays* (Englewood Cliffs, N.J., 1963)

Works — The Novels of Jane Austen, ed. R.W. Chapman, 5 vols. (London, 1923; repr. 1926, 1933; rev. eds., 1943, 1946, 1948, 1954, 1959, 1965); *The Works of Jane Austen*, ed. R.W. Chapman, Vol. VI: *Minor Works* (London, 1954; repr. 1958; rev. eds., 1963, 1965)

Chapter Notes

Chapter 1

Cassandra Austen's account of her sister's death and funeral, on which the present one is largely based, may be found in letters to her niece Fanny Knight written two and eleven days, respectively, after Jane Austen's death. See *Letters* (20 and 29 July 1817), pp. 514–17, *passim*.

J.E. Austen-Leigh is quoted from the *Memoir*, pp. 228, 226, 2, 230–1, and 46–7, respectively. Jane Austen's niece—not otherwise identified—is quoted in *Life and Letters*, p. 83. Henry Austen's 'Biographical Notice' of his sister (dated 13 December 1817) is quoted from *Works*, V, pp. 5–8, *passim*.

The critics quoted in the text are Hodge, p. 13; Chapman, p. 99; Mudrick, p. vii; Elizabeth Hardwick, 'Afterword' to *Northanger Abbey* (New York, 1965; Signet paperback edition); Watt, in Watt, p. 50 (speaking of *Sense and Sensibility*); Donald Greene, 'Jane Austen's Monsters,' in Halperin, p. 271; Lawrence, 'A Propos of *Lady Chatterley's Lover*,' reprinted in *Sex, Literature and Censorship*, ed. Harry T. Moore (1953; rpt. New York: Viking Press, 1959), p. 109; Ives, p. 26; Harrison is quoted by Pinion, p. 25; O'Connor, 'Jane Austen: The Flight from Fancy,' in *The Mirror in the Roadway* (London, 1957), p. 25; the next three quotations are taken from David Daiches, 'Jane Austen, Karl Marx and the Aristocratic Dance,' *American Scholar*, 17 (Summer 1948), 289; Lionel Trilling, 'A Portrait of Western Man,' *The Listener*, 49 (11 June 1953), 971; and Donald Greene, in Halperin, p. 264; Brissenden, 'La Philosophie dans le boudoir; or, A Young Lady's Entrance into the World,' *Studies in Eighteenth-Century Culture*, 2 (1972), 128 (Proceedings of the American Society for Eighteenth-Century Studies); Moore, *Avowals* (London, 1924), pp. 57–8; Virginia Woolf, 'Jane Austen at Sixty,' a review of Chapman's edition of the novels, originally published in the *Nation* (15 December 1923), 433, and reprinted as 'Jane Austen' in *The Common Reader* (London, 1925)—I am quoting from Watt, p. 16, and Ives, p. 27.

Chapter 2

Plumb is quoted from p. 12; see also pp. 14, 93, 82, 147, and 33, respectively. Cecil is quoted from p. 14. Much of what I say in these opening paragraphs is indebted to Plumb, *passim.*, and to Cecil, especially pp. 14–15. See also Hodge, pp. 29–33. Kennedy is quoted from p. 8. And see the *Memoir*, pp. 50–1.

On Steventon, see Lascelles, p. 1; Chapman, p. 20; Pinion, p. 4; Cecil, pp. 23 and 24; Jenkins, p. 6; and the *Memoir*, pp. 32–4.

On the Austen family, see Cecil, p. 25; Chapman, pp. 2–4; Jenkins, p. 7; Laski, pp. 6 and 8; Gillie, p. 5; and Smithers, Chapter 1, *passim*. On the Walters, see *Life and Letters*, pp. 5–6.

On the Leigh family, see Laski, p. 9; the *Memoir*, pp. 11–12; Rees, p. 19; and Pinion, p. 3. On the Leigh Perrots, see the *Memoir*, pp. 86–7.

The quoted passage about the Austens is taken from Cecil, p. 25. On the Austens' honeymoon, see *Life and Letters*, p. 10. Philadelphia Hancock's letter about the trial of Warren Hastings is quoted from *Life and Letters*, p. 41.

On Jane Austen's noble connections, see Donald Greene, 'Jane Austen and the Peerage,' *PMLA*, 68 (December 1953), 1017–31, reprinted in Watt, pp. 154–65. My discussion is indebted to Greene's in Watt, pp. 156–7. On Brydges's 'Bourgh' boast and Jane Austen's 'conservatism,' see Butler (II), pp. 98–9 and 108.

My account of Jane Austen's brothers and sister is indebted principally to Chapman, pp. 7–19, *passim.*; also to Pinion, pp. 8 and 23; the *Memoir*, p. 42; Lascelles, p. 3; and Jenkins, p. 10. Mrs Austen on the subject of her mentally handicapped son is quoted from *Life and Letters*, p. 20; her letter is dated 9 December 1770.

On Jane Austen's 'narrow' life, see Kennedy, p. 23. On George Austen's income, see *Life and Letters*, pp. 52 and 18.

On the Abbey School, see *Life and Letters*, p. 27. Jenkins is quoted from p. 12. The critic quoted on Jane Austen's education is Hodge, p. 23. *Pride and Prejudice* is quoted from *Works*, II, p. 165. On Jane Austen back home, see Kennedy, p. 24.

On the furnishings of Cassandra and Jane's rooms at Steventon, see Gillie—citing Anna Austen Lefroy, the novelist's niece—p. 8.

See Laski, p. 8, on the freedom of Jane Austen's upbringing.

Section II. On the Austens' politics, see Hodge, p. 29. On their neighbours, see Chapman, pp. 25–9, *passim.*, and—on Ben Lefroy's ordination—Smithers, Chapter 1. The quotation from Brydges's autobiography is taken from the *Memoir*, p. 64; that from Jane Austen's poem, 'To the Memory of Mrs. Lefroy' (1808), is taken from the *Memoir*, p. 78.

On the theatricals, see Pinion, p. 9; Laski, p. 29; and *Life and Letters*, pp. 64–6. Sir William Heathcote is quoted from *Life and Letters*, p. 66.

Section III. On the visit to Sevenoaks and London, see *Life and Letters,*
p. 58. Philadelphia on Jane is quoted from Rees, p. 29, and *Life and Letters,*
p. 59. The Comtesse de Feuillide is quoted in Gillie, p. 11, and Hodge, p. 25.
Sir Egerton Brydges on Jane Austen is quoted from the *Memoir,* p. 64. J.E.
Austen-Leigh is quoted in Gillie, p. 11. The niece quoted here is Louisa
Knight, daughter of Edward; in later years Louisa married Lord George Hill,
youngest son of the second Marquess of Downshire—Lord George's first wife
was Louisa's younger sister Cassandra Jane; I quote from a letter, in the
archives of Castle Howard, from one Pamela Fitzgerald to Lord Carlyle
(dated 26 March 1856) in which Lady George Hill's conversation is reported.
See 'Some Notes on Background,' p. 26.

The passage from the 'Biographical Notice' appears in *Works,* V, p. 5.

Chapter 3

On the Juvenilia, see *Works,* VI, p. 1; Bush, p. 18; and Pinion, p. 9. For
general accounts of the Juvenilia, see Southam, Chapter 1; Litz's discussion,
passim.; and John Halperin, 'Unengaged Laughter: Jane Austen's Juvenilia,'
in the *South Atlantic Quarterly,* 81, No. 3 (Summer 1982), 286–99, *passim.*

On Jane Austen's adolescent personality, the following are quoted in the
text; Brown, p. 50; Richard Simpson, in the *North British Review,* 52, No. 13
(April–July 1870), 130; George Levine, 'Translating the Monstrous:
Northanger Abbey,' in *Nineteenth-Century Fiction,* 30, No. 3 (December
1975), 337; Mudrick, pp. 57 and 62; Greene, in Halperin, p. 276; Mudrick, pp.
91, 36, 1, 3, and 36, respectively; and Robert M. Polhemus, *Comic Faith: The
Great Tradition from Austen to Joyce* (Chicago, 1980), p. 27. Jane Austen's
Sir Charles Grandison is discussed by David Cecil in his Foreword (p. x) to
Grandison.

I quote Schorer from 'An Interpretation' of *The Good Soldier,* originally
published in the *Princeton University Library Chronicle* in April 1948 and
reprinted since in *Horizon* in August 1949 and again as an introduction to the
Vintage paperback edition of Ford's novel (New York: Random House,
n.d.), p. xiii.

Southam is quoted from pp. 30 and 21, respectively.

'Frederic & Elfrida' is quoted from *Works,* VI, pp. 4 and 11.

'Jack & Alice' is quoted from *Works,* VI, pp. 15–16 and 27–8.

The quotation from 'Edgar & Emma' is taken from *Works,* VI, p. 33.

Quotations from 'The Three Sisters' are taken from *Works,* VI, pp. 58–9,
61, 63, 67, and 69. Rees, p. 36, makes several points about Jane Austen's
concerns in 'The Three Sisters' similar to those I make in the text.

Quotations from 'Love and Freindship' are taken from *Works,* VI, pp. 85,
89, 102, and 99, respectively. On 'Love and Freindship,' see Southam, p. 26.

Quotations from 'Lesley Castle' are taken from *Works,* VI, pp. 122 and
132.

Quotations from 'The History of England' appear on pp. 141 and 148 of *Works*, VI. See also Southam's commentary, p. 29.

The quotation from 'Scraps' may be found in *Works*, VI, pp. 171-2.

The subtitle of *Volume the Third* is quoted from *Life and Letters*, p. 55.

On 'Evelyn' and its attack on 'benevolence,' see Litz, pp. 31-6, *passim.*, and Rees, p. 40. Litz is quoted from p. 34. On Jane Austen's parody of landscape-descriptions and her dissatisfaction with early Gothic fiction, see Southam, pp. 36-8.

Quotations from 'Catharine' are taken from *Works*, VI, pp. 210-11, 198, 207-8, 226, 227-8, 222, 236, 198, 221, 216, and 194, respectively.

On Catharine as a heroine, see Southam, p. 41, and Mary Lascelles's article in the *Review of English Studies*, N.S., 3 (1952), 184.

On the dating of 'Lady Susan,' see Southam, Chapter 3. Quotations from 'Lady Susan' are taken from *Works*, VI, pp. 250, 248, 269, 274, 293, 300, 303, 307, 248, 268, 311, and 313, respectively.

Southam is quoted from p. 51. Farrer is quoted from 'Jane Austen,' *Quarterly Review*, 228 (July 1917), 15.

The chronology I give for *Sir Charles Grandison* is that suggested to me by Brian Southam. Orton is quoted from an interview he gave in connection with his radio play *The Ruffian on the Stair*; the interview first appeared in the *Radio Times* for 29 August 1964. Rees is quoted from p. 45. The quotation from 'Catharine' at the end of this section appears in *Works*, VI, p. 212. Virginia Woolf is quoted from Watt, p. 17; see above, under Notes for Chapter 1, for the full citation.

Section II. The quotation from 'Catharine' is taken from *Works*, VI, pp. 232-3.

My account of the 'love-making' going on around Jane Austen during her late 'teens, and of her life during this time, is indebted largely to Jenkins, pp. 46-8. On the forgeries perpetrated by Jane Austen in her father's parish registers, see Rees, pp. 45-6. Jenkins is quoted from a 1965 Report to the Jane Austen Society.

The extent of Jane Austen's visits in the early 1790s is recounted by Lascelles, pp. 10-11, and in *Life and Letters*, p. 78. On the death of the Comte de Feuillide, see *Life and Letters*, pp. 44-5.

On Jane Austen, spinsterhood, and Charlotte Lucas, see *Works*, II, pp. 122-3 and 125; Duckworth, pp. 3 and 88; and Kennedy, p. 27.

The quotation from Cecil appears on p. 68. The penultimate sentence of the penultimate paragraph of this chapter is a paraphrase of Hodge, p. 45.

Chapter 4

The opening quotation from Rees is taken from pp. 48-9. The dating of Jane Austen's first three novels is of course disputed. I follow that by Cassandra

Austen (see Southam, p. 53), whose authority in such matters can hardly be denied, and Southam, p. 54. I quote Gilson from the Introduction to his edition of *Five Letters from Jane Austen to Her Sister Cassandra, 1813* (Brisbane, 1981), p. iii.

Chapman is quoted from *Letters*, Introduction, p. xl; Pritchett from *George Meredith and English Comedy* (London and New York, 1970); Hodge from p. 128; Auden from 'Letter to Lord Byron,' in *Collected Longer Poems* (London, 1968), p. 41; H.W. Garrod from *Essays by Divers Hands* (Royal Society of Literature, 8 [1928]); and Nicolson from Chapman, p. 93. Bradley, writing in *Essays and Studies by Members of the English Association*, Vol. 2, p. 10, is quoted in *Life and Letters*, p. 83. *Persuasion* is quoted from *Works*, V (Vol. IV), p. 204.

The letters of 9 and 14 January 1796 are quoted from *Letters*, pp. 2–6, *passim.*; the later letter referring to Tom Lefroy (17 November 1798) is quoted from p. 27.

On Tom Lefroy, see Bush, p. 26 (quoting Jane Austen's niece Caroline); and Chapman, pp. 57–8, quoting Caroline Austen and T.E. Lefroy.

The letter of 5 September 1796 is quoted from *Letters*, pp. 12–13. The letter of 15 September 1796 is quoted from pp. 14–15.

On *Camilla*, see Jenkins, p. 49. On the death of Thomas Fowle, see Rees, p. 61, and *Life and Letters*, p. 105.

Eliza de Feuillide and Cassandra Leigh Austen are quoted by Rees, p. 58.

Section II. On the titles, chronology, and offer of publication of *Pride and Prejudice*, see Southam, p. 60; Bush, p. 90; Litz, p. 101; Chapman, p. 43; and Chapman's Introductory Note and Appendices to *Works*, II, especially pp. xi and 406–9. On elements of literary parody in *Pride and Prejudice*, see Q.D. Leavis, 'A Critical Theory of Jane Austen's Writings,' *Scrutiny*, 10 (June 1941), 61–87 (the passage quoted appears on 71); Butler (I), p. 199; and Southam, pp. 59–62, *passim*.

The connections between Chevening Park and its parsonage with Rosings and Hunsford in *Pride and Prejudice*, as well as those between Lady Catherine de Bourgh and the Stanhopes, were examined systematically for the first time by Sir David Smithers in *Jane Austen in Kent* (1981), on which my discussion is chiefly based (see especially Chapter 3). I am grateful to Sir David for talking to me about these probable connections, and for making available to me, as I was writing the present study, the typescript of his own book, then in press. My conclusions are drawn primarily from his. Sir David's views are also published in abbreviated form in an article, 'Where Was Jane Austen's Rosings?: The Case for Chevening,' *Country Life*, 158, No. 4341 (30 October 1980), 1568–71.

On the position of women writers in the 1790s, see Rees, p. 49, from which much of what is said in this paragraph is adapted.

The first two quotations in the text from *Pride and Prejudice* are taken from *Works*, II, pp. 58 and 279.

On autobiographical elements, see pp. 60, 14, 57, 12, 91, 154, 221, 312, 325, 376, and 165, respectively. The critic quoted is Mudrick, p. 95.

On 'detachment' and related questions, see *Works*, II, pp. 42-3, 57, 371, 230, 299, 236-7, and 364, respectively. On Mr Bennet—I have quoted or paraphrased Butler (I), p. 210; Mudrick, p. 113; Litz, p. 105; Greene, in Halperin, pp. 269-70; and Morgan, p. 96. Additional accounts of Mr Bennet's significance are given by Morgan, pp. 98 and 102; Duckworth, p. 128; and Brown, p. 75.

On irony, cynicism, etc., see *Works*, II, pp. 3, 6, 108, 152, 309, 21-2, 125, 153, 58, and 135, respectively.

On wit, see pp. 141, 152, 225, 373, 377, 381, and 379, respectively.

On the novel's didacticism, see pp. 23, 373, 312, 48, 136, 369, 289, and 343, respectively.

Section III. The letter of 27 October 1798 is quoted from *Letters*, pp. 23-6, *passim*.

The letter of 17 November 1798 is quoted from pp. 28-9. On Blackall, see Chapman, p. 60; *Letters*, pp. 317 (letter of 3 July 1813) and 486-7 (letter of 23 March 1817); and *Grandison*, Introduction, p. 27.

The letter of 25 November 1798 is quoted from pp. 32-3. That of 1 December 1798 is quoted from pp. 34-6. The letter of 18 December 1798 is quoted from pp. 38-41.

The letter of 24 December 1798 is quoted from pp. 42-4 and 46.

Section IV. On the chronology of the development of *Sense and Sensibility*, see Southam, pp. 54-5; see also Jenkins, p. 64. The critic who quotes Sartre in connection with *Sense and Sensibility* is Brown, p. 58.

The opening quotations from the novel are taken from *Works*, I, pp. 304 and 376. Craik is quoted from p. 49. On Lucy Steele, see *Works*, I, pp. 366, 127, 140, and 263. On general 'nastiness,' see pp. 32, 55, 215, 229, 232, 160, 175, 250, and 233. On the money theme, see pp. 91, 226, and 275. On Brandon, see p. 94.

On the marriage theme, see pp. 38, 140, 59, 118, 184, 263, 141, and 302. On Elinor and Jane Austen, see pp. 79, 93, 369, 339, 122, and 120. On Marianne and Jane Austen, see pp. 46, 304, 17, and 8. On anti-romanticism and excessive emotionalism, see pp. 7, 189, 56, 261, 201-2, 345, 378, and 98—and Butler (I), p. 196. I am grateful to Professor Alistair M. Duckworth for helping me to gloss Jane Austen's probable attitude toward the 'picturesque' as it is articulated in *Sense and Sensibility* and discussed in my text. On Barton and Steventon, see *Works*, I, pp. 40, 97, and 380.

On the ending of *Sense and Sensibility*, see pp. 361, 378, 327, 324, 329, and 331.

References for citations at the end of this section are as follows. See Edmund Wilson, 'A Long Talk About Jane Austen,' in *Classics and Commercials: A Literary Chronicle of the Forties* (New York, 1950), first published in *The New Yorker* for 13 October 1945; I am quoting from Watt, p. 35. The other critic quoted on the ending of *Sense and Sensibility* is Odmark, p. 99. Moore is quoted from *Avowals* (London, 1924), pp. 39–40. See Kingsley Amis, 'What Became of Jane Austen?', in *Spectator*, No. 6745 (4 October, 1957), 339–40; I am quoting from Watt, p. 141. See D.W. Harding, 'Regulated Hatred: An Aspect of the Work of Jane Austen,' in *Scrutiny*, 8 (1940), 346–62; quoted from Watt, p. 170. And see Virginia Woolf, 'Jane Austen at Sixty' (see above, under Notes for Chapter 1, for full citation); I am quoting from Watt, p. 20.

Section V. The letter of 8 January 1799 is quoted from *Letters*, pp. 48–53, *passim*. The letter of 21 January 1799 is quoted from pp. 53–8, *passim*. On Harris Bigg Wither, see Chapman's discussion in *Letters*, note for p. 56. On the Williamses, see Rees, pp. 63 and 68. My discussion of Bath is indebted to Plumb, p. 15. The letters of 17 May and 2 June 1799 are quoted from *Letters*, pp. 59–66, *passim*. The letters of 11 and 19 June 1799 are quoted from pp. 66–73, *passim*.

On the Leigh Perrot affair, see Laski, p. 44; Cecil, pp. 86–8; Ives, pp. 23, 21, and 16; and *Life and Letters*, Chapter IX. Richard Lovell Edgeworth's letter is quoted from *Life and Letters*, p. 139.

Section VI. On the history, chronology, and possible revisions of *Northanger Abbey*, see Southam, p. 61; Chapman's Introductory Note to *Works*, V, pp. xii–xiii; and Butler (II), p. 106. Jane Austen's 'Advertisement' for *Northanger Abbey* is quoted from *Works*, V, p. 12. Craik is quoted from p. 7.

On Henry Tilney, see Andrew H. Wright, *Jane Austen's Novels* (London, 1953), p. 108; Litz, pp. 67 and 69; Craik, p. 16; Mudrick, pp. 43, 49, and 51; and *Works*, V, pp. 219, 25, 79, 206, 114, 132–3, and 59, respectively. On the destruction of romance, see Gooneratne, p. 55; George Levine, *The Realistic Imagination: English Fiction from Frankenstein to Lady Chatterley* (Chicago, 1981), p. 67; *Works*, V, p. 212; Butler (I), p. 173; and *Works*, V, pp. 167, 173, 193, 197, 199, 201, 200, and 232, respectively. On the picturesque, see p. 111.

On the 'botched' ending, see pp. 243, 250, and 252; see also Odmark, p. 92, and Mudrick, p. 58. On autobiographical elements, see *Works*, V, pp. 15, 109, and 138. On Catherine, see pp. 234, 165, 182, 141, 191, and 211, respectively.

On Jane Austen's 'bitterness' in *Northanger Abbey*, see pp. 16, 40, 98, 73–4, 110–11, 122, 124, 146, 202, and 241, respectively; Mudrick, pp. 52, 58, and 59; and *Works*, V, p. 198.

On novels and novel-writing, see pp. 106 and 37–8.

Chapter 5

The chronology of Jane Austen's *Sir Charles Grandison* is argued persuasively by Southam in his Introduction to *Grandison*, especially p. 15. On Jane Austen's knowledge of Richardson and *Sir Charles Grandison* and her ownership of a first edition of the novel, see Jenkins, p. 34; the *Memoir*, p. 89; and *Grandison*, Southam's Introduction, pp. 9-10. The reference to Richardson's novel in *Northanger Abbey* may be found in *Works*, V, pp. 41-2. On Charlotte, Isabella, Catherine, and Henry, see Southam's Introduction, pp. 33-4n. On eighteenth-century abridgements of *Sir Charles Grandison*, see Southam's Introduction to *Grandison*, pp. 21-2 and p. 33n. On the prayer-book business, see *Grandison*, pp. 43 and 138n. On Harriet's nature and her marriage prospects, see the quoted passages in *Grandison*, pp. 52, 54, and 55, respectively.

Section II. On the activities of the Austens during the year 1800, see Jenkins, pp. 120-3, *passim.*, and Rees, pp. 75-8, *passim.*

The letter of 1 November 1800 is quoted from *Letters*, pp. 79-81; that of 8 November 1800 from pp. 84-5 and 87; that of 12 November 1800 (to Martha Lloyd) from pp. 87 and 89; that of 20 November 1800 from pp. 90-2; and that of 30 November 1800 from pp. 96-7.

On the Austens' decision to move to Bath and Jane Austen's reaction, see Jenkins, p. 124; Rees, p. 80; *Life and Letters*, p. 156; the *Memoir*, p. 78; and Hodge, p. 75. On the Digweeds, see Rees, p. 80.

The letter of 3 January 1801 is quoted from *Letters*, pp. 99-103, *passim.*; that of 8 January 1801 from pp. 104-5; that of 14 January 1801 from pp. 108-11, *passim.*; that of 21 January 1801 from pp. 112 and 114-15; that of 25 January 1801 from pp. 117-18; and that of 11 February 1801 from pp. 120-1.

On the move to Bath and the new house, see Jenkins, p. 126; Rees, p. 83; and Hodge, p. 80. On Bath in 1801, see Cecil, p. 92.

The letter of 5 May 1801 is quoted from *Letters*, pp. 122 and 124; that of 12 May 1801 from pp. 127-9; that of 21 May 1801 from pp. 130 and 132-4; and that of 26 May 1801 from pp. 135-7. On the amber crosses and *Mansfield Park*, see Jenkins, p. 128.

Section III. On the mysterious summer romance of 1801, see Jenkins, pp. 129-30; Cecil, p. 97; and Laski, p. 53. On the convenient location of the house at Bath, see Rees, p. 89. On the Bigg Wither affair of December 1802, see Chapman, pp. 61-2; Rees, p. 90; G.H. Tucker, *A Goodly Heritage* (Manchester, 1983), p. 159; *Life and Letters*, pp. 92-3; Laski, p. 54; and Reginald F. Bigg Wither, *Materials for a History of the Wither Family* (Winchester, 1907). On *Persuasion*, see Hodge, p. 82. Bush is quoted from p. 27.

On Frank Austen's engagement and the visit to Ramsgate, see Jenkins, p. 134. On the sale of 'Susan,' see Jenkins, p. 148, and Hodge, p. 85.

On 'The Watsons,' see Rees, p. 92, and Southam, pp. 65-6 and 64.

Quotations from 'The Watsons' are taken from *Works*, VI, pp. 327, 328, 335, 361, 318, 346, 317, 351, 343, 342, 325, 345, 361, and 362, respectively.

On 'The Watsons,' see Mudrick, pp. 145-52, *passim*.; Gooneratne, p. 43; and Litz, pp. 89 and 87.

Section IV. On Frank Austen's activities in 1804-5, see Rees, p. 94, and Cecil, pp. 101-2.

On the Austens' stay at Lyme during the summer of 1804, see *Life and Letters*, pp. 76-7.

The letter of 14 September 1804 is quoted from *Letters*, pp. 139-42, *passim*.

On the move to Green Park Buildings and George Austen's decline and death, see Rees, pp. 96-7; Laski, p. 60; and Pinion, p. 15. The letters of 21, 22, and 29 January 1805 are quoted from *Letters*, pp. 144-7, *passim*. On Jane Austen and the 'bad parents' theme, see Hodge, p. 88.

On the family council during the winter of 1805 and its results, see Cecil, p. 109, and Hodge, p. 89.

Section V. The letters of 8 and 21 April 1805 are quoted from *Letters*, pp. 148-52, 154-7, and 159, *passim*.

The letters of 24, 27, and 30 August 1805 are quoted from pp. 160-4, *passim*., 166, and 169. The quotation about Frank Austen and the account of his activities in 1805 are taken from *Life and Letters*, pp. 192-3. Caroline Austen on her aunts is quoted by Hodge, p. 91.

On the activities of the Austens during the summer of 1806, see Rees, p. 101. Mrs Austen is quoted from various sources: *Life and Letters*, p. 196; Cecil, p. 113; and Rees, p. 103.

My account of the Castle Square location in Southampton is indebted to Laski, p. 63. The *Memoir*, on the Southampton house, is quoted from p. 100. Miss Mitford is cited in Chapman, p. 54. The critic quoted on the Austens' life at Southampton is Cecil, pp. 115-16.

Chapter 6

The letter of 7 January 1807 is quoted from *Letters*, pp. 171-3 and 175, *passim*.; that of 8 February 1807 from pp. 176-81, *passim*.; and that of 20 February 1807 from pp. 182, 184, and 186, *passim*.

Section II. On the Austens' evenings at home in Southampton and Charles Austen's marriage, see Cecil, pp. 116 and 119; *Life and Letters*, p. 204; and Hodge, p. 100. An account of James Austen's income and Henry Austen's

London address is given by Laski, p. 64. The visit to Chawton House is well-documented—e.g., Pinion, p. 16. On Jane Austen's activities during the spring of 1808 and the possible suits of Edward Bridges, see Hodge, pp. 100 and 103.

Quotations from the letter of 15 June 1808 are taken from *Letters*, pp. 186, 188-9, and 191, respectively; that of 20 June 1808 is quoted from pp. 194-7, *passim.*; that of 26 June 1808 from pp. 199 and 201-4, *passim.*; and that of 30 June 1808 from pp. 205-9, *passim.* On the silver knife in *Mansfield Park* and Caroline Austen on Godmersham, see Chapman's note for Letter 54.

The letter of 1 October 1808 is quoted from pp. 209-14, *passim.*; that of 7 October 1808 is quoted from pp. 215-17 and 219, *passim.*; that of 13 October 1808 from pp. 219-21, *passim.*; that of 15 October 1808 from pp. 221-4, *passim.* On Edward Austen's failure to remarry, see Rees, p. 112.

The letter of 24 October 1808 is quoted from pp. 225-8, *passim.* On Jane Austen and the Beckfords, see Chapman, pp. 71-2. The letter of 20 November 1808 is quoted from pp. 231-3, *passim.*; that of 9 December 1808 from pp. 235-6 and 238, *passim.*; and that of 27 December 1808 from pp. 240-4, *passim.*

Section III. The letter of 10 January 1809 is quoted from *Letters*, pp. 244-6 and 248-9, *passim.* On the Peninsular Campaign and the retreat in Spain, see Pinion, p. 17. On 1808 editions of *Marmion*, see Chapman's note to Letter 63. The letter of 17 January 1809 is quoted from *Letters*, pp. 249-51 and 253-4, *passim.* Jane Austen on Edward Cooper's sermons is quoted by Rees, p. 119. The letter of 24 January 1809 is quoted from pp. 254-8, *passim.* Jane Austen on evangelicalism, according to a contemporary, is quoted in Hodge, p. 110. The letter of 30 January 1809 is quoted from *Letters*, pp. 259-62, *passim.* On the deathbed conversation of General Sir John Moore, see Chapman's note to Letter 66.

The letter to Crosby of 5 April 1809 is quoted from *Letters*, p. 263. Crosby's response of 8 April 1809 is quoted from p. 264. The poem addressed to Frank Austen, dated 26 July 1809, is quoted from *Letters*, pp. 265-6.

Section IV. On Chawton and Chawton Cottage, see Lascelles, p. 25; Chapman, p. 70; *Life and Letters*, pp. 236-7; Laski, p. 74 (Edward Austen-Leigh is also quoted here); Cecil, pp. 126-31, *passim.*—the descriptions of the garden and the road are based on his, p. 129; Jenkins, p. 206, and Rees, p. 123, both quoting Caroline Austen; and the *Memoir*, p. 105.

J.E. Austen-Leigh is quoted by Hodge, p. 114. The critic commenting on Cassandra's portrait is Hodge, p. 114. Caroline Austen's comparison of Jane and Cassandra is quoted by Jenkins, p. 209.

On Jane Austen in her mid-thirties, see Cecil, p. 131. Anna Austen Lefroy is quoted in *Life and Letters*, pp. 239-40. The subsequent discussion of her

personality is indebted to *Life and Letters*, p. 240. Caroline Austen on Jane
Austen's personality and personal appearance is quoted by Laski, pp. 78 and
76, respectively. J.E. Austen-Leigh is quoted by Lascelles, p. 28. Caroline on
her mother's warning is taken from Jenkins, pp. 208-9. Virginia Woolf is
quoted from the essay called 'Personalities,' in *Collected Essays*, Vol. II
(London and New York, 1966).

On Jane Austen's life at Chawton, see Cecil, pp. 131-6, on whose account
mine is largely based. I am indebted to Donald Greene for alerting me to the
work of J.B. Cramer and the possible connections with Beethoven. Anna
Austen on her two aunts may be found in *Life and Letters*, p. 240. Caroline on
Jane Austen's 'charm,' etc., is quoted by Cecil, p. 140. On Jane Austen and
her neighbours, see Hodge, p. 113 (quoting Caroline Austen), and Cecil,
pp. 140-1 (Caroline is quoted here on p. 141). The critic cited on Jane
Austen's 'detachment' is Cecil, p. 141. On Jane Austen at the Alton library,
see *Life and Letters*, p. 241. On J.E. Austen-Leigh's ignorance of his aunt's
early work, see Bush, p. 31. The passage quoted from the *Memoir* may be
found on pp. 142-3 and 146. Lascelles on Chawton is quoted from p. 29.

Chapter 7

On the April 1811 visit to London, see Cecil, p. 154. On the financial
backgrounds of the publication of *Sense and Sensibility* and 'vanity'
publishing, see Hodge, p. 120. Jane Austen's earnings are discussed by
Hodge, p. 123. On the novelist's probable state of mind in the spring of 1811,
see Rees, p. 127.

The letters of 18, 25, and 30 April 1811 are quoted from *Letters*,
pp. 267-79, *passim*.

The letters of 29 and 31 May and 6 June 1811 are quoted from *Letters*,
pp. 280-91, *passim*. Mrs Austen on mourning clothes is quoted from *Life and
Letters*, p. 257. The visit of the Charles Austens to Chawton is recounted in
various sources; see, for example, Cecil, p. 155. The expected September
1811 publication of *Sense and Sensibility* is suggested in *Life and Letters*,
p. 254.

Cassandra's description of Fanny Austen (Charles's wife) is quoted by
Hodge, p. 131.

Section II. On Fanny's diary entry, see *Life and Letters*, p. 254; Rees, p. 129;
and Jenkins, p. 219.

On the publication of *Sense and Sensibility*, see *Life and Letters*, p. 255;
Jenkins, p. 218; Laski, p. 82; and Rees, p. 130.

On Lady Bessborough's reaction, see Hodge, p. 130; Laski, p. 82; and
Cecil, p. 156—the quotation on the Whig aristocracy is taken from him.

On the earnings of *Sense and Sensibility*, see Rees, p. 130; Hodge, p. 122;
and *Life and Letters*, p. 255.

The discussion of the place of fiction in the second decade of the nineteenth century is taken from the 'Introduction' by the present writer to Halperin, pp. 4–5. Altick is quoted from *The English Common Reader* (Chicago, 1957), pp. 63–5, *passim*. On literature as a 'seducer,' see the *Methodist Magazine*, 42 (1819), 606–9, and the *Westminster Review*, 2 (1824), 346. On the bad repute of novels in 1800 and their resuscitation by the time of Trollope, see Q.D. Leavis, *Fiction and the Reading Public* (London, 1932), pp. 145 and 161–3. Coleridge is quoted from *Lectures on Shakespeare and Milton*, The First Lecture.

Reviews of *Sense and Sensibility* (*Critical Review*, February 1812, n.s. 4, i, 149–57, and the *British Critic*, 1812, 39, 527) are quoted from *Critical Heritage*, pp. 35–40, *passim*.

Section III. On Edward and his mother in 1812, see Pinion, p. 19, and *Life and Letters*, p. 256. On Charles and Edward Austen and their families, and the visit of Jane and her mother to Steventon, see Hodge, p. 132. On Edward's move to the Great House in the autumn of 1812, see Jenkins, p. 239. Anna Austen's relationship with her aunt and Jane Austen's reading in 1812 are discussed by Cecil, pp. 158–9.

The letter to Martha Lloyd (29 November 1812) is quoted from *Letters*, pp. 499–502, *passim*. The lines on Camilla Wallop are discussed by Chapman in his note to Letter 74.1.

The letter (to Cassandra) of 24 January 1813 is quoted from *Letters*, pp. 291–6, *passim*. On the publication of *Pride and Prejudice*, see Jenkins, p. 240, and Laski, p. 85.

Reviews of *Pride and Prejudice* by the *British Critic* (unsigned, February 1813, 41, 189–90) and the *Critical Review* (unsigned, March 1813, 4th series, 3, 318–24) are quoted from *Critical Heritage*, pp. 41–7, *passim*. The comments of various private individuals on the novel are quoted from Southam's Introduction to *Critical Heritage*, pp. 7–9.

The letters to Cassandra of 29 January and 4 and 9 February 1813, and that to Martha Lloyd of 16 February 1813, are quoted from *Letters*, pp. 296–305 and 503–5, *passim*. On the length of the various volumes of *Pride and Prejudice*, and on hedgerows and realism, see Chapman's note to Letter 76.

In his note to Letter 78, Chapman declares that 'Maria' must be Maria Heathcote of Manydown, but the reference is more likely to be that which I suggest in the text.

On Cottesbrooke and *Mansfield Park*, see Chapman's note to Letter 78.1. My interpretation of Jane Austen's comments on the affairs of the Prince and Princess of Wales is indebted to advice given me by Donald Greene.

Section IV. On the death of Eliza Austen and Jane Austen's visit to

London, see Jenkins, p. 243; *Life and Letters*, p. 265; Hodge, p. 141; and Pinion, p. 19.

The letter of 20 May 1813 is quoted from *Letters*, pp. 306 and 308, that of 24 May 1813 from pp. 309–13, *passim*.

On Miss Burdett, see Hodge, p. 141. On Henry's promotion, see Rees, p. 140. On Fanny Knight's growing intimacy with her aunt, see Jenkins, p. 246, who quotes Fanny's diary entries.

The letter to Frank Austen (3–6 July 1813) is paraphrased and quoted from *Letters*, pp. 313–18, *passim*. On Jane Austen's use of the names of Frank Austen's ships in *Mansfield Park*, see Jenkins, p. 248.

Quotations from the letter of 15 September 1813 are taken from *Letters*, pp. 320–4, *passim*.; those from the letter of 16 September 1813 are taken from pp. 326–8; those from the letter of 23 September 1813 from pp. 329–31, 333, and 335; and those from the letter of 25 September 1813 (to Frank Austen) from pp. 336–41, *passim*.

On Anna Austen's engagements in the autumn of 1813, see Laski, p. 90. On the reprinting of Jane Austen's novels, see Southam's Introduction to *Critical Heritage*, pp. 4–5. The letter of 11 October 1813 is quoted from *Letters*, pp. 342–7, *passim*. (on goose and Michaelmas Day, see Chapman's note to Letter 86); that of 14 October 1813 is quoted from pp. 348–51 and 353–5.

The references in connection with the discussion of Jane Austen and children are to Brigid Brophy, 'Jane Austen and the Stuarts,' in *Critical Essays on Jane Austen*, ed. Brian Southam (London, 1968), p. 33; Christopher Ricks, 'Jane Austen and the Business of Mothering,' Address given at the Annual General Meeting of the Jane Austen Society (Report for the Year 1982); and Nina Auerbach, 'Artists and Mothers: A False Alliance,' in *Women and Literature*, 6 (1978), 8. I am grateful to Professor Ricks for kindly allowing me to read an early draft of his essay in manuscript.

The estimate of the number of Jane Austen's letters known (at one time, at least) to exist, but missing now, was made for me by Brian Southam, in a note dated 20 August 1981.

The letter of 21 October 1813 is quoted from *Letters*, pp. 357–8; that of 26 October 1813 is quoted from pp. 359 and 361–3; and that of 3 November 1813 is quoted from pp. 365–9, *passim*.

Marianne Knight's memory of Jane Austen at Godmersham is cited in *Life and Letters*, p. 290. On the reference to Cowper, see John Halperin, 'The Worlds of *Emma*: Jane Austen and Cowper,' in Halperin, p. 198. The reference to Johnson is cited by Chapman in *Letters*, note to Letter 90. The letter of 6 November 1813 is quoted from *Letters*, pp. 370–2. On Vittoria and the response of Parliament, see Chapman's note to Letter 91.

Section V. Quotations from *Mansfield Park* are taken from *Works*, III. The quotations in the opening paragraphs appear on pp. 68, 367, 459, 464, 468, 358, 209–10, 449, 467–8, 131, 147, 155, and 187, respectively.

The critics quoted here are as follows: Amis, in Watt, pp. 141–2; Tave, pp. 182, 164–5, 194, 175, and 178; Bernard J. Paris, *Character and Conflict in Jane Austen's Novels: A Psychological Approach* (Detroit, 1978), p. 22; Duckworth, p. 76; and Mansell, p. 110.

On Newman and *Mansfield Park*, see Park Honan, *Matthew Arnold: A Life* (New York, 1981), p. 60.

On the brothers, see *Mansfield Park*, pp. 236 and 64. On sibling rivalry, see p. 235. On the mothers, see pp. 35, 285, 427, 371, 389–90, and 50–1. On Mrs Norris and Mrs Leigh Perrot, see Ives, p. 26, and *Mansfield Park*, pp. 283 and 387. Ives quotes Alexander Dyce on Mrs Leigh Perrot in a note to the present writer.

On dancing, see *Works*, III, pp. 270 and 281. On the circulating library, see p. 398. On 'improvements,' appreciation of nature, and hatred of cities, see pp. 244, 93, 439, 113, 209, 446–7, 381–2, 391, 431–2, and 392, respectively. On the Portsmouth chapters of *Mansfield Park*, see John Halperin, 'The Trouble with *Mansfield Park*,' in *Studies in the Novel*, 7, No. 1 (Spring 1975), 6–23, *passim*.

On marriage, lack of consequence, and related topics, see *Mansfield Park*, pp. 318–19; 'Some Notes on Background,' p. 26; and *Mansfield Park*, pp. 467, 324, 353, 3, 202, 46, 26, 152, 221, 280, 297, 370, 201, 51, 159, 463, and 473, respectively.

On questions of comfort and attacks on materialism, see pp. 213, 289, 434, 394, 436, 361, and 323.

The final quotations on autobiography in *Mansfield Park* are taken from pp. 289, 425–6, and 473.

On the general topic of autobiography in *Mansfield Park*, as well as a discussion of the ordination theme, the theatricals, and 'acting,' see John Halperin, 'The Novelist as Heroine in *Mansfield Park*: A Study in Autobiography,' in *Modern Language Quarterly*, 43, No. 2 (Summer 1983), *passim*.

On 'ordination' and church matters, see *Mansfield Park*, pp. 92, 110, 93, 248, and 112. The critic referred to in the text is Butler (I), p. 243.

On acting and theatricals, see *Mansfield Park*, p. 349; Chapman's note on *Lovers' Vows*, p. 474; Arlin Turner, *Nathaniel Hawthorne: A Biography* (New York and Oxford, 1980), p. 26; and *Mansfield Park*, pp. 145, 137, 121, 124, and 126.

On the 'botched' ending and related topics, see Odmark, p. 102; and *Mansfield Park*, pp. 461, 470–2, and 443.

Section VI. On the trip to London, see Laski, p. 94, and Pinion, p. 20.

The letter of 2 March 1814 is quoted from *Letters*, pp. 376–8. On the prospect of peace in Europe in March 1814, see Hodge, p. 151. The letter of 5 March 1814 is quoted from *Letters*, pp. 379–82 and 384, *passim*. The letter of 9 March 1814 is quoted from pp. 385–6.

On the publication of *Mansfield Park*, see Laski, p. 94; Rees, pp. 150–1;

and Chapman's Introductory Note to *Works*, III, p. xi. On the novel's earnings for Jane Austen and John Murray, see Hodge, pp. 124-5.

Jane Austen's comment on Scott's review of *Emma* is quoted from *Critical Heritage*, p. 53.

On Jane Austen's collecting of opinions on *Mansfield Park*, see Hodge, p. 153. The collected opinions are reprinted by Chapman in Volume VI of *Works*; I quote them from *Critical Heritage*, where they are reproduced on pp. 48-53, *passim*.

On Bookham and *Emma*, see Jenkins, pp. 281-2. On 'Which Is the Heroine?', see Chapman's note to Letter 95 in *Letters*.

The letter of 14 (misdated 13) June 1814 is quoted from *Letters*, p. 389. On the Tsar, the King, and the Prince Regent in London in June 1814, see Hodge, p. 154. The letter of 23 June 1814 is quoted from *Letters*, pp. 390-1.

The letter (to Anna) of 10 August 1814 is quoted from pp. 393-5. The letter to Cassandra of August 1814—exact date uncertain, but probably 23 August—is quoted from pp. 397-9. The letter to Martha Lloyd (2 September 1814) is quoted from pp. 506-8. The letter of 9 September 1814 (to Anna) is quoted from pp. 400 and 402. The letter of 28 September 1814 is quoted from pp. 403-6, *passim*.

On Fanny Knight, John Plumtre, and Jane Austen, see Rees, p. 161. The letter of 18 November 1814 is quoted from *Letters*, pp. 408-11, *passim*.

The letters of 22 and 29 November 1814 (to Anna Lefroy) are quoted, respectively, from pp. 413 and 425.

The letter of 30 November 1814 (to Fanny Knight) is quoted from pp. 416-20, *passim*.

The three letters of December 1814 (exact dates unknown) to Anna Lefroy are quoted from pp. 420, 422, and 423, respectively.

On the events of March 1815, see Rees, p. 164.

Section VII. On the advertisements and sales of the first edition of *Emma*, see Chapman's Introductory Note to *Works*, IV, p. xi. Mudrick is quoted from p. 181.

On the schools, see *Works*, IV, pp. 21-2, and Jenkins, pp. 289-90. On the charades, see Jenkins, p. 288. On Miss Bates and Mrs Miles, see Jenkins, pp. 302-3. On Mr Weston and Henry Austen, see *Works*, IV, p. 15.

On Mr Woodhouse and Mrs Austen, see pp. 387, 7-8, 37, 21, and 146.

For general autobiography, see pp. 7, 23, 52, 166, 155, 363, 249, 92, 64, 82, 117, and 261.

On the governess business, see pp. 300, 165, 384, 400 (and p. 493n), and 382.

On marriage and 'tenderness,' see pp. 11, 54, 60, 63-4, 84-6, 203, 320, 269, and 482.

On Jane Austen and James, see p. 347; Duckworth, p. 148; and Butler (I), p. 251. On Emma's failure to travel, see Mansell, pp. 146-7; see also Craik, p. 125. The quotation from Brown may be found on p. 101.

On wit, see *Works*, IV, pp. 181, 271, and 434.

On fancy and the imagination, see pp. 98-9, 345, 57, 37, 335, 344, 412, and 343; and John Halperin, 'The Worlds of *Emma*: Jane Austen and Cowper,' in Halperin, pp. 197-206, *passim*.

On clarity and openness, see *Works*, IV, pp. 59, 226, 288-9, 341, 394, 397, 431, 446, 460, 475, and 399.

On 'scene' versus 'description,' and the ending of *Emma*, see p. 431.

The story of Edward Knight and the apple trees is recounted by Jenkins, p. 288.

Section VIII. On Napoleon's escape, the probable effects of the war on the Austens, and Charles's letter to Jane, see Hodge, p. 163, and Rees, p. 164; the letter from Charles is quoted by Rees, p. 164. On Lord Holland, see Hodge, p. 163.

On the Lefroys' new house, see Hodge, p. 163, and Pinion, p. 21. The letter of 29 September 1815 is quoted from *Letters*, p. 424.

The letter of 17 October 1815 is quoted from pp. 425 and 427. Gifford's report to Murray is given by Rees, p. 166, and Hodge, p. 165. Henry Austen's letter to Murray is quoted by Hodge, pp. 163-4. Hodge on Jane Austen's earnings is quoted from pp. 124-5. On Seymour, see *Letters*, Chapman's note to Letter 111. The letters of 30 October (to Caroline Austen) and 23 November 1815 (to John Murray) are quoted from pp. 428 and 432.

On Jane Austen, J.S. Clarke, and the Prince Regent, see the following: Pinion, p. 21; Laski, p. 100; Jane Austen's letter to Clarke dated 15 November 1815 and his response of the next day—quoted from *Letters*, pp. 429-30.

The letters to Cassandra (24 and 26 November and 2 December 1815) are quoted from pp. 433-41, *passim*. On Madame de Staël and the evening-party, see Jenkins, p. 362.

The letter to Clarke (11 December 1815) is quoted from *Letters*, p. 443. Clarke's reply (21 December 1815) is quoted from pp. 444-5.

On the repurchase of 'Susan' and the French translations of Jane Austen's works, see Laski, p. 108.

For the exchange of letters between Jane Austen and the Countess of Morley, see *Letters*, pp. 448-9. Maria Edgeworth's letter is quoted in Laski, pp. 105-6. The letter to Anna Lefroy is quoted from *Letters*, p. 449.

For 'Opinions of *Emma*: collected and transcribed by Jane Austen,' see *Critical Heritage*, pp. 55-7, *passim*. For contemporary reviews of *Emma*, see *Critical Heritage*, pp. 58-72. Scott's essay may be found on pp. 58-69.

On Charles Austen, see Hodge, p. 176. On Henry Austen's bankruptcy, see *Life and Letters*, pp. 332-3; Laski, p. 109; Hodge, p. 175; and Rees, p. 174.

The letter to Caroline Austen (13 March 1816) is quoted from *Letters*, p. 450. Clarke's letter to Jane Austen (27 March 1816) is quoted from p. 451. The novelist's response (1 April 1816) is quoted from pp. 452-3. I am grateful to Donald Greene for reminding me of the contemporary relevance of the House of Cobourg. The critic mentioned in the text is Southam, p. 81. The letter to Murray (1 April 1816) is quoted from *Letters*, p. 453.

On the 'Plan of a Novel,' see Bush, p. 33, and Southam, pp. 80, 82–3, and 85. The 'Plan' is quoted from *Works*, VI, pp. 429–30.

The letters to Caroline Austen (both 21 April 1816) are quoted from *Letters*, pp. 454–6.

On the visit to the Fowles, see Rees, p. 177.

On Chawton during the summer of 1816, see Rees, p. 177.

The letter to J.E. Austen (9 July 1816) is quoted from *Letters*, pp. 457–8. The letter to Caroline Austen (15 July 1816) is quoted from p. 460.

On the revisions of *Persuasion*, see *Life and Letters*, pp. 334–5; Laski, p. 110; Pinion, p. 22; Lascelles, p. 37; Hodge, p. 179; and Southam, Chapter 6, pp. 86–99, *passim*. On the question of the titling of *Persuasion*, see Morgan, p. 167, and Hodge, p. 179.

Section IX. The letter to Cassandra (27 December 1808) is quoted from *Letters*, p. 240.

On Lady Russell, persuasion, and 'seeing,' see *Works*, V (Vols. III and IV), pp. 11, 249, 202, 88, 61, 247, 244, 246, and 29–30.

On anti-romanticism, see pp. 85, 101, 100, and 109.

On 'openness,' insincerity, parties, the theatre, female education, and related topics, see pp. 207, 161, 226, 180, 223, 40, and 234.

On miscellaneous autobiography, see pp. 198–9, 17–19, 99, 64, 50–1, and 68. Duckworth is quoted from p. 181.

On bad parents and other 'personal' connections, see *Persuasion*, pp. 56, 218, 220, 26, and 96; Chapman's notes to *Persuasion*, p. 272; and p. 161.

On direct autobiography and related topics, see Jenkins, pp. 354–7, *passim*.; Hodge, p. 181; Tave, p. 256; and *Works*, V (Vols. III and IV), pp. 5–6, 82, 61, 42, 150, 232, 47, 14, 135, 138, 33, 26, 29, 28, 235, and 243.

Reviews of *Persuasion* are quoted from *Critical Heritage*, pp. 79–84 and 266–8, *passim*. For nineteenth-century views of Jane Austen's work, see John Halperin, 'Jane Austen's Nineteenth-Century Critics: Walter Scott to Henry James,' in Halperin, pp. 3–42.

Chapter 8

The letters to Cassandra of 4 and 8 September 1816 are quoted from *Letters*, pp. 461–2 and 464–7. The letter to James Edward Austen (16 December 1816) is quoted from pp. 467–70, *passim*. The suggestion that Jane Austen's 'two inches of ivory' may be a reference in part to her daily engagement book has come to me from Mrs Alice D'Angelo. The letter to Anna Lefroy (either 19 or 26 December 1816) is quoted from *Letters*, p. 470.

Section II. The letters to Caroline Austen (23 and ?29 January 1817) are quoted from *Letters*, pp. 471-4. The letter to Alethea Bigg (24 January 1817) is quoted from pp. 474-7, *passim*. On Southey, see Chapman's note to Letter 139.

On the manuscript of *Sanditon*, see Rees, p. 184.

The letters to Fanny Knight (20 February and 13 March 1817) are quoted from *Letters*, pp. 478-85, *passim*. My account of the Pagets and the Waterloo story is taken from Hodge, p. 195. The story of the rat in the bottle was told to me by Donald Greene.

Section III. Rees is quoted from p. 184; she discusses here too the possible origins in Jane Austen's life of *Sanditon*'s attack on hypochondria and hypochondriacs. Duckworth is quoted from p. 210. Southam is quoted from p. 102. I then go on to paraphrase, in the opening paragraph, a section of another essay by Southam called '*Sanditon*: The Seventh Novel,' in *Jane Austen's Achievement*, ed. Juliet McMaster (London, 1975), p. 2. This essay includes an interesting discussion of some possible connections between *Sanditon* and Peacock's *Headlong Hall* (1815). Southam is quoted once again from p. 115. The quotation from Butler (I) is taken from p. 286. I am grateful to Professor Donald Greene for calling my attention to Sandling as a possible model for Sanditon, Dr Clyde Binfield for suggesting Sandgate, Ms Glenda Hudson for suggesting Sandwich, and Professor Peter J. Manning for helping me to gloss the exchange between Charlotte Heywood and Sir Edward Denham on Burns. Jenkins on Sir Edward Denham is quoted from pp. 386-7.

Quotations from *Sanditon*, in *Works*, VI (*Minor Works*), are taken, respectively, from pp. 371, 422, 369, 373, 387, 412-13, 364, 396-8, 403-5, 391, 406, 421, 376, 401, and 382.

On the publishing history of *Sanditon*, see Chapman's Introductory Note to *Works*, VI, p. 363.

For a general discussion of *Sanditon*, see John Halperin, 'Jane Austen's Anti-Romantic Fragment: Some Notes on *Sanditon*,' in *Tulsa Studies in Women's Literature*, 2, No. 2 (Fall 1983), *passim*.

Section IV. The *Memoir* on the manuscript of *Sanditon* is quoted from *Life and Letters*, p. 382.

The sources for my account of Jane Austen's fatal illness are as follows: letters to me on the subject from Sir David Smithers (17 November 1981), Dr Abraham Braude (18 August 1982), and Dr Michael Safdi (1 September 1982); discussion of the subject with Dr Donald Atlas; Smithers, Chapter 6, *passim*.; Herbert S. Parmet, *Jack: The Struggles of John F. Kennedy* (New York, 1980), p. 191; and Zachary Cope, 'Jane Austen's Last Illness,' *British Medical Journal* for 18 July 1964, pp. 182-3 (I quote from p. 183). The case for Hodgkin's Disease is made in F.A. Bevan's rejoinder to Cope in the *BMJ* for 8 August 1964, p. 394.

On Jane Austen's invalidism, see the *Memoir*, p. 217, and Jenkins, p. 378.

The letter to Fanny Knight (23 March 1817) is quoted from *Letters*, pp. 486-9, *passim*. The letter to Caroline Austen (26 March 1817) is quoted from pp. 490-1.

On the death of James Leigh Perrot and the aftermath, see Rees, p. 187; Hodge, p. 197; and Jenkins, pp. 389-90.

The letter to Charles Austen (6 April 1817) is quoted from *Letters*, pp. 491-2. His writing on the letter is cited by Jenkins, p. 391. On Edward Cooper's letter to Jane Austen, see Hodge, p. 199.

Caroline Austen's account of the last visit is quoted from *Life and Letters*, pp. 386-7.

Section V. Jane Austen's will (27 April 1817) is given in full in *Letters*, p. 519. On Madame Bigeon, see Hodge, p. 199; on the later memorandum, see Laski, p. 114. On Lyford, see Laski, p. 114; the *Memoir*, p. 220; and Jenkins, p. 333.

The letter to Anne Sharp (22 May 1817) is quoted from *Letters*, pp. 493-5.

On the removal to Winchester and the lodgings there, see Cecil, p. 195, and Jenkins, p. 393. *Life and Letters* is quoted from pp. 388-9. On the Heathcotes, see the *Memoir*, p. 221.

The letter to James Edward (27 May 1817) is quoted from *Letters*, pp. 496-7. The final (censored) letter (? May 1817) is quoted from pp. 497-8.

Mrs Austen's letters to Anna Lefroy (n.d.) are quoted from *Life and Letters*, pp. 391-2. James Austen's letter to his son and Caroline's addendum are quoted from *Life and Letters*, pp. 392-3. Mrs Austen's letter to Anna Lefroy is also quoted from *Life and Letters*, p. 398.

Persuasion is quoted from *Works*, V (Vols. III-IV), p. 156.

The *Memoir* is quoted from p. 225. On the service of Holy Communion, see *Life and Letters*, p. 393.

On Jane Austen's activities in June 1817, see Cecil, pp. 197-8.

The novelist's last verses are taken from Rees, p. 191; the characterisation of them quoted in the text is that by Laski, p. 119.

Persuasion is quoted from *Works*, V (Vols. III-IV), p. 154.

On Jane Austen's last conscious hours, see Rees, p. 191, and Jenkins, p. 395. They, however, should not be held accountable for what is said in the final paragraph.

Index

About the Author

John Halperin is Centennial Professor of English at Vanderbilt University. He has also taught at the State University of New York at Stony Brook, the University of Southern California, and the University of Sheffield.

Born in Chicago in 1941, Mr Halperin attended Bowdoin College, the University of New Hampshire, and The Johns Hopkins University, which awarded him a doctorate in 1969.

His publications include *The Language of Meditation* (1973), *The Theory of the Novel* (editor; 1974), *Egoism and Self-Discovery in the Victorian Novel* (1974), *Jane Austen: Bicentenary Essays* (editor; 1975), the highly acclaimed *Trollope and Politics* (1977), *Gissing: A Life in Books* (1982), hailed on both sides of the Atlantic as the definitive critical biography, *Trollope Centenary Essays* (editor; 1982), and *C.P. Snow: An Oral Biography* (1983). He has also edited works by Trollope, Meredith, Gissing, and Henry James. His essays, articles, and reviews have appeared in the leading journals of America and Europe.

Mr Halperin was a Guggenheim Fellow in 1978–79. He has also held fellowships from the Rockefeller Foundation, the American Council of Learned Societies, and the American Philosophical Society.